Stirring Words:

Reflections and Recipes from A Harte Appetite

Tom Harte, 12-12-06

by Tom Harte

Bon Appetit to one who, like me, has found the friendship of Joe Law to be more nourishing than all these recipes.

Best wishes,
Tom Harte

Southeast Missouri State University Press
2006

Stirring Words: Recipes and Reflections from A Harte Appetite

ISBN-10: 0-9760413-40
ISBN-13: 978-0-9760413-4-4

First published in the United States of America, 2006.

Southeast Missouri State University Press
MS 2650, One University Plaza
Cape Girardeau, MO 63701
http://www6.semo.edu/universitypress

Cover photos of the author at the Royal N'Orleans restaurant
in Cape Girardeau, Missouri, by Susan Swartwout.

Cover design by Liz Lester.

To my wife, Jane—after 41 years, still my favorite dish.

We gratefully acknowledge the *Southeast Missourian* in which the food column "A Harte Appetite" first appeared.

We would like to acknowledge the following newspapers and magazines, from which some of the recipes in this book were adapted:

Atlanta Journal-Constitution, Better Homes and Gardens, Bon Appétit, The Buffalo News (Angie Toole), *Chocolatier, Cooking Light, Cooks Illustrated, Eating Well, Executive Health's Good Health Report, Family Circle, Food and Wine* (Linda Merinoff), *German Life, Glasgow Herald, Good Food, Good Housekeeping, Gourmet, Heart and Soul, Highlights for Children, Ladies Home Journal, Lighter Tastes of Aspen, McCall's Magazine, New Orleans Times-Picayune* (Marcelle Bienvenu), *New York Times, Parade Magazine* (Julia Child)*, Prevention, Salon, St. Louis Post-Dispatch, Sunset, Vegetarian Times.*

We would also like to acknowledge the following books, from which some of the recipes in this book were adapted:

Pamela Asquith, *Pamela Asquith's Ultimate Chocolate Cake Book*; Nancy Baggett, *The International Cookie Cookbook*; Rick Bayless, *Mexico: One Plate at a Time*; James Beard, *James Beard's American Cookery*; Lee Edwards Benning, *Oh, Fudge!: A Celebration of America's Favorite Candy*; Rose Levy Beranbaum, *The Cake Bible* & *The Pie and Pastry Bible*; Mary Bergin & Judy Gethers, *Spago Desserts*; Carole Bloom, *All About Chocolate: The Ultimate Resource for the World's Favorite Food*; Anne Byrn, *The Cake Mix Doctor*; Narcissa Chamberlain, *The Omelette Book*; Jane Charlton & Jane Newdick, *A Taste of Honey*; Julia Child, *The French Chef Cookbook*; Linda Collister & Anthony Blake, *The Baking Book*; Caroline & Terence Conran & Simon Hopkinson, *The Essential Cook Book*; Jesse Ziff Cool, *Toast: 60 Ways to Butter Your Bread and Then Some*; Elaine Corn, *Gooey Desserts: The Joy of Decadence*; Shirley O. Corriher, *CookWise: The Secrets of Cooking Revealed*; Rosalind Creasy, *The Edible Flower Garden*; Gail Damerow, *The Perfect Pumpkin: Growing/Cooking/ Carving*; Linda Dannenberg, *Paris Boulangerie-Pâtisserie: Recipes from Thirteen Outstand- ing French Bakeries*; Elizabeth David, *An Omelette and a Glass of Wine*; Marcel Desaulniers, *The Burger Meisters*; Matthew Drennan, *Classic Irish: A Selection of the Best Traditional Irish Food*; Henry Haller, *White House Family Cookbook*; Marcella Hazan, *The Classic Italian Cookbook*; Sharon Tyler Herbst, *Cooking Smart*; Junior League of Boise, *Beyond Burlap*; Junior League of Fort Walton Beach, Florida, *Sugar Beach Cookbook*; Junior League of St. Louis, *Saint Louis Days . . . St. Louis Nights*; Marie Kimball, *Thomas Jefferson's Cook Book*; Teresa Layman, *Gingerbread for All Seasons*; Faye Levy, *The New Casserole*; Leslie Mansfield, *The Lewis & Clark Cookbook*; Zarela Martínez, *The Food and Life of Oaxaca: Traditional Recipes from Mexico's Heart*; Gail McPherson, *Passion for Peaches*; April Moon, *The Flying Biscuit Café Cookbook: Breakfast and Beyond*; Kitty Morse, *Cooking at the Kas- bah: Recipes from my Moroccan Kitchen*; Nabisco, *Oreo with a Twist*; The National Council of Negro Women, *The Historical Cookbook of the American Negro*; Judith Olney, *The Joy of Chocolate*; Dorian Leigh Parker, *Pancakes: From Flapjacks to Crêpes*; Elsa Peterson-Sche- pelern, *Smoothies and Other Blended Drinks*; Rick Rodgers, *365 Ways to Cook Hamburger and Other Ground Meats* & *Kaffeehaus: Exquisite Desserts from the Classic Cafés of Vienna, Budapest, and Prague*; Julee Rosso & Sheila Lukins, *The Silver Palate Cookbook* & *The New Basics Cookbook*; Elisabeth Rozin, *Blue Corn and Chocolate*; Chris Schlesinger & John Willoughby, *The Thrill of the Grill: Techniques, Recipes, and Down-home Barbecue*; Diane Seed, *Italian Cooking with Olive Oil*; Mimi Sheraton, *Visions of Sugarplums: A Cookbook of Cakes, Cookies, Candies & Confections from All the Countries that Celebrate Christmas*; Jen- nifer & Mo Siegel, *Cooking With Tea: The Celestial Seasonings Cookbook*; Marie Simmons, *Bar Cookies A to Z*; St. Louis Jewish Hospital Auxiliary, *Cooking in Clover*; Patricia Wells, *Patricia Wells' Trattoria: Simple and Robust Fare Inspired by the Small Family Restaurants of Italy*; Victoria Wise & Susanna Hoffman, *The Well-Filled Tortilla Cookbook*; Paula Wolfert, *Couscous and Other Good Food from Morocco*; Clarissa Dickson Wright & Jennifer Paterson, *Cooking with the Two Fat Ladies*; *The World's Fair Souvenir Cook Book.*

Acknowledgements

I think it was Molière who observed that some men eat to live while other men live to eat. I know which category I fall into. I love food, glorious food. The word "diet" has always been a particularly offensive four-letter word as far as I'm concerned. (And did you ever notice that the first three letters of that word spell "die"?) Samuel Johnson could just as well have had me in mind when he said, "A man seldom thinks with more earnestness of anything than he does his dinner."

Thus, when Joe Sullivan and Joni Adams, editors of the *Southeast Missourian*, came to me some ten years ago and asked if I'd be interested in writing an occasional food article for the newspaper, I answered yes in less time than it takes to blanch an almond. In the most fundamental way, then, they are responsible for this book, for had it not been for them, my newspaper columns would never have existed and, consequently, neither would this collection of them. So, first and foremost, I thank them for getting me started.

I'm also indebted to many others at the newspaper for their support and encouragement, especially Sam Blackwell, Heidi Hall, Laura Johnston, Callie Clark Miller, and, not least, the Rust family.

I'm particularly appreciative of the efforts of the newspaper's talented photographers—Lou Pikert, Stephan Frazier, Don Frazier, Fred Lynch, and Diane Wilson—who over the years have produced many mouth-watering pictures to accompany the columns. I owe a special thank-you to Fred and Diane for helping me sort through all those photos to select the ones you'll find in this volume.

I'm enormously grateful to Dr. Susan Swartwout of the Southeast Missouri State University Press for taking an interest in this book in the first place and to Mandy Henley for all her hard work.

I also want to express my gratitude to my wife, Jane, and my daughter, Jill, who never complain when I ask them, as I always do, to look over a column, taste-test a recipe, and make suggestions. I couldn't ask for better consultants.

Finally, I want to say thanks to my readers. Without them there would be no reason to write in the first place.

—Tom Harte

The Essays

Recipe Table of Contents

Sides   291

Desserts   301

Recipe Writing

Some years ago a lady wrote to the *London Daily Telegraph* and reported, "The hymn 'Onward Christian Soldiers' sung to the right tune and in a not too brisk tempo makes a very good egg timer. If you put the egg into boiling water and sing all five verses and chorus, the egg will be just right when you come to Amen."

This may well be the most unconventional recipe I've ever run across, and it underscores the fact that while a recipe is essentially "a formula or written set of instructions for preparing food," to quote Joan Whitman and Dolores Simon, authors of a handbook for cookbook writers, some ways of writing those instructions are better than others.

The matter of writing style, I've discovered, is no less important in recipes than in any other form of prose. And it may be even more perplexing when it comes to recipes. Where else, for example, do the words "sit" and "stand" mean the same thing? (Thus, "add yeast to warm water and let sit five minutes" and "add yeast to warm water and let stand five minutes" are interchangeable.) No wonder cookbook author Carol Field suggests writers need guidance through what she calls "the dense and intricate thicket of writing recipes and cooking instructions."

Believe it or not, recipe writers and cookbook authors occasionally get into spirited arguments over questions of style and grammar. For example, as Whitman and Simon note, "Capitalization, a seemingly noncontroversial issue in the population at large, can cause heated debate in food-writing circles." So too, apparently, can the matter of the serial comma, how to best indicate the measurement of butter or margarine, and the question of whether to use "of" after words like "dash" or "pinch." (Whitman and Simon say yes, but Barbara Gibbs Ostmann and Jane L. Baker, authors of *The Recipe Writer's Handbook*, say no.) A dash, by the way, is anything less than ⅛ teaspoon.

Food writers have developed a smorgasbord of technical rules governing the language of recipes. Among other things, they decree that the correct term for an angel food cake pan is "tube pan," that bread crumbs are not one word, that ketchup is the preferred spelling for catsup, that soft cheeses are "shredded" while hard cheeses are "grated," that chocolate chips are properly referred to as chocolate morsels, that there is no generic name for Tabasco sauce, that decimal points should never be used in recipe writing, and that when a wine is named after a grape it should not be capitalized unless the grape is named after a place and the wine comes from there.

The language of recipes is worth such fussing over. That's because recipes are practically indispensable tools for just about anyone who likes to cook. It's true, of course, that some cooks are more dependent on recipes than others and that two different cooks can take the same recipe and produce two different results. Pie crust is a perfect example of that principle. But just because recipes can never fully account for the level of skill of the cooks who use them or record every subtle nuance of a dish's preparation does not mean they are unworthy of careful crafting. After all, the same thing is true of a musical composition. As the great British food writer Elizabeth David put it, "One certainly cannot learn the technical details of cookery entirely from books, but if the cooks of the past had believed that written recipes were unnecessary, we should now be in a sad plight indeed."

So recipes are vital documents, and as such they need to communicate clearly and accurately. As the dust jacket on *The Recipe Writer's Handbook* admonishes, "Every recipe . . . has the power to make or break a meal—and a cook's reputation!" And this is especially true today when, according to Ostmann and Baker, "an overwhelming number of today's recipe users are cooking illiterates; that is, they haven't learned to cook alongside their mothers or grandmothers, and they lack knowledge of what many food professionals consider basic food terminology and skills." As proof, they cite a recent national poll in which fully three-fourths of the people surveyed, almost all of whom considered themselves excellent cooks, failed a basic cooking quiz. They didn't know how many ounces were in a cup, how many teaspoons were in a tablespoon, or the standard measure of a stick of butter.

It shouldn't be surprising, then, that over the years various food writers have received some rather astonishing calls from their readers. For instance, Ostmann and Baker tell of one caller who wanted to know how far to drop drop cookies. They cite another who had just bought a new oven and wondered whether it was preheated. And they report that still another couldn't understand why a cake recipe produced such a gritty result. Amazingly, it turned out that the caller had used whole eggs as the recipe had specified—shells and all!

But even if we weren't dependent on them for instruction, recipes would still deserve to be written with a careful editorial eye. After all, a recipe is more than just a blueprint. It's a creative undertaking. And though the primary focus of any recipe is, admittedly, physical sustenance, like other forms of creative writing, it has the potential to nourish the soul as well.

And who's to say a recipe is any less noble a form of self-expression than other works of art? Indeed, I'd argue it's the ultimate way to give of yourself. (I guess that's why I have little use for people who refuse to share their recipes and downright disdain for those who leave out vital ingredients when they do.) As a matter of fact, sharing recipes is a uniquely American tradition; printed cookbooks were almost unknown in this country during the first 150 years of our colonial history. Rather, housewives relied on their own trusted collections of handwritten "receipts" which they handed down from generation to generation. Thus, no less than other artistic works, recipes are a means of achieving some measure of immortality. As the main character in the wonderful Mexican novel *Like Water for Chocolate* says, great aunt Tita lives so long as someone cooks her recipes.

So while I wouldn't claim that recipes are in the same league as the Great Books, I would maintain that they are certainly a respectable literary genre, which raises the question, what makes a recipe well written? Ostmann and Baker devote a whole section of their book to this question, what they call recipe philosophy, and they quote numerous food authorities on the subject. For example, Jennifer Darling, a food editor for Meredith Books, says, "The basic ingredient of every good recipe is clear, concise directions." She's right. As Whitman and Simon point out, "A recipe must meet the same standards of English as any other piece of explanatory prose. . . ." But beyond that, Carol Haddix, food editor of the *Chicago Tribune*, observes, "Any recipe that makes someone want to cook is good. The rest is just details." Cookbook author Greg Patent agrees. He declares, "Reading a good recipe makes me want to head straight for the kitchen and start cooking."

Not every recipe, of course, can live up to that standard, but, as the novelist Joseph Conrad noted, they nevertheless constitute a unique form of communication. He called them "the only product of the human mind altogether above suspicion." As he pointed out, "The intention of every other piece of prose may be discussed and even mistrusted, but the purpose of a cookery book is one and unmistakable. Its object can conceivably be no other than to increase the happiness of mankind."

American Desserts

What could be more American than apple pie? How about a slump, buckle, or grunt? Though these might sound like expletives from a Saturday morning cartoon, they are, along with pandowdy, crisp, crunch, cobbler, and brown betty, some of the "strange" names, to use the word of the late gourmet James Beard, which Americans have over the years given to their down-home fruit desserts.

As the new *Joy of Cooking* points out (in a chapter supervised by pastry chef Jim Dodge, the man who helped turn the restaurant in Boston's Museum of Fine Arts into a showplace for culinary masterpieces), the ancestors of these desserts are puddings on the one hand and pies on the other. Though they exhibit considerable variation in ingredients and methods (they may use pie crust, biscuit dough, and even dumplings, and the fruit may be cooked over, under, or inside the dough), they have a common denominator. As the *Joy of Cooking* states, "However they are made, these are plain, uncomplicated desserts—almost folklore, passed down from one generation to the next. . . ."

Pandowdies may be the quintessential version of these American fruit desserts. Even the name suggests plainness. Sharon Tyler Herbst, in her *Food Lover's Companion*, claims that the name may indeed refer to the dish's dowdy appearance. Others say that it alludes to the act of "dowdying" the pastry, the process of breaking up the partially baked crust and submerging it into the filling, a step usually taken about halfway through the cooking process. Whatever the case, a pandowdy is a deep-dish dessert made of fruit and spices, topped with a biscuit or pie dough which gets crisp and crumbly when baked. The *Joy of Cooking* tells us that pandowdies were originally eaten for breakfast, having baked overnight in the embers of a fireplace. They are often served warm with ice cream. Though apples are the typical fruit used in a pandowdy (many cookbooks treat pandowdy and apple pandowdy synonymously), other fruits, blueberries for example, can be used as well.

A grunt is essentially a concoction of steamed or stewed fruit and dumplings, and, like many of these old-fashioned desserts, it originated in New England. Although Herbst says the names "grunt" and "slump" are interchangeable, the *Joy of Cooking* makes a distinction between them. A grunt, it says, is steamed in a mold and inverted when served. A slump, on the other hand, is cooked in a covered pan and served in a bowl with the dumplings on top. The term "grunt" presumably comes from the sound which the dish makes when unmolded. No one is quite sure what the origin of the term "slump" is, but the *Joy of Cooking* observes that the word describes the eventual fate of the dumplings.

A buckle is a type of cake. Fruit is folded into the batter and streusel topping is scattered over it before baking. This causes the cake to crumple or "buckle" in spots, hence the name. Blueberry buckle may well be the most common variety, but peaches are a good choice too.

A betty or brown betty is fundamentally a baked pudding in which fruit is layered with buttered bread crumbs. The most common version is Apple Brown Betty, but other fruits can also be used. The *Joy of Cooking*, for example, has a recipe for Banana Brown Betty in which graham-cracker crumbs are substituted for bread crumbs. As James Beard noted in his book *American Cookery*, "Apple Brown Betty has many different guises. I don't think any two of the recipes are alike. They all have unusual bits of personality attached to them."

Crisps and crunches (the British call them "crumbles") are perhaps the simplest fruit desserts of all. They consist of sweetened fruit which, in the case of a crisp, is covered with a crumbly topping or, in the case of a crunch, sandwiched between it. As cookbook author Lee Bailey suggests, these rugged desserts must have been the mainstays of frontier America when there was little time to make something fancy. Made from readily available ingredients, they are, he notes, "just the sort of thing people need after a hard day of carving out a new life for themselves and their families."

Finally there are cobblers. These are merely deep-dish fruit desserts topped with a crust. A biscuit crust is more common today, but in earlier times cobblers were most often made with pie dough. The derivation of the name "cobbler" is uncertain, but the authors of the *Joy of Cooking* maintain that it may refer to the act of patching, or cobbling, the ingredients together just as a shoemaker might. As Bailey points out, "The cobbler is a dessert with no secrets except its simplicity." He warns against overzealous cooks who think it necessary to fancy up such desserts with complicated crusts or extra ingredients. "Whenever you see too many ingredients in a cobbler recipe," he cautions, "put the whole thing down to a cookbook writer's ego (or desperation)—and move on."

That's probably good advice for any of these indigenous concoctions, for, as Beard indicates, they are all the result of experimentation, borne of a shortage of more refined ingredients in early America. And their very homespun nature is what makes them so special. Give them a try and see why, as Beard reminds us, "We have been one of the most dessert-minded of all countries. . . ."

Aphrodisiacs

They say the way to a man's heart is through his stomach. It's a truth worth contemplating when Valentine's Day approaches. After all, as the writer Turgenev observed, "The genius of love and the genius of hunger . . . are the two moving forces behind all living things." In other words, all living things must feed and reproduce, or to put it bluntly, the two most important things to the human race are eating and sex. (As to which is more important, perhaps Talleyrand had it right when he said, "Show me another pleasure like dinner that comes every day and lasts an hour.")

Given the centrality of food and sex, it's hardly surprising that they are often associated. That association is ancient and universal. As Isabel Allende notes, "Ever since the first humans dropped a vulture or rat carcass on glowing coals and then celebrated that agape with festive fornication, the bond between food and sex has been constant in all cultures." Biblically, as the London newspaper the *Independent* remarks, "Food and sex have been bedfellows ever since Adam and Eve tasted the forbidden fruit."

Consequently, despite the availability of nonfood substances ranging from Spanish Fly to Viagra, food has become the natural precursor to romance. As the 16th-century French physician François Rabelais proclaimed, "Venus taketh cold when not accompanied by Ceres and Bacchus," which is to say that love is muted when not in the company of food and drink. Suzi Godson and Mel Agace of *The Sex Book* are surely correct when they claim, "Sharing food and wine must be the most common act of foreplay on the planet."

The search for foods which foster romance—called aphrodisiacs after Aphrodite who, not coincidentally, was the goddess of both love and crops—is age-old. And there's hardly a food, including green M&Ms, that at one time or another hasn't been identified as one able to create, in the words of an early *Encyclopaedia Britannica* article on the subject, "an inclination to venery."

As *The Cambridge World History of Food* explains, some foods have been labeled aphrodisiacs because of their resemblance to genitalia. Asparagus is a case in point. Thus, according to Bert Greene, in 19th-century France a bridegroom's prenuptial dinner traditionally contained three servings of the vegetable. (I suppose those who could afford such extravagance were objects of asparagus envy.)

The aphrodisiacal reputation of other foods is based on mythology. For example, since sparrows were said to be sacred to Aphrodite, their eggs were often prescribed in love potions. Still other foods were assumed to "provoke lust," merely because of their remote origin. Thus, even the American potato was seen as an aphrodisiac when introduced to Europe.

Allende, whose book *Aphrodite: A Memoir of the Senses*, by the way, includes a recipe for "Soup for Orgies" (it serves ten), suggests that anything with a French name seems aphrodisiacal while the late Johan Santesson, creator of a website on the subject, argues that anything expensive does.

Whatever the case, and bearing in mind the Roman prostitute's insight that kissing and hugging are the most powerful aphrodisiacs, you might want to serve the following foods on Valentine's Day:

- Oysters: The most famous aphrodisiac, its reputation persists from ancient times. Oysters contain zinc, which, it turns out, increases testosterone.
- Figs: There's probably a reason this was Cleopatra's favorite fruit.
- Garlic: For thousands of years garlic has been alleged to prompt women to fall in love and to make men powerful. And perhaps it does, but most likely only when both partners consume it. We do know that chickens lay better when fed garlic.
- Truffles: The gastronome Brillat-Savarin identified truffles as erotic back in 1825. More recently, cookbook author Paula Wolfert has echoed the saying that those who wish to lead virtuous lives had better abstain from them.
- Champagne: An old saying has it that whiskey makes a girl stop arguing, beer soothes her, gin disarms her, rum cajoles her, but champagne arouses her. Casanova must have thought so, for he poured the bubbly for all his conquests.
- Chocolate: Long ago, chocolate was banned from monasteries, and for good reason. It may be the champion of aphrodisiacs. The Aztec ruler Montezuma drank fifty cups of the stuff each day to maintain his virility, and Madame DuBarry served it to every suitor. Today we know that chocolate contains a chemical that stimulates euphoria.

The erotic potential of these foods notwithstanding, perhaps Allende is right when she says, "Everything cooked for a lover is sensual." (For insurance, she recommends shedding a garment or two as the meal is prepared.) Certainly there's no denying her conclusion that "the only truly infallible aphrodisiac is love."

Better than Better-than-Sex Cake, 302

Army Cooking

On Veteran's Day, at eleven o'clock, the 11th hour of the 11th day of the 11th month, Americans pause to acknowledge the debt we owe to fellow citizens who have served in our armed forces, including the more than 40 million who have served in wartime and the more than 1 million who have given their lives in that service.

The time and date of this observance, originally called Armistice Day on the order of President Woodrow Wilson, commemorates the exact time and date of the signing of the truce that ended World War I. That war was supposed to be the "war to end all wars," but, alas, by the time Congress got around to declaring November 11 a federal holiday in 1938, World War II was only a year away. In 1954, following the signing of yet another truce, this time in Korea, Congress changed the name of the holiday to Veterans' Day in honor of all who have served their country in uniform. They all deserve our gratitude.

If you ask Veterans about their experience in the military, you are not likely to hear much praise for the food they ate. In fact, mess-hall cuisine (the term is probably an oxymoron) was frequently derided. Coffee was referred to as "battery acid," sausages were called "bags of mystery," and that military staple, chipped beef on toast, was labeled "SOS." (If you were in the service, you know what that stands for.)

Feeding the troops has always been a formidable challenge, going all the way back to the days of the American Revolution when the weekly ration included a pound of beef or salt fish or ¾ pound of pork, a pound of bread or flour, a pint of milk or a quart of cider, and three pints of peas or beans. The soldiers of the Civil War fared no better. The mainstay of their diet was something called hardtack, a square biscuit made of flour and water. Soldiers called them "sheet iron crackers" because they were so hard they had to be broken up with a rock or rifle butt, soaked in water, and fried in bacon grease to make them soft enough to eat. By comparison, the fast food served by the "Wolfmobile" of the Persian Gulf War seems like haute cuisine.

While nobody would pretend that military food ever really approaches haute cuisine, my late Uncle Don, who was an army first-cook in Korea, told me that the mess hall afforded opportunities for occasional culinary highs, like the time one evening when he scrounged up some lard and flour to make doughnuts. The men in his company were so delighted with the unexpected treat that they quickly gobbled up the hot doughnuts right out of the fryer, leaving the six gallons of icing meant to glaze them unused.

Or there was the day, between frying eggs five dozen at a time and opening fifty cans of bacon with a hatchet, that he found time to prepare and decorate a cake to enter in a contest at a base twenty miles away. Though the cake did not survive the trip in Korea's 106-degree heat, he nonetheless received an award for the attempt. Moreover, among the rations there were isolated delicacies, like Australian tub butter, and, unlike the other cooks in the mess hall, Uncle Don managed to attractively garnish the food he served, an inclination which made him popular with his men.

Uncle Don, by the way, who had never cooked a day in his life before joining the army, took awhile to adjust to the home kitchen after he came back from the war. One of the first meals he fixed upon his return was a pot of chili for 4 which he inadvertently salted for 250!

But sporadic culinary achievements notwithstanding, most servicemen (and women), especially if they weren't officers, will probably find the Cookie character in the Beetle Bailey cartoon a little too close to the truth. After all, besides chipped beef on toast, the armed forces are still a major consumer of Spam. During the Second World War, 100 million pounds of the stuff was shipped to Russian, European, and American troops. (No wonder Nikita Khrushchev in his memoirs credited the canned luncheon meat with insuring the survival of the Russian army.) Indeed, Spam is inextricably linked with World War II because not only did the soldiers of that era eat a lot of it but, due to rationing, it became popular on the home front as well. The butt of a classic Monty Python sketch, it is not usually considered gourmet food, though Margaret Thatcher, former prime minister of Great Britain recalls it as a "wartime delicacy" served on Boxing Day.

But chipped beef and Spam have probably been unfairly maligned over the years. Despite their sometimes unsavory association with the military and their identification with wartime scarcity, they are ingredients which can have a flavorful role in contemporary dishes. In fact, Spam sales are increasingly strong, and statistics show that in this country alone something like four cans of Spam are eaten every second. Since it was first introduced in 1937, over 5 billion cans have been sold, making it one of the nation's most popular foods. In Korea, believe it or not, there's even a black market for Spam, and the product, sold in fashionable gift boxes, is as highly prized as jewelry. Chipped or dried beef likewise still has a following and no less a gourmet than the late James Beard included a trio of recipes for it in his book *American Cookery*. So why not give these two veteran foodstuffs another look? You might be surprised at how good they can taste in the right recipe.

Hot Chipped Beef Dip, 220
Hot and Spicy Spam Stir-fry, 290
Tex-Mex Dried Beef Supreme, 263

Asparagus

I'm not a vegetarian, but one of the most memorable meals I've ever eaten contained no meat and consisted entirely of a single vegetable.

It was during a springtime visit to Maastricht, the southernmost city in the Netherlands, a town practically within walking distance of the German border. It was Spargelzeit (asparagus time) in Germany, so one afternoon my wife and I hopped a train, and before we knew it we were shopping at a delightful German outdoor market which featured row upon row of that luxurious stalk. We splurged and bought several pounds of the vegetable and then hurried back to our Maastricht apartment to cook it.

That night we gorged ourselves on asparagus, nothing but asparagus, following the late James Beard's advice not to serve it sparingly and proving to ourselves the truth of his observation that "if asparagus is fresh and properly cooked, it needs nothing but freshly ground pepper and salt, and it is best eaten with the fingers." That meal was as satisfying and opulent as any I've ever had in a three-star restaurant.

It seems perfectly sensible to me to make an entire meal out of asparagus and to consider such a repast extraordinary. After all, asparagus is, as the French say, the king of vegetables and the vegetable of kings. Louis XIV liked it so much he had it grown in the royal greenhouse so he could eat it all year long. For most of us, though, it's a treat limited to just a few weeks during spring, which makes it all the more special. (It's hard to believe, as Rosso and Lukins tell us in *The Silver Palate Cookbook*, that in Russia the spears are so abundant that cows graze on them! I'm envious.)

We ought to feel special when eating asparagus, because, according to Maguelonne Toussaint-Samat, author of the *History of Food*, during the 19th century, asparagus, like meat, was food for the privileged. "Few country people ever tasted either," she notes, "and even in towns only a very small minority . . . could eat such things." The famous French gastronome, Anthelme Brillat-Savarin, reported that the vegetable sold for as much as forty francs a bundle at the Paris shop of Mme Chevet, a horrifically high price for the typical workingman of the era who earned only two and a half francs a day. Just as now, the cost reflected the fact that asparagus, especially the white variety preferred in Europe, is expensive to cultivate. Often requiring daily harvests, which must be done by hand, it may take as many as five years to establish a crop that will turn a profit, since spears can't be cut until three years after they are planted. Add to that the fact that after trimming, often only about half of it is edible and you realize just how extravagant a treat asparagus is. No wonder that in his book, *American Cookery*, Beard complained about the practice of cutting asparagus "shockingly long" just to increase its weight and up its price.

But its expense notwithstanding, asparagus has been a coveted vegetable for centuries. There is evidence, for example, that the Egyptians even presented bundles of it as offerings to their gods. The ancient Greeks, from whom we get the name of the vegetable (it means "sprout" or "shoot"), preferred wild asparagus and as early as 200 BC the Romans developed techniques to cultivate it, sometimes growing stalks as large as three to a pound, much to the dismay of Pliny, who contended that nature ordained it should grow untamed.

The Romans also pioneered freezing asparagus by sending chariots full of it up the Tiber River to the Alps where it would be kept in snow for months. Appropriately, they would serve it on the Feast of Epicurus. Roman emperors such as Caesar Augustus (whose phrase for urging haste was "quicker than you can cook asparagus") even designated special boats, the asparagus fleet, for transporting the vegetable.

Apparently the Arabs introduced asparagus into Spain, and from there it spread to France, the largest producer in Europe, where the town of Argenteuil near Paris became famous for it. Dutch and English colonists brought asparagus to North America in the 1700s, and by the middle of the next century it was being cultivated in California, now the country's major producer, though Oceana County in Michigan has proclaimed itself the asparagus capital of the nation.

Though one of the most popular varieties of asparagus is named after Martha Washington, when it comes to appreciating the plant, we're still amateurs compared to Germany where, during the season, virtually every restaurant features a special asparagus menu (a Spargelkarte), magazines are filled with recipes for it, and organized tours to asparagus farms (asparagus weekends) are not uncommon. There's even an asparagus museum near Munich.

Besides being delicious, asparagus has other virtues. The ancients believed it had medicinal qualities, as did the early Native Americans. Today we know it is a rich source of folate, a vitamin that may lower the risk of heart disease and certain types of cancer, and it contains lots of potassium, which can have a salutary effect on blood pressure. It is a natural diuretic.

But still the best reason to devour asparagus is because it tastes so good, and the truth is, like a ripe tomato or a fresh raspberry, the less done to it the better. Thus, Edith Jones of Cape Girardeau, Missouri, a German-born Spargel aficionado who fondly remembers her father growing the vegetable, recommends simply steaming or boiling it and serving it in classic Teutonic fashion with thinly sliced ham, hard-boiled egg, and melted butter. That's good advice. Asparagus, after all, is a member of the lily family and it hardly needs gilding.

Here are some asparagus tips for selecting and cooking perfect spears. Choose firm, bright green stalks with compact tips and no ridges. Store asparagus with the ends submerged in water or swaddled in damp paper towels and serve it as soon as possible, preferably the day you buy it. Trim each stalk by simply bending it until the tougher end breaks off with a snap. You need not peel asparagus unless it is especially thick. The thickness of the stalk, by the way, is merely an indication of the plant's maturity. Contrary to popular wisdom, there is no reliable relationship between thickness and tenderness. Cook asparagus on its side in barely boiling water in a large frying pan until just done. You really don't need one of those fancy vertical cookers. Or you can drizzle asparagus with olive oil and roast it in a 500-degree oven for 8–10 minutes.

Though it's hard to beat plain asparagus prepared this way, it's also only fair to note that the vegetable can elevate a quiche, enrich a risotto, enhance a frittata, embellish a plate of pasta, or jazz up a bowl of potato salad. And it makes a heavenly soup, too.

Stir-fry of Asparagus with Pears and Chicken, 270
Asparagus and Rhubarb Custard Pie, 335
Asparagus and Ham Brunch Bread, 252

Baklava

Burhan Cagdas, a third-generation pastry-maker in the city of Gaziantep, the pistachio capital of Turkey, likes to tell the story about two feuding 19th-century families who specialized in baklava, the layered dessert of thin filo pastry (also spelled fillo or phyllo) and nuts drenched in honey or flavored syrup. As he recounted the story recently for the *Los Angeles Times*, the son of one family married the daughter of the other. After the groom took his new in-laws a tray of baklava, in keeping with wedding etiquette, the father of the bride gathered his seven sons together and asked them what was wrong with it.

One suggested that the syrup was too thick, another that improperly clarified butter had been used, and still another that the pastry was too damp. One by one, each critiqued the dish. But the father said, "No, you are all wrong. The correct answer is: When you bite into a baklava, it should go 'hush,' but this one goes 'moojook.'"

As this story suggests, a well-made baklava feels and therefore sounds different than one that has been made ineptly. It is delicate and crisp, not soggy. You can almost sense each individual layer of filo as you bite into it. The story also reveals that in Turkey they take baklava seriously.

It shouldn't be surprising that Turks are passionate about baklava, for they invented it. Variations of the dessert are now found in Syria, Lebanon, Greece (where it was traditionally served at Easter, made with forty layers of pastry to represent the forty days of Lent), and neighboring countries. But it was in the kitchens of Istanbul's Topkapi Palace where the sweet was first concocted.

On a recent pilgrimage to the palace, I stood amid its ten double kitchens (two were reserved exclusively for desserts), which now house the finest collection of Ming Dynasty porcelain outside of China, and tried to imagine what it must have been like some 500 years ago when baklava was first created for the sultans of the Ottoman Empire. Hundreds of cooks scurried about, creating all manner of exotic dishes, preparing meals for as many as 20,000 people a day, and in the process, developing a cuisine that rivals French or Cantonese. I could picture in my head the grand Baklava Procession conducted annually by Suleyman the Magnificent to honor his palace guards. Others may envy the sultans their vast wealth or, perhaps, their harems, but I am jealous of their culinary riches.

Though baklava was created only 500 years ago, as confirmed "filophile" Marti Sousanis, author of *The Art of Filo*, points out, its roots can be traced back another 500 to when nomadic Turks in Central Asia developed the habit of stacking an unleavened tortilla-like bread called *yufka* (the same word used today to refer to a single sheet of filo) with butter and other fillings. Gaining access to ovens, they began filling these bundles ("baklava" means "a bundle") with nuts and baking them, and a few centuries later they hit upon the idea of stretching the dough until it was paper-thin. And the rest, as they say, is history. Filo dough itself, by the way, went on to become the base for strudel when the Turks invaded Hungary, and as Rose Levy Beranbaum, author of *The Pie and Pastry Bible* tells us, it is the mother of French puff pastry as well.

Most people are familiar with baklava made with walnuts and cut into diamond shapes. But at the 128-year-old baklava shop run by the Gulluoglu family in Istanbul (reputed to be the best in the city), I discovered that there are many kinds of fillings and shapes. Besides baklava with walnut stuffing (*cevizli*), there is baklava with pistachio nuts (*fistikli*) and baklava with clotted cream (*kaymakli*), to name just a few. Almonds are another popular stuffing, and I know of at least one bakery, near Boston, that uses cashews. Sousanis even reports an Ethiopian version made with peanuts! As to shapes, besides the familiar diamonds, baklava can be rolled up like a cigar, cut into wedges, or coiled into nests called *bülbül yuvasi* (nightingales' nests).

Examining this myriad of baklavas, you might conclude that making the dessert at home would be rather daunting. It can be, but it needn't be, as I discovered in talking with one of Cape Girardeau, Missouri's most gracious hostesses and the best baklava maker I know, Beverly Noffel. She comes by her baklava skills honestly, being of Lebanese descent, and can even recall grandparents making their own filo dough. Over decades and countless pans of baklava, she has perfected the process and offers the following tips.

First, use fresh filo dough if possible. If the dough has been frozen, the leaves may stick together and tear when pulled apart. This is especially true if the dough has been allowed to thaw and refreeze in the grocer's case, an all-too-common occurrence. In using frozen dough, however, I have discovered that little tears here and there, as long as they are not gaping, really don't matter that much in the final product. But fresh dough is much more fun and far less frustrating.

Second, filo leaves should be well coated with melted butter so they don't dry out, but they should not be sopping or the finished product will be greasy. Clarified unsalted butter (where the milk solids and water have been allowed to separate out) is preferable when making baklava because the reduced water content abets a crisp baked dough. (This is just the opposite of puff pastry where unclarified butter with its extra water content is needed to create steam to separate the layers.)

Third, chill the assembled baklava before baking, and bake until very golden. Avoid underbaking.

Fourth, always put cool syrup on hot baklava. The reverse will work too, but a contrast in temperatures is crucial if the baklava is to soak up all the syrup.

Finally, Beverly recommends being orderly and systematic. Clarify the butter, make the syrup, and chop the nuts in advance and have all of your materials at hand in an uncluttered work space. Then you can work efficiently before the unused dough dries out, which it quickly will, to the point of shattering, if not covered with a damp towel.

Your first attempts at baklava may not be worthy of a sultan's table, but in using these tips you'll discover that preparing this regal sweet is not as difficult as you might imagine. The following recipes are designed to give you plenty of practice.

Balsamic Vinegar

Perhaps you've heard of the vinegar diet which promises that you can lose weight without counting calories or going hungry. The hitch is, you have to drink vinegar (you're apparently allowed to lace it with a little honey) several times daily.

I haven't tried the regimen, but I suspect it would sour me even further on dieting. Unless, however, I could substitute that most unvinegar-like of vinegars, the balsamic variety.

Authentic balsamic vinegar, a conspicuous exception to the old adage that you can catch more flies with honey, is as highly prized by gourmet cooks as caviar, truffles, or saffron and, in terms of price, in the same category. A three-ounce bottle of the very best balsamic vinegar can fetch as much as $500. Thus, cookbook author Diane Seed reports that when her house was burglarized a few years ago, she knew the thieves were gentlemen of discernment. They took a bottle of her best *balsamico* with them. No wonder that in Italy, where it is used as an aperitif, it is often part of a wedding dowry. One manufacturer in Modena, in Northern Italy, the birthplace of balsamic vinegar, even produces a chocolate candy filled with the stuff.

The origin of balsamic vinegar (the word may relate to balm, suggesting its comforting qualities) is impossible to pin down precisely, though clearly it's a recent development as vinegars go. Generic vinegar goes back thousands of years and was probably discovered accidentally when some unsuspecting cook left an uncovered jar of wine, itself the product of fermented grape juice, out in the open where it underwent a second fermentation. (The word "vinegar" is derived from the French, *vin aigre*, for "sour wine.") Vinegar's origin is so ancient that there are no less than eight references to it in the Bible (four in the Old Testament and four in the New), not counting the inadvertent reference in an edition published in Oxford in 1717 when the word "vineyard" was misprinted as vinegar. That edition has been known ever since as the Vinegar Bible.

The first reference to balsamic vinegar dates to the 11th century when a Benedictine monk wrote about a barrel of vinegar given as a gift to King Enrico II of Franconia. But it was not until 1598, when the Duke of Este moved his court and his barrels of vinegar to Modena, that the elixir gained wider attention, though it was reserved for the upper classes. By the 18th century, word of the potion had spread elsewhere in Europe. Still the condiment was largely unknown in this country until recently, when noted cooking teacher Marcella Hazan and opera superstar Luciano Pavarotti, a native of Modena, both began to sing its praises. Now it is the rage.

The celebrity status of balsamic vinegar has not been without its drawbacks. Demand for the product has resulted in a flood of cheap imitations of the real thing, and perhaps nowhere in the world of cuisine is there a greater difference between the real thing and an imitation than when it comes to balsamic vinegar. By contrast, the disparity between margarine and butter is trivial.

Genuine balsamic vinegar is an artisanal product made from grapes, chiefly the Trebbiano variety, cultivated in the provinces of Modena and Reggio in northern Italy. No additives are legally permitted, and the grapes must be cooked over a direct flame in an open pot. They are then stored in wooden barrels and aged over a period of years (twelve is the minimum), usually in an attic called an *acetaia*. The attic allows the vinegar to take advantage of the climate of the region, letting in hot air in the summer and cold air in the winter to promote the desired chemical changes. As the liquid thickens, it is decanted into progressively smaller barrels, sometimes several hundred years old, made of oak, chestnut, cherry, mulberry, or juniper, and which impart subtle flavors. Before it can be sealed in exclusively designed bottles, the finished product must pass a blind tasting and be certified as *aceto balsamico tradizionale*, the words which guarantee that it is the genuine article.

The truth is, the very best balsamic vinegar is priceless and often not sold, but kept in the family for special occasions. For instance, Italian families that maintain vinegar attics often put up a barrel of balsamico at the birth of a child and serve it on the child's 21st birthday, or at Christmastime they taste a spoonful of the oldest brew on hand in memory of loved ones who have died. But demand for balsamic vinegar has increased production and there is still plenty left if you are willing to pay for it. Look for the word *tradizionale* on the label and expect to pay per ounce what you would for fine perfume. *Extra vecchio* (or extra old) balsamic vinegar must be aged at least 25 years instead of the minimum 12 and, obviously, will cost more, but Darryl Corti, an importer in Sacramento, advised the *New York Times* that any bottle selling for less than $50 is probably inferior.

The high cost of the real thing has resulted in a slew of cheaper so-called balsamic vinegars, which isn't so bad in itself because you probably wouldn't use the $75-an-ounce stuff to make a salad dressing anyway. Save that, as the Italians do, to drizzle over finished dishes such as grilled meats or vegetables or even over fruit or ice cream. (A sublime treat is genuine Parmigiano-Reggiano cheese splashed with balsamic vinegar.) But even though there is a place for the cheaper industrially produced balsamic vinegar, finding a good one is problematic because, unlike the genuine article, its production is largely unregulated.

In 1965 the Italian Ministry of Agriculture legally defined balsamic vinegar, but the statute contained several loopholes which permit commercial manufacturers to use vinegar aged only for days, not years, dilute it with wine vinegar, and sweeten it with caramel and still quite legally call it "balsamic vinegar of Modena." And that's just in Italy. In the United States, just about any vinegar can be called balsamic and the manufacturer can say almost anything on the label. Even statements of age may be suspect. The result is that for commercial balsamic vinegar, even price is not a reliable guide to quality. Generally speaking, however, an artisan-style balsamic, which is aged, but not for as long as a true balsamic, will be superior to the commercial variety you typically find in the supermarket. At $16 and up per bottle, it's more expensive, but still affordable. Wood-aged is preferable. If the vinegar was made in Modena or Reggio (the label will say API MO or API RE), so much the better. Finally, you needn't be above doctoring an inferior so-called balsamic vinegar to suit you. A trick some restaurants use to create something reminiscent of true balsamic vinegar is to mix 2 tablespoons light brown sugar with ⅓ cup of the cheap stuff and boil it down to ¼ cup.

Whether it's inexpensive or costly, it's a shame to relegate the balsamic vinegar you have at your disposal just to the salad bowl. As the following recipes demonstrate, it can add subtle nuances to a variety of foods. Even though it's vinegar, as Jackie Gleason would have said, "How sweet it is."

Balsamic Glazed Pasta, 265
Roast Chicken and Potatoes with Balsamic Black-Pepper Sauce, 275
Poached Pears with Ricotta, Walnuts, and Balsamic Vinegar, 374

Bananas

"So when the woman saw that the tree was good for food, and that it was a delight to the eyes, and that the tree was to be desired to make one wise, she took of its fruit and ate; and she also gave some to her husband, and he ate." Thus begins the Biblical account of the fall from grace of Adam and Eve.

Many of us think that the fruit of the tree of knowledge referred to in the story of the Garden of Eden was an apple, but speculation has centered around a variety of other fruits as well, including pomegranates, quinces, tomatoes, figs, and oranges. Islamic tradition has it that the forbidden fruit was actually a banana, and consequently, it is said that after their fall, Adam and Eve covered themselves with banana leaves rather than fig leaves.

Well, why not? The banana is about the closest thing there is to the perfect fruit. Though low in calories (typically around ninety) it is high in nutrition. The only staple food that is not a grain, it is an especially good source of vitamin C, fiber, and potassium. No wonder an old saying has it that "a banana is as good as a steak."

At one time, bananas were an exotic luxury in North America. Waverly Root and Richard De Rochemont, authors of *Eating Well in America: A History*, note that had it not been for the simultaneous development of transportation and refrigeration, they might still be. Back around the time of the Civil War, for example, when bananas were all but unknown in this country, they were sporadically shipped to New Orleans from the West Indies, wrapped individually in tinfoil as befits a precious commodity, and sold for a dollar apiece.

Though bananas wouldn't be officially introduced to Americans until 1876 at the Philadelphia Centennial Exhibition, they were already well known in other parts of the world and had been for a long time. In fact, some historians maintain that bananas were the first fruit farmed by man.

Since there are so many varieties of bananas found in Malaysia, it's likely that they originated there thousands of years ago. They then traveled to India, where in 327 BC they were discovered by Alexander the Great and brought to the Western world. As early as 200 AD they had reached China, and eventually they arrived in Madagascar. Before long, they spread across tropical Africa from east to west. In the 15th century, Portuguese sailors took them from Guinea to the Canary Islands, and from there in 1516, the Franciscan monk Tomas de Berlanga brought them to Santo Domingo. They spread so quickly and extensively throughout Central and South America that later explorers actually thought they were native to the region.

Lorenzo Baker, the captain of the schooner *Telegraph*, began the banana trade to the United States in 1870 when he brought a couple of bunches from Jamaica to Boston and discovered how profitable their sale could be. Today, bananas are the most popular fruit in America. We import more than 4 million tons of them every year. The average person eats some thirty-three pounds annually. It appears we've become a Banana Republic after all.

Grilled Banana Split, 372

Basil

Had television been around then, both Jerry Springer and Martha Stewart might have fought to have as guests on their show Lorenzo and Isabella, the hero and heroine of a Keats poem based on a story by Boccaccio.

Isabella lived with her two brothers following the death of their father. Despite the insistence of the brothers that she marry well and collect a sizable dowry, she fell madly in love with Lorenzo, a carpenter who worked on the family estate. To keep their plans from being foiled, the brothers lured Lorenzo into the woods and killed and buried him there. Subsequently, his ghost appeared to the distraught Isabella, told her what happened, and gave her a map to his shallow grave in the woods.

Isabella dug up Lorenzo's body, cut off its head, and took it home with her where she promptly planted it in a large basil pot along with some basil seeds. She watered the seeds with her tears, and in time the plant grew so lavishly that it rivaled the finest specimens in Florence. Isabella's brothers became concerned about her attachment to the plant and stole it away. Cracking the pot open they saw the head of Lorenzo and, realizing what had happened, left town. Meanwhile, Isabella, unable to locate her precious pot of basil, died of misery.

Fortunately for us, it is not necessary to go to such lengths to grow basil, an herb with a fragrance and flavor far more delightful than this macabre tale might suggest.

Basil has always been an herb with symbolic significance. In Crete it represented "love washed with tears," as in the story of Isabella and Lorenzo. In ancient Rome it was thought to provide protection against the fire-breathing dragon or Basilisk. In ancient Persia and Malaysia it was scattered on graves. In Rumania a man is considered officially engaged when he accepts a sprig of it from his girlfriend. In India, where the plant actually originated, one variety (appropriately named Holy Basil) is considered sacred. Likewise, the ancient Greeks thought that only the king himself, using a golden sickle, should harvest basil (the name comes from the Greek word for king, *basileus*.) As Maguelonne Toussaint-Samat points out in the *History of Food*, the harvesting process was steeped in ritual. Women were not allowed to pick the herb, and the priest who officiated at the harvesting ceremony had to purify his right hand with water from three different springs.

The 3,000-year-old plant also has therapeutic value. It is an antidote to venom, is reputed to contain antiviral compounds, and has been used as an insect repellent. An article on home remedies in *Mother Earth News* reports that a world-renowned French herbal folk healer named Maurice Messegue prescribes a basil tea for migraines. He also claims it is good for the eyes and suggests that if merely drinking the hot tea doesn't do the trick, it should be cooled to lukewarm and used as an eyewash.

But, of course, basil's greatest role is in food. There are more than a dozen varieties of the herb, ranging from sweet to spicy, that can be used in cooking. Sweet basil, with its broad, green leaves is probably the most familiar, but there's also opal basil which is deep purple in color, as well as cinnamon basil, lemon basil, licorice basil, Thai basil, and lettuce-leaf basil, so called because of its large leaves.

We love them all at our house, because, with the possible exception of cilantro, basil is our favorite herb. And luckily for us, it is a lot easier to grow than cilantro. In fact, basil is one of the easiest herbs to grow. The Romans even believed that the more the plant was abused the more it would thrive. It grows well in full sun, prefers dry soil, since it is sensitive to excess moisture, and tends to be prolific. (Even now, scientists in Italy, where basil is a multimillion dollar industry, are hard at work developing a frost-resistant strain that would allow for an even longer growing season.)

You can begin harvesting basil when the plants are as small as six inches tall and have only 6 or so pairs of leaves. As Thomas DeBaggio and Susan Belsinger point out in *Basil: An Herb Lover's Guide*, this early pruning will actually trick the plants into being more productive. That's because basil plants are programmed to produce only a certain number of leaves before they start flowering and then quit growing leaves altogether. If you harvest early enough to keep each stem from developing its target number of leaves, you can delay the flowering process and get more leaves per plant. And you can grow basil year-round. All you need is a warm, sunny window. (Fresh basil is now routinely available, even in winter, at the supermarket as well.)

Growing the herb year-round is a good idea because, frankly, no method of storage can keep its just-picked essence from fading. Dried basil is almost totally devoid of the true character of the fresh herb. A traditional way of preserving basil is to layer the leaves in an airtight jar, salt them, cover with olive oil, and keep in a cool place or refrigerate. A more modern method involves puréeing the leaves with water or oil and freezing the mixture in ice cube trays for later addition to soups and sauces.

Probably the best thing to do with excess basil is to infuse its flavor into vinegar or oil or, better yet, turn it into the classic Italian basil sauce, pesto, and freeze it. Invented in Genoa where there's plenty of basil and olive oil to go around, pesto consists of basil, garlic, pine nuts, Parmesan cheese, and oil ground together in a food processor or by hand in a mortar. (The name comes from the Italian word *pestare* which means "to pound.")

But at our house, the problem of what to do with leftover basil is not really an acute one. Our appetites usually tend to outstrip the production of the two pots we have growing out on the patio. That's because during the summer months we eat lots of the classic Insalata Caprese (literally, "the salad from Capri") which is simply a layering of fresh tomatoes, basil, and mozzarella dressed with olive oil. And also because we put basil in everything, including risotto, pasta, pasta dough, soup, salad, potatoes, salmon, chicken, iced tea, melon, and even sorbet (we fell in love with the stuff after sampling it at a booth at the Union Square Greenmarket in New York City). We've yet to run across a dish that in our judgment isn't improved by the addition of fresh basil. Try the following recipes and see if you don't agree.

Berries

"Doubtless God could have made a better berry," opined Dr. William Butler writing in the 16th century about the strawberry, "but doubtless God never did."

His position is tenable, but I wonder whether it represents careful analysis or mere prejudice. Did he consider the akala, a sweet berry from Hawaii, or the wild whortleberry of England, a tart relative of the blueberry? Did he take into account the Scandinavian cloudberry or the Japanese wineberry? Did he ponder the cranberry or its cousin the cowberry? Did he take note of the gooseberry, the indispensable ingredient in that classic English dessert, gooseberry fool?

Obviously he did not study the loganberry or the boysenberry, because the former was not discovered by Judge J. H. Logan of California until around the turn of the century, and the latter, a cross between a loganberry, a raspberry, and a blackberry was not invented by Rudolph Boysen until 1923. And what about blackberries and raspberries, and for that matter, elderberries and mulberries? Did he factor these into his deliberations?

Clearly, Butler's assertion about the strawberry may have been a bit, well, rash. Not that the strawberry isn't a strong candidate for the title of best berry. Surely the residents of Wepion, the Belgian town which claims to be the world capital of strawberries and which houses a strawberry museum, would give it their vote. So, too, most likely, would the citizens of Strawberry, Arizona, and Strawberry, California.

And who would argue that strawberries aren't wonderful? The ancient Romans even thought they could cure gastritis and other illnesses. (I don't know if that's true, but, on the other hand, I won't dispute the notion that a large dish of strawberries, perhaps covered with heavy cream, can be therapeutic.)

Strawberries are members of the rose family and grew wild for hundreds of years before being cultivated in the 15th century. Today there are some seventy varieties. The best ones still grow wild in the woods of France and are known as *fraises des bois* (strawberries of the woods). The French word for strawberry, *fraise*, as well as the Italian word, *fragola*, and the Spanish word, *fresa*, derive from the Latin term, *fragaria*, applied to strawberries because of their scent or fragrance. We call them strawberries probably because of the straw used to cover the berry beds to keep down weeds, though there is another theory that because strawberries were ripe at the time hay was mowed, the "straw" comes from the Anglo-Saxon word, *streow*, for hay.

Whatever they are called, there is no question that the strawberry is a beautiful fruit worthy of accolades. After all, how bearable would summers be without strawberry shortcake? But then there are blackberries.

To me there is hardly a sight more beautiful than a basket of just-picked blackberries, especially if I didn't have to pick them. Blackberries grow on thorny shrubs, which is why they are sometimes called brambles. Admittedly, they contain large seeds, but that's a small price to pay for their tart, intense flavor. Too bad these gorgeous berries seem to be scarcer than others, for they make the definitive cobbler and, as far as I'm concerned, a few fresh ones can transform even the most pedestrian bowl of cereal into gourmet food.

Not that the blueberry doesn't have much to commend it. Curiously, it's one of the few foods where the color blue is appetizing (actually, a blueberry is light green on the inside). Blueberries last longer after picking than other berries, and they seem to freeze better too. And when it comes to baking, blueberries are far more adept than other berries, particularly strawberries, which quickly lose flavor, color, and texture when subjected to heat (unless you boil them down into jam or jelly). Blueberries may well be the ultimate addition to pancakes and muffins.

But despite the allure of strawberries, blackberries, and blueberries, when it comes to selecting the best, I'd have to cast my ballot for the raspberry, for it seems to me the raspberry represents the best of all possible berry worlds: a color more intense than a strawberry's, a shape more refined than a blackberry's, a texture more melting than a blueberry's, and a taste more ambrosial than any of them.

Though raspberries come in three major varieties—black, golden, and red—the red are the most delicious in my judgment, and the most elegant. As food writer Barbara Kafka rightly observes, "Nobody can be insulted by raspberries and cream." Indeed, because of their limited availability and typically high price, raspberries are often considered a luxury. But what wonderful extravagance!

So with all due respect to the good Dr. Butler, I think he may have overstated the case for strawberries, though, perhaps, not by much. The truth is, I wouldn't want to spend a summer without strawberries, blackberries, blueberries, or raspberries. I'm grateful for all of them.

Blackberry Cake, 305
Strawberries and Ice Cream with Balsamic Vinegar, 373
Blueberry Torte, 308
Raspberry Cheese Tart, 336

Biscuits

What could be better than having your cake and eating it too? How about having your cake and eating pie crust too! That, according to Rose Levy Beranbaum, is exactly what you have when you eat a biscuit. And she should know, for Beranbaum is the author of both *The Cake Bible* and *The Pie and Pastry Bible*.

As Beranbaum explains, biscuits are actually the bridge between pastry and cake. While they are prepared like flaky pie dough, they contain the same basic ingredients as cake. No wonder they are so good.

At our house, as a result of culinary overzealousness, we rediscovered the appeal of homemade biscuits. Faced with the need to use up the remains of a 22-pound ham prepared for ten people at Easter, we whipped up some traditional Southern ham biscuits, little ham sandwiches made with biscuits instead of bread. The ham disappeared in no time, and in the process, we were reminded how delectable a biscuit can be.

As Marcelle Bienvenu, writing in the *Times-Picayune* of New Orleans, points out, biscuits have been popular in this country since just before the Civil War when the introduction of commercial baking powder made it easy to prepare them and other so-called "quick" breads (quick because they do not require the long-rising times of yeast breads). And, as she also notes, nothing is more Southern.

That's not to say that folks living above the Mason-Dixon line don't know how to make them, but there really is a difference between a Northern biscuit and a Southern one. As food scientists at Oregon State University indicate, biscuits vary with cultural background and geographical location. They suggest that the ideal Southern biscuit has a rough pale golden crust with a uniform fine crumb whereas the standard Northern biscuit has a golden brown, smooth, tender and crisp crust without brown specks.

Furthermore, most Southern cooks will tell you that the secret to perfect Southern biscuits is in the flour, and they warn that "Yankee" flour just won't do. Flour milled in the North, which includes most national brands, is made from hard wheat which is high in protein. Beranbaum, for example, reports that Pillsbury and Gold Medal all-purpose flours typically contain 11% protein; bread flour, such as King Arthur's, is even higher at 14%. Southern flour, sometimes called biscuit flour, such as Martha White or White Lily, on the other hand, is made from soft wheat which contains less protein, around 9% according to Beranbaum.

The more protein, the more strands of gluten, the elastic substance formed when the protein in flour combines with liquid. Gluten is desirable in yeast breads where it traps the carbon dioxide released through fermentation and gives the bread structure. But it tends to make biscuits tough. Originally some biscuits were meant to be hard. In fact, as Sharon Tyler Herbst notes in *The Food Lover's Companion*, the word "biscuit" comes from the French *bis cuit* which means "twice cooked," which is what was done to sea biscuits to keep them crisp. But these days we like our biscuits tender and flaky. Indeed, as breadmaking expert Beth Hensperger observes, it is this flakiness, the result of a layering effect not unlike that in puff pastry, that makes biscuits (and scones, for that matter, which are essentially biscuits in a different shape) unique among quick breads.

Geographic differences aside, there are several types of biscuits. There are rolled biscuits, which are cut from dough which has been kneaded and rolled out. These are typically cut into rounds, but they can also be cut into squares, rectangles, or sticks, an approach which eliminates scraps.

There are drop biscuits which, as their name indicates, are made by simply dropping batter directly onto a baking sheet. Drop-biscuit dough is usually made with more liquid than rolled dough. You can bake drop biscuits in muffin tins for the sake of uniformity if you like.

There are cream biscuits, which rely on heavy cream rather than butter or shortening to provide the fat. They are perhaps the easiest of all biscuits to prepare since the fat does not have to be cut into the dry ingredients separately.

There are buttermilk biscuits, such as those for which Mother's Restaurant in New Orleans is famous. They are a classic Southern specialty. According to Mother's chef Jerry Amato, in an interview in *Restaurants and Institutions* magazine, buttermilk makes a dough that requires less handling, resulting in a more tender biscuit.

There are combination biscuits, such as angel biscuits or cloud biscuits, which contain yeast as well as baking powder or some other leavener. Technically, these are not really biscuits at all, but something closer to a yeast roll.

There are fried biscuits which are cooked in hot oil, and there are beaten biscuits, which, true to their name, are beaten vigorously before being baked. Beaten biscuits, which may actually predate Colonial times, tend to be dry, and can be served like cocktail crackers. Originally, cooks pounded the dough with a hammer, mallet, or the side of an axe until the invention of the biscuit brake, a device which used hand-cranked rollers to do the job. Today a food processor can reduce the beating time from the customary 15–30 minutes to only 2–3.

Regardless of type and despite the mystique often surrounding them, biscuit recipes, as the *Joy of Cooking* notes, tend to be forgiving. As long as you are careful to avoid overworking the dough, you'll probably get good results. And though refrigerated biscuits produce quite satisfactory results (no less an authority than the late James Beard even wondered if they rendered homemade ones obsolete), making your own is surely more rewarding. Moreover, when you mix the ingredients yourself, you can add a wide variety of flavorings such as cheese, herbs, hot peppers, nutmeats, wild rice, fruits and vegetables, and even cocoa powder. The following recipes can get you started while demonstrating why, in the words of Beth Hensperger, "In some households, biscuits are still the bread."

Blue Cheese

"Well, I never felt more like singing the blues," went a Guy Mitchell tune that rose to the top of the charts in the late 1950s. Though Mitchell's song was plaintive, when it comes to cheese, the blues can be positively joyous.

However, blue cheese can take some getting used to. As Harvey Day condescendingly observed, people may shy away from cheeses like Roquefort and Stilton because "the plebeian proboscis is not equipped to differentiate between the sordid and the sublime." But even an aristocrat might side with David Frost when he asks, "Why is it that Swiss cheese has the holes when it's Gorgonzola that needs the ventilation?"

After all, you wouldn't think that a food which is by definition "moldy" could be so delectable. And let's face it, with the exception of blueberries, blue is normally not a sought-after color in food. Indeed, when most foods turn that shade, it's time to throw them out!

But blue cheese is a different matter. It's my favorite choice as an appetizer, in a salad, on top of a burger, or paired with a good port for dessert. (In fact, an outstanding cheese will make you think an ordinary wine is better than it really is.) And trust me, blue cheese raises apple pie, or better yet pear pie, to majestic heights. I wouldn't be at all surprised if Clifton Fadiman was thinking about the blue genre when he defined cheese as "milk's leap toward immortality."

Blue cheese gets its distinctive flavor by being treated with molds that facilitate the development of its characteristic blue, really blue-green, veins. (In the case of the Spanish blue cheese, Cabrales, they're almost purple.) For example, France's famed Roquefort cheese is produced by stirring into the curd Penicillium roqueforti which is actually moldy rye-bread crumbs.

There are many varieties of blue cheese. There's even a blue version of England's classic Cheshire cheese. But the most well known are Danish blue, Roquefort, Stilton, Gorgonzola, and Cabrales, all imports. Vying with these and on a par with them is Maytag blue, made at the Maytag Dairy Farms in Newton, Iowa (the same town where they make the washing machines). Though you might call these the "Blues Brothers" of the cheese world, they differ significantly. Some, for example, are made with cow's milk, others with sheep's milk. Some are crumbly, others soft and almost spreadable. Some are mild, others strong.

If you want to learn all there is to know about these cheeses, and any others for that matter, I recommend the *Cheese Primer* by Columbia, Missouri, native Steven Jenkins, the first American to be awarded France's Chevalier du Taste-Fromage, among the highest honors to which a cheesemonger can aspire. (An autographed copy of his book is among my prized possessions.)

Jenkins points out that Danish blue cheese provides excellent value and consistent quality, if not complex flavor, and is one of the few mass-produced cheeses that decidedly does not represent what Bob Brown, in referring to processed cheese, calls "the triumph of technology over conscience." The Danes invented one of my favorite cheeses, Saga blue, a wonderfully creamy cheese that is also made in this country.

Roquefort cheese, according to Jenkins, may be the most intensely flavored cheese of all. "I cannot think of any other food that possesses such complexity of flavor," he says. This cheese, which was a favorite of Charlemagne, is made with sheep's milk and ripened for months in the limestone caves of Combalou, near the town of Roquefort-sur-Soulzon in southwestern France. Its name is protected by law.

Stilton, my favorite cheese, is England's only name-protected cheese. Though it was actually never made there, it took its name from the Bell Inn at Stilton where 18th-century travelers got their first taste of it. Jenkins echoes my sentiments when he observes that "Stilton's greatest glory comes at the end of a grand meal with a glass of Port or a fine red wine, good bread, and sweet fruit." It has a firm yet crumbly texture.

Gorgonzola is named for a town south of Milan where it was originally produced. Its aroma can be quite powerful. It comes in two varieties, dolce (sweet) or naturale (sharp). Jenkins recommends it for salads and as a primary ingredient in stuffed chicken or veal, pasta sauces, and pizza, or with pears and figs for dessert. "I am constantly grateful a cheese this good exists," he says.

Cabrales, one of Spain's great cheeses, is made from a mixture of goat's, cow's, and sheep's milk. Its flavor "immediately electrifies the tongue," according to Jenkins. This is a strong cheese which, Jenkins advises, demands your full attention. Therefore, he recommends it be eaten by itself with, perhaps, only some bread, walnuts, fruit, or wine as an accompaniment.

Finally, there is Maytag blue cheese, a domestic cheese which, according to Jenkins, represents "one of the brightest aspects of American cheese production." This creamy cheese is sold mostly through mail order.

When it comes to selecting a good specimen of any of these cheeses, probably T. S. Eliot gave the best advice when he said, "Never commit yourself to a cheese without having first examined it." Once they pass that test, these blue cheeses are the ingredient which makes the following recipes special. Try them to see why the late cookbook author and gastronome James Beard called cheese of any kind "probably the friendliest of foods."

Upscale Macaroni and Cheese, 268
Low-fat Blue Cheese Dressing, 223
Baked Apples in Blue Cheese with Walnuts and Leeks, 299

Boston Cream Pie

"What's in a name?" Shakespeare asked. Apparently quite a bit, especially if the name doesn't fit. That's called a misnomer, and, depending on your point of view, you see and hear them every day. For instance, to members of a symphony orchestra, the term "rap music" might be a misnomer. To one political party, the other party's use of the term "tax reform" might be a misnomer. To people in the newspaper business, the term "television news" might be a misnomer.

The culinary world is no exception. From personal experience, I've concluded that the term "diet delight" on a menu or as the title of a recipe is invariably a misnomer. And when it comes to food, there are lots of them that are inaccurately labeled. For example, there's wild rice, which isn't really rice at all, but a form of grass. And peanuts, which aren't really nuts but legumes. And Chinese duck sauce and oyster sauce, neither of which contains what sounds like it ought to be the principal ingredient. And then there are Jerusalem artichokes, which aren't from the Holy Land and are really members of the sunflower family, plus plum pudding, which contains nary a plum.

But perhaps the greatest culinary misnaming of all is Boston cream pie, a concoction which anybody can tell just by looking is not a pie but a cake. In fact, it's two layers of sponge cake filled with pastry cream and topped with a chocolate glaze. How it got its name is a matter of some debate, and a clear-cut answer is not easy to find. You'd think the award-winning cookbook author Rose Levy Beranbaum would know, but neither her *Cake Bible* nor her *Pie and Pastry Bible*, both of which I've read religiously, are much help. Boston cream pie doesn't appear in either one of them.

The origin of Boston cream pie is easier to determine than the origin of its name. The first recorded mention of it, according to *The Dictionary of American Food and Drink*, was in the *New York Herald* in 1855, and most observers say Boston's Parker House Hotel, where they still bake nearly 200 of them each week, invented the version we know today, though there is disagreement over which hotel employee was responsible. The *Joy of Cooking* credits a German baker named Ward who was also the originator of the Parker House roll. The *New York Times* says the mastermind behind the dessert was a French chef named Sanzian who simply took a two-layer custard-filled sponge cake, already known as Boston pie, and topped it with chocolate frosting.

Some evidence suggests a concoction known as Boston cream pie predated the one at the Parker House. According to the late James Beard, it was a two-layer custard-filled butter cake merely sprinkled with powdered sugar. The Parker House chocolate-iced version was simply a variation. Christopher Kimball, writing in *The Dessert Bible*, lends credence to Beard's account by noting that the venerable *Fannie Farmer Cookbook* includes a recipe for something called a Boston favorite cake and treats the Boston cream pie as a modification.

But why were any of these cakes called "pie"? No one seems to know for sure, but the best guess is that they were so labeled because they were baked in pie tins, which were more common in 19th-century America than cake pans. Indeed, more than a few old American recipes for pie are really for cakes baked in a pie tin. For example, one of my favorite imposters, Nantucket Cranberry Pie, is made by spreading cake batter over sweetened cranberries. The dividing line between cake and pie was not so clear-cut in early America.

After all these years it's unlikely that Boston cream pie will be rechristened Boston cream cake, certainly not in Massachusetts where a few years ago it was anointed the state dessert, beating out the Toll House cookie and Indian pudding during a spirited political battle. One thing's for sure, however; when applied to Boston cream pie, the word "delicious" is no misnomer.

Parker House Boston Cream Pie, 320

Brown Sugar

Though Mick Jagger and the Rolling Stones had something very different in mind when they sang in praise of brown sugar, I maintain that the stuff I put on my oatmeal each morning is every bit as worthy of a tribute.

Whether it's enriching a crock of baked beans, adding density to a pan of brownies, or elevating a grapefruit half from mere diet food to something sublime, brown sugar makes me wonder why people just didn't leave well enough alone instead of refining sugar to the point where it turns white.

Without refining, all sugar would be brown. In fact, the earliest attempts at refining sugar, which began in Persia in the 4th century, produced large golden brown blocks. But today the natural brownish color is lightened by washing and bleaching. Juice is first pressed out of shredded sugarcane, then boiled until it becomes a thick brown syrup. The sugar which crystallizes out of this syrup is still brown, even after it has been through a centrifuge to remove the molasses from it. Only after further refining and decolorizing with phosphoric acid and charcoal does the sugar become white.

Alas, these days the brown sugar you are likely to find at the supermarket is actually white sugar with some of the molasses added back in instead of genuine unrefined brown sugar crystallized from a molasses syrup. (You can actually make your own by merely adding two tablespoons of molasses to one cup of granulated sugar.) But the real thing is another matter. Harkening back to the sugar of thousands of years ago, it is richer in color and taste, with complex underlying flavors. The best unrefined brown sugar is said to come from sugarcane grown in volcanic ash on the tropical island of Mauritius in the Indian Ocean off the coast of Africa.

There are many different kinds of brown sugar. Some are available in health-food stores and at ethnic markets, and others through mail order.

Muscovado sugar is also known as Barbados sugar because that's where it originated. It has a rich flavor with hints of rum and caramel. It can be used in baking (it's great in gingerbread) and goes well with broiled fruit such as bananas or pineapple. Though ordinarily the darkest of Western sugars, it does come in a light form.

Demerara sugar is named for the place in Guyana where it originated. It is lighter in color than muscovado and has coarse, hard crystals. Despite its light color, it imparts a definite molasses flavor. Its sandy texture makes it less desirable for creaming in cake batters, but it is ideal as a topping for coffee cake, sugar cookies, ice cream, or a bowl of hot oatmeal.

Turbinado sugar is a relative of Demerara sugar. It is raw sugar that has been washed with steam and resembles refined white sugar except for its honey color. It is especially well suited to caramelizing atop crème brûlée.

Chinese rock sugar may range in color from clear to amber and comes in large or small lumps. Chinese cooks use it in dishes ranging from soups to puddings.

Jaggery is dark palm sugar from India. It has a fairly solid consistency and comes in blocks. Depending on the type of palm sap used, its flavor varies, but is always strong and distinctive with smoky overtones and a nutty aroma. Wealthy Indian families might serve a dozen or more varieties of it with tea.

Mexican brown loaf sugar comes in two varieties. *Panela* is an unrefined loaf sugar found in southern Mexico. It comes in flat, rounded chunks which are so hard, they have to be beaten into smaller pieces with a hammer. *Piloncillo* is similar to panela except that it is milder in flavor and comes in a conical shape. It is a classic ingredient in Mexican spiced coffee.

Brownulated sugar is a trade name for Domino's brand of free-flowing brown sugar which has been hydrolyzed so that it doesn't dry out or cake. Great for sprinkling on cereal or fruit, it cannot be substituted for regular brown sugar in baking because it doesn't measure out in the same way.

Cup for cup, brown sugar and white sugar have the same sweetening power, but for an accurate measure, brown sugar must be packed into the measuring cup to eliminate air pockets. Because it contains 2.1% water compared to only 0.5% for white sugar, it adds moisture as well as flavor to baked goods. This is generally a good thing unless you're making something fragile or delicate, such as a meringue, where the added weight can be counterproductive.

If a recipe doesn't specify whether to use light or dark brown sugar, the safest thing to do is opt for light to avoid overwhelming the other flavors in the dish, but, frankly, because I like the more pronounced molasses flavor of dark brown sugar, I tend to use it unless a recipe directs otherwise.

One problem with brown sugar is that it can turn rock hard if it loses moisture, which is why nowadays it usually comes packaged in a resealable plastic bag. Favorite methods for softening hardened brown sugar range all the way from putting it in the refrigerator to putting it in the oven. Actually, heating the sugar in a microwave provides a quick but temporary fix by softening the molasses "mortar" which is created when brown sugar dries out. A longer-term solution involves replacing the moisture. A convenient way to do this is by putting the sugar in a container with a slice of apple. In a day or so the water vapor from the apple will have softened the sugar. Of course, the best way is to avoid the problem altogether by using brown sugar so frequently that it doesn't have a chance to dry out in the first place. The following recipe is a delightful way to pursue that objective.

Marge Janssen's Brown Sugar Brownies, 356

Brownies

The late Mary Jane Rathbun, a.k.a. Brownie Mary, was a beloved California crusader for the legalization of marijuana for medical use. A courageous pioneer in the fight against AIDS, she routinely gave away to people suffering from the disease batch after batch of her own prescription—cannabis-laced brownies. Accustomed to being occasionally busted for illegal possession of drugs, she was nonetheless outraged when following one of her early arrests, the local newspaper reported that police had confiscated from her home 20 pounds of high-grade marijuana, 50 pounds of flour, 50 pounds of sugar, 22 dozen eggs, and 35 pounds of margarine. Mary was mortified. She was not embarrassed to have been caught violating a law which she thought was unjust, but she was chagrined by the implication that she used margarine as an ingredient in her notable confections. "The narcs may not know any better," she testily complained, "but that was the finest quality butter."

At the risk of being misunderstood, I want to say that Brownie Mary was my kind of baker. And brownies are my kind of cookie.

Actually, brownies aren't really cookies and they aren't really cake. They are a cross between the two. Though *The Oxford Companion to Food* concludes that the origin of the bars is unclear, like so many culinary inventions, they were probably discovered by accident. One legend has it that brownies were invented when a clumsy baker dropped a chocolate cake, but most theorists suggest that the first brownie was the result of someone forgetting to put baking powder in cake batter which was, perhaps, already overloaded with chocolate, butter, and sugar. No one seems to know who this serendipitous inventor was, though some claim it was a librarian in Maine by the name of Brownie Schrumpf. Whatever the case, the cake did not rise and may well have been considered a failure, until someone took a bite. The name, by most accounts, comes from the brownie's deep brown color and is not a tribute to Ms. Schrumpf or anyone else.

James Trager, in *The Food Chronology*, claims that the first published recipe for brownies appeared in, of all places, the *1897 Sears, Roebuck Catalogue* and *The Oxford Companion to Food* agrees. But a recipe for the confection appears in the *1896 Boston Cooking-School Cook Book* (the original *Fannie Farmer Cookbook*) which was published a year earlier in 1896. To make matters just that much more confusing, however, that recipe contains no chocolate.

Whatever their origin, brownies have been popular ever since their creation. Kristin Miller, a food historian for Oprah's Oxygen Network, says they were the favorite treat of the Roaring Twenties. Moreover, as she also points out, they are uniquely American. Every culture has its cookies, she observes, but only we have brownies.

Perhaps that's why in this country they often outsell much fancier desserts, even in the most upscale of restaurants. Indeed, no less a celebrity chef than Wolfgang Puck has become a convert. According to Mary Bergin, a pastry chef at Puck's fashionable restaurant, Spago, when she first tried to put brownies on the Los Angeles restaurant's menu, Puck resisted. "You know, I don't think I like these square chocolate things," he would say. But when Spago opened a Las Vegas branch, she concocted a brownie sundae and got Puck's permission to give it a try. During the first month of operation, it outsold every other dessert! Fittingly, the *Spago Desserts* cookbook, authored by Bergin, contains an entire chapter devoted to brownies.

Conventionally, brownies are classified as either fudgy or cakelike, but Joan Steuer and Rick Rodgers, authors of the immodestly titled cookbook *Best-Ever Brownies*, have identified three distinct varieties: fudgy, chewy, and cakey.

Fudgy brownies, as their name implies, are gooey with an intense chocolate flavor. They are the classic version and are traditionally made with unsweetened chocolate and a very small amount of flour. They are seldom iced. They are removed from the oven while the center of the brownie still seems unbaked and a toothpick inserted one inch from the side of the pan comes out with a moist crumb.

Chewy brownies are also soft and moist, but are usually thicker than the fudgy variety. They tend to be crusty around the edges. Typically made with semisweet chocolate and creamed butter, as opposed to melted, they frequently contain nuts. They are baked until a toothpick inserted into the center of the brownie comes out with a moist crumb.

Cakey brownies are springy to the touch and resemble a firm devil's food cake. They will usually contain baking powder or some other leavening agent and often feature thick, creamy frostings. They are baked until a toothpick inserted into the center of the brownie comes out clean.

Despite their homespun appearance, baking brownies is actually more exacting than you might expect. Variations of as little as a tablespoon or two of flour can make a fundamental difference in the finished product. Oven temperature is critical. And just two or three minutes of baking time can spell the difference between success and disaster. As dessert virtuoso Maida Heatter, whose reputation as a pastry chef started with her brownies, observes, "Perfectly timed brownies are a great accomplishment!"

Probably the most important thing to remember when baking brownies is to avoid overbaking, but here are some other brownie points to keep in mind. The easiest way to remove brownies from their baking pan is to line it with aluminum foil. Allow a two-inch overhang of foil to use as a "handle" to remove the entire brownie from the pan before slicing. Cool brownies completely before cutting. Though it may be hard to resist the temptation of a warm brownie, they tend to improve in taste and texture after sitting for at least four hours and will be even better after twenty-four.

Remember that the flavor of brownies can vary dramatically when different brands of chocolate are used because there is no industry standard for the amount of sugar in semisweet and bittersweet chocolate. The use of cocoa powder will affect not only the flavor of a brownie but, because it contains less cocoa butter than chocolate does, its texture as well.

If a recipe calls for soft butter to be creamed with other ingredients such as sugar and egg, avoid letting it get too soft or the resultant mixture will lack fluffiness and this will affect the texture of the brownies.

The best way to tell when a brownie is done, according to cookbook author Jim Fobel, is to carefully monitor baking time, which is established through trial and error. The toothpick test is a good guide, but it is not foolproof.

Be creative with additions to your brownie batter. A cup or so of grated zucchini added to a standard-sized batch of brownies will make them incredibly moist (and provide a welcome auxiliary outlet for zucchini). Believe it or not, as Mexican cooks who have long known the affinity of spice and chocolate will tell you, a teaspoon of black pepper adds a delightful kick to a batch of brownies. More conventional additions include peanut butter, marshmallows, chunks of white chocolate, coffee, various liqueurs (Grand Marnier is nice), swirls of cream cheese, Peppermint Pattie candies, and, of course, nuts. One of my favorite additions is chopped candied ginger.

But the truth is, you don't have to go overboard with additions to make a great brownie. If made with fresh ingredients and the highest quality chocolate, even a plain brownie, contrary to Brownie Mary's experience, is sufficient for any gourmet to get high on. I think you will find the following perfectly legal recipes particularly exhilarating.

Burgers

In some countries cows are sacred. Here, it's the hamburger. While Germany has its sausages and Austria its schnitzels, in the United States the burger is king.

Every year billions of hamburgers are sold in American restaurants. In fact, five of the biggest restaurant chains in the country have hamburgers at the core of their menu. McDonald's alone has sold enough burgers to feed the world a dozen times over. Given this popularity, it's not surprising that in Texas, a state where they take burgers seriously, official records show that nearly a third of inmates sentenced to death choose a hamburger for their last meal.

Even professional chefs crave burgers. As Marcel Desaulniers, executive chef at Williamsburg's Trellis Restaurant, observes in his award-winning cookbook *Burger Meisters*, "I am amazed at how often food conversations with my colleagues invariably turn from what is 'in' to what is personally preferred. The food most widely proclaimed as the choice away from work is a burger."

Clearly, John Mariani was correct to write in *The Dictionary of American Food and Drink* that "hamburgers, along with hot dogs, are considered the most identifiably American of food items." Moreover, burgers have been outselling hot dogs since the 1940s.

Despite our nation's love affair with the burger, as Jeffrey Tennyson points out in his book, *Hamburger Heaven: The Illustrated History of the Hamburger*, the hamburger's origin is embroiled in controversy. Its roots can easily be traced back to the nomadic tribes of Tartary in 13th-century Asia who invented steak tartare by placing raw beef fillets under their horses' saddles where it got pounded and minced as they rode into battle. And it is clearly a descendant of Hamburg Steak, a broiled chopped steak brought to this country and popularized by immigrants from Hamburg, Germany, in the 19th century. But it is not so clear who first thought of placing the hamburger patty between slices of bread. No fewer than four people lay claim to that distinction.

First, there is Louis Lassen who supposedly, on a moment's notice, created a sandwich of thinly sliced steak trimmings and bread for a rushed customer at his New Haven, Connecticut, luncheonette in 1900. Then there is Charlie Nagreen ("Hamburger Charlie") of Seymour, Wisconsin, who is said to have invented the first burger in 1885 at his ox-drawn concession stand at the Outagamie County Fair in response to customers wanting to wander the fairgrounds and eat lunch at the same time. Similarly, two brothers, Charlie and Frank Menches of Akron, Ohio, are often credited with creating the hamburger at the county fair there, only in this case somewhat by accident. When they were unable to get sausage for their popular sandwiches, as a last resort they substituted ground beef. (By the way, even if Charlie Menches isn't the real father of the hamburger, his place in culinary history is still secure. He claims to have also invented the ice-cream cone.)

And finally there is Fletcher Davis of Athens, Texas, who is most frequently cited as the man responsible for the debut of the burger—at the St. Louis World's Fair in 1904. He garnered the attention of the New York press when he and his wife opened up for business on the midway.

Whoever it was that begat the burger, the major credit for popularizing it belongs to Billy Ingram, who along with his business partner J. Walter Anderson (quite likely the inventor of the hamburger bun) founded the country's first hamburger chain, White Castle. As history professor David Gerard Hogan remarks in his book on the subject, *Selling 'Em by the Sack*, "It could be said that what Henry Ford did for the car and transportation, Billy Ingram did for the hamburger sandwich and eating."

White Castle upgraded the image of the burger and legitimized it through its hundreds of restaurants designed after Chicago's famous Water Tower. And though other chains have overshadowed it, there are millions of Americans, like myself, who are still passionate about "belly bombers" or "sliders," as White Castle burgers are affectionately called. For example, Kim Kelly-Bartley, marketing director for the firm, tells about one customer who has a provision in his will calling for White Castles to be served at his funeral. I have no question that he is of sound mind.

But allegiances to fast-food burgers notwithstanding, there is nothing like the burger you make yourself, as most of us rediscover each summer. Thus, the National Cattlemen's Beef Association reports that during the summer months more than 50 percent of Americans grill out at least once a week. Doubtless they often grill hamburgers.

But, as Stephanie Witt Sedgwick of the *Washington Post* notes, making a simple hamburger can be a complex task. This is partly because barbecue grills produce uneven heat that is difficult to gauge. The result, she says, is often "more hockey puck than patty." Then, too, as Bill Jamison, co-author of *Born to Grill* points out, backyard cooks often take a rather casual approach to cooking. "You would never turn an oven to any old temperature, not measure it, stick something in to cook, walk away and not look at it until you thought it was done," he remarks. Yet this is precisely what many do when they grill.

Sedgwick offers several tips for making great burgers. First and foremost, start with the right meat. If too lean, you'll be guaranteed a dry burger. Sedgwick recommends no less than 15% fat and ideally 24%. If you find that much fat hard to stomach, as I do, you can use a trick I first learned from Cape Girardeau, Missouri, barbecue maven, the late Charlie Knote. He understood that the heat of a grill can evaporate lots of moisture from a burger and, typical of Charlie, he knew exactly how much—111 milliliters per pound. So to compensate he recommended adding about 6 tablespoons of water to each pound of meat before cooking. I've discovered that you can produce much the same effect by mixing a similar amount of crushed ice with the hamburger. Sedgwick also recommends grinding your own meat, a step which, I agree, is well worth the trouble. It's also best to season the meat beforehand. Salt won't draw out moisture if it's applied just a few minutes before cooking.

In addition, there are some things you shouldn't do. First, don't compact the burger tightly. This will just make it more dense and dry. Second, don't make the burgers too big. They'll become burned on the outside waiting for the inside to get cooked. Sedgwick recommends burgers no bigger than 6 ounces, but as one who fondly recalls downing a full-pound burger at a restaurant in Arizona some years ago (I still have the souvenir picture to prove it), I think an 8-ounce burger is manageable. (That's still a lot smaller than the Guinness record holder for the biggest burger ever made, which was 5,000 pounds and cooked on a grill the size of a two-car garage.)

Third, don't press down on the burgers as they cook. This just squeezes more moisture out of them. And fourth, don't eyeball the burgers for doneness. Use an instant thermometer to make sure they are cooked to a safe 160 degrees.

Finally, remember that, despite the advertising war between McDonald's and Burger King in the 1990s, some chefs, such as Christopher Kimball, founder of *Cooks Illustrated* magazine, believe that a pan-cooked burger is superior to one prepared on the grill. I know they can be just as good, especially if topped with cheese. (Three restaurants, by the way, one in California, one in Kentucky, and one in Colorado, claim to have invented the cheeseburger.) One technique I've found useful for enhancing burgers cooked in a skillet was inspired by the Cape Girardeau, Missouri, Rotary Club's famous salt steak cookout. I sprinkle a light layer of coarse salt over the pan and let it start to smoke before placing the burgers on top.

Try these suggestions in the following recipes, all designed, as Jimmy Buffet might say, to take you to burger paradise.

Missouri Sirloin and Blue Cheese Burger, 262
New American Bistro Burger, 262
Chicago Beer Burger, 263

Butter

The *Milwaukee Journal Sentinel* recently reported the exploits of a Sheboygan man who snuck into the basement of a tavern in the wee hours of the morning, intent upon stealing some beer, and who found himself locked inside with no way out except for a small opening in a door. It was a tight squeeze, but by smearing himself generously with some butter, which was also being stored in the basement, the slick would-be thief was able to make his escape.

Perhaps the culprit could have just as easily eluded the authorities had he relied on Parkay, but to me his story just goes to show what I have always maintained: When you've got a lot at stake, there is no substitute for real butter.

Yes, I know there's a product on the market now called "I Can't Believe It's Not Butter!" I can. That's not to say that ICBINB is not a perfectly good spread. It's just that when it comes to butter versus margarine, I side with Joan Gussow, a nutrition professor at Columbia University. She says, "I trust cows more than chemists."

From a health standpoint, it would appear that her faith is well placed. Concerned about their profiles, both visual and lipid, many Americans have become wary of butter, adopting an attitude almost as intolerant as the one Martin Luther alleged represented the position of 16th-century Church officials bent on selling dispensations. He complained, "Eating butter, they say, is a greater sin than to lie, blaspheme, or indulge in impurity." (Accordingly, as Jean-Louis Flandrin observes, those countries of the world which rely on butter for cooking are pretty much the ones which broke away from the Catholic Church at that time.) But now medical science tells us that margarine may not be so good for us either. For one thing, it contains trans fatty acids, which can increase cholesterol levels.

But it's not really health concerns that prompt me to prefer butter over substitutes. Fundamentally, it's the taste involved. As *The Oxford Companion to Food* notes, "Butter is a fine cooking medium; the excellent flavour which it imparts to food is matched by no oil or other fat." Food writer Al Martinez goes even further. He says, "Without butter, fine cooking would disappear from the face of the earth." He doesn't overstate the case by much, as far as I'm concerned. I concur wholeheartedly with his observation that butter is to food what love is to romance. "Without it," he declares, "there is only lard and emptiness."

Realization of this truth, perhaps, accounts for the fact that people have been making butter for centuries. The first documented mention of the process is in the sacred songs of dwellers of Asiatic India, dating back almost 2,000 years before Christ. But Maguelonne Toussaint-Samat notes that long before that, around 3500 BC, the vertically designed churn was in use, an improvement over the even more archaic Mongolian method of churning cream horizontally in a leather flask. By biblical times, butter was well known, and apparently well regarded, as confirmed by a line in the Old Testament: "She brought forth butter in a lordly dish" (Judges 5:25).

Curiously, the ancient Greeks and Romans didn't care much for butter, preferring oil instead. Pliny, in fact, called butter a food of the barbarians. In medieval France, it was even thought to make a person susceptible to leprosy. Thus, according to Toussaint-Samat, butter was all but unknown in Italy until around the 15th century, and, incredibly, Taillevent's classic French cookbook of the late 14th century, *Le Viander*, calls for it in a mere 2 percent of its recipes. Even today the relative popularity of butter and oil differs geographically. People in English-speaking countries tend to favor butter while those in Hispanic countries favor oil. The French are evenly divided. (Even so, their per capita consumption of butter is three times ours.)

Countries differ also when it comes to the animal sources they rely on for their butter. In the United States butter is made with cow's milk. But in India they use water buffalo's milk; in parts of Asia, sheep's milk; in Egypt, goat's milk; and in Tibet, yak's milk. Horse, donkey, and camel butter are the rule in some parts of the world. Not surprisingly, the species employed affects the flavor of the butter produced, as does its diet. For example, the prized butter of Normandy gets its distinctive flavor from aromatic herbs ingested by the cows there.

Cultural preferences notwithstanding, butter has become the object of spreading fame. In fact, it has even been seen as sacred. East Indians of the Vedic era petitioned it as a deity and used butter made from the milk of sacred cows for religious ceremonies. Tibetans used to simmer their dead priests in it prior to embalming them. (Talk about buttering someone up!) Moreover, butter has been used for cosmetic and medicinal purposes as well. Cleopatra reportedly bathed in the stuff, and not that long ago it was thought that a pat of butter placed near a person suffering from cancer would absorb the disease.

But it's clearly what butter does to food that has sealed its reputation as a substance for which there is no rival. In baked goods, as a medium for sautéing, as the basis of a sauce, or just slathered on good bread, nothing can compare to it. As Los Angeles chef Suzanne Goin properly proclaims, "Life would be so lonely without butter."

Gooey Butter Cake, 311

Cajeta

The heavy-set son ushered us down a narrow hallway toward a 15-gallon, hammered copper pot (the traditional cazo used for candy making) filled to the brim with today's goat milk. As we moved past it, the passage opened onto a narrow room with a 2-foot-high, bricked-in stove along one side. There, four more huge cazos boiled over strong gas jets. A barrel of sugar stood nearby with a wooden paddle propped up beside it; in the small bottling room at the end was a shelf that held baking soda, cinnamon, vanilla and alcohol, plus glass bottling jars in sizes from a cup to a quart.

Thus, Rick Bayless, owner of Chicago's Frontera Grill, perhaps this country's best Mexican restaurant, relates his first visit to the Cajeta Vencedora factory in Celaya, Guanajuato, where they make the definitive version of cajeta: the rich, thick, golden caramelized goat-milk confection that is as quintessentially Hispanic as apple pie is American.

Nearly thirty years ago, my own first encounter with cajeta, during a visit to Mexico City, was not nearly as ceremonious, but it had every bit as much impact. One taste and I knew I would never again be satisfied with ordinary caramel sauce.

Lydia Martin, writing in the *Houston Chronicle*, calls cajeta (known variously as *dulce de leche*, *fangullo*, *manjar blanco*, and *arequipe*) the Ricky Martin of Latin desserts. "We don't all eat tacos; we don't all go for black beans and rice," she explains. "Some of us are into mango and guava; others prefer, well, chocolate," she continues. But cajeta, she maintains, is "the one thing almost all Hispanics, whether they're from Mexico, Cuba, Nicaragua or Argentina, can vibe together on." No wonder Häagen-Dazs' *dulce de leche* ice cream outsells vanilla 3:1 in Miami. For that matter, it's doing pretty well everywhere else, too. It's now the company's second-best-selling flavor.

As Martin observes, cajeta is "kind of like caramel, only a whole lot sexier." Though it looks like caramel sauce, there the similarity ends. According to Bayless, in his latest book, *Mexico: One Plate at a Time*, because it contains goat's milk, its flavor is more intricate; and because it is allowed to reduce in volume through slow simmering, it is more concentrated in taste and color. He likens it to good wine: "silky-smooth, balanced and complex."

Technically speaking, cajeta isn't really caramel (which, as Maguelonne Toussaint-Samat tells us, was invented by the Arabs and used early on as a depilatory for harem ladies) because it does not contain caramelized sugar. Rather, its flavor and color are the result of browning milk solids, a process not unlike browning butter. Thus, cajeta recipes often call for the addition of baking soda which neutralizes acidity and promotes the browning. Indeed, Bayless reports that baking soda produces a golden brown color even when there is no sugar in the cajeta mixture. Occasionally, just for good measure, however, a bit of already caramelized sugar is added to the cajeta as it completes cooking, producing what is sometimes termed *cajeta quemada*, or burnt cajeta. According to the online *World on a Plate*, the name "cajeta" itself comes from the name of the small balsa-wood box or case (*cajita*) especially made to store the product before refrigeration was prevalent. Nowadays you're more likely to find the stuff packaged in glass jars.

Though cajeta can be found in abundance nearly anywhere south of the border, perhaps the most legendary version comes from the small town of Celaya in central Mexico. Cajeta was once such an integral part of that city's culture that, as Howard LaFranchi notes, writing in the *Christian Science Monitor*, children there were traditionally taught to believe that the town's landmark turn-of-the-century water tower was filled to the top with it. Though factories have displaced many of Celaya's small family producers, there are still local cajeta-makers there determined to keep the old custom alive. Spurring them on are enough goats inhabiting the town's surrounding farmland to collectively produce some 10,000 quarts of milk a day.

You can follow the lead of the *dulceros* (sweet-makers) of Celaya and make your own cajeta. All that's required is a heavy pot, some goat's milk, and a lot of patience. But it's well worth doing, for homemade cajeta is bound to be superior to commercially produced versions which, as Diana Kennedy, America's maven of Mexican cuisine, notes, invariably suffer from shortcuts such as the addition of cane syrup.

In a pinch you can always take a can of sweetened condensed milk and submerge it in boiling water for a few hours (be careful—the danger of explosion is real enough that cans of Eagle Brand now carry a warning), but starting from scratch will produce something even more delicious—and addictive.

Once you've made your first batch, use it in place of pedestrian caramel sauce, and you'll discover that cajeta makes a terrific topping for ice cream, a marvelous companion to fresh fruit such as pineapple, pears, or figs, a decadent filling for crêpes, a transforming addition to your favorite pound-cake recipe, and the secret ingredient to the best Bananas Foster you'll ever taste. You'll gladly discover these and many other uses for this caramely concoction, that is, if you can restrain yourself from simply eating it right out of the jar.

Cajeta (Goat-Milk Caramel), 362

Cake Mixes

I have a confession to make. For years I have been making a chocolate cake that everybody raves over. Once I took it to a committee meeting and one of the committee members said it was absolutely the best chocolate cake he had ever tasted. Another time I took it to a party and people actually fought over the last slice. Without fail, whenever I serve it, somebody asks for the recipe. Well, the cake does contain some flavorful ingredients—Kahlua, sour cream, and almost a pound of chocolate. But, and here's the confession, it begins with a mix.

I was prompted to let this skeleton out of my oven by the publication of Anne Byrn's *The Cake Mix Doctor*, which suggests that I should no longer be ashamed of myself. Apparently I'm not the only one parlaying a cake mix into something special. When Byrn asked readers of the Nashville *Tennessean* for ideas for doctoring cake mixes, she received 500 recipes within just one week.

I've always had a disdainful attitude—ok, snobbish—toward cake mixes. I steadfastly maintained that no mix can rival what you get when you bake from scratch. That's because I've eaten my share of box cakes that didn't need a doctor, they needed a priest! But Byrn has me questioning my assumptions. I'm now convinced that proper embellishment can make a cake mix taste as good as homemade.

Partly, this is because cake mixes have come a long way since their introduction almost sixty years ago. Actually, the origin of the cake mix can be traced back further than that, to 1842 and the invention of self-rising flour. Other precursors include corn-muffin mix, developed in 1920, and gingerbread mix, created in 1929.

Cake mixes, outgrowths of baking mixes used to feed troops in World War II, were introduced by General Mills and Pillsbury in 1949. Initially they did not catch on, despite the fact that postwar America seemed a ripe market for them. Consumer research revealed that they induced guilt in housewives who, having to add nothing more than water, did not feel they were living up to expectations and really baking. But when Nebraska's Consolidated Mills introduced its Duncan Hines brand just three years later, it captured almost 50 percent of the market within just three weeks and after six months sold six times what had been projected for the entire year. The mix, devised by company chemist Arlee Andre, required consumers to add their own eggs and that, apparently, made all the difference. In fact, called the Three Star Special, it could be the basis of a white, yellow, or devil's food cake depending on whether the baker added egg whites, whole eggs, or cocoa powder. So jazzing up a packaged cake mix with additional ingredients is not altogether new.

Over the years, manufacturers have tirelessly experimented with cake mixes. For example, Byrn tells the story of a senior home economist at Pillsbury who drove 3,000 miles around Montana with a load of cake mix in her car to determine firsthand how the product would hold up during shipping. In 1977, after noticing how many winners of its Bake-Off relied on pudding mix to enhance their entries, Pillsbury reformulated its product and put the pudding in to begin with. General Mills followed suit.

Because of such improvements, cake mixes are now used by more than 60 percent of American households, and as Byrn notes, they have some real advantages over homemade. For instance, they're much more forgiving. Overbeat the batter, and they still bake up fine. Underbeat it, and the result is nonetheless perfectly acceptable. Take a box cake out of the oven sooner than you should and all will be well. Plus, cake mixes contain emulsifiers that prevent fat and liquid from separating, guaranteeing a moist cake. In a scratch cake, the only emulsifier is egg yolk. Moreover, at home you have only baking powder or baking soda at your disposal, whereas cake mix manufacturers employ other leavening agents that insure a high-rising cake even if you don't follow the directions precisely. And because eggs are not a source of leavening in a cake mix, you don't need to take the time to let them come to room temperature as you should when baking from scratch. You can even prepare cake-mix batter, refrigerate it, and bake it later. Finally, all you need is a simple hand-held mixer. In fact, a sturdy commercial-style mixer would be overkill. No wonder a once popular tearoom in Cape Girardeau, Missouri, noted for elegant and delicious layer cakes, relied heavily on mixes.

You can capitalize on these strengths while using judicious additions that give the cake a homemade quality, and even a former purist like myself may never guess your secret. For example, for chocolate mixes, Byrn recommends adding a few tablespoons of cocoa powder and some instant coffee, and substituting buttermilk for the water. For white mixes she advises using melted butter instead of oil and whole eggs instead of just the whites called for in the package directions. From there, let your imagination run wild. There's hardly a limit to the things you can add to a cake mix to deliciously camouflage its ancestry. Extras such as chocolate chips, fruit, liqueurs, cream cheese, lemon curd, grated zucchini, Jell-O, and even Coca-Cola can help you turn a cake mix into a signature dessert.

But though these days you can make a credible cake from a box, Byrn insists you follow a rule handed down from her mother: "You can get away with baking a cake from a mix, but you absolutely must make homemade frosting."

Melted Ice Cream Cake, 304

Carrots

"I never worry about diets," observed Mae West. "The only carrots that interest me are the number you get in a diamond." Considering the source, such a view is perhaps understandable, but it is certainly shortsighted, as the Easter Bunny would surely tell you. After all, the carrot is among the most multifaceted of all root vegetables.

Added to soups and stews, the carrot lends sweetness; boiled, steamed, or roasted, it makes a great side dish; put in a stir-fry, it adds color and crunch; its flavor is enhanced by herbs and spices as diverse as thyme, dill, mint, parsley, chervil, ginger, and nutmeg; its juice makes a healthy drink; and given that the carrot contains more sugar than any other vegetable except the beet, it can even function as dessert. Indeed, well before the invention of carrot cake (my favorite way to eat my vegetables), carrots were being used in candies and puddings. Carrots don't even have to be cooked to be enjoyed. They're great raw in a salad or as a crudité.

No wonder the carrot is the second-most-popular vegetable in the world after the potato—not bad for a plant which, according to *The Oxford Companion to Food*, "had an unpromising origin." It is, after all, merely a refined version of a common weed—Queen Anne's lace. In fact, originally the carrot wasn't even orange—just about every color but. In Roman times carrots were purple or white. In Ancient Egypt they were often yellow, green, black, or red. Actually, the word "carrot," a word of Celtic origin, means "red of color."

The orange carrot didn't appear on the scene until the 16th century, and it was the result of patriotic fervor. Dutch growers, among the leading carrot breeders of the time, developed it in colorful tribute to the House of Orange, the Dutch royal family. It shows up with some regularity in Dutch paintings of the 17th century. Ironically, today purple carrots are staging a comeback. They're now widely available in Great Britain, where the carrot is the No. 1 vegetable.

Its color notwithstanding, the carrot has been around a long time. Fossilized pollen from the carrot family of plants has been dated to as far back as the Eocene period millions of years ago, and traces of carrot seeds have been found at prehistoric lake dwellings in Switzerland. But the root itself was probably first cultivated in what is now Afghanistan some 5,000 years ago. Thus, Egyptian temple drawings from 2,000 BC depict what look suspiciously like carrots, albeit purple ones. By the 8th century BC, the carrot was included in a list of vegetables grown in the royal garden of Babylon.

Initially, the carrot was prized merely for its aromatic leaves and seeds. Moreover, it was used medicinally long before it was used as food. The Greeks, for example, thought the carrot was both an aphrodisiac and a cure for venereal disease. (It was the former belief that prompted the demented Roman emperor Caligula to once serve the entire Roman Senate a banquet of nothing but carrots.)

It wasn't until the 12th century that carrots began to be taken seriously as food, thanks to the Spanish, who later introduced them to the New World. Today the United States is the second-largest producer of carrots in the world after China, where it is not unheard of for some species to routinely grow as long as three feet. The longest carrot ever recorded, by the way, was nearly seventeen feet.

Modern science has confirmed that the ancients were wise to consider carrots health food. Carrots have the highest content of vitamin A of any vegetable. They also contain high amounts of beta-carotene, which is converted into vitamin A in the body, and certain phytochemicals. Thus, they boost immunity, protect the skin from sun damage, fight infection, and may even reduce the risk of heart disease, high blood pressure, osteoporosis, and cancer, as well as lower cholesterol levels. They're also a good source of fiber. No wonder Bugs Bunny can always beat Elmer Fudd!

It turns out also that your mom was right when she claimed that carrots are good for your eyes. Both the vitamin A and the beta-carotene in carrots lower the risk of eye disease, including cataracts and macular degeneration, and help counter night blindness. Thus, along with radar, specially bred high-carotene carrots were a secret weapon of British RAF pilots in World War II.

Though the best carrot is still an organically grown one with its green top still attached (remove it before storing so it doesn't draw excess moisture out of the root), these days carrots are available in a variety of sizes and shapes, including curls, wave-cut slices, and so-called baby carrots, which aren't babies at all, but full-sized carrots cut on a lathe to look like babies. In whatever form, it would be a shame to think of them merely as rabbit food.

Consummate Carrot Cake, 306

Casseroles

"In the history of cookery, there are few names more blighted than casserole," says Russ Parsons of the *Los Angeles Times*. "Mention it, and heads politely turn away. Stomachs just turn."

I know firsthand what Parsons is talking about. I can recall vividly the time some thirty years ago when I suggested to my colleagues on a committee planning a banquet for a national convention that we consider something on the order of a casserole. I was very nearly ejected from the room. What I had in mind, of course, was not what the celebrated food writer M.F.K. Fisher called "a careless or stupid mishmash of unrelated foods hiding in what may be our national dish," but something, in my judgment, far more noble.

But I probably should have anticipated the negative reaction, for most people have doubtless been subjected to some awful casseroles, though, I hope, none so dreadful as the one delightfully recounted by Ruth Reichl, former *New York Times* restaurant critic and now the editor of *Gourmet*, in her memoir. Made by her mother, a notoriously bad cook, it sent twenty-six people to the hospital.

But everyone can probably remember eating a casserole which, though digestible without medical attention, nonetheless was bad enough to justify the term's unsavory reputation. (The tuna strata my wife made for me the first year we were married, and which she has never made again, comes to mind.) Perhaps that explains why the new edition of the classic *Joy of Cooking* contains scarcely a mention of the term casserole (though it does retain the recipe for Turkey Tetrazzini), whereas the previous edition devoted several paragraphs to the concept and included nearly fifty casserole recipes. Fisher is right, I suppose, when she remarks that casseroles are "an American phenomenon, like Cokes and chewing gum, and by many traditionalists they are put somewhat disdainfully into the same category."

It's both ironic and unfortunate that the casserole is not universally well regarded. Ironic, because at one time it was thought to be haute cuisine, identified by Alexander Dumas in his *Grand Dictionnaire de Cuisine* as the "principal ornament" of the culinary art. (Though in fairness, he may not have had in mind what has evolved into the American casserole of today.) More to the point, the disrepute of the casserole is unfortunate because, properly conceived and executed, it can be one of the most palatable dishes imaginable. Indeed, Faye Levy, author of *The New Casserole*, points out that casseroles capitalize on something called the "flavor exchange principle," wherein ingredients cooked together impart flavor to each other to produce a new taste.

A casserole, after all, is merely a combination of foods cooked together and usually served in one dish. *Larousse Gastronomique* defines it more or less that way—and then goes on to add, "Such a dish is very popular in homes where there are no servants to help prepare or serve meals." Clearly, this definition embraces a host of grand culinary creations. Lasagna is a casserole. So is jambalaya. So is Greek *moussaka*. So too are the classic French *cassoulet* and the national dish of Spain, *paella*, not to mention Mexican *chilaquiles* and Moroccan *tagine*. In no way whatsoever are these second-class concoctions, and people are beginning to discover that, as *Restaurant Business* magazine reports. Casseroles and one-dish meals have become fashionable items at restaurants around the country. For example, shepherd's pie is a staple at the California-based Cheesecake Factory chain. Maybe that's because casseroles are fundamentally comfort food. A few bites of, say, Campbell's Green Bean Bake, or just the sight of it piping hot from the oven, can flood us with good memories. (Incidentally, that classic casserole of green beans, mushroom soup, and French-fried onions is still, more than fifty years after it was invented, the Campbell Company's most requested recipe.)

So it's time, I think, to give casseroles their due. Not only are they delicious and satisfying but they're simple to prepare, can be made well in advance and even frozen, take well to reheating (some even taste better the second time around), are ideal for feeding a big crowd, and are a great way to use leftovers. (Don't think that using leftovers, called cross-utilization in the industry, isn't as much a concern for restaurants as it is for home cooks.) And what is more, as Faye Levy observes, casseroles are well suited to entertaining because they hold "a certain element of surprise." She says, "Your guests don't always know what flavors they will discover under the crust or the top layer of bubbling sauce." I predict you'll like what you discover in the following recipes.

Tagine of Lamb with Prunes, 284
King Ranch Chicken Casserole, 277
Apple Apricot Noodle Pudding, 365

Chef's Table

The best seat at a baseball game is behind home plate. The best seat in a theatre is often in the balcony. And the best seat in church, judging by parishioner behavior, is a pew in the back.

But where's the best seat in a restaurant? That depends on a number of factors, but until recently everyone agreed that it was one far away from the kitchen.

Not anymore. Today the hottest restaurant seat (figuratively and literally) is not merely close to the kitchen, but right in the kitchen itself. It's called the chef's table.

A chef's table provides diners personal attention from the chef and a meal designed exclusively for them. Because guests at the chef's table can see what is going on in the kitchen (some restaurants even employ television monitors to give close-up coverage while others position the table overhead in a "skybox" for a bird's-eye view), the experience is as much theatrical as culinary.

The growing popularity of the chef's table is probably the inevitable result of our growing fascination with food. First came the "open" kitchen (i.e., right out in the open where everybody can see food being prepared) pioneered by restaurants such as Joyce Goldstein's Square One in San Francisco, where many years ago I experienced it for the first time. The chef's table is just the next logical step.

Though a contemporary phenomenon, the chef's table actually has roots in medieval times when royalty would hold dinner parties in the palace kitchen so guests could interact with the king's personal chef. Some argue that the concept really emerged during World War II in France when chefs there, trying to retain some measure of privacy under the watchful eyes of the Nazis, began dining in their own kitchens atop a butcher block. (Many Left Bank restaurants still offer such tables to regulars.) An even more recent legend says the concept was born at Los Angeles' Hotel Bel-Air when the chef placated a celebrity, who wanted to avoid the paparazzi, by personally serving him at a table set up in the kitchen.

You don't have to visit California to experience this phenomenon, or, fortunately, New York, where Alain Ducasse charges $500 per person to eat in his kitchen. The trend has now spread to the rest of the country, including the Midwest, though, alas, the most charming version of the phenomenon I've ever experienced, Sunday brunch served at tablecloth-draped prep tables amidst kitchen paraphernalia at Marty's Baking in St. Louis, is no longer operating.

Even in my hometown of Cape Girardeau, Missouri, James and Patricia Allen execute the concept at Celebrations, where every night they offer a special tasting menu served in a cozy private room across from the kitchen.

The chef's table truly is the best seat in the house, even when compared to the one in your own kitchen. After all, somebody else does the dishes.

Flank Steak with Crispy Polenta and Roasted Shallot Vinaigrette, 283

Chili

As California restaurant critic Merrill Shindler observes, "Like politics and religion, nobody agrees about the one true chili." It's a dish that's easy to get into an argument over. For example, some people vehemently claim that real chili does not contain beans while others claim just as vehemently that it does, and, what is more, they'll specify the particular type of bean which must be used. Some contend that pork, chicken, and even lamb can be used while others insist that true chili contains only beef. And among those there will likely be arguments about whether the beef should be ground or chopped into chunks.

Even the color of "real" chili is not above controversy. While the International Chili Society (a nonprofit organization which for over forty years sponsored the World's Championship Chili Cookoff) recognizes only red chili, green chili abounds in the Southwest, particularly in New Mexico where someone has facetiously suggested that the official state question should be "Green or red?" because that's what they'll ask you if you order a bowl of chili there. (In fact, one of the best versions of chili I've ever eaten is the green chili stew served at the little Kiva Coffee Shop in Taos.) Surely cookbook author John Thorne was not exaggerating when he wrote in a recent issue of *Chile Pepper* magazine, "There is no way of making chili, no food or flavor, not even a cooking implement, that can be named as essential to the dish that won't provoke an argument."

Even the origins of the dish are the subject of some dispute. Though Cincinnati can claim to be something of a chili capital because of the unique style of the dish served there, *chili con carne* probably was invented in Texas. At least that was the site, before the turn of the century, of the first chili parlor (irreverently defined by Beard and McKie in *Cooking: A Cook's Dictionary* as "a fistfight at which cooked beef is served"). According to one theory, the dish originated in Texas prisons as a way to make inexpensive meat palatable. Another theory maintains that it was first prepared in San Antonio prior to the Civil War. And another contends that it was first envisioned by a 17th-century Texas nun as she came out of a trance.

But, though disputes about chili tend to run as hot as a jalapeño, there is no debating that chili, however it is made, belongs on the cold-weather menu.

Chocolate Tasting

"All I really need is love, but a little chocolate now and then doesn't hurt." That sentiment, uttered by Lucy Van Pelt of the Peanuts cartoon strip, is an appropriate one. But Miranda Ingram goes even further when she asserts, "It's not that chocolates are a substitute for love. Love is a substitute for chocolate. Chocolate is, let's face it, far more reliable than a man." Apparently, she's not alone in her views. A recent Gallup poll conducted in Great Britain revealed that more women would prefer to give up sex than to give up chocolate.

In any case, the relationship between love and chocolate has always been a powerful one. In Mexico, where chocolate originated and was thought to be the divine gift of the god Quetzalcoatl, the Aztec emperor Montezuma reportedly consumed some fifty cups of it a day, usually prior to visiting his harem of 600 women. In the ancient Mayan culture which preceded the Aztecs, cocoa beans were traditionally exchanged between bride and groom as part of the marriage ceremony. Moreover, chocolate was a favorite drink of Casanova. He clearly knew what he was doing. A scientific conference on chocolate held at London's Royal Institution examined the nature of the substance and found that it contains methylxanthine and theobromine (both stimulants), phenylethylamine (a mood elevator), anandamide (which opens synapses in the brain), and magnesium (which can aid in the production of serotonin and a feeling of well-being). So why shouldn't chocolate make us feel the same way we do when we fall in love?

Recent surveys suggest as much. They show that couples who regularly eat chocolate are three times more likely to engage in romantic activity than those who never eat chocolate, and, what is more, men who drank hot chocolate after dinner were far more likely to give their mate a massage that evening than those who drank something else. No wonder the Marquis de Sade fed his party guests chocolates, though taking no chances, he laced them with Spanish Fly. Nor is it surprising that some expensive perfumes, such as Rush by Gucci, incorporate chocolate aromas.

Chocolate, as it turns out, is the single-most-craved food, especially among women. So it's no coincidence that on Valentine's Day close to $1 billion is spent to purchase almost 40 million boxes of the stuff. A recent poll by the Chocolate Manufacturers Association revealed that nearly 80% of us identify Valentine's Day as the number one occasion for chocolate-gift giving.

But how do you know whether you should pay $4 per pound, the price of Hershey's bar chocolate, or $56 per pound, the price of a Godiva assortment in a heart-shaped box? A chocolate tasting is one way to find out.

Just as a wine tasting can help further your appreciation of fine wine as you explore its many varieties, the same organized approach to sampling chocolate can enhance your knowledge and enjoyment of it. Even some of the lexicon is the same, as professional chocolate tasters routinely refer to the acidity and astringency of chocolate, whether its flavor is heavy or light, whether it is marked by woody or mossy notes or the flavor of fruit, and whether it has a good "finish." After all, as Debra Waterhouse, author of *Why Women Need Chocolate*, points out, "Chocolate contains more than 500 flavors, which makes it more complex than any other food." To analyze those complexities requires some systematic investigation.

That was precisely the rationale underlying a so-called "Grand Cru" chocolate tasting conducted at the Shangri-La Hotel in Singapore. Participants savored single-bean chocolates from Venezuela, Equador, and Madagascar and compared them to chocolate made from a blend of cocoa beans. But you hardly need to go to such lengths to set up a chocolate tasting of your own. All you need is a handful of different brands or types of chocolate and a little organization.

You could limit yourself to several brands of the same kind of chocolate, such as bittersweet or milk, for example. Or you could sample several different kinds of chocolate—extra-bittersweet, semisweet, milk, white—all from the same manufacturer. Or you could taste chocolates from a single country or from many countries. You don't want an overwhelming number; three to five types should be sufficient.

Chop each chocolate into small chunks, place them on separate plates, and label by number only, concealing their identity until after the tasting is completed. Issue tasters score cards to keep track of their judgments. Universally recognized criteria for tasting include appearance (good chocolate is shiny, not dull), aroma (there should be no chemical or musty smell), snap (good chocolate breaks firmly and cleanly and doesn't crumble), texture or mouthfeel (poor chocolate is waxy), melting point (good chocolate melts evenly), sweetness (sugar is sometimes used to mask inferior flavor), and overall taste.

Tasters need nothing more than water as a palate cleanser between samplings, but champagne adds a festive note. After all chocolates are tasted, have guests share their impressions and determine the overall rankings, which are occasionally surprising. At a tasting at our house, for example, France's vaunted Valrhona chocolate came in only third after Lindt from Switzerland and Perugina from Italy. Ghirardelli, on the other hand was, predictably, beat out by the imports. Other good brands to try in a tasting are Callebaut, Poulain, Droste, Guittard, Scharffen Berger, and Karl Bissinger. It can be instructive to also include something cheap like Hershey's.

Though hardly necessary, at our house we like to engage in a bit of overkill and follow the tasting with several desserts made from the chocolates that were sampled. An even simpler approach, and perhaps even more fun, is to make fondue out of the remaining chocolate. In any case, guests will come to appreciate why Carl Linnaeus, the father of modern botany, gave cocoa the scientific name *Theobroma*, meaning food of the gods.

Chocolate Fondue, 374

Cinnamon

The Roman emperor Nero had a mercurial personality. For example, as Maguelonne Toussaint-Samat tells us in her *History of Food*, he killed his wife Poppaea by kicking her when she was pregnant, but then he gave her the most lavish funeral imaginable. He burned on her pyre all of the cinnamon in Rome.

Perhaps the gesture was the product of guilt, but whatever the case, there could have been no higher honor. The Romans believed cinnamon was sacred, and every Roman emperor stocked cinnamon in his treasury. The empress Livia even built a temple in honor of her husband Augustus around a huge chunk of the spice sealed in a gold vessel.

The Romans weren't the only ones who valued cinnamon. The ancient Egyptians used it for sorcery and embalming. Their references to it in Sanskrit manuscripts make it the first spice to be specifically mentioned in history. It also appears in the Old Testament.

Over the years cinnamon has been prized for its medicinal properties, and the Chinese actually believed it was able to confer immortality. Recent studies indicate that it may inhibit the progression of type 2 diabetes, so much so that one researcher recommends that people at risk take a teaspoon per day.

No wonder cinnamon was once more precious than gold or that it was partly responsible for the beginning of world trade. And no wonder traders such as Marco Polo deliberately kept its origin secret. Nor is it surprising that the Portuguese resorted to terror to preserve their monopoly on the substance.

What might be surprising, however, is the fact that in this country, most of what passes for cinnamon is not really cinnamon at all. And perhaps more startling still, a taste-test conducted by *Cooks Illustrated* magazine indicates that's just the way we like things.

Cinnamon is the dried bark of various laurel trees, but the genuine article comes only from *Cinnamomum verum*, a tree indigenous to Sri Lanka. Because of high cost (as much as $100 per pound back in the early 1900s), it has not been readily available in this country for nearly a century. Instead, the bark of a similar tree, *Cinnamomum cassia* (sometimes called bastard cinnamon), is most often imported here. The term "cinnamon" can be legally applied to both, though in Britain only the real stuff, which is prized for its special flavor, can be sold as cinnamon. (It's not too hard to spot the difference. Cinnamon is tan, while *cassia* is reddish brown.)

Though there is only one true cinnamon, there are several varieties of *cassia*, the chief ones being from Indonesia, Vietnam, and China. Most of what is sold as cinnamon in the United States is *cassia* from Indonesia. Chinese *cassia* tends to have a stronger flavor while the Vietnamese variety, only recently available in this country, has gained a reputation for being among the world's finest.

Needless to say, given all this variation, the taste of competing brands of cinnamon can differ dramatically, as *Cooks Illustrated* discovered. It conducted a blind tasting of nearly a dozen samples of cinnamon, including true cinnamon from Sri Lanka. Some twenty people took part in two separate rounds of tasting.

Ironically, the true cinnamon was rated only "acceptable," finishing in eighth place. Almost every brand of *cassia* finished ahead of it. Some testers actually complained that the real stuff was not "cinnamon-y" enough! Apparently, Americans have become accustomed to the more robust flavor of *cassia*. By the way, the difference in taste between *cassia* and real cinnamon has to do with their essential oils. True cinnamon contains eugenol, a chemical which gives cloves their flavor, while *cassia* does not.

The top-rated brand, incidentally, was Penzey's China Cassia Cinnamon. The top rated supermarket brand was McCormick's, an Indonesian *cassia*. Interestingly enough, McCormick's Vietnamese *cassia*, though more expensive, was rated lower. Penzey's Vietnamese *cassia*, however, finished in second place overall, ahead of both McCormick versions.

You can buy cinnamon-bark chips and grind them yourself (William Bounds, Ltd. of California is one supplier), but typically cinnamon is sold in stick or powdered form. The sticks generally have less flavor because they come from the tree's upper branches, whereas ground cinnamon is typically made from the more strongly scented older bark lower on the tree.

Though cinnamon is probably the most common baking spice, it's a shame to confine it only to cakes and pastries, as is typical in European and American cookery. In the Middle East, however, it's often found in meat stews such as the Moroccan tagine. In fact, in Lebanon and much of Syria, cinnamon and allspice are the only spices used to flavor meat. A bit of cinnamon can also transform a rice pilaf and enhance the taste of vegetables and fruits. It's the bark that makes for a great bite.

Lucille's Caramel/Cinnamon Rolls, 258

Community Cookbooks

The novelist Joseph Conrad once remarked that a recipe was "the only product of the human mind altogether above suspicion." He said, "The intention of every other piece of prose may be discussed and even mistrusted; but the purpose of a cookery book is one and unmistakable. Its object can conceivably be no other than to increase the happiness of mankind."

I agree with Conrad wholeheartedly, and I think his observation is especially applicable to community cookbooks, those collections of recipes from church groups, garden clubs, junior leagues and other organizations, usually published locally as fundraisers. They are familiar items in most kitchens, and they invariably have frayed edges, food-splattered pages, and other signs of wear and tear because, perhaps more so than any other type of cookbook, they are bought to be actually used. And that, of course, is part of their great appeal. As Glen Wimmer, a Memphis publisher of such books, notes, a cookbook by, say, Emeril Lagasse can be rather intimidating. But a recipe from Mrs. Smith of the Junior League for something she cooks in her own home offers a level of comfort.

But community cookbooks offer more than just foolproof recipes that have been tested and modified by everyday cooks. According to Anne L. Bower, a professor of English at Ohio State University whom I met at a conference in Nashville, community cookbooks tell stories, stories about the lives of the people who put them together, their history, values, and culture.

Certainly these cookbooks tell us about the changing role of women in our society. As Virginia Bartlett, a culinary historian who has examined more than 500 community cookbooks, points out, in previous eras men took the dominant role in households, and it was the woman's job to cater to their appetites. Indeed, a woman's very self-concept might be rooted in her husband's position. Thus, in the early community cookbooks, women rarely used their first names but instead referred to themselves through their husbands, sometimes going so far as to sign recipes as Mrs. Dr. Smith or Mrs. Judge Walker. One, Bartlett reports, even identified herself as Mrs. Ex-Governor Harden.

Early cookbooks frequently carried advertisements, and these ads, likewise, chronicle the changing status of women. Originally they were for items such as soap and makeup. As women began to assume greater decision-making power in the home, ads for major items such as farm implements started to appear. And as women began to enter the labor force, the cookbooks once again reflected their changing status by emphasizing convenience foods and quickly prepared recipes.

According to Bartlett, community cookbooks may have even contributed to women's suffrage by giving women the opportunity to develop useful skills as they solicited recipes, sold ads, and edited their volumes. She notes that one community cookbook, published in Boston in 1888, "reads like a 'Who's Who' of women's suffrage."

Community cookbooks are a uniquely American institution whose origins can be traced back to the Civil War, when Ladies' Aid Societies sold cookbooks to raise money for wounded soldiers and their families. The tradition continued after the war ended, and it really took off in the late 1860s and early 1870s. Today nearly 15,000 new community cookbooks are published every year. No wonder some bookstores now specialize in them; there's even a national competition, the equivalent of the Academy Awards for community cookbooks, to determine the best of the genre.

Almost everybody is getting into the act. For example, the Texas Rangers have published a cookbook. So have the nation's firefighters and the Family Advisory Board of the Central Intelligence Agency. Schools, churches, sports teams, symphony orchestras, museums, and garden clubs have published cookbooks. There's a community cookbook from Alaska with recipes inspired by the television show *Northern Exposure*. There's one put out by a San Francisco PTA which features recipes for Spam. Even East Hampton, New York, a town you wouldn't think would need to do much fundraising, has one. It features recipes from, among other members of that community, Christie Brinkley, Chevy Chase, and Martha Stewart.

A particularly intriguing community cookbook I've run across is the recipe collection published by the River Heritage Quilters Guild of Cape Girardeau, Missouri. It makes perfectly good sense that a group of quilters should assemble a cookbook, for cooking and quilting are both activities which involve an amalgamation of varied components into a glorious whole. Moreover, quilts, no less than cookbooks, can be considered texts worth reading for the insights they yield about the life and culture of the women who produced them.

Paul McIlhenny of the Tabasco Company, which sponsors the annual community cookbook awards, says such books are "a truly American, democratic phenomenon that celebrates the great mélange—the bouillabaisse, if you will—of American cooking and the local groups that put [them] together." The following recipes are good ways to celebrate both.

Thelma Stone's Apricot Chicken, 274
Blintz Casserole, 335
Elvera Weber's Jell-O Salad, 240

Corn

"Sex is good," Garrison Keillor has observed, "but not as good as fresh sweet corn." Betty Fussell, author of *The Story of Corn*, probably wouldn't disagree. After researching the subject for five years, she concluded, "I can't think of anything sexier than corn."

Sexy or not, nothing is more basic to American cuisine and culture than corn. As Elisabeth Rozin observes, "Corn is the ultimate, the essential American food, the one that began here, the one that stayed here, the one that nourished all who came here." She adds, "It remains today the single food most closely identified with the American character and the American myth." Indeed, without it there might not have been an America as we know it. As Waverly Root and Richard De Rochemont note, "Plymouth and Jamestown alike would have disappeared before they had taken root if their settlers had been unable to bring themselves to eat corn."

Today the country they settled produces over 10 billion bushels of corn each year, and their ancestors consume, in one form or another, over three pounds of corn per person per day. In an average year each of us will eat something like sixty quarts of popped corn.

And yet corn in its natural state makes up less than one percent of the American corn market. Fifty-seven percent of the crop is fed to animals, which is to say it's converted into cows, hogs, and chickens. If you had eggs for breakfast this morning (assuming you didn't have a bowl of that most American of breakfast foods, corn-flakes), the chicken who laid them was probably fed corn. Moreover, corn derivatives are major ingredients in a host of food products, including soft drinks, ice cream, and even hot dogs. And don't forget the role corn plays in making America's favorite whiskey, the bourbon of Kentucky (where, they say, the corn is full of kernels and the colonels full of corn).

Beyond the dinner table, corn figures in a wide variety of products ranging from shoe polish to embalming fluid. At last count there were at least 600 products made from corn. Like Native Americans who made moccasins out of corn husks and used the cobs for fuel, we do more with corn than eat the kernels, and we'd be hard pressed to live without it.

Those natives, of course, had been growing corn long before Columbus arrived in 1492 and "discovered" it. As far back as prehistoric times, they were already making popcorn, the oldest known corn in the world. In fact, were it not for them, the crop we know today would not exist, for corn is a plant that is not found naturally in the wild. It cannot reproduce itself. It must be cultivated and developed by humans.

That cultivation began at least 7,000 years ago in central Mexico when natives serendipitously crossed two grasses, teosinte and gamagrass. The result, with small kernels spaced far apart, didn't look much like modern corn, but through systematic cultivation Native Americans promoted the development of ears or cobs like those we see today.

Before long, corn took on symbolic significance for these peoples. For example, among the Mayans the growing cycle of maize was a metaphor for life, the root of their language, and the basis of their calendar. In every indigenous culture, corn was planted amidst ceremony and prayer, and thought to be a gift of the gods. One taste of a freshly picked golden ear of summer corn dripping with butter, and it's hard to argue with that.

Grilled Corn on the Cob with Cheese and Lime, 292

Couscous

"A handful of couscous is better than Mecca and all its dust." So says a famous Moroccan proverb about almsgiving.

The maxim cannot be tossed off as mere chauvinism about the tiny balls of dough that are Morocco's national dish. You don't have to be from Africa to appreciate couscous. The late Craig Claiborne, for example, called it one of the dozen greatest dishes in the world. Paula Wolfert, who over thirty years ago wrote what is still, in my judgment, the definitive treatise on the subject, claimed that couscous can be compared without exaggeration to such great specialties as Japanese *sukiyaki*, Peking duck, bouillabaisse, and paella Valenciana and called it the "crowning achievement" of Moroccan cuisine. It is to Morocco what pasta is to Italy. Indeed, some of the local names used for it there are identical to the word for "food" in general.

No wonder the French, who know a thing or two about fine food, have embraced it. The *Atlantic Monthly*, noting that couscous has outstripped both rice and potatoes as the country's favorite side dish, maintains that it is arguably the national food of France. As the *Christian Science Monitor* recently observed, "Bouillabaisse may be Marseille's most famous dish, but couscous is its most popular."

Likewise in this country, couscous, once considered an exotic ingredient, has become fashionable, upstaging even polenta at trendy restaurants. You can now find it at almost any grocery store, and it is quickly becoming part of the home cook's repertoire.

It's about time couscous got its due. While *The Oxford Companion to Food* insists that there is no evidence for its existence before the 13th century, it nonetheless speculates that it was invented as far back as the 11th. Some say it even predates pasta and goes back to the 10th. (The name may be derived from the Arabic word *kiskis*, which refers to the steamer pot in which couscous is traditionally cooked, or it may be onomatopoeic, mimicking the hissing sound which the steam makes.)

Now perhaps you've tried couscous, soaking the granules in water for five minutes and then fluffing them with a fork as the instructions on the box typically direct, and wondered what all the fuss is about. I felt the same way until a recent visit to Tangier, where I learned that Moroccans would never think of using such an approach. Rather, as they have for centuries, they steam their couscous, sometimes as many as seven times, in a specially designed piece of equipment resembling a double boiler, called a couscousiere.

In the shadow of the Kasbah I bought a couscousiere, and when I got home I discovered that the difference between couscous made with it and couscous made by mere soaking is nothing short of astonishing. Steamed couscous turns out light, fluffy, and tender and not at all gummy as it sometimes does with mere soaking.

Once you've tasted properly prepared couscous you'll understand why it's always served at feasts and celebrations in Morocco to ensure that guests achieve what is called *shaban*, or total satisfaction.

Cranberry Pecan Couscous, 294

Cranberries

Ever heard of the cranberry bounce? No, it's not a dance step from the Roaring Twenties, but a method for sorting good cranberries from bad ones.

According to Ocean Spray, Inc., the cranberry bounce was discovered in the 1880s by John "Peg Leg" Webb, a New Jersey farmer. Because he was one-legged, he was unable to carry his cranberry crop down the stairs from the storage loft in his barn and so simply poured the berries down the steps. He noticed that the best fruit bounced to the bottom of the steps while spoiled or bruised ones remained where they were. Today cranberry processors still sort cranberries, sometimes called bounceberries, by their springiness.

Had it not been for Webb's advance, cranberries might not be so readily available today and that would be a shame. For what would Thanksgiving be without cranberries? More so than sweet potatoes or pumpkin pie or even the turkey itself, it seems to me that cranberries are the most indispensable food to this holiday. And that's probably as it should be, because, though there is some controversy about the menu for the first Thanksgiving celebration, historians are pretty sure that cranberries, one of only three major fruits indigenous to North America, were on it. (The other two, by the way, are the blueberry and the Concord grape.)

As Jack Robertiello writing in *Americas* magazine reasons, it's likely that Native Americans brought cranberries to the first Thanksgiving because the cranberry was already an important fruit to tribes, such as the Wampanoags of Cape Cod, long before the Pilgrims arrived at Plymouth Rock. They not only used it for food, combining it with fat and ground venison or bear meat to create something called *pemmican*, which was formed into cakes and dried in the sun, they used it in a variety of other ways as well. They dyed rugs and blankets with cranberry juice, boiled the berry in poultices used to treat arrow wounds, and settled their differences over a cranberry offering. Indeed, the name of the Delaware chief, Pakimintzen, who distributed cranberries at peace feasts not unlike the first Thanksgiving, came to mean "cranberry eater."

Though various Native American tribes had different names for the cranberry (the Wampanoags' *ibimi*, meaning bitter berry, was an appropriate one), most authorities give the Pilgrims credit for coining the term "cranberry." Originally they referred to them as "crane-berries" because the pink blossom of the fruit resembles the head of a crane. Later the term was shortened to "cranberry."

It didn't take long for the Pilgrims to catch on to the value of cranberries. Recipes for cranberry sauce appear as early as 1663 in *The Pilgrim's Cookbook*, and the recipe for the first cranberry-juice cocktail can be found in the *Compleat Cook's Guide*, published in 1683. The settlers also used the berries for decorative purposes, such as to adorn Christmas trees. Soon enough, the cranberry became one of the three most-prized commodities of the Puritans along with corn and codfish. In fact, in 1773 the colonists passed a law making it a crime for anyone on Cape Cod to pick more than a quart of cranberries before the peak harvest in September.

Thank goodness the berries are not rationed today, for living as we do in an area where they are available only mid-September through December, I routinely freeze ten to fifteen bags of them every year around that time. They'll keep in the freezer for close to a year. Generally, it's best not to thaw them before using. If I run out, I can always resort to those wonderful dried cranberries, sometimes marketed as "craisins," which are available in supermarkets.

We eat cranberries year-round at our house because they are one of my favorite fruits. It's shortsighted, I think, to enjoy them only at the holidays or to relegate them to the relish tray. I like to put them in chocolate-chip cookies, cheesecake, sorbet, bread pudding, pies, scones, muffins, gingerbread, coffee cakes, fruitcakes, brownies, fudge, and, believe it or not, tiramisu. (Give me cranberries jubilee over the cherries version any day!) They make an excellent accompaniment to main dishes such as pork, chicken, burgers, curry dishes, and, of course, turkey, and they can enliven a bowl of chili or a salad. Their juice adds an interesting touch to champagne, sangria, mixed drinks like Mai Tais and margaritas, not to mention punch, iced tea, and even hot buttered rum. No wonder that when we last visited Plymouth, Massachusetts, I was more excited about touring Cranberry World than the replica of the *Mayflower*.

Though I would be the last person to scorn a jellied cylinder of cranberry sauce coaxed right out of the can, these recipes, take the "bog ruby" to an even higher level.

Cruise Ship Dining

"You come on as a passenger, but you leave as cargo!" So goes a quip uttered at one time or another by every cruise director who has ever sailed. After having taken more than a dozen cruises over the years, I can attest that the remark exaggerates things—but not by much.

It's hard to eat sensibly on a cruise. Indeed, the phrase "cruise diet" is the ultimate oxymoron. And to people like me, that is a primary appeal of traveling on an ocean liner.

I well remember the first cruise our family took years ago. There was a midnight buffet every evening, and I didn't miss a single one. To guard against total gluttonous embarrassment, each night a different sleepy-eyed member of the family would accompany me to provide supervision.

Things have changed considerably since then. Today, most ships no longer offer a midnight buffet every night. That's the bad news. The good news is they now provide food virtually twenty-four hours a day and, furthermore, my family has long given up trying to restrain me.

Pigging out on board is a tradition almost as old as cruising itself. Passengers on the *Titanic*, for example, dined on a ten-course meal shortly before the ship went down. The fare included oysters à la Russe, consommé Olga, poached salmon with mousseline sauce, chicken Lyonnaise, lamb with mint sauce, pâté de foie gras, and chocolate-painted eclairs.

Even the very first pleasure cruise in American history, which, according to Samuel Eliot Morison, took place in 1536, is remembered for what the passengers ate. Sadly, the excursion, a sailing to Newfoundland, ended in tragedy as voyagers were left in such desolate conditions that they resorted to cannibalism.

Cruising has come a long way since then. Today it's experiencing a revival with bigger ships, more exotic destinations, and, happily, more bounteous dining than ever before. The *Queen Elizabeth 2*, for example, sports five main restaurants. Norwegian Cruise Line has ships with as many as ten. Holland America boasts a Dutch chocolate extravaganza, Princess a steakhouse, and Carnival a 24-hour pizzeria. Sushi bars are common. Three of the last four ships I've sailed on have had one.

And, of course, there's always a poolside grill, a self-service buffet, and room service. Why, a person could eat all day long! And lots of us do. Statistics reveal that cruise-ship passengers spend 33 percent of their time afloat eating. It makes you wonder if some of them have signed up for both the early and the late seating in the main dining room. (Actually, you can't. I've tried.)

Not surprisingly, it takes enormous storehouses of food, giant kitchens, and numerous tireless workers to satisfy the appetites of seafaring passengers. For example, during a private galley tour on my last cruise, I learned that the ship's nine butchers, thirteen pastrycooks, nine bakers, ten salad preparers, plus dozens of other workers slaving away in the fruit and cheese larder, the soup station, and the garde manger (cold kitchen) went through 1,100 pounds of fish, 1,500 pounds of beef, 1,000 pounds of pork, 2,100 pounds of vegetables, 4,860 pounds of fresh fruit, 1,142 servings of ice cream (all made right on board), and 4,285 cakes and pastries each and every day. The bakery alone used 1,300 pounds of flour (the equivalent of 260 bags like we buy at the grocery store) daily. No wonder the crew had to wash 50,000 dishes every day. Moreover, they do all of this while at sea, which has been likened to working in a land-based kitchen while on roller skates.

I've heard similar figures while visiting kitchens on other ships, but perhaps the most stunning statistic comes from the venerable *QE2*. On its around-the-world cruises, it routinely sails with a ton of caviar on board, making Cunard, its parent company, the third-largest purchaser of the stuff in the world, after the governments of Russia and the Ukraine.

But the quantity and availability of food is not the only focus on cruises. Today many lines even retain famous chefs to elevate the cuisine on board. Crystal employs Piero Selvaggio, the proprietor of Los Angeles' famed Valentino restaurant; Celebrity has hired 3-star Michelin chef Michel Roux (he was in charge of the wedding reception for Prince Charles and Princess Diana); and Seabourn has teamed up with Charlie Palmer, founder of New York's renowned Aureole. And, in the unlikely event that the food on board is not special enough, a few ships will even arrange for you to dine at top restaurants shoreside while the vessel is in port.

Of course, you can watch your waistline while on a cruise because most ships offer healthy menus that even carry the endorsement of the American Heart Association. But a spokesman for Royal Caribbean estimates that if they didn't, 80 percent of passengers would never complain. As Gerry Abraham of Carnival observed in a recent issue of the *South Florida Business Journal*, "It's a nice subject for conversation."

No, most passengers are like me. I've sailed on the Atlantic, the Pacific, the Mediterranean, the Gulf of Mexico, the Caribbean, the North Sea, and the Mississippi, Danube, and Yangtze Rivers, but what I like best is the Sea of Calories.

Scallops Sautéed with Garlic and Herbs, 288

Culinary Disasters

Perhaps you've heard the story about the lady who marched into the dining room on Thanksgiving Day with a magnificently prepared turkey and then accidentally dropped it on the floor in full view of her horrified guests. Without missing a beat, she picked up the bird and headed back to the kitchen, telling everyone not to worry. In the kitchen she wiped off the turkey, basted it again with pan drippings, then returned to the dining room with it and announced, "Here's the other turkey!"

Not everyone has the quick-wittedness to recover so confidently from culinary disaster, but such moxie sure beats the reaction of François Vatel, chef to the Minister of Finance under Louis XIV. Mortified at running out of food when the king himself and his retinue came calling, he vowed to redeem himself at their next meal. Taking no chances, he placed orders with nearly every fisherman in the region. Later, upon receiving a delivery, he inquired apprehensively of the supplier, "Is that all there is?" Not realizing that it was just a portion of his order, the deliveryman mistakenly told him yes. Unable to bear the thought of being humiliated two meals in a row, Vatel went to his room and ran himself through with his sword. His body was discovered by another deliveryman coming to tell him the rest of the fish had arrived.

Cooking disasters are unavoidable, even for the best of cooks. As Karen Mamone of the *Hartford Courant* writes, "Any cook who doesn't have failures must be cooking the same old predictable boring stuff over and over. Experiments must come to no good from time to time." For that matter, even when you're cooking tried-and-true fare, disaster may strike.

Take, for example, the lady who got a new stove. Knowing that slow cooking enhances tenderness, she decided to cook the meat for a dinner party for several hours overnight. She put it in her oven and then flipped what she thought was a lever that merely sealed the oven door, trapping excess heat. The lever, of course, activated the oven's self-cleaning cycle and in the morning she was greeted with the charred remains.

The question, then, is not whether you'll ever experience a culinary mishap, but, rather, what you will do about it when it happens. Short of suicide, as it turns out, there are measures you can take when confronted with culinary catastrophe.

The easiest thing to do when a dish does not turn out right is to simply pretend that nothing is wrong and serve it anyway. Occasionally you can even find virtue in the defective result. Thus, in her beautiful book *Chocolate and The Art of Low-fat Desserts*, Alice Medrich features a recipe for Fallen Chocolate Soufflé Torte. There it is, pictured on page 32 in all its glory, with a note from the author saying, "I like the sunken-soufflé look of this torte served right side up with a dusting of sugar." You have to wonder whether the dessert was planned to sag in the middle or if the shrewd Medrich is merely putting a favorable spin on things.

Similarly, Marcel Desaulniers, in his lavish book *Desserts to Die For*, offers a recipe for Fallen Angel Cake. The cake is named, he explains, for "the precipitous fall it undergoes after being removed from the oven." Desaulniers advises, "Do not despair when this happens—it gives the cake its interesting appearance and dense texture." Further grasping victory from the jaws of culinary defeat, he adorns each slice with a spun-sugar halo.

Obviously, not every culinary disaster can be peddled as a triumph. Sometimes corrective action is required. That is what Stanislas Leszczynski took when he poured rum over a yeast bun that was too dry for him. He also invented *baba au rhum*, now a classic dessert, in the process.

Food writer Judy Walker advises that few dessert mishaps are beyond salvaging. Though you may not invent a classic, she suggests that if your fudge is runny, you can simply serve it over ice cream; if your cake falls apart, you can layer it with fruit and custard to make a trifle; if your pie is runny, you can serve it in a bowl and garnish it appropriately.

Marina and John Bear, in their book *How To Repair Food*, recommend that every kitchen be equipped with a first-aid kit—not for the cook but for the food. Among the items to include are Parmesan cheese ("a hurry up topping"), instant mashed-potato flakes (for thickening failed sauces), sherry (to add gourmet taste to just about anything), canned cheese soup (to dress up lackluster vegetables), baking soda (to sweeten soured cream or milk) and canned hollandaise sauce. "Who would ever dream you had made a mistake," they ask, "when you bring something to the table smothered in hollandaise?" They even suggest that burned food can usually be reclaimed by judicious scraping or, in desperate cases, adding barbecue sauce to complement the "smoky" taste.

In the final analysis, however, perhaps the best defense against culinary calamity is to keep the number for Domino's Pizza posted prominently on your refrigerator door.

Tart Tatin, 337

Culinary Exam

If you can't teach them, test them. I used to wonder if my students thought that view represents my philosophy of education, because I gave frequent quizzes. But examinations are important. After all, we wouldn't take a cake out of the oven without testing it, would we?

I couldn't resist preparing the following culinary quiz. Try your hand at it, but remember that a fool can ask more questions than a wise man can answer.

Culinary IQ Test

Q: Which of the following instruments is used to finely slice and julienne food?

a) banjo
b) guitar
c) mandoline
d) harmonica

A: c) mandoline. The mandoline is a hand-operated machine with adjustable blades that slice paper-thin. It cuts potatoes into French fries or waffle cuts with ease and julliennes better than a food processor. I suppose it would be a natural in a kitchen band as well. Most professional chefs wouldn't be without one.

Q: Which of the following is a copycat?

a) Oreo
b) Hydrox
c) neither of these
d) both of these

A: d) both of these. Because the Oreo cookie is America's favorite and the best selling cookie in the world, many people mistakenly believe that the Hydrox (now called Droxies) is an imitation. But it actually was introduced four years earlier than the Oreo. Both cookies, however, were patterned after cookies first made in England. No one is quite sure how the Oreo got its name, though some suggest that since they first came in a gold-colored package, the name is derived from the French word for gold. Hydrox, on the other hand, is a combination of the first letters of the ingredients that constitute water—hydrogen and oxygen. The makers were looking for a name that was associated with cleanliness and purity and which would complement the image created by the company's name, Sunshine Biscuit.

Q: One stick of butter is equal to:

a) 1 cup
b) ½ cup
c) ⅓ cup
d) ¼ cup

A: b) ½ cup. Butter comes in one-pound boxes containing four sticks. Each stick is therefore ¼ pound but the equivalent of ½ cup or 8 tablespoons. No wonder Barbara Gibbs Ostmann and Jane L. Baker in *The Recipe Writer's Handbook* observe, "How to indicate the measurement of butter and margarine is a controversial topic." Most recipes will give at least two measurements just to make sure the instructions are clear.

Q: Which of the following was discovered by accident?

 a) chocolate-chip cookies
 b) fudge
 c) puff pastry
 d) all of these

A: d) all of these. Culinary accidents have been responsible for almost as many wonderful food innovations as culinary inspiration. The chocolate-chip cookie was born in 1930 when Ruth Wakefield of the Toll House Inn in Massachusetts ran out of baker's chocolate and mixed a cut-up candy bar into her cookie batter, expecting it to melt and mix with the dough. It didn't. Fudge was the result of a botched batch of caramel or toffee. And puff pastry was discovered in 1654 by a French pastrycook apprentice who forgot to add butter to his dough and attempted to incorporate it after the fact.

Q: When should you definitely not order fish in a restaurant?

 a) Sunday
 b) Monday
 c) Friday
 d) Saturday

A: b) Monday. According to Chef Anthony Bourdain in his exposé, *Kitchen Confidential*, you should never order fish in a restaurant on a Monday evening, especially if it's the special. That's because the chef orders fish on Thursday for delivery on Friday morning, hoping he can sell it on Friday and Saturday night. If he doesn't and it still smells all right and he's reasonably sure it won't poison you, the fish he bought on Thursday is what you'll be served on a Monday night! Seafood on Sunday, Bourdain says, can also be risky, especially at brunches, which he calls dumping grounds for leftovers.

Q: Philadelphia Brand Cream Cheese originated in:

 a) Pennsylvania
 b) California
 c) New York
 d) Illinois

A: c) New York. The concept of cream cheese was invented in 1872 by William E. Lawrence and Son of Chester, New York, in Orange County. The Philadelphia Brand was adopted as a trademark in an attempt to capitalize on that city's reputation as the home of high-quality foodstuffs.

Q: A meal consisting of foods named after John D. Rockefeller, Caesar Cardini, François Chateaubriand, Alfredo Di Lelio, and Ali Baba would include:

   a) oysters, iceberg lettuce, broiled beef, spaghetti, poached peach halves with ice cream and raspberry sauce
   b) oysters, romaine lettuce, broiled beef, fettuccine, rum-soaked sponge cake
   c) oysters, avocado salad, lobster, fettuccine, sliced bananas in a warm butter and rum sauce
   d) two all-beef patties, special sauce, lettuce, cheese, pickles, onions on a sesame seed bun

A: b) oysters (Oysters Rockefeller), romaine lettuce (Caesar Salad), broiled beef (Chateaubriand), fettuccine (Fettuccine Alfredo), rum-soaked sponge cake (Baba au Rhum). Oysters Rockefeller, invented at Antoine's Restaurant in New Orleans, were originally served on a bed of scallions, tarragon, and celery which turned them so green that the Rockefeller name, indelibly associated with greenbacks, seemed appropriate. Caesar Cardini, a Tijuana restaurant owner, improvised his salad out of a practically bare cupboard and originally called it Aviator Salad in honor of his brother, a veteran of the Italian Air Force. Chateaubriand, long a specialty at Cape Girardeau, Missouri's Royal N'Orleans Restaurant, is thickly cut tenderloin served with bearnaise sauce, a dish invented by its namesake's personal chef. Italian restauranteur Alfredo Di Lelio first prepared his rich pasta dish in an effort to spark his wife's appetite after childbirth. King Stanislas of Poland is said to have first doused a kugelhopf with rum. Some say the name comes from the Polish word for good woman and not the fictional character from *A Thousand and One Arabian Nights*. Frankly the desserts in the other choices would suit me fine too, whether the Peach Melba in option a, or the Bananas Foster in option c.

Q: Which of the following is a vegetable?

   a) tomato
   b) squash
   c) cucumber
   d) all of these
   e) none of these

A: d) or e). This is a trick question. Botanically speaking, all of the above are fruits. But legally they are all vegetables. The distinction can be an important one for trade purposes. Back in 1893, for example, there was a tariff on imported vegetables, so an importer argued that his shipment of tomatoes from the West Indies should be exempt since the tomato is a fruit. The case went all the way to the Supreme Court where Justice Horace Gray ruled that tomatoes are vegetables because, unlike fruits which are generally served as dessert, they are typically served with the principal part of dinner. The ruling established a legal precedent which has also been applied to squash, cucumbers, and peppers.

Q: Which of the following terms denotes a preparation containing truffles?

a) Dubarry
b) Florentine
c) Périgourdine
d) noisette

A: c) Périgourdine. The term refers to the Périgord region of France which is famous for its black truffles. A dish with "Dubarry" in the title, after a courtesan of Louis XV, contains cauliflower. A dish labeled "Florentine," or "in the style of Florence," contains spinach. The word "noisette" refers in French to hazelnuts, but more than likely, if you order a dish with that term in the description, you'll get fish or meat with browned butter that mimics the nutty flavor of hazelnuts.

Q: The best thing to do with leftover champagne is:

a) throw it out
b) make vinegar out of it
c) deglaze a sauté pan with it
d) take a bath in it

A: d) take a bath in it. As reported in the *Washington Post* recently, a woman in Arlington, Virginia, revealed to her cooking class that she liked to soak in leftover champagne and found it very soothing. Her approach, which I suppose you could call a bubbly bath, sounds like a good idea to me.

Scoring

Each question is worth 10 points. Grade yourself as follows:

90–100: There could be an opening for you at the CIA (Culinary Institute of America).

80–90: Though Julia Child probably wouldn't feel threatened to have you in her kitchen, Betty Crocker might.

70–80: It might be a good idea for you to curl up for a while with *Larousse Gastronomique*.

60–70: You're a good cook as long as you stick to TV dinners and cake mixes.

0–60: Fortunately for you, Denny's is open 24 hours a day.

Culinary Queries

"A little learning is a dangerous thing," Alexander Pope remarked. I don't disagree, but clearly no knowledge at all can be just as hazardous. Especially in the kitchen.

If you can't tell a *coulis* from a *clafoutis*, don't know whether it's better to chop garlic or mash it in a press, or fail to appreciate the role of a *mirepoix*, you could be setting yourself up for culinary catastrophe. What's more, to the extent your lack of knowledge makes you less adventurous, you could be missing out on some flavorful experiences.

Fortunately for the "epicurious" among us, food writer Nancy Rommelmann has cooked up an informative volume that comprises, as its title proclaims, *Everything You Pretend to Know about Food and Are Afraid Someone Will Ask*. Among the more intriguing culinary queries she deals with are the following.

What's the most humane way to cook a lobster?

Rommelmann asserts that lobsters must feel pain because they flail about so when plunged into boiling water, but the authors of the *Joy of Cooking* disagree. Whatever the case, Jonathan Bartlett, in his *Cook's Dictionary and Culinary Reference*, argues that the lobster's death is instantaneous and entails no suffering. Still, there are precautions that can be taken if for no other reason than to ease the guilt of the cook. One method is to sever the lobster's spinal cord before cooking, though, as Rommelmann notes, this hardly seems more humane than boiling. Another technique involves anesthetizing the lobster by putting it in water and slowly increasing the temperature. A third approach is to submerge the crustacean in wine so that it is too intoxicated to care. Finally, in an effort to summon the courage necessary to prepare dinner, the cook might consume the wine instead of giving it to the lobster.

Is a sweet potato the same thing as a yam?

You might think so, judging by the two varieties of sweet potatoes typically found in the supermarket and the fact that yams and sweet potatoes are generally prepared in much the same way. For example, *The Oxford Companion to Food* recommends steaming, boiling, mashing, roasting, or frying yams, just what you'd do to sweet potatoes (though the *Joy of Cooking* warns that yams do not take well to puréeing). But a true yam is a totally different vegetable than a sweet potato, which, as Bartlett notes, is not really a potato at all.

What is a Scoville unit?

Devised by pharmacologist Wilbur Scoville, a Scoville unit measures how hot a chile pepper is. The higher the number, the hotter the chile. Thus, a bell pepper scores 0 (no heat whatsoever) on the Scoville scale. A poblano chile registers between 1,000 and 1,500 units (mild burn). The state pepper of Texas, the jalapeño, is medium hot, or around 2,500 to 5,000 units. The fiery cayenne pepper scores between 30,000 and 50,000, and the hottest pepper known to humankind, the habanero or Scotch bonnet, scores a whopping 100,000 to 300,000 on the Scoville scale. Scoville units, thus, scientifically validate the familiar principle that the smaller a chile pepper, the hotter it is likely to be.

Does champagne come in bottles bigger than a magnum?

A magnum is equal to two standard bottles of champagne, but there are much larger bottles than that, all named after Biblical kings: a Jeroboam is the equivalent of four bottles, a Rehoboam of six bottles, a Methuselah of eight bottles, a Salmanazar of twelve bottles, a Balthazar of sixteen bottles, and a Nebuchadnezzar, the largest of all, of twenty bottles.

Must a wine have "legs" to be good?

The tendrils of wine that adhere to and slowly slide down the sides of a wine glass are its "legs" or "tears." The more viscous the wine, the better the legs. However, viscosity breaks down with age, so an old bottle of wine may be excellent and have no legs at all. Hence, a wine's legs are all but irrelevant in assessing its quality and nowhere near as important as its three essential attributes—color, nose, and taste.

What is the most expensive food in the world?

Beluga caviar, selling for $800 per pound, is the world's most costly food, but saffron, at $600 per pound, is close behind. It is made up of the stigmas of the purple-flowered crocus, and it takes some 70,000 of them to make a pound. As they must be picked by hand, the harvesting of saffron is labor-intensive, therefore making for a high-priced spice. French truffles, at about $500 per pound, are also among the world's most precious foods. By comparison, genuine balsamic vinegar at only $75 per ounce or Parmigiano-Reggiano cheese at a mere $17 per pound seem like real bargains.

Rommelmann's little book deals with many other culinary issues, ranging from why arabica beans are never used in instant coffee (they're too good) to whether sun-dried tomatoes really are dried in the sun (not likely) to why cashews are never sold in the shell (the shell is toxic). And it tells you why in the kitchen a china cap is never worn on the head and a mandoline is never strummed. (The former is a conical sieve and the latter is a guillotine-like slicer.) But ultimately, when it comes to culinary knowledge, the best tutor is a good recipe like the following one.

Grappa Semifreddo, 368

Culinary Sleuthing

The corpse exuded the irresistible aroma of a piquant, ancho chili glaze enticingly enhanced with a hint of fresh cilantro as it lay before him, coyly garnished by a garland of variegated radicchio and caramelized onions, and impishly drizzled with glistening rivulets of vintage balsamic vinegar and roasted garlic oil; yes, as he surveyed the body of the slain food critic slumped on the floor of the cozy, but nearly empty, bistro, a quick inventory of his senses told corpulent Inspector Moreau that this was, in all likelihood, an inside job.

That sentence was a 1998 winner in the annual Bulwer-Lytton Fiction Contest which challenges entrants to compose the opening sentence to the worst of all possible novels. But bad though it may be, it serves as a reminder of just how far the genre of the culinary mystery has come since the days of Rex Stout's heavyweight detective Nero Wolfe. The popularity of contemporary writers like Diane Mott Davidson and Michael Bond (who writes deliciously about culinary sleuth Monsieur Pamplemousse and his dog Pommes Frites) testify to the fact that some of us enjoy reading cookbooks like novels and vice versa.

And why shouldn't we? After all, both detectives and cooks are often confronted with mysteries: For the former it's a question of "whodunit?" and for the latter it may be a question of why the soufflé fell or the cake failed to rise.

Fortunately, there's help for solving those food mysteries from Anne Gardiner and Sue Wilson, two Canadians who have collaborated on a book and website called *The Inquisitive Cook*. Of course, not all food mysteries (like what's really in Spam) are penetrable, and others (like why grandmother always cut the ends off the ham before she baked it) don't require a Sherlock Holmes to solve. (Turns out she didn't have a big enough pan!) But as Gardiner and Wilson demonstrate, an understanding of the fundamentals of food chemistry can explain many culinary puzzles.

For example, why do some recipes call for both baking powder and baking soda, and what's the difference between them anyway? Both leaven baked goods by chemical reactions that generate carbon dioxide. But baking soda is an alkali and it needs acid to work. That's why a recipe will usually contain some acid ingredient if it also calls for baking soda. But if the proportion of acid and baking soda are not balanced or, worse yet, if there is no acid at all, you'll wind up with a disaster. So you couldn't use regular milk in place of buttermilk in your pancake batter and expect good results. Instead, you'd need to sour the milk by adding a tablespoon of vinegar.

Baking powder, on the other hand, contains its own acid. In fact, the double-acting kind contains two, one that reacts with liquid and another that reacts with heat. This makes it especially useful for batters which must stand for a while before baking. Sometimes a recipe calls for both baking soda and baking powder because the amount of soda needed to balance the acid ingredient doesn't provide enough leavening for the amount of flour used, so baking powder is added to provide a boost. (Generally you need ¼ teaspoon of baking soda and ½ cup of an acidic ingredient for each cup of flour.) For example, a banana-bread recipe might take this approach because overripe bananas contain less acid than ripe ones (a pH of 7 vs. one of 4.6), weakening the baking-soda reaction. But don't think that you can achieve extra-high muffins and breads simply by adding a little more baking powder. The reverse is true. Too much leaven overinflates the batter and causes it to collapse.

A little knowledge of culinary chemistry can solve other food mysteries as well. For example, why are some chocolate-chip cookies soft and others crisp? It has to do with the ingredients and baking procedures. Soft cookies have a high moisture content, rely on margarine or shortening which spreads less than butter, and bake at a higher temperature for a shorter time. Crisp cookies exhibit a low liquid-to-flour ratio, use butter, and bake at a lower temperature so they take longer to brown and, thus, dry out more in the process.

Why does the typical sauce recipe instruct you to sauté onions separately before adding other ingredients like tomatoes, even if the dish will require further cooking? That's because tomatoes are acidic and will prevent the onions from softening if you cook them both at the same time. Similarly, if you add the typically acidic molasses-based sauce to baked beans before they've softened, they never will. On the other hand, adding the sauce after the beans have had a chance to soak and soften will firm them up and keep them from getting mushy.

How can meat that's cooked in moisture still be dry? That's because even though the connective tissue in meat begins to dissolve at temperatures as low as 175 degrees, high heat shrinks muscle fibers and squeezes out juices, which makes the meat tough. Thus a gentle simmer rather than a boil is better for braising and stewing.

Why do muffin recipes tell you to stir the batter only until the ingredients are just moistened? Because the more you stir the batter the more gluten you develop and the tougher your muffin. Gluten is an ingredient that's formed when liquid is added to flour and it's needed in yeast breads to give the dough elasticity and strength. But if you want tender muffins, you need to downplay its characteristics. Low-protein flour, like Martha White brand, develops less gluten than high-protein flours, further enhancing tenderness. That's why it's always been the choice of Southern cooks for biscuit-making.

Why should you never beat egg whites in a plastic bowl? Because grease can adhere to it and the whites won't foam if there is even a trace of fat in them. Why is the surface of packaged hamburger bright red when inside it's brown? Because it contains myoglobin, a pigment that stores oxygen and becomes brighter when exposed to air. The plastic film used by the supermarket is pervious to oxygen just for that reason. Why should you store onions and potatoes separately? Because onions emit gasses that make potatoes deteriorate rapidly. Why should you add sugar to applesauce only after the apples have been cooked? Because if you do it sooner, the apples, in accordance with the principle of osmosis, will hold their shape and merely poach rather than stew. Why does food seem to have little taste when you have a cold? Because flavor is mostly dependent on odor. Pinch your nose, and an apple and a potato taste the same.

Solving mysteries such as these help us improve dishes and avoid disasters. The result is recipes like the following.

Banana Pecan Muffins, 253
Versatile Chocolate Chip Cookies, 349
Szechuan Spinach Sauté, 295

Danish Pastry

As the globe becomes increasingly interconnected and societies everywhere more diverse, it's no longer always necessary to visit the country of origin to taste authentic versions of so-called foreign foods. For example, arguably the best sushi in the world is served in New York City (at Nobu's), not in Japan.

But there are still a few items which are altogether different in their home countries than anywhere else. French bread is one. Gelato, or Italian ice cream, is another. And so is Danish pastry.

Having visited Copenhagen, I can readily attest to the fact that what often passes for Danish pastry over here bears little resemblance to the real thing over there. As Karina Porcelli, an American living in Denmark who writes for Fodor's Travel Publications, observes, "I believe above and beyond every gastronomic specialty a country offers, there is one, just one, perfect, delicious bit or bite or drop of something or another that sums up everything the country is and ever has been." And she goes on to argue that the essence of Denmark can be found in its pastries.

As she puts it, "A Danish is effortlessly elegant, unobtrusively hedonistic and often packed with a surprise—an edible metaphor of the Danish experience." I couldn't agree more. After diligently searching out and sampling the wares at the best bakeries in Hans Christian Andersen country (there's a bakery named after him near Tivoli Gardens), I discovered that the stories I'd heard about the virtues of true Danish pastry were not fairytales.

American pastry maven Rose Levy Beranbaum declares, "Danish pastry is truly one of the world's great pastries." Not at all like the cakey American-style version, it is crisp on the outside, and tender and slightly flaky on the inside. The best Danish bakeries make it as many as two or three times a day to insure that whenever you buy it, that's the way it will be. One taste of the real thing and you won't be surprised to learn that along with the likes of Paul Bocuse, Emeril Lagasse, and Jacques Pépin, Joseph Amendola has also been inducted into the Distinguished Visiting Chefs Hall of Fame at Rhode Island's Johnson and Wales University College of Culinary Arts. His specialty is Danish pastry, and his repertoire includes nearly one hundred varieties based on two different doughs.

As Beranbaum points out in her authoritative *The Pie and Pastry Bible* (a work worth studying religiously), Danish pastry is in the same family as filo, strudel, croissant, and brioche doughs because all consist of the same basic ingredients (flour, liquid, and fat) in different proportions and assembled in varying ways.

Specifically, Danish dough is a variation of puff pastry, which was invented in 1654 by a French pastrycook apprentice named Claudius Gele. Apparently he forgot to add butter to his dough and attempted to correct his mistake by folding lumps of it into the dough after the fact. To the astonishment of everyone, when the dough was baked, the butter did not leak out of it, but instead the butter's moisture produced steam, which lifted the pastry into distinct layers. Gele went on to perfect his invention, creating a technique wherein butter is wrapped with dough, then rolled out and folded several times. With each fold, the number of layers in the dough increases exponentially. Typically, puff pastry is given six folds, or "turns" to use the pastrycook's terminology, to produce 729 layers. With only one more fold, the number of layers jumps to over 2,000!

Though there were experiments with it at the royal court as early as 1840, the conversion of puff pastry into Danish dough took place during the latter part of the 19th century when Danish bakers went on strike, protesting the fact that they were paid with room and board rather than real wages. Austrian bakers were brought in to do the work, and they popularized the layered-dough technique. After the strike, Danish bakers started making layered doughs, only they added yeast and eggs to the recipe. Their debt to the Viennese is recognized by the fact that Danish pastries are still known as *Weinerbrod* (Viennese bread) in Denmark. Just to make it more confusing, in Vienna they're called Copenhageners.

Danish dough, then, differs from straight puff pastry because it contains both yeast and egg. Actually, if you add only yeast to puff-pastry dough, you have croissant dough, so Danish dough is really croissant dough with the addition of egg. This makes it less flaky (yet it still has some 27 layers), but richer and more tender.

More critical to the success of Danish pastry than its ingredients, however, is procedure. As Robert Capon writing in the *New York Times* points out, "There are some culinary triumphs that are at least three-fourths technique. . . . Nowhere is this more true than in the confection of homemade Danish pastry. The actual formula is almost a triviality compared with the labor of mastering the method involved." Having tried my hand at puff pastry, I understand what he means. But the process really isn't all that difficult. The most important thing to keep in mind is that the butter needs to be just the right temperature. Too cold and firm and it will tear the dough. Too soft and it will melt into the dough, eliminating any layering.

They know the technique well at the *konditori* La Glace, for they've had plenty of practice. The establishment, operating in the same spot since 1870, is the oldest confectionery in Copenhagen. My wife and I became a familiar sight to the aproned ladies at this genteel pink, green, and gold tearoom since we visited at least twice a day during our stay. (Had they not closed at 5 PM, we might have gone more often.) Before I left town, I had tried practically every variety of Danish which they offer. And with each one, my resolve to start making my own Danish became stronger. I know I'll never attain the level of perfection exhibited at La Glace, but the following recipes, one truly authentic and the others quite simple but exceedingly good imitations, will produce pastries far better than anything I am likely to buy at the store. Try them if, like me, you're no longer willing to settle for anything less than wonderful, wonderful Copenhageners.

Department Store Dining

Creamed spinach is not something you'd normally associate with Christmas. But at our house it is. It goes back several years to when our family used to journey to St. Louis on the day after Thanksgiving to kick off the holiday season by shopping downtown—a tradition for us until the kids grew up, downtown began to decline, and merchants started pushing Christmas sales the day after Halloween.

For me, food was a central part of this holiday ritual. I made sure that interspersed among inspections of store windows, sojourns through the toy department, and a visit to Santa Claus were plenty of hot-chocolate breaks, cookie samplings, and candy-counter tastings. No wonder my favorite year was the one when Famous-Barr (now Macy's) constructed a real candy kitchen on the eighth floor of its store and gave out fresh candy canes to all who came through.

But the culinary highlight of the trip was always lunch, and our choice of a place to go was never lightly considered. Sometimes it was one of the fancy department-store tearooms, occasionally it was the Chinese restaurant across the street from the parking garage, and often as not it was Miss Hulling's, on 8th and Olive, where creamed spinach was a specialty. To this day when the holiday season rolls around, my daughter vividly remembers how I raved about that dish, and I fondly recall introducing it to her when she was six-years-old and just the two of us had made the outing, leaving Mom and newborn brother at home in Cape Girardeau, Missouri.

It doesn't seem possible that more than twenty-five years have passed since then, but they have, and holiday shopping has changed considerably. As Tom Heilman, who used to manage the Patuxent Room in a Woodward and Lothrop store near Washington, D.C., told the *Washington Post*, "Years ago, you spent your entire afternoon, your whole Saturday at a department store. Department stores had a self-interest in having restaurants. They wanted to keep their customers in the store, refresh them and send them out to shop some more. People don't shop like that today."

Now we shop at a hurried pace at cookie-cutter malls, and if we stop to eat at all, we whisk through the food court and grab something on the run. Gone are the days when Christmas shopping was a social event, complete with full-course meal, for which you made sure to dress properly. And consequently, department-store dining rooms, and department stores themselves, have had trouble surviving.

I became nostalgic about shopping and dining while finishing off a Frango Mint sundae at Marshall Field's in Chicago (now also Macy's), one place where shoppers can still experience some of the graciousness of bygone days. The store restaurant, the Walnut Room, is still going strong, and if you want to witness the annual lighting of the great tree there, you'll have to stand in a long line to make a reservation. Marshall Field's has operated a tearoom on the premises since 1890, when the food was prepared in a private home because there was not a store kitchen large enough. Though then there were only fourteen tables staffed by eight waitresses and four pantry helpers (that ratio should give you some idea of the level of service you could expect), the store's famous chicken pie was already on the menu. Initially, Marshall Field himself was opposed to the idea of ladies eating in his store, but he was talked into opening the tearoom by his associate, Harry Gordon Selfridge, who would later go on to found his own great department store in London.

Sadly, not many stores have been able to carry on in the fashion of Marshall Field's. I was in Vancouver when the famed Eaton's finally declared bankruptcy, and was led to wonder about the fate of its premier restaurant on the ninth floor of the Montreal store. The restaurant, commissioned by the late Lady Eaton who had made numerous crossings on the legendary *Ile-de-France*, was a reproduction of the first class salle à manger of the ship. Fortunately, if riding French trains instead of French ocean liners is what you like, Le Train Bleu, a reproduction of a 19th-century luxury French dining car, is still open in Bloomingdale's on 59th Street in New York. So far, to my knowledge, nobody has opened a restaurant that duplicates the interior of the French Concorde, which is probably just as well.

Not surprisingly, larger stores have had better luck keeping their tearooms open. That explains why Marshall Field's, which claims to be the world's largest store (in floor space) is still in the restaurant business, and so is Macy's, which also claims to be the world's largest store (in interior volume). Macy's, in fact, opened the first department store "ladies lunchroom" this side of the Atlantic back in 1878.

Upscale stores also fare better in the dining department. Thus, Bloomingdale's Petrossian Restaurant in Boca Raton serves fine caviar and champagne, Nordstrom's in San Francisco has a bar on every floor (I prefer the café for its view), and a Bullock's store in Los Angeles lured Wolfgang Puck into trying his hand in what used to be the sock department. Curiously, the Saks Fifth Avenue store in New York City did not have a restaurant until fairly recently, but now operates one of the more ambitious of any department store. Neiman Marcus' Zodiac cafés still do well, specializing in genteel dining (my mother swears by the popovers with strawberry butter served with every meal at the Frontenac location), and even became the stuff of urban legend when a mythical story circulated about a woman supposedly charged $250 for their cookie recipe. (The story should have raised suspicions because it also claimed the lady bought a scarf at the store, whose initials some claim stand for Needless Markup, for only $20!)

Thankfully the greatest department store of them all, Harrods in London (their motto is *Omnia, Omnibus, Ubique*—Everything, for everybody, everywhere) shows no signs of getting out of the food business, which is fitting since it is the only department store that started out as a grocery. It operates more than a dozen restaurants and bars, including the elegant Georgian Restaurant which seats 400 people.

But many other department-store dining spots have not been so lucky. Gone, for example, is the refined Missouri Room in the St. Louis Stix, Baer and Fuller store where my wife as a child first tasted lamb. In fact, gone is Stix itself. Even Wanamaker's, the Philadelphia institution which invented fixed pricing, a major contribution to retailing by the modern department store, is now Macy's. The department store, started in Paris with The Bon Marche in 1838 as the product of social and economic change, may itself become the victim of such change.

Change, of course, is inevitable. With the Internet we may some day find we don't need stores at all. But if you, like me, are just a bit wistful for the old days of gracious shopping and dining, perhaps the following recipes, all vestiges of that bygone era, can help satisfy your longing.

Famous-Barr Onion Soup, 248
Nordy Bars, 352
Miss Hulling's Creamed Spinach, 295

Edible Flowers

"A rose by any other name would smell as sweet," said Shakespeare. But after a visit to Holland's Floriade, the once-in-a-decade event that is a veritable World's Fair of flowers, I got to wondering if it would still taste as good.

The Floriade showcases more than 300 floral exhibits from around the world. Nations from four continents are represented, but the star of the show may be the Dutch themselves with their display of 130,000 tulips, the national hallmark.

You can work up quite an appetite roaming around the Floriade's 160 acres, I discovered, so it's not surprising that someone like me would begin to think about the culinary possibilities blooming around me. But I'm hardly the first person to do so. Cooking with flowers is age-old.

In ancient Rome, as Cathy Wilkinson Barash notes, the lower classes, who could not afford saffron, used powdered calendula petals instead. (Saffron itself is made from the stigmas of the crocus flower.) In ancient Persia some 2,000 years ago, as *The Oxford Companion to Food* notes, they made wine from rose petals. (In Iran today, rose petals are still preserved in jams and added to *advieh*, a spice mixture used in savory dishes.) Even the Bible, as Peggy Trowbridge points out, refers to the dandelion as an edible, albeit bitter, herb.

Different cultures have embraced edible flowers in different ways. In the Orient they prize daylilies and chrysanthemums, in Italy they stuff squash blossoms, and in Britain, where the culinary use of flowers is seen as charmingly old-fashioned, they have a taste for nasturtiums, violets, and marigolds. (John Gerard's 17th-century book on herbs maintains that "no broths are well made without dried Marigolds.") Even the classic French liqueur Chartreuse boasts carnations as a unique ingredient.

Yet many people are still hesitant to bite into the idea of eating flowers. Perhaps they think it isn't safe or maybe they think it's just bizarre. Rosalind Creasy, a leading authority on the subject who confesses to occasionally stooping to sneak a bite of her host's centerpiece, suggests a novel explanation. She says, "People believe that flowers are almost magical, so beautiful that only the eyes should feast on them. To those folks, eating flowers seems a bit greedy."

Such people might be surprised to learn that in one form or another they've probably been eating flowers all along without realizing it. Broccoli is technically a flower, though an immature one. So is cauliflower. So are artichokes.

So how big a step can it be to advance from broccoli to begonias, from cauliflower to carnations, or from artichokes to apple blossoms? Marsha Toll, who runs the elegant Bellevue Bed & Breakfast in a beautifully restored 111-year-old house in Cape Girardeau, Missouri, thinks it's a step that ought to be taken. She delights in serving her guests dishes featuring fresh flowers.

Among Marsha's favorite edible flowers are nasturtiums. The entire plant—flowers, leaves, and seed pods—is edible, but she prefers the blossoms, which have a tangy flavor reminiscent of watercress. Nasturtiums can be incorporated into butters and soft cheeses or used to flavor oils, dressings, and vinegars. They're wonderful in cucumber sandwiches and canapés, sprinkled over a salad, or even in pasta dishes. And, of course, they make beautiful garnishes.

Roses, according to *The Oxford Companion to Food*, are the most widely used of all flowers having culinary applications. All types are edible and their taste reminds some of strawberries. They can be frozen into ice cubes, candied and used to decorate desserts, made into syrups and jellies, or used, as they were in a classic scene in the movie *Like Water for Chocolate*, as the secret ingredient in poultry dishes. Moreover, rosewater, said to have been discovered by the famous 10th-century Persian physician Avicenna, is used as a flavoring in several foods.

Lots of other flowers can be used in cooking, including begonias (their stems can substitute for rhubarb), carnations, marigolds, gardenias, gladiolas, lavender (imparts wonderful fragrance to cheesecake or ice cream), dandelions, daylilies, chrysanthemums, English daisies, tulips (stuff them whole with chicken salad for a spectacular presentation), pansies, hibiscus, violets (great for candying), and even scented geraniums.

Whichever varieties you chose, Marsha suggests you grow them yourself, as she does. That way you'll have a reliable and inexpensive source and, more importantly, you'll know they are safe to eat, something you can't count on if you buy flowers from a nursery, florist, or garden center. Their products are likely to have been treated with pesticides and should be avoided.

Always double-check that a given flower, or part of it, is edible. Sometimes one part is, but another is not. (Rhubarb stalks, for example, are edible but their leaves are poisonous.) Remove a flower's pistil and stamens before eating because they may contain pollen which can lessen flavor or cause allergic reactions. Also, some flowers, such as roses, taste better if you remove the bitter white part at the base of the petals. Don't forget, too, that just like other produce, the fresher the better. Pick flowers as close to mealtime as possible. And, finally, it's always a good idea to taste a flower before serving it. Just because it's edible doesn't mean you'll like it. For example, though some sources say marigolds have a delightfully citrus flavor, to Creasy their taste falls "somewhere between skunk and quinine."

Use edible flowers in your cooking and you may come to agree with Creasy that they are as essential to good cuisine as salt and pepper. And like Marsha Toll, you'll delight in your guests' reaction when you ask them to "please eat the daisies."

Flower Confetti Salad, 234

Escoffier

It was aboard the liner *Imperator* shortly before the start of World War I, as *Larousse Gastronomique* tells it. The kaiser, Emperor William II, was so impressed with the job that the supervisor of the ship's imperial kitchens had done that he turned to him and said, "I am the Emperor of Germany, but you are the Emperor of chefs."

And so he was. He was the "king of chefs" and the "chef of kings." At his death he was hailed as "the most famous cook in the world." He was Georges Auguste Escoffier.

Escoffier was born in France in the village of Villeneuve (now Villeneuve-Loubet) near Nice in 1846, the son of a blacksmith, and grew up to be the first cook in French history to receive the cross of the Legion of Honor. Along the way he transformed our ideas about fine dining and revolutionized the professional kitchen. One of his biographers, Timothy Shaw, says, "He was the presiding genius of a whole gastronomic epoch."

Though Escoffier had originally intended to be a sculptor, he had always been interested in food, even as a young boy. His grandmother was an excellent cook, and at the age of ten, Escoffier would spend hours in the kitchen with her, observing her cooking techniques. Sometimes he would experiment on his own.

But it was not until his uncle François agreed to take him on as a kitchen apprentice at his successful restaurant in Nice that Escoffier became serious about cooking as a profession. (He was too small to work in the family trade as a blacksmith. In fact, as a youth he had to wear elevator shoes in the kitchen to avoid getting burned or being overcome by the intense heat.) He would recall later, "They just told me I was going to be a cook, and that was that!"

And he did. As Shaw notes, his career was "one of the most illustrious in food history." After a six-month stint at his uncle's restaurant, he went to work at other local establishments and in his spare time learned the art of pastry making at a nearby patisserie. During this time, he impressed a visiting restaurateur from Paris who recommended him for a job in that city, a significant career move.

From there he served as a cook in the army (where he learned that "horsemeat is delicious when you are in the condition to appreciate it"); joined with César Ritz to open great hotel restaurants in Monte Carlo, Rome, Paris, and London (at the Savoy he invented the revolutionary concept of background music by bringing in Johann Strauss); became the Edwardians' favorite chef (catering to the likes of the Prince of Wales, Sarah Bernhardt, and Oscar Wilde); wrote books (his *Le Guide Culinaire*, containing some 5,000 recipes, is still a standard reference work), and eventually, retired after 62 years (perhaps the longest professional career in cooking in history, his rival Prosper Montagne notes in *Larousse Gastronomique*). And even in retirement, he remained active, writing *Ma Cuisine*, a cookbook focusing on bourgeois cooking for chefs working in private homes and featuring, among others, recipes that hearken back to his birthplace, such as *Poulet Grandmere*, a simple chicken dish like his grandmother used to make.

Escoffier changed the very way we eat today with his innovations. Previously, ostentation was the standard for dinner service, a tradition dating back to the medieval banquet. A large number of different dishes would be set on the table at once and changed during the meal. The purpose was to impress by lavish display. Escoffier helped changed the practice to the style we know today where dishes are served consecutively instead of all at the same time. He also introduced the fixed price menu. Moreover, he disliked excessive garnishes and aimed for a balance of a few good ingredients as opposed to a glut of too many. He believed such simplification represented an advancement in cooking rather than a decline.

Still, a typical Escoffier meal would be considered opulent by today's standards. For example, a representative dinner at the Carlton Hotel in London, Escoffier's last post, might include blini and caviar, consommé, sole in white-wine sauce, partridge and noodles with *foie gras*, lamb noisettes with artichoke hearts and peas, champagne sorbet, turkey with truffles, endive and asparagus salad, and a variety of desserts. Believe it or not, this is a far smaller number of courses than might have been served at a typical meal in the previous century.

Behind the scenes, in the kitchen, Escoffier instituted significant changes too, perhaps in reaction to the terrible conditions he remembered when he was a kitchen apprentice in an era when, according to medical reports, cooks were more vulnerable to occupational diseases than miners. Among the hazards of the profession were tuberculosis, varicose veins, chronic alcoholism, and asphyxiation. (The common practice was to seal the kitchen so the dishes would not cool as they were being served, thus exposing cooks to undiluted gas from the open charcoal burners.) Add to that the serf-like conditions under which most cooks worked, and the professional kitchen was a fairly brutal place. Escoffier, in contrast, insisted on a more civilized atmosphere in keeping with his inherently gentle demeanor and completely reorganized the kitchen into independent stations to promote efficiency, essentially the system still in use. As Shaw notes, Escoffier is remembered today as much for what he did to elevate the status and working conditions of the ordinary cook as for his recipes.

And throughout it all, Escoffier managed to create recipes which are still famous today, many of them named for the most prominent celebrities of his era. He was the inventor of Coupe Yvette, Poularde Adelina Patti, Consommé Favori de Sarah Bernhardt, Salad Tosca, Tournedos Rossini, Soufflé Rothschild, Sole Alice, Fried Eggs a la Verdi, and the most famous of all, Pêches Melba, named after opera singer Nellie Melba who also inspired, during one of her recurrent diets, Melba toast.

Food Etymology

"What's in a name?" asked Juliet gazing down upon Romeo from her balcony. Apparently plenty, as any lexicographer will tell you.

Dr. Peter Hilty, who for years taught English at Southeast Missouri State University, observes that words come from somewhere. "The outright creation of a word is rare," he says. And this is certainly true when it comes to words about food.

Consider, for example, the word "pumpernickel." According to Webster's, it comes from two German terms: *pumpern*, to pass wind, and *Nickel*, a goblin. Etymologists explain that the name refers to the bread's presumed ability to produce flatulence worthy of the devil himself.

Not all food words have origins this intriguing, but the study of how foods got their names can be fascinating. Moreover, as Hilty notes, "We are creatures who use words, and the more we know about words, the more we know about ourselves." Dr. Henry Sessoms, a colleague of Hilty's who teaches a course in the history of the English language, agrees. He points out that studying English words is particularly illuminating because our language is arguably the most accepting of foreign terms. And this is increasingly true as our population grows more diverse. Interestingly enough, our national motto, *E pluribus unum*, first appeared in an ancient Roman recipe for salad. Today, perhaps not coincidentally, authorities on multiculturalism argue that the salad bowl is a better metaphor than the melting pot to describe America.

Martha Barnette, a writer who studied classical languages for a dozen years, has compiled a delicious work entitled *Ladyfingers and Nun's Tummies* which tantalizingly chronicles the origins of hundreds of food-related terms. (The word "tantalize," by the way, derives from Tantalus, who in Greek mythology stole the gods' ambrosia and as punishment was consigned to an eternity in which food and water were always just out of reach.) As Barnette demonstrates in her book, there are "unforgettable pictures and surprising tales tucked into the words we put into our mouths every day."

Sometimes it takes considerable sleuthing to determine what those tales are. Take *canapé*, for example. Barnette explains that in French it means "couch," and, indeed, an edible *canapé* is a piece of bread or toast upon which other items sit. But the word goes all the way back to the Greek term *konopion*, for "a bed or couch surrounded by mosquito netting," which in turn derives from the Greek *konops*, meaning "gnat or mosquito."

In other cases the relationship between a food and its name is pretty clear. For instance, many foods are named for what they look like. Thus eggplant is so named because the white variety resembles eggs. Likewise, the Italian word *orecchietti* means "little ears" and refers to a pasta of similar shape. The word "pretzel" can be traced back through the German *brezel* to the Medieval Latin word *brachitellum* meaning "little arm," a reference to the fact that pretzels are supposed to resemble arms folded in prayer. The word "avocado" is a direct descendant of the Aztec word *ahuacatl* which denotes an avocado-shaped portion of the male anatomy. (Mash the avocado, add the Aztec word for "sauce," *molli*, and with a little modification you get *guacamole*.)

Among the more interesting derivations of food words are those which are the result of misunderstandings. These, says Barnette, can often show how language works. Cherries and peas are good examples. Both are the consequence of what linguists call "back-formation," one type of which involves the mistaken assumption that a singular word is actually plural. It was this confusion which led to the British using the word *cheri* instead of the Norman *cherise* and the word *pea* instead of the Middle English *pease* to refer to individual specimens of those foods.

Sometimes changes in pronunciation can be misleading. For instance, those candy-coated nuts, Jordan almonds, are not from Jordan as their name might suggest. Their name actually derives from an anglicized pronunciation of the Old French word *jardin* for "garden." Similarly, Cold Duck, the German sparkling wine, started out as *Kalte Ende* or "cold end," possibly suggesting that it should be drunk at the end of the day or after a meal. Before long, the word *ende* was corrupted to *ente*, which means "duck." Sometimes the naming process simply invites misunderstanding, regardless of grammar and pronunciation. German chocolate, for example, has nothing to do with Germany, being named instead for its creator Samuel German.

Foods named for people are perhaps the easiest to trace. As Barnette shows, these "edible eponyms" abound. There's Salisbury steak, developed by Dr. James Salisbury, an advocate of shredded food; Fettucine Alfredo, invented by an Italian restaurateur of the same name, and made famous by Hollywood stars; the Cobb salad, invented by none other than Bob Cobb, a Los Angeles restaurant owner; Bananas Foster, a dessert dreamed up by Brennan's Restaurant in New Orleans to honor a regular customer, Richard Foster, an awning salesman; and the beef, mushroom, and sour-cream dish named in honor of the 19th-century Russian diplomat Count Paul Stroganoff; not to mention the Sandwich, Earl Grey tea, the Napoleon, and Beef Wellington.

Perhaps the most successful developer of dishes named after people was the legendary New York restaurant Delmonico's, which often created specialties in honor of its customers. It is credited with devising Eggs Benedict for Mrs. LeGrand Benedict, Chicken à la Keene (later chicken a la king) for Foxhall P. Keene, and Lobster Newburg. The latter was really the creation of a wealthy shipping magnate named Benjamin Wenburg, and for a while the dish was called Lobster Wenburg. However, after Wenburg took part in a drunken brawl in the dining room, the name was altered.

As this feast of words illustrates, etymology can often provide real food for thought. As Barnette notes, when words are, in the phrase of poet Owen Barfield, "made to disgorge the past that is bottled up inside of them," we learn how our predecessors tried to make sense out of the world. And, I'd add, where food words are concerned, we develop a deeper appreciation for what we eat. Whether you're a food lover or a word lover, I hope you find the following recipes appetizing.

Linguine with Lobster, 267
Saltimbocca, 280
Sweet Hominy Chimichangas with Fruit Purées, 375

Foods of the Millennium

To everybody's relief, Y2K arrived without incident. Even our cable service went uninterrupted! Apparently those dire predictions about what might happen at the dawn of a new millennium were wrong.

Having survived the transition from 1999 to 2000, it's only natural to contemplate the events of the past. Thus, we have since been subjected to lists of the most influential persons or occurrences of the last thousand years. But notably absent from these rosters are the major culinary figures and episodes of the last millennium, an egregious oversight, it seems to me. Perhaps *Time* magazine is right to call Albert Einstein the person of the century or A&E to designate Gutenberg the person of the millennium, but did they really have more impact on their times than Julia Child or Taillevent? Of course not! So for balance, I herewith offer a subjective catalogue of the major culinary happenings of the last one thousand years.

We begin with the 11th century. Iron plows were beginning to replace wooden ones; the Normans, following the Battle of Hastings, were changing our culinary language with the introduction of French words like *boeuf* which was morphed into "beef"; and some say Roquefort cheese was discovered. But clearly the event of the century was the invention of the fork. The device, introduced in Venice in 1071, would take a while to catch on. It would not be until early in the 18th century that Englishmen would discontinue eating with their fingers.

The 12th century witnessed no less a major food event, the founding of Les Halles, the great French food market, in 1110. Louis VI, known as Louis the Fat, gave some peasant women permission to set up fish stalls outside his palace in Paris, and one thing led to another. In little more than 25 years, Les Halles, called "the belly of France" by Emile Zola, would become the largest food market in the world, operating in the same spot until 1969 when it moved because of traffic congestion.

From a culinary standpoint, things picked up in the 13th century. A number of incidents could legitimately vie for the title of most significant food-related event of the period. For historians it might be the famines which swept through the century. For dieters it might be China's exporting of tofu to Japan in 1212. For drink connoisseurs it would undoubtedly be the first distillation of brandy at the Montpellier medical school in France. For the rest of us it might be the fruits, both literally and figuratively, of Marco Polo's travels. But I think a better case can be made for the Viennese bakers of 1217 who prepared crescent-shaped rolls for Duke Leopold VI as he embarked on a Fifth Crusade. A variation of this treat would be brought to Paris years later by Marie-Antoinette and, with some alterations by French bakers, become the croissant. I'll take puff pastry over tofu and even brandy any day!

Despite the Black Death, the 14th century produced some noteworthy culinary advancements, not least among them the commercial production of pasta in Italy where noodles had formerly been only a luxury food. But even so, the most remarkable triumph had to be the career of Taillevent, the great French chef who began as a kitchen helper and ended up as France's first royal chef. His manuscript, *Le Viander*, finished in 1380, contains the basic formulas for meat stocks, the foundation of classic French cuisine, which have changed little to this day.

All culinary events of the 15th century, which include the world's first printed cookbook, by a Vatican librarian in 1475, are eclipsed by what is arguably the most important culinary event of the entire millennium—Columbus' voyage to the Western Hemisphere. His discovery of over a hundred New World foodstuffs, including tomatoes, potatoes, chiles, corn, and beans, and his introduction to the New World of Old World foods literally transformed the eating habits of everyone on the planet.

But just ten years later, in the 16th century, on his fourth and final voyage in 1502, Columbus outdid even himself when he discovered chocolate. Granted, he thought little of it and only as a curiosity brought it home where it would take another 300 years or so for it to be developed into the candy we love today, but to my way of thinking, no other event of the century outranks this breakthrough—not the first *cassoulet* in 1533, not the founding of the American beef cattle industry by Coronado in 1540, not even the perfection of tempura by the Japanese in 1585. As a confirmed chocophile, I pay homage to this delicious culinary milestone every Columbus Day.

The 17th century had its share of important advancements in the art of cuisine, including the invention of the bagel, the codification of regulations governing Dijon mustard, and the creation of Louis de Bechamel's famous sauce. But it would be hard to imagine a more important contribution to civilization than the one made by Benedictine monk Dom Pierre Perignon in 1698. Sparkling wines had been around for years, but it was he who perfected *la méthode champenoise* wherein a secondary fermentation process takes place in a tightly corked bottle, creating the distinctive "pop" when it is uncorked and earning him the title "father of champagne."

The tempo of culinary progress accelerated in the 18th century as French cooking came into full flower, Cajun cuisine got its start, King Stanislas invented both the *madeleine* and *baba au rhum*, the first modern English cookbook—Hannah Glasse's *The Art of Cookery Made Plain and Easy*—was published, *pâté de foie gras* was created, mayonnaise was invented, London's Fortnum and Mason's opened, and, according to some accounts, sushi was devised. But perhaps the most far-reaching development of the century took place in 1762 at London's Beef Steak Club above the Covent Garden Theatre when John Montagu, the fourth Earl of Sandwich, reluctant to take a break after 24 hours of nonstop gambling, ordered some meat and slices of bread, put them together, and ate as he went on betting. Where would Subway, Oscar Mayer, or Dagwood be without him!

The 19th century was a period of such dizzying culinary innovation that a whole book could be written about it. Among the more noteworthy achievements were the patenting of the tin can in 1810, the publication of the first recipe for tomato-based ketchup in 1812, the creation of the Sacher torte in 1832, the invention of the hand-crank ice-cream freezer in 1846, the birth of the potato chip in 1853, the concoction of Baked Alaska in 1876, the formulation of Tabasco sauce in 1868, the invention of the hamburger in 1885, and the debut of Coca-Cola the very next year, not to mention the invention of peanut butter, Waldorf salad, Fig Newtons, Tootsie Rolls, Cracker Jacks, cherries jubilee, Jell-O, the Dobostorte, and brownies. But for sheer refinement, it would be hard to beat the introduction in 1840 by Anna, wife of the seventh Duke of Bedford, of the tradition of British high tea as a tide-me-over between lunch and dinner. To this day, no mere coffee break can compare.

That brings us finally to the 20th century. It witnessed a veritable explosion of wide-ranging culinary developments. It is the century that saw in the same city, Philadelphia, separated by only 67 years, the opening of the first coin-operated automat and the opening of what many regard as the finest restaurant in the country, Le Bec-Fin. It saw the creation of vichyssoise and Caesar salad and White Castles. It witnessed the debut of TV dinners and cake mixes and Julia Child. It saw demand created for frozen foods and free-range chickens. It saw the birth of the ice-cream cone and the Dairy Queen, the Oreo and the fortune cookie. It noted the introduction of Land O' Lakes butter, Imperial margarine, and Crisco. It marked the invention of the pop-up toaster, the pressure cooker, Pyrex, and the food processor. It observed the arrival of *Larousse Gastronomique*, *Gourmet* magazine, and Mr. Food. It saw the advent of Teflon and Tupperware. It beheld the coming of My Daddy's Cheesecake. For anyone who loves food, it was an exciting hundred years.

Can one event out of all of this culinary activity be called the highlight of the century? Perhaps not. But if I had to pick one, it would probably be the serendipitous accident committed in 1933 by Ruth Wakefield, owner of the Toll House Inn at Whitman, Massachusettes. She chopped up a chocolate bar and stirred it into her cookie batter erroneously expecting the chocolate to melt during baking. Surely her fortuitous invention of the chocolate-chip cookie holds some claim to being the watershed culinary event of the last century.

No one really knows what the watershed culinary events of the next one hundred or one thousand years will be, but judging by the events of the past millennium, they are likely to be exciting.

Millennial Chocolate Chip Cookies, 350

Fools

Ambrose Bierce has defined an April fool as "the March fool with another month added to his folly." Mark Twain went even further when he declared, "The first of April is the day we remember what we are the other 364 days of the year."

Both of these observations, perhaps, hit a little too close to home; for after all, as Wilson Mizner reminds us, even a person who's always professing he's no fool "usually has his suspicions." April Fool's Day is the day when those suspicions may be realized. It is a day when your friends, family, and coworkers may feel free, even obligated, to play pranks and practical jokes designed to make a "fool" of you.

The origin of April Fool's Day is not exactly certain. Some historians argue that it can be traced back to the Roman empire when the Christians came into power and replaced the traditional April 1 spring ritual with Easter. Those who didn't fall in line with the new doctrine were ridiculed and made to feel foolish. Others claim that April Fool's Day began with the adoption of a new calendar in France in the 16th century. Charles IX proclaimed that New Year's Day would be observed on the first day of January instead of the first day of April, as it had been during medieval times. Those who resisted the change and continued to celebrate in April were taunted as fools.

Whatever its origins, the custom of a day of foolishness has become widespread. It's observed, among other places, in France, Germany, England, Scotland (where it is a 48-hour holiday), India (on March 31, the final day of the Feast of Huli), and Mexico (in December on El Día de los Inocentes).

I can think of no better way to suffer fools gladly than to create one, an English fruit fool, that is. A "fool," as *Larousse Gastronomique* defines it, is merely chilled cooked fruit crushed into a purée and mixed with whipped cream. (The term, "fool," may, in fact, come from the French word for "crushed or pressed," *foule*.) *Larousse Gastronomique* calls for a ratio of two parts whipped cream to one part fruit purée, but other recipes call for equal parts.

The origin of the fruit fool is decidedly less obscure than the origin of April Fool's Day. It is a classic English dessert that dates back to the 15th century. Originally a blend of custard and puréed fruit, the fool has evolved today into an amalgam using only whipped cream and fruit. Though gooseberry fool is the traditional variety, fools can be made from almost any fruit, including raspberries, strawberries, rhubarb, cranberries, dried apricots, and even plums. The recipe stays essentially the same regardless.

According to James Beard in his *American Cookery*, the fool spread throughout this country, first in the South and then in New England, after being introduced by the English. "It is still a great delicacy," he writes. And, as British food writer Elizabeth David points out, the fool may well have been the precursor to ice cream. One of the earliest printed recipes for ice cream, in Hannah Glasse's 18th-century cookbook, *The Art of Cookery Made Plain and Easy*, is essentially a recipe for a raspberry fool which is then frozen.

One word of warning about the following recipes. Though it has been observed that there's no fool like an old fool (as Jacob Braude says, "You can't beat experience"), the maxim definitely doesn't apply to dessert fools. It's best to serve them immediately after preparation so you can fully appreciate what fools these morsels be.

Fruitcake

The late humorist Erma Bombeck used to maintain that there were actually only four or five fruitcakes in the world and that they made the rounds during the holidays like a chain letter. "If you don't give away your fruitcake before the year is up," she warned, "something terrible will happen to you."

This theory that the majority of fruitcakes given as Christmas gifts are handed down from year to year is made not entirely implausible by the fact that fruitcake does keep well and even improves with age. As Rombauer and Becker point out in the venerable *Joy of Cooking*, when properly doused with liquor, buried in powdered sugar, and tightly sealed in tins, fruitcakes have been known to last for as long as twenty-five years!

Moreover, because fruitcakes are so dense that a little goes a long way, even when opened and eaten they often seem to take forever to consume. Thus, a few years ago, *Gourmet* magazine concluded its December issue with an article entitled "Recycling Fruitcake." Among their suggestions were fruitcake soufflés, fruitcake and ice cream terrine, chocolate-covered fruitcake balls, pork chops with fruitcake stuffing, and fruitcake trifle.

Clearly, as demonstrated by comments like Bombeck's and recipes like *Gourmet*'s, fruitcake is a much maligned food. The etiquette czar Miss Manners even offers advice on how to politely discourage a relative from bringing you a fruitcake for the holidays.

But this wary attitude toward fruitcake is unwarranted, I believe. Granted, as Rose Levy Beranbaum points out in *The Cake Bible*, "Fruitcake is one of the most personal cakes." People either love it or hate it, and even those who love it disagree over whether it should contain more fruit than cake or vice versa. No wonder, then, that the Pentagon's guidelines for procuring fruitcake run to fourteen pages!

But I suspect that fruitcake's tarnished reputation stems from the fact that too many people know only inferior versions of this traditional confection, versions made with skimpy amounts of fruits and nuts or, worse yet, mediocre cake batter. Good fruitcake, after all, has a noble heritage. For example, Dundee cake, the rich Scottish fruitcake, was a favorite of Mary Queen of Scots. And if there were no such thing as a good fruitcake, how could the Collin Street Bakery of Corsicana, Texas, the nation's largest purveyor of fruitcake, manage to sell over 1.5 million of them (all new, none recycled) this year?

So perhaps it's time to give fruitcake another chance. And herewith are some recipes which you just might find redeeming. The first is for a fruitcake which has proved itself a winner for over fifty years, the second for the kind of fruitcake that is practically all fruit and nuts, the third for one that is more cakelike, and the fourth for one that, with the addition of chocolate, elevates classic fruitcake to a new dimension. I think I can safely predict that if you make one of these recipes, you will produce a fruitcake that will not become the object of jokes or be passed on to someone else, but a fruitcake that will be truly enjoyed and appreciated.

Fudge

Of all the culinary accidents in human history, which include the chocolate-chip cookie and, if you believe Charles Lamb's account, roast pork, surely fudge must rank among the most serendipitous.

Nobody knows for sure just who made the first pan of fudge, but most everybody agrees it was invented by mistake. Probably it was the result of a botched batch of caramel or toffee. We do know that it is a relatively recent discovery and that it is uniquely American.

As Lee Edwards Benning notes in *Oh Fudge: A Celebration of America's Favorite Candy*, her exhaustive treatise on the subject, fudge is little more than a hundred years old and was unknown outside this country, even by those who might have been expected to discover it first. Thus, the Chinese, who in the 7th century sent ambassadors to India to learn the secrets of sugar refining, did not know of fudge. Neither did the Spanish, despite the fact that they were the ones who introduced sugarcane seedlings to the New World. Not even the French, who gave birth to the confectionery arts, can take credit for devising fudge. As Benning observes, "Despite their knowledge of marzipan and marshmallows, nougats and pastilles, fondant and caramel (the latter two, father and mother to fudge, respectively), the French learned of that most popular of all confections from America during this [20th] century." Speculation has it that fudge was introduced to France and the rest of Europe by U.S. soldiers in World War I when their mothers sent over packages of the homemade candy.

A little detective work reveals that fudge most likely was invented sometime after 1849. That is the date of publication of the second edition of J. M. Sanderson's *Cook and Confectioner*, a work of nearly 400 pages which details techniques and recipes for making all manner of candy and sweets. Yet it contains nary a word about fudge. As Benning argues, this book was simply too complete to have made such an omission, unless the candy did not exist then.

So when did fudge initially appear on the candy scene? The first printed recipe for it appears to be the one included in a pamphlet of homemade candy recipes by a Mrs. Janet McKenzie Hill and published in 1909. But there is evidence that people were making the stuff a few years before that.

The first verifiable account of the origin of fudge is the one given by Emelyn B. Hartridge, an 1892 graduate of Vassar College who claims to have obtained the recipe from a classmate whose cousin made and sold it at a Baltimore grocery store. She whipped up 30 pounds of the confection to sell at the Senior Auction in 1888, and from there it caught on across the campus and spread to Smith and Wellesley Colleges, where girls would concoct it over the gas lamps which hung in their dormitory rooms. Vassar students even devised a song to sing in tribute to "the fudge-pan bright."

It wasn't long before fudge spread westward to places like Mackinac Island off Michigan's Lake Huron coast, sometimes referred to as the fudge capital of the United States. Recipes for it became standard literature on the backs of cocoa cans and containers of marshmallow fluff, and it became a culinary rite of passage for teenage girls, not to mention a surefire way to attract the attention of teenage boys.

During World War II, Mamie Eisenhower's popular version raised so much money for the fighting effort that her husband named it Million Dollar Fudge. And today the making of fudge is a tourist attraction at theme parks, fairs, and shopping centers. Even the Brigittine Monks of the Priory of Our Lady of Consolation in Oregon do a brisk mail-order business selling the confection.

While we cannot be absolutely certain who made the first batch of fudge, it is reasonable to conclude that its name derives from the use of the term "fudge" as an expletive. It's not hard to imagine a candymaker at the turn of the century bungling a recipe and in frustration exclaiming, "Oh, fudge!" Webster's still defines the term as meaning "nonsense" when it's a noun or "to make or put together . . . carelessly" when it's a verb. Either definition might accurately apply to the circumstances of fudge's discovery.

Expletives, probably of a less tame variety, might well be uttered even by someone intentionally attempting to produce a batch of fudge, because the confection has a reputation for being difficult to make. That's because the secret to good fudge is to control the "candying" or graining process, and there are a number of things that can affect that. If the fudge mixture is not boiled long enough, it won't set up properly. If it's boiled too long, it will be too firm and dry. If the mixture is beaten before it is cool enough or beaten too long or too hard, the fudge will become grainy. If it cools too fast it will turn to caramel. If it's made on a humid day it may not harden completely. And if you don't watch it carefully for telltale signs that it is perfectly ready to pour into the pan, you may miss the opportunity.

Fortunately, there are a number of precautions you can take to increase the likelihood of success. Use a candy thermometer to keep better track of the boiling mixture's progress. Stir with a wooden spoon instead of a metal one which, because it is a conductor, causes the syrup to heat unevenly. Butter the sides of the pot in which you cook the syrup to facilitate wiping away stray sugar crystals. Use butter instead of margarine to insure creaminess, and freeze it if the recipe calls for adding it to the boiled mixture to "seed" it after it reaches the correct stage. Instead of adding final flavorings to the boiled syrup, pour it over them in a separate container to avoid agitating excess sugar crystals. Turn the fudge into a glass rather than a metal pan to keep it from cooling down too quickly. And you can cheat, or should I say "fudge" a little, by choosing recipes that call for marshmallow creme which, while not really foolproof, are far more forgiving. And if worse comes to worst, you can turn disaster into triumph by simply using the failed fudge for something else, like topping for ice cream. After all, as Benning points out, since fudge began as an accident, if yours doesn't come out right, you didn't fail; you were just too successful for your own good!

Vassar Fudge, 360
Cookies and Cream Fudge, 360
Pumpkin Fudge, 361

Funnel Cakes

For over 150 years people have been drawn to the annual SEMO District Fair in Cape Girardeau, Missouri. Some go for the tractor-truck pull or the crosscut-saw contest. Others go to be entertained by the Oak Ridge Boys or the gospel sing. And still others are attracted by the poultry/rabbit dress-up or the barrow carcass judging.

I, on the other hand, go for the cotton candy, the lemonade, the taffy, the snow cones, the smoked turkey legs, the corn dogs, the fried potato spirals, the kettle corn, the cheesecake on a stick, and the funnel cakes. I take no umbrage at all when Garrison Keillor describes a fair as "a herd of hefty folks in shorts wandering in search of animal fats."

Though I was raised in a good-sized city, have never driven a tractor, and have only seen a barrow in the dictionary (which I had to consult to find out what it was), fair food and I go back a long way.

In high school and college I worked in the concession stand at a major St. Louis amusement park in the days before such places succumbed to Disneyesque gentrification. There, in a setting much like our annual district fair, I learned the intricacies of spinning cotton candy and the secret to forming perfectly shaped and properly doused snow cones. And there I learned that despite its humble origins, fair food can be far from average.

Take cotton candy, for example. Bruce Feiler, a former circus clown, writing in *Gourmet* magazine, calls it "America's most overlooked contribution to world cuisine." Today this confection has become the trademark dessert at New York's famed The Four Seasons restaurant. In that temple to *haute cuisine*, where diners pay $125 for a serving of white-truffle risotto, what was first sold at the St. Louis World's Fair under the name "fairy floss" apparently is right at home.

The restaurant makes its cotton candy in the same sort of machine I learned on, a device invented in Nashville in 1897. Little did I realize all those years ago, as I routinely fabricated towering columns of fluffy spun sugar resembling Marge Simpson's hairdo, sometimes in color as well as in shape, that I was perfecting skills which might one day be sought after by a fashionable New York eatery.

But I shouldn't have been surprised. As Feiler points out, many classic American foods had their origin in the circus or the fair. He cites as an example pink lemonade, which according to legend was accidentally invented by a circus clown turned drink purveyor who made a batch of his beverage using a tub of water in which one of the circus performers had been soaking her red tights.

More to the point, many of the foods served at the fair don't need to be transformed or transported to a fancy restaurant to become worthy of an Epicurean; they already are. I call them "gourmet fair." And there's no better example than the funnel cake.

Ken Hoffman, who writes the "Drive-thru Gourmet" column in the *Houston Chronicle*, calls funnel cakes "the greasiest, slimiest, hardest-to-eat, choke-your-arteries, wipe-your-chin treat on the carnival midway." Of course, that's a substantial part of their appeal. But let's not forget that a funnel cake is not that far removed from the presumably more sophisticated French *beignet*, the classic New Orleans treat traditionally served with chicory-flavored coffee. Fundamentally, they're both fried dough. And that, obviously, is why they are so wonderful!

It's no wonder there's hardly a culture that doesn't have its own version of fried dough. The French, as already noted, have their *beignets*, the Mexicans their *sopaipillas*, the Italians their *zeppole*, the Polish their *Pulacki*, the Scandinavians their rosettes, and we our hush puppies, just to name a few. Whoever it was that first thought of throwing food into a vat of hot, bubbling oil (most likely animal fat in a cast-iron pot over an open fire) ranks right up there, in my opinion, with the greatest of culinary pioneers.

The funnel cake, as its name suggests, is fried dough made by pouring batter through a funnel, typically in a spiral pattern, into hot oil and letting it brown. The classic garnish is a liberal dusting of powdered sugar, but fruit and maple syrup are also good toppings.

Sharon Tyler Herbst in *The New Food Lover's Companion* says funnel cakes are a Pennsylvania Dutch specialty, which makes sense since in Germany they make a very similar fried dough called "tangled britches." The Amish, who call them *Drechter Kuche*, specialize in them also. But Maguelonne Toussaint-Samat, in her *History of Food*, tells us that the Greeks were piping ribbons of dough into hot oil through a funnel as far back as the time of Demosthenes. The pastry was called *euchytes* and was taken by Greek colonists to Spain where it became *churros*, a breakfast specialty in that country and in Mexico to this day. Somehow or another the same treat turned up in German-speaking areas of Switzerland where it is called *trichterkuchli*. Greek *euchytes* formed various shapes as they cooked, but the Greeks also made a spiral shaped fritter called *streptes* which was cooked in honey.

Whatever its lineage, the funnel cake is now a staple at fairs and festivals around the country. In fact, a whole industry has been born to supply equipment and materials to the countless funnel-cake booths in operation on the nation's carnival midways. Perhaps the granddaddy (or should that be fry daddy?) of professional funnel-cake companies is the Original Pennsylvania Dutch Funnel Cake Company, Inc., which started in 1968 when its owner, Elizabeth Bechta, and her late husband first tasted the treat in Pennsylvania Dutch country. The company's headquarters is in New Jersey. It claims to produce the world's best funnel cakes, but then so does the upstart Funnel Cake Company of Gatlinburg, Tennessee, in business since 1988. Their spokesperson Tommy (Pappy) Goolsby has openly challenged his competitors to an independent taste test. If they're looking for a judge, I would be happy to volunteer.

Though part of the undeniable enjoyment of funnel cakes is eating them amidst the atmosphere of the fair (where as Keillor remarks you can get a whiff of hot fat, animal manure, and diesel exhaust all at the same time), one of the nice things about them is that they can also be made at home with ordinary kitchen equipment. (Cotton candy, on the other hand, requires a $1,000-machine to produce.) In fact, few recipes are easier.

Though recipes for funnel-cake batter vary somewhat (I've even heard of chocolate and pumpkin varieties), they're all pretty much the same: a blend of milk, flour, eggs, and baking powder, and sometimes sugar. So the real trick in producing the genuine article is not the batter but the frying. It takes a little practice, but, as the *Joy of Cooking* notes, "Done with care, a wide number of delicacies can emerge from hot oil crisp on the outside, moist within." That's a perfect description of the ideal funnel cake.

The most important thing to keep in mind when frying funnel cakes, or anything else for that matter, is proper temperature. If the oil is not hot enough, it will soak into the cake and make it greasy. If it's too hot, it will brown the outside of the cake before the inside is done. Moreover, if oil gets hot enough to smoke, it begins to break down. The best frying temperature for funnel cakes is somewhere between 365 and 375 degrees.

Here are some other tips to help you get over the fear of frying:

- Use a good flavorless oil such as corn oil or peanut oil.
- Don't skimp on the oil, but don't fill the fryer more than half full.
- Heat the oil gradually.
- Only cook one funnel cake at a time, unless your fryer is really large, so the oil temperature does not decline rapidly.
- Allow sufficient time between the frying of each funnel cake to let the oil resume its ideal temperature.
- Skim crumbs out of the oil periodically so they don't affect color and flavor.
- Take proper precautions.
- Place funnel cakes on paper toweling to drain excess fat, if you can wait that long.

Funnel Cake, 310

Gingerbread

"And I had but one penny in the world, thou shouldst have it to buy gingerbread," says Costard in the last act of Shakespeare's *Love's Labor's Lost*. Though Costard was a clown, I take seriously the implication that gingerbread is something on which it is worth spending one's last cent. Served warm from the pan, it is for me the quintessential comfort food.

Gingerbread was a well-known confection by Shakespeare's time. There's even a reference to "gyngebreed" in Chaucer's *Canterbury Tales*. In fact, Rombauer, Becker, and Becker in the latest edition of the *Joy of Cooking* maintain that gingerbread "can be traced back further than any other baked good with the exception of bread."

Tarla Fallgatter, a California caterer and restaurant consultant who was the first foreign woman allowed to cook in the kitchens of Maxim's in Paris, points out that the term "gingerbread" originally meant merely "preserved ginger" (and in Medieval Europe, ginger was the second-most-coveted spice after pepper). Today, however, the term usually refers either to dense molasses cookies cut into whimsical shapes such as gingerbread persons (the politically correct term now in use at some markets) or, typically in this country, to a moist spice cake usually baked in a square pan. (By the way, Queen Elizabeth I supposedly invented the gingerbread man, which can take a number of shapes as demonstrated by gourmet food purveyors Dean & Deluca, who at their Georgetown outlet once sold gingerbread Bill Clintons.)

Though I have decorated and eaten my share of gingerbread cookies, it is the cake that I have in mind here. And I recall vividly the best version of it that I have ever eaten. It was some years ago on the Big Island of Hawaii at a little bakery and cafe in the renovated Aloha Theatre. It was midmorning and the cake was served warm from the oven, redolent of fresh ginger. I spent the next several years trying to duplicate that cake at home.

And in the process I discovered several techniques and hundreds of recipes (Fallgatter, for example, contends that the United States has a larger repertoire of gingerbread recipes than any other country). One particularly useful technique for infusing that marvelous ginger flavor throughout a cake is one I ran across about five years ago in an issue of *Bon Appétit* magazine. It involves mixing chopped fresh ginger with a little sugar (two parts ginger to one part sugar is a good ratio) and letting it sit for about 30 minutes to form a syrup which is then incorporated into the cake batter. I've also learned that because of its assertive flavor, gingerbread is one baked good that adapts well to low-fat cooking. In almost any recipe you can successfully substitute applesauce for half or more of the fat.

But the main conclusion I've come to is that there are few things in this world more satisfying, particularly on a cold February day, than sitting in front of a roaring fire with a glass of milk or a cup of coffee and eating a slice of gingerbread simply dusted with powdered sugar or, for real decadence, slathered with whipped cream. The following recipes, I trust, will demonstrate the validity of that conclusion.

Girl Scout Cookies

One of the most eagerly anticipated days of the year at our house is the start of the annual Girl Scout Cookie sale. And apparently ours is not the only household that looks forward to this American tradition; statistics show that during the first quarter of every year, when Girl Scouts go door to door peddling them, Girl Scout Cookies rank number two in sales, rivaling Keebler and Nabisco.

The custom of selling cookies to raise funds to subsidize Girl Scout camps and other programs is almost as old as Girl Scouting itself. It wasn't long after the organization's founding in 1912 by Juliette Gordon Low, otherwise known as Daisy, (one variety, Reduced Fat Iced Ginger Daisies, is named after her) that individual Girl Scout troops began selling home-baked cookies. The original version was a simple shortbread cookie made with equal amounts of butter and sugar, a couple of eggs, some flour, and a little milk.

As early as 1928 an issue of *Girl Scouts Leader* magazine reported that one enterprising troop had raised as much as $1,400 through cookie sales, an impressive figure, especially in pre-depression dollars. In 1932 the organization made available an official Girl Scout insignia cookie cutter so that troops around the country could produce a uniform product. Before long, the girls had to turn to commercial bakeries to fill the increasing demand for their cookies.

Laura Hinkebein, Resource Development Director for the local Otahki Girl Scout Council, points out that in addition to being eaten straight out of the box, Girl Scout Cookies can also be used as an ingredient in a variety of dishes. For example, when crumbled, they can be used to make crusts for pies, swirled through your favorite cheesecake batter, combined with butter and sugar to make a streusel topping, or used to coat chocolate truffles. In fact, for a more sophisticated taste, try substituting Thin Mints (the best-selling variety by far) in almost any recipe which calls for Oreos. And if you're looking for a good excuse to buy some extra boxes of Girl Scout Cookies to store in the freezer, consider the following approaches to "cooking with cookies."

Lemon Cookie Chicken Salad, 235
Spicy Thai Pasta with Chicken, 267
Chocolate Coconut Caramel Dessert, 333

Graham Crackers

Life is full of ironies, and the culinary world is no exception. Take graham crackers, for instance. Developed in 1829 by Sylvester Graham, the nation's first health nut, as a whole-grain alternative to baked goods made with refined flour, they are now the most common base for cheesecake, a concoction which the fitness-minded Graham would have no doubt railed against.

It is no accident that this country should have produced a diet fanatic such as Graham, for as Dennis Roth writing in *Food Review* points out, "No other country has had our variegated history of nutritional theories, diets, food fads, and, more recently, eating disorders." Europeans by and large eat for enjoyment, he argues, but Americans have a long-standing concern for nutrition and health.

Partly this is because we sometimes feel further removed from the sources of our food supply and therefore more suspicious of them than people are in other countries. The United States, after all, was the first continental market where food products could be shipped over thousands of miles. Then too, our very bounty sometimes conspires against us. As the country became more urbanized and its citizens more sedentary, unlike other countries we had to actually begin to curb our appetites in the face of abundant food supplies. Roth says, the political climate has also played a role, noting that nutritional reforms often coincide with political ones. Finally, there is what he calls our frontier-honed ethos of self-improvement. As Charles Tart, a psychologist at the University of California at Davis, puts it, "Americans . . . have the delusion that we can eat our way to enlightenment."

It is perhaps no wonder, then, that this country should have spawned a character like Sylvester Graham, a man Bee Wilson in an article in the *New Statesman* calls the father of all modern diet crazes. His legacy, according to Frederick Kaufman in a review of several diet books for *Harper's Magazine*, can still be felt in prescriptions such as the Pritikin diet and *Sugar Busters!*

Sylvester Graham, by any account, was something of an eccentric. For example, among his beliefs about nutrition were the notions that ketchup could cause insanity and that cholera was the result of chicken pie and excessive lewdness. (Apparently either was a sufficient cause.)

Born on July 4, 1794, in West Suffield, Connecticut, he was one of seventeen children. His father, a local minister who was 72 at the time of his birth, died two years later, leaving Graham and his mother to the care of relatives in New Jersey. He attended Amherst Academy for a while, but was expelled on a false charge trumped up by classmates who were turned off by his egotistical personality. (In later life he bragged that he never read books and perfected his theories completely on his own.) Studying with a private tutor, he was eventually ordained and before long was lecturing for the Pennsylvania Society for Discouraging the Use of Ardent Spirits. A compelling speaker, he lectured to packed houses up and down the East Coast, often getting paid as much as $300 per night, the equivalent of thousands in today's dollars.

Though derided by some (Ralph Waldo Emerson, for example, called him "the prophet of bran bread and pumpkins," and some newspapers dubbed him "a nut among the crackers"), Graham developed quite a following. Grahamite hotels, serving only meals that followed his dietary prescriptions, sprang up to serve his disciples. Special stores opened to sell his graham (whole-wheat) flour and later graham crackers, which became a New England fad. Oberlin College for a time required all students to subsist on a diet of only graham crackers and water. Some of Graham's converts included, at least temporarily, Henry David Thoreau, Horace Greeley, and Joseph Smith, the founder of the Mormon Church. His influence is still felt in part on Seventh Day Adventists and Christian Scientists. The Kellogg brothers took some of his ideas and created the cold-cereal industry. (Grahamites invented the first cold cereal, Granula, made of crumbled graham crackers.)

Graham compared humans to orangutans and concluded that a vegetarian diet was best for both of them. In his regimen, spices, including salt and pepper, were forbidden. So were butter, cream, tobacco, coffee, tea, molasses, honey, fish, mustard, sugar, and warm food. Even soup was to be avoided. He also preached daily tooth brushing, fresh air, exercise, seven hours of sleep on hard beds and regular cold baths. (Graham would occasionally walk to a river near his home to take a dip, strolling down the street sporting only a bathrobe.)

But the cornerstone of Graham's system was that whole-grain bread, not white, should be the mainstay of the diet, and it should be home-baked, not store-bought. Not surprisingly, this edict did not endear Graham to the professional bakers of his day. Along with butchers who, understandably, were likewise not enamored of Grahamite vegetarianism, they staged a riot outside a Boston hotel during one of Graham's lectures.

Graham didn't stick just to advice about food. He believed that anything "stimulating" was injurious to health, including alcohol and what he called sexual excess, a consequence, he contended, of eating fats. He argued that men should remain virgins until the age of 30 and once married should have sex only once a month. In his famous "Lecture to Young Men" he warned against "lascivious day-dreams," and he invented the graham cracker because he thought its ingredients would reduce lust and tame teenage hormones, particularly in young girls.

Well, at least he appears to have been right about whole grains. Recent studies indicate that women who consume mostly refined grains have a 16 percent higher likelihood of early death compared to those who regularly eat whole grains. Apparently Graham's other theories have not been as rigorously tested, owing, I suspect, to a lack of willing experimental subjects.

For all his abstinence from the good things in life, Graham, whose Massachusetts home is now a very ungraham-like restaurant, died at the rather young age of 56. And though in retrospect some people view him as a crackpot, he nonetheless left his mark on the American diet, even if it clearly wasn't the mark he had intended. His namesake crackers can now be found everywhere, not just in so-called health-food stores. Ben and Jerry put them in their ice cream, Russell Stover makes a candy concoction out of them, and there's even a honey graham-cracker Jelly Belly. And, of course, legions of Girl Scouts, oblivious to the cracker's origins, devour them around the campfire with toasted marshmallows and chocolate. John Steele Gordon, writing in *American Heritage*, claims that Graham inadvertently created the American diet-fad industry. Maybe so. But surely his graham cracker is a far better legacy. The following recipes are delicious ways to celebrate it.

Homemade Graham Crackers, 355
Graham Cracker Streusel Cake, 310
Sawdust Pie, 331

Grits

"On every breakfast plate in the South there always appears a little white mound of food. Sometimes it's ignored. Sometimes insulted. But without it, the sun wouldn't come up, the crops wouldn't grow, and most of us would lose our drawl." That's what Bill Neal and David Perry said in *The Good Old Grits Cookbook*. They were talking, of course, about grits. And, at least from a Southerner's point of view, they didn't overstate the case by much.

The standing which grits have in the South (where they are even served at some McDonald's) was first driven home to me some twenty-five years ago on one of our family's first visits to Memphis. Breakfast and brunch buffets were our choice of dining experiences back then, and at every food line we went through, we spotted what we thought was Cream of Wheat. We fed our son, who was but an infant at the time, bowl after bowl of it before we discovered much later in the week that the substance was really grits. In retrospect, I realize how much luckier he is than I. As a Northerner, I had to wait until adulthood to taste my first serving of this uniquely American food.

It's a shame that, despite an occasional upsurge of interest in them, grits have not traveled much outside the South. Though often the object of wisecracks (The *New York Times* says grits may be the third-longest-running joke in food, right behind Vegemite and chitterlings) and frequently scorned as bland, peasant food (no less an authority than the great gourmand, the late James Beard, pronounced the breakfast version "revolting"), grits are deserving of the attentions of any gourmet.

It's somewhat ironic that grits get so little respect while polenta, a slightly more refined (that is, less coarsely ground) cousin is all the rage. Maybe the name has something to do with it. Polenta, after all, is really just cornmeal mush, but the name and the fact that it is associated with fashionable Italian cooking confer upon it a certain degree of status. Yet grits, though possessing less prestige, have just as many possibilities for dressing up.

Grits also have greater historical significance. As Tim Warren writing in the *Smithsonian Magazine* points out, they were arguably America's first food. The Powhatan Indians of Virginia introduced grits to the early settlers, and Captain John Smith took note of them in his journal as early as 1629. Corn, the New World food which forms the basis of grits, was domesticated at least as far back as 5,000 years ago in central Mexico, and by the time of the arrival of the American colonists, the Indians were cultivating the crop as far north as what is now the state of Maine. As Warren observes, Pocahontas would have been no stranger to what Smith called "bruized Indian corne pounded, and boiled thicke." The term "grits," by the way, comes from the Old English word for "the bran and chaff of grain."

Warren explains that grits became the signature staple of the South primarily because of necessity. Corn, unlike wheat, the dominant starch of the North, was a crop that could withstand the heat of Southern summers and be planted almost regardless of terrain. Economic restrictions following the Civil War made grits, an exceedingly cheap food to prepare, even more popular than they had been before. Soon they became, to borrow an image from Professor John Shelton Reed of the University of North Carolina at Chapel Hill, the glue that held the South together.

Reed's choice of words is unfortunate, or apt, if you think grits resemble library paste. But if you think that, you obviously have never tried the real thing—true grits, if you will. Authentic grits require stone-ground grain. Experts point out that when corn is ground using steel rollers, flavor-sapping heat is produced. Stone-ground grits are the consistency of coarse sand, not at all like the instant grits which most Southerners find absolutely resistible. They take much longer to cook, of course, but aficionados say they are worth the extra time.

Whether you start with stone-ground or instant grits, the important thing to remember is that grits should rarely be eaten by themselves (though I think the stone-ground variety is delicious on its own). That's because they're relatively neutral in flavor. But that neutrality is a blessing. It allows them to soak up other flavors and serve as a foil for other ingredients. The classic example of this principle is Carolina shrimp and grits, but there are plenty of other complex dishes in which simple but versatile grits can play a major role.

And increasingly, restaurants around the country are discovering this fact. In New York they're serving grits with wild mushrooms, truffle oil, and smoked duck. In Washington, D.C., they're offering fried grits cakes with portobellos and goat cheese. In Chicago they're doing grits with andouille sausage or jalapeños and cheddar cheese. In Atlanta they're making smoked tomato grits. In Louisville they're marrying grits and Mediterranean veal shanks.

So perhaps there is hope that one day grits will get the same level of respect above the Mason-Dixon Line that they now get below it. It's doubtful, though, that any Northern city will hold a grits festival like the one in St. George, South Carolina, where participants consume nearly 3,000 pounds of grits as they engage in grits-eating contests, plunge into a pool of grits to see who can coat themselves with the greatest amount of the stuff, and cheer on the Grits Queen and Baby Miss Grits as they ride down the parade route. Another favorite of parade-goers is a crew called the Grits Sisters, nine women who, from atop their float, toss sample packets of instant grits to the crowd.

On the other hand, if Northerners were to try some of the following recipes, they might very well feel like engaging in such shenanigans.

Jimmy Carter's Baked Cheese Grits, 229
Grits Milanese, 293
Baked Grits with Sun Dried Tomatoes, 292

Guinness Beer

"It's not easy being green," Kermit the Frog lamented. Except, of course, on St. Patrick's Day, when green is the color of choice.

Though green is the color of spring, shamrocks, and the Emerald Isle itself, let me suggest that on St. Patrick's Day, as we pay homage to the patron saint of Ireland (who, by the way, was not really Irish, being born in either Wales, Scotland, or Roman Britain), there's another color that should come to mind: black. Black is the color of that yeasty ale with the creamy white head that is without question the most popular beverage in Ireland. I'm referring, of course, to stout, specifically Guinness, which is, in any Irish pub, an equivalent term. (Actually, as Monica Sheridan notes in *The Art of Irish Cooking*, the term "beverage" is a misnomer when applied in Ireland to anything other than a warm bedtime drink, lemonade, or Coca-Cola. The correct term is "drink.")

Guinness Stout is a drink that has become something of a rage in this country too, despite the fact that, for American beer drinkers at any rate, it is sort of an acquired taste, though that may be true for beer in general, as Winston Churchill once noted: "Most people hate the taste of beer—to begin with," he said. "It is, however, a prejudice that many people have been able to overcome." Such appears to have been the case with Guinness, which is now brewed in thirty-five countries and is consumed 10 million times a day around the world.

Stout gets its characteristic dark color from malted barley that is roasted not unlike coffee beans. It is classified as an ale, broadly speaking, one of only two kinds of beer, a libation which beer historian Alan Eames points out changed the course of human history by inducing our forebears to abandon their nomadic lifestyle. "Mankind was lured by intoxication into tending crops and establishing settlements," he observes. The other beer type is lager. Lagers are made with bottom-fermenting yeast, while the fruitier and more complex ales are made with a yeast that ferments on top. Stout is darker, stronger, and more full-bodied than just about any other beer (at the opposite end of the spectrum from, say, Heineken Lager, though its alcohol content is relatively light).

The drink was not that well known in Ireland when Arthur Guinness began brewing it in 1759, in a dilapidated plant which he leased for 45 pounds per year on the outskirts of Dublin. Actually developed in London, the drink was known as porter because of its popularity with the porters and stevedores of Covent Garden. Within ten years, Guinness porter, later referred to simply by the adjective "stout," dominated the market in Ireland and had made such inroads into the English market that by 1799, the brewery ceased producing other kinds of beer and specialized in this one kind. Before long, Guinness was exporting millions of barrels of the stuff all over the globe, and for a time its St. James' Gate Brewery was the largest in the world. It is still the largest producer of stout. And in an effort to increase its reach in 1989, the company launched a so-called draft-in-a-can product that purports to offer the taste of freshly tapped beer in a can. The device which makes this possible, something called a widget, a plastic insert containing nitrogen, won the Queen's Award for Technological Achievement, a first for a brewer.

Perhaps some of this phenomenal success can be chalked up to the luck of the Irish, but in any case, Guinness has achieved near-cult status among beer aficionados worldwide. Some of them claim that Guinness really is good for you, in keeping with a company advertising slogan hearkening to an earlier era when the drink was prescribed as "liquid bread" for nursing mothers and wounded soldiers. They cite recent research done at the University of Wisconsin which shows that dark beer, just like red wine, contains flavonoids which are supposed to prevent blood clots and thereby reduce the incidence of heart attack. Other devotees argue that you can determine the nationality of a Guinness drinker by examining the residue or rings left on the inside of the glass with each swig of the brew. Conventional wisdom has it that whereas Americans leave 17–20 rings because they tend to sip (behavior frowned upon by true connoisseurs), the Irish leave only 5–6, and the English 8–10. Australians, it is said, leave none, preferring instead to drink the entire glass in one quaff!

All agree that attaining the perfect pint of Guinness depends upon precisely followed ritual. The drink must be served in a 20-ounce glass which under no circumstances has been chilled. And it must be poured in two stages wherein the glass is first filled to about 80 percent capacity and then topped off once the beer has settled completely. (The uninitiated, to the amusement of veterans, often start drinking after the first stage.) Tradition also maintains that one should never drink just one Guinness, but at least two.

But you don't have to be a fanatic to agree that in Guinness, which claims to be Ireland's most famous export, the Irish have yet another source of pride, another example of how, in William MacQuitty's words, "Ireland throughout her centuries has made a contribution to the world out of all proportion to her size and numbers." Indeed, the harp that symbolizes the country and appears on the back of its coins now adorns every Guinness product, albeit facing in a different direction. (Folklore suggests that in return for using this logo, which also appears on the Trinity College Dublin coat of arms, the company provides a complimentary glass of Guinness for Scholars and Fellows of the College at their traditional evening meal.)

So what better way to celebrate St. Patrick's Day than with a pint or two of Guinness, either consumed directly out of a glass or as an integral ingredient in recipes such as the following?

Honey

The "heavenly gift of honey," as the poet Virgil referred to it, has always been one of my very favorite foods. Indeed, I was stung to learn recently that the late M.F.K. Fisher, arguably the greatest food writer in the English language, detested it. So does Ruth Reichl, former *New York Times* restaurant critic and now the editor of *Gourmet* magazine.

With all due respect, it's hard for me to imagine how anyone could not like honey. I agree with Claude Lévi-Strauss who, in his *Origin of Table Manners*, observed about this miraculous substance, "So powerful is its gastronomic appeal that, were it too easily obtained, mankind would partake of it too freely until the supply was exhausted." And, as food historian Maguelonne Toussaint-Samat points out, the effort we must expend to obtain honey is perhaps part of its appeal. "Hidden away like treasure, it has an element of reward about it," she says, as she proudly begins her magnificent volume, *History of Food*, with a chapter on the subject.

Human beings have apparently been stuck on honey for as long as recorded history and probably even before then. As food writers Jane Charlton and Jane Newdick suggest, "The date when man enjoyed his first taste of honey is not known—we can only surmise that the earliest hunter-gatherers must have come across a wild bees' nest in a hollow tree or bank of soil and plundered it. A few bee stings would be quickly forgotten, but the sweetness of the honey would remain in the memory, in contrast to their normally unpalatable diet of game, plants, and nuts."

The oldest advertisement in the world is what Toussaint-Samat calls a rock painting in the Cave of the Spider near Valencia, Spain, that depicts a man gathering honey with bees swarming around him. It is 12,000–15,000 years old. Representations of bees, which came to symbolize royalty, are not uncommon in Egyptian hieroglyphs, such as those at the temple of Karnak. (Napoleon would later take the bee for his emblem as well.) The Egyptians, in fact, occasionally paid their taxes in the form of honey, and they sent their Pharaohs off to the after-life with a pot of it. It was even used as an embalming agent. Rameses III offered 15 tons of the stuff in sacrifice to the Nile god Hapi in the 12th century BC.

The ancient Greeks, just like their descendants today, made honey a staple of their diet. So did the Romans. In the 1st century AD, the Roman gourmet Apicius included honey in more than half of the recipes he recorded in his cookbooks. Among them were honey-baked tortoise and peacock in honey sauce. His honey sauce for fish is considered a classic. Honey-baked ham, a dish so popular today that there is even a whole chain of stores devoted to its sale, actually goes back to the Romans.

Throughout the Middle Ages, as the only sweetener available in a pure state and far less a luxury than cane sugar, honey continued to be an important ingredient, not just as a sweetener but as a condiment. It was used in the preparation of beer in Germany in the 11th century and cultivated in the American colonies in the 17th century. Though Native Americans had already developed beekeeping using an indigenous strain of bees which lack stingers, settlers brought hives of European bees with them. They adapted well to the new climate and ultimately spread across the continent.

Though taste may be its foremost feature, honey and its by-products have also been used for a variety of nonculinary purposes, chiefly medicinal and cosmetic. As early as 2,500 BC, honey was used to treat wounds and burns, and indeed, it does contain an antibiotic element. The ancient Greeks fed it to their Olympic contestants to boost their energy. The Romans prescribed it both as a laxative and as a cure for diarrhea. An old English treatment for an earache involved inserting a piece of honey-coated onion into the ear. Honey is still used today to treat sore throats and coughs and is the principal ingredient in a common household remedy for a hangover. Modern medical research reveals that consuming honey can help ward off hay-fever symptoms, especially if the honey contains small amounts of pollen. Honey has been an ingredient in skin treatments at least since Cleopatra's day and was popularized as a hair lotion in the 18th century by British royalty. Bee glue, a by-product of honey, was one of the secrets in the varnish used by the violin makers of Cremona.

Given our long fascination with honey, it is not surprising that the substance and the bees who manufacture it have often figured prominently in myth, legend, and ritual. The Bible, of course, refers to the land of milk and honey, and we are told bees fled the Garden of Eden after the fall of Adam and Eve. (Candles used during a Roman Catholic Mass must still contain a proportion of beeswax for that reason.) Mohammed claimed the bee was special because it was the only animal addressed by the Lord himself. The Hebrew term for "bee" means "word," an indication that the bee's mission is to reveal the Divine Word or truth which honey signifies. The ancient Greeks believed Zeus was born in a sacred cavern guarded by bees and used honey to make his father Kronos sleepy prior to chaining him up and dethroning him. The *Popul Vuh*, the sacred text of the Mayan Indians, talks about the Universal Hive at the center of the earth.

Toussaint-Samat tells of an Eastern custom whereby honey is poured on the hands of just-married couples. Likewise, the Hindu wedding ceremony sometimes employs a bowl of honey and a mention of it in the marriage vow. Clearly, in either case the newlyweds should be ready for the "honeymoon."

Dr. Frank Nickell of Southeast Missouri State University's Regional History Center remembers, as a youngster, a neighbor who always went to "tell the bees" about a death in the family, an old English custom memorialized in a Whittier poem. The bees had to share in the family news, lest they would either die themselves or leave. In England in the 18th century, sometimes a piece of funeral cake would be left at the hive and the bees formally invited to the services.

It seems only fair to include the bees in family happenings. They are, after all, models of domestic tranquility. And where would we be without them? Someone has calculated that if bees were to become extinct, all world crops, not just garden flowers, would expire due to lack of pollination, and what is more, human beings, dispossessed of food sources, would not last longer than two years. No wonder, then, that a Cornell University study concluded that the value of the work honeybees perform for U.S. agriculture amounts to nearly $10 billion. The figure makes sense when you consider that it takes 864 worker bees an entire lifetime to produce one pound of honey and as many as 100,000 trips for them to bring a liter of nectar back to the hive.

So during September, which is National Honey Month, when the harvest is at its peak, I say we should show our appreciation by making a beeline to the kitchen to whip up some recipes containing that magical elixir.

Hot Chocolate

Humorist Dave Barry once declared, "When I heated my home with oil, I used an average of 800 gallons a year. I have found that I can keep comfortably warm for an entire winter with slightly over half that quantity of beer."

Though it probably won't please the heating oil industry or Anheuser-Busch, I respectfully suggest that when it comes to keeping warm in the winter, Barry should consider the virtues of hot chocolate instead.

Few things are as satisfying on a cold winter night, or a cold winter morning for that matter, as a mug of hot chocolate, topped, perhaps, with marshmallows or, if you're in a particularly decadent mood, whipped cream. Moreover, few beverages are as nourishing and, if you hold the whipped cream and use skim milk, so relatively low in fat. Hot chocolate has much less caffeine than tea or coffee, too, 17.5 milligrams versus 100–200 milligrams for a 12-ounce cup.

Perhaps that's why hot chocolate, an ancient drink, is experiencing something of a resurgence these days. Even the French company, Valrhona, maker of what some claim is the world's finest chocolate (I wouldn't necessarily disagree), has gotten into the act with a bottled premixed chocolate drink. "We began to see a big demand from fine restaurants and hotels for an upscale, refined hot-chocolate drink," Bernard DuClos, executive vice-president of the company was quoted as saying in *Newsday*. Similarly, Cadbury, Great Britain's chocolate giant, has signed on Errol Brown, lead singer of the band Hot Chocolate (his tune, "You Sexy Thing" was featured in the award-winning British film *The Full Monty*), to promote their chocolate drinks in a £2.2 million advertising campaign.

The truth is, chocolate was being enjoyed as a beverage for hundreds of years before anyone ever thought of eating it, and the invention of "eating chocolate" was really just a by-product of attempts to make a better beverage. Even before it was discovered that chocolate could be turned into an edible solid, the question of whether it was food or drink was the topic of spirited ecclesiastical debate for a couple of centuries, as a succession of Popes contemplated whether its consumption would constitute breaking a Lenten fast. A priest of Madrid even wrote a whole treatise on the subject. Finally, Cardinal Francesco Maria Brancaccio, the Bishop of Rome, declared in 1662 that hot chocolate was a drink and not a food, presumably to the delight of some parishioners, chiefly upper-class ladies, who actually had their maids serve them the drink during church services.

Though it bore little resemblance to the hot chocolate of today, the original chocolate drink can be traced back to the Ancient Mayans of Central America. Their predecessors, the ancient Olmecs, not the Aztecs as is commonly thought, were the first to cultivate the cocoa tree which has grown in that part of the world for over 4,000 years. Indeed, the world's first chocoholics, as Marcia and Frederic Morton point out in their book, *Chocolate: An Illustrated History*, may have been the birds and monkeys who ate the fruit of the tree and helped spread its seeds.

The Mayans believed the pods growing from the trunk of the tree were an offering from the gods and created a drink out of the seeds or beans which it contained. They and the other peoples of Central America also used the cocoa bean as a form of currency. Ten beans would buy a rabbit and twelve the services of a prostitute. As a measure of the importance of the crop to them, the name of one of the last three rulers at Tikal was Lord Cacao, a fact which served only to intensify my admiration for this civilization when, a few years ago, I trekked into the Guatemalan jungle to climb Tikal's highest pyramid and watch the sunrise.

The Toltecs and Aztecs who followed also prized the cocoa bean and the beverage made from it. And it was this bitter, unsweetened drink, called *xocoatl* by the natives and often containing chile peppers, that Christopher Columbus was the first European to sample. He didn't much care for it. Perhaps he can be forgiven since the concoction was nothing like what we think of as hot chocolate today; in fact, it was served cold. Thus, Giramolo Benzoni, a 16th-century botanist, pronounced the drink "more fit for the pigs than like a beverage for human beings," and Jose de Acosta, a Jesuit priest of the time, called it "loathsome to such as are not acquainted with it." Still, those of us who are confirmed chocophiles might reason that even if Columbus could be forgiven for all the other errors he made and the often frightful consequences of his encounter with the New World, he should not get off lightly for failing to appreciate the potential of chocolate.

That would have to wait a few more years for the arrival in Mexico of Spanish explorer Hernán Cortés. He too was probably not especially fond of the drink itself, but the conditions under which he was introduced to it served to impress him, and he realized its economic potential. In fact, according to Maguelonne Toussaint-Samat in the *History of Food*, when Cortés asked his hosts to show him their treasures, they took him to the royal plantation at Maniapeltec and presented him with mountains of cocoa instead of the mountains of gold he had expected. He must have known that something about this substance was special. Surely his suspicions were confirmed when he witnessed the role which *xocoatl* played in native rituals wherein the drink was served in golden cups by naked virgins, a circumstance which might make one appreciate even Nestle's Quick. No wonder Cortés called the substance "the divine drink," and no wonder that after he went home in 1527, he routinely kept a chocolate pot on his desk.

No sooner had Cortés brought hot chocolate back to Spain, along with Aztec utensils such as the *molinet* or *molinillo* used to beat it to a froth (you can still buy wooden ones almost anywhere in Mexico today), than it caught on, especially after being doctored with sugar at the suggestion of the king, Charles V. The Spanish tried to keep their discovery secret and enjoyed a virtual monopoly on chocolate throughout much of the 16th century. (I'm convinced that this headstart on perfecting hot chocolate explains the fact that to this day the best cup of the brew I have ever been served was in Madrid.) But something as wonderful as hot chocolate could not be kept concealed for long, and soon the beverage, aided by the favor of royalty, was being served in chocolate houses, precursors of today's Starbuck's, all across Europe. And eventually, of course, the drink made its way back to the New World where we can enjoy it in recipes such as the following.

Castillian Hot Chocolate, 382
White Hot Chocolate, 383
Parisian Hot Chocolate, 383
Mexican Hot Chocolate, 382

Ice Cream

History is full of famous duos: Romulus and Remus, Gilbert and Sullivan, Batman and Robin. But of all the prominent pairs over the ages, perhaps my favorite is Ben and Jerry. That's because the ice cream produced by that Vermont institution is the closest to homemade of any store-bought brand I know. And what could be better during the hot summer months than a scoop of homemade ice cream? (Unless it's two scoops.)

Though ice cream may be the quintessential American dessert (with over 30 quarts per capita consumed on average, it is our favorite sweet), it actually originated in ancient China. There, a combination of mountain snow and saltpeter was used to freeze containers of syrup, a process said to have been brought to Italy by Marco Polo. How much credit should be given to him is unclear, but in any case, Italians, especially in Venice, have traditionally specialized in making iced confections. Their predecessors, the ancient Romans, knew how to make sorbet, or what we call "sherbet," though sometimes the two are distinguished by the fact that a sherbet usually contains milk while a sorbet usually does not. (Actually, *sorbet* is a French word; Italians call it *sorbetto*.) Sorbet is typically lighter than ice cream but richer than an ice, or what Italians call *granita*, a concoction which is more granular than sorbet or ice cream.

Despite the noble efforts of Herrell's in Boston, Lappert's in Hawaii, and Blue Bell in Texas (all among my favorites, not to mention Ben and Jerry's), the best ice cream in the world, as far as I am concerned, is still made in Italy. On several occasions I've explored the ice-cream parlors of Italy (a task to which I took naturally, having lived as a child next door to the Bang's ice-cream plant in St. Louis), and as a result, I can fully understand why legend has it that King Henry II of France married Italy's Catherine de Médicis for her ice-cream recipes.

Gelato (the Italian word for "ice cream") is generally richer, more intensely flavored, and creamier than our ice creams because it typically contains less air. The amount of air in ice cream does make a difference (as does the amount of butterfat—the FDA requires a minimum of 10 percent, but some premium brands have over twice that). Some air is necessary to prevent ice cream from being hard as a rock, but too much air makes it spongy and light. The less air, the denser and creamier the ice cream. The legal maximum is 50 percent, and brands vary widely in the amount of overrun, a term used to refer to the amount of air they contain. That's why a half gallon of one brand may not weigh the same as a half gallon of another.

Generally, the heavier the ice cream per volume, the more satisfying it will be, though, of course, other factors like the nature of the ingredients will also come into play. So as a public service, I painstakingly conducted an ice cream weigh-in among several readily available brands. The results reveal that Breyer's, Edy's, and Schnuck's house brand all weigh roughly the same per half gallon (around 2½ pounds, give or take an ounce or two), while Ben and Jerry's and Häagen-Dazs tip the scales at 4 pounds per half gallon, meaning they contain roughly half as much air as the other brands. No wonder they taste so rich, and no wonder they cost so much.

Of course, the richest, densest, and most satisfying ice cream is the kind you make yourself. Turning the crank of an ice-cream maker by hand, or even letting an electric motor do it, will likely not aerate the mixture to the same degree that an industrial machine in a factory will. Besides, when you make ice cream at home, you can enhance the final product by using only the finest of ingredients in generous quantities. (I once burned out the motor on an ice-cream maker by adding too many chocolate chunks to the container. I have no regrets!)

Making homemade ice cream, however, is a time-consuming process, and it does require a certain amount of effort, even hassle (unless you have one of those modern, and very expensive, machines that eliminate hand cranking and don't even require ice and salt). Still, it's probably worth it. But producing something homemade that is extra special does not necessarily require using an ice-cream maker.

You can create great homemade ice creams by using one of two other quick and easy techniques. One involves freezing the ice-cream base until almost solid, then breaking it into chunks and placing it in a food processor where it is blended until smooth and then put back in the freezer until firm. This technique works best for frozen yogurt, sherbet, or sorbet. Alternately, you can freeze chunks of fruit and blend them in the food processor with milk or other liquid to get much the same result.

The other easy homemade-ice-cream technique is even simpler. Just fold extra ingredients into softened store-bought ice cream and transform it into something special. For example, at our house, favorite ingredients to blend into ordinary vanilla ice cream include ground cinnamon, chunks of candied ginger, and fresh cherries with chopped chocolate.

Risotto Gelato, 370
Blackberry Sorbet, 368
Peanut Rocky Road, 373

Irish Soda Bread

"Eaten bread is forgotten," says an old Irish proverb. Figuratively speaking, there's probably something to that observation, but if you've ever eaten good Irish soda bread, you know that literally it's not true.

Irish soda bread, says award-winning cookbook author Jeanne Lemlin, is Ireland's greatest culinary legacy, one of the three things she remembers most from her visits to the country. (The other two are the friendliness of the people and the scenery.)

Soda bread has been a specialty of Ireland since the late 19th century, a traditional accompaniment to the so-called "immutable trio" of meat, vegetables, and potatoes that until recently constituted the typical Irish dinner. Even today in fashionable restaurants in Ireland, where food is as sophisticated as anywhere else in the world, they still make Irish soda bread. Nobody in Ireland would think of eating smoked salmon or Galway oysters without a few slices of brown soda bread on the side.

Soda bread, of course, gets its name from the fact that it employs bicarbonate of soda rather than yeast as the leavening agent, an idea which was born of necessity in Ireland. The Emerald Isle's climate is characterized by a small range of temperature changes (one reason why it's always so green there). Without extreme heat and cold, hard winter wheat, the kind required if yeast is to do its work, does not thrive there. Instead, soft wheat prevails, and it produces soft flour that simply does not work well with yeast. Consequently Ireland did not develop a yeast bread tradition.

Contributing to the evolution of a soda-bread culture was the fact that years ago Irish families typically cooked over glowing coals in their hearths, not in ovens. They used a device called a *bastible*, a three-legged iron pot with a flat lid, which was nestled in the coals. Hot coals were placed on top of the pot to ensure even baking. Alternatively, especially in the northern part of the country, they employed a flatiron griddle placed on a trivet at the side of an open fire with glowing coals underneath. Both utensils are ideally suited to the preparation of baked goods leavened by baking soda. Indeed, purists claim they are unsurpassed, even by modern gadgets, when it comes to making the most flavorful soda bread.

Traditionally, Irish soda bread contained nothing more than flour, salt, soda, and buttermilk (the acid which when combined with bicarbonate of soda produces carbon dioxide that makes the dough rise), but over the years, especially as immigrants brought the bread to these shores, all kinds of variations emerged. Today recipes might call for raisins, caraway seeds, dried figs, olives, sugar or honey, herbs like basil or rosemary, and even chocolate chips.

Whether traditional or trendy, nothing could be easier to make than Irish soda bread. All you do is sift together the dry ingredients, add buttermilk, mix, plop onto a baking sheet, cut a cross into the top (to frighten away the devil or to let the fairies out), and bake. It's almost easier than running out to the store to buy a loaf. And it's almost as quick. So even if you follow the Gaelic admonition, "*Ná mól an t-arán go mbruithtear é*" ("Don't praise the bread until it is baked"), you can be applauding your efforts in no time.

Golden-Raisin Irish Soda Bread, 253

Jefferson the Gourmet

On the Fourth of July, food is as important as fireworks. And why not? After all, the American Revolution had deep culinary connections. Moreover, the chief author of the document we commemorate would think Independence Day victuals no trivial matter.

As writer James Comer notes, along with American political independence came independence in cookery as Yankee cookbooks replaced old English ones. Though Root and De Rochemont argue persuasively that Americans willfully ignored the opportunity to achieve complete independence from one of the least-admired institutions of the British Isles—its cuisine—it is nonetheless true that the Revolutionary War prompted significant changes on America's tables.

For example, many people, as a sign of national loyalty, began to drink coffee instead of tea. Indeed, just a couple of years before declaring independence, the colonists had dumped loads of English tea into Boston Harbor. As Nathan Schachner declares, "It was tea—the fragrant brew associated with fragile cups, crooked fingers and cozy gossip—that finally sent the ball rolling on the road to revolution."

Similarly, whiskey became more popular than rum, another beverage which figured in its share of tense relations with the mother country. As Root and De Rochemont suggest, "If the Revolution had not been sparked by tea, it might have been by rum. . . ." They note, too, that the institution of moonshine whiskey had its roots in the Revolution. (Even George Washington and Thomas Jefferson operated distilleries on their estates.) It also inspired a brand of whiskey, "Old 1776," claiming on its label to have been "Born with the Republic."

From the Marquis de Lafayette (who fittingly became enamored of the American cause over a grand lunch with the Duke of Gloucester) we learn how pivotal a role hunger assumed in the outcome of the Revolutionary War. Ultimately, Cornwallis surrendered at Yorktown because he and his men, in contrast to the better-fed troops commanded by Washington, were starved into submission.

Finally, emphasizing the culinary underpinnings of America's fight for independence, Root and De Rochemont, noting that the firebrand Samuel Adams suffered from ulcers, speculate that America's road to independence might have been less tortuous had every colonial leader been well-fed and blessed with agreeable digestion like Thomas Jefferson.

Maybe so. But even with healthy stomachs, none of the Founding Fathers could rival Jefferson when it came to gastronomy, because in addition to being a statesman, a philosopher, a diplomat, a legislator, a man of letters, an architect, an inventor, a lawyer, and a citizen of the world, the author of the *Declaration of Independence* was also America's first gourmet.

As Root and De Rochemont put it, Jefferson was "a pushover for the seductiveness of food." An avid collector of recipes, his interest in the delights of the table was so great that Lucy Barajikian, a food- and travel-writer, maintains he counted his introduction of certain crops to the South nearly as important as his writing of the *Declaration*.

Historian Marie Kimball says Jefferson was among the greatest epicures of his day. His passion for good cooking was so great that he took one of his slaves to

Paris with him for culinary training and only freed him later, on the condition that he would in turn train another to take his place. That slave was James Hemings, brother of Sally, for whom Jefferson is alleged to have also had a passion.

As Margaret Brown Klapthor of *Smithsonian Magazine* notes, every detail of gracious living merited Jefferson's personal attention, and he was equally at home whether coordinating the social life of the capital or overseeing the destiny of the country. According to Kimball, he gave as much thought to selecting a chef as he did to choosing a minister plenipotentiary. He copied down recipes as solemnly as he signed a treaty. Even while president, he found time to carefully monitor the wares at the Washington market, and it was not uncommon for him to accompany his head steward on shopping excursions. No wonder that during Jefferson's administration, dinner at the White House, as Edythe Preet points out, "was a gustatory as well as a political tour de force."

But, as Kimball documents, Jefferson's reputation as a gourmet was secure long before he was elected president. Living in Paris as minister to the court of Louis XVI, he became engrossed in French cooking. As he traveled around the rest of Europe, he assiduously sampled indigenous foods. In Holland, after tasting waffles for the first time, he lost no time in acquiring a waffle iron. In Amsterdam, pleased with the taste of Hyson's tea, he took half a pound along with him. At Nancy he bought chocolate, in Nice he purchased Ortolans, at Rozzano he took painstaking notes on the making of Parmesan cheese, in southern France he undertook a comparative study of various oranges, out of Piedmont he smuggled a special strain of rice (in direct violation of Italian law).

Such curiosity made Jefferson a culinary trailblazer. He introduced macaroni to this country. He was the first to plant tomatoes in the United States. Because of him, the potato finally got its due. By routinely serving his guests ice cream wrapped in warm pastry, he, in effect, invented Baked Alaska nearly a century before it made its first appearance at New York's Delmonico's Restaurant.

As Kimball notes, under Jefferson the executive mansion was as famous for its cellar as for its cuisine. Klapthor calls him the greatest wine connoisseur ever to live in the White House. Accepted among his contemporaries as the ultimate authority on the subject, he studied viniculture and was conversant with the finest wines of the world. Not surprisingly, all but six lines of his congratulatory letter to newly elected President Monroe is devoted to recommended wines for official entertaining.

Thomas Jefferson may have immortalized the words "all men are created equal," but his own culinary biography clearly demonstrates that not all palates are.

Thomas Jefferson's Recipe for Ice Cream, 371

Jell-O

It's the Rodney Dangerfield of the culinary world. The *Epicurious* website, which with over 16,000 listings boasts that it is the world's greatest recipe collection, contains only six citations for it. Some users think even that is too many and have chastised the site for including any at all.

Not surprisingly, foodies are less apt to know about its uses in the kitchen than its many alternative uses—as a wrestling medium, a hair dye, or the secret behind the movie special effects. (It was the substance that constituted the parted Red Sea in Cecil B. De Mille's *The Ten Commandments*.)

Yet despite its less than haute status, it has become a national icon, arguably America's most famous dessert, so famous and so typically American, in fact, that it was served to immigrants entering Ellis Island. Ten boxes of it are sold every second. The Smithsonian Institution has even sponsored a conference on it. No wonder astronaut Shannon Lucid felt compelled to serve it to her Cosmonaut colleagues every Sunday while she was aboard the Russian space station *Mir*.

It's Jell-O, of course, and sales of it peak every year at Thanksgiving. At our house, for example, the holiday wouldn't be the same without my mother-in-law's cranberry Jell-O mold, as essential an ingredient to our festivities as the turkey or the pumpkin pie. Like many households, however, once the holidays are over, we all but forget about Jell-O. That's short-sighted, I have concluded.

I came to this realization after my wife underwent a tonsillectomy, a procedure for which post-operative care demands only soft and soothing foods. Thus, while she recuperated there was lots of Jell-O at our house—in a wide variety of flavors, colors, and shapes. As a result of this experience, we began taking Jell-O more seriously. We found it can be, in the words of early ads, "delicate, delightful, delicious, and dainty."

This really shouldn't have surprised us, because jelled desserts and aspics were once all the rage. The Victorians loved them. Great chefs like Câreme and Escoffier gave them an honored place at the table. They were typically served on silver trays and in cut-glass dishes. The embodiment of elegance, they were normally found only on the tables of the wealthy, mainly because only they could afford to hire someone to go through the rigors of preparing the stuff, a labor-intensive and, frankly, unappetizing process before the invention of Jell-O changed all that.

Prior to the availability of Jell-O, if you wanted to make a gelatin salad or dessert, you first had to obtain a couple of calves' feet, then scald them, remove the hair, split them and remove the fat from between the claws, and boil them for six or seven hours, periodically removing the scum that would accumulate on top. Then you'd have to strain the liquid, skim off the fat, boil some more, and purify the mixture with egg shells. Only after further straining and skimming would you be ready to add sugar and flavorings. As one early cookbook author put it, the process took "everything a cook has in her repertoire and beyond."

That all changed in 1890 when Charles Knox, motivated by the spectacle of his wife slaving over a batch of calf's-foot jelly, invented unflavored gelatin powder, the most well-known brand of which still bears his name. He launched what cookbook author Jean Anderson calls "the Age of the Molded Salad" when he sponsored a recipe contest (Fanny Farmer was one of the judges) in which Pennsylvania's Mrs.

John Cooke entered her Perfection Salad. It only won third prize, but printed and distributed around the country by Knox, the recipe inspired legions of home cooks.

Then, on the heels of Knox, Pearl B. Wait, a cough-syrup manufacturer from Le Roy, New York (now home of the Jell-O museum), made it even easier to create gelatin salads and desserts when he came out with a prepackaged product containing not only powdered gelatin, but sugar and flavorings as well. Now all the home cook needed to make spectacular molded gelatin dishes was boiling water. Wait's wife, May, named the product Jell-O.

But it wasn't until the turn of the century that the product began to jell with the American public. In 1899, lacking the capital to successfully market his invention, Wait sold the formula to a fellow townsman, Frank Woodward, for a mere $450. Woodward, who had considerable experience marketing patent medicines, used extensive advertising and a Jell-O recipe book to parlay the product into a million-dollar-a-year business by 1906. Before long his food company was renamed the Jell-O Company and later it became the foundation of the General Foods Corporation. Aggressive advertising, complete with a "Jell-O girl" designed by the creator of the Kewpie doll and jingle-laden ads on Jack Benny's popular radio program, helped congeal the product's reputation as a stylish dish. Today the Jell-O brand is recognized by fully 95 percent of Americans.

Not a bad record for a food that is rumored to be made out of horse hooves. (Actually, it's now made out of "hide trimmings," which sounds even worse, but it's so purified that the FDA doesn't even consider it a meat product.) But somewhere along the way, as Americans became increasingly sophisticated eaters, Jell-O lost its cachet and became perceived as a concoction suitable only for children and hospital patients, and welcomed only once a year or so at the holiday table. Perhaps it's time to reconsider that view. Famed French chef Jacques Pepin, after all, admits to loving the stuff. And why not? With the right touch, Jell-O can add shimmer and sparkle to any menu.

Sangria Jell-O Salad, 240

Julia Child

It was an ordinary day in 1968. I turned on the little black and white television set to watch my favorite show. The program's host, in her unmistakable voice ("a voice that could make an aspic shimmy," it's been called), was showing how to make a French chocolate, rum, and almond cake called Queen of Sheba.

For 28 minutes and 52 seconds, this woman, who has been likened to a dowager doing a burlesque routine, demonstrated with characteristic aplomb everything you needed to know to create the dish. As soon as the show was over, I headed straight for the grocery store to buy the ingredients to make the cake that very evening.

That was not the only time this program would have such an effect on me, nor was I the only one. For example, after the show on broccoli, every store within 200 miles of the Boston television studio where it originated sold out of the vegetable. Following the program on omelettes, there was a run on omelette pans at every specialty store in the area. Clearly, millions of others like me were similarly inspired by this show, *The French Chef*, and its host, Julia Child.

Julia Child changed the way we relate to food, for, as Kathryn Kellinger observes, it is impossible to exaggerate her influence. Karen Lehrman equates her impact to that of Alfred Kinsey and Elvis Presley. No wonder *Ladies Home Journal* listed her among the most important women of the 20th century—along with Rosa Parks, Eleanor Roosevelt, and Helen Keller.

"Julia Child invented modern life," proclaimed *U.S. News & World Report*. Before she came on the scene, as *Newsweek* put it, "America was tuna-casserole land." Women did all of the cooking, and for many of them, preparing meals was not a joy but a chore. They relied on recipes in so-called ladies' magazines, which touted quick preparations using canned soups and frozen vegetables, or they resorted to TV dinners. A bestseller of the day was Peg Bracken's *I Hate to Cook Book*.

Julia Child changed all of that. As Pia Nordlinger observes, "She replaced the perception of eating as nourishment and cooking as punishment with the idea that food exists mainly for enjoyment." Jane and Michael Stern credit her with transforming cooking into entertainment. Lehrman declares that she raised home-cooking to the level of art. Frances Dowell rightly concludes, "Julia Child changed the face—and flavor—of American cooking."

Ironically, when Julia McWilliams was born, few would have predicted that she would become, in Kellinger's words, "the most important culinary figure this country has produced." Indeed, as Nordlinger notes, she spent her first 36 years as a food philistine. Born to privilege and wealth, she did not need to venture into the kitchen to prepare her meals. There was a hired cook for that.

However, during World War II she joined the Office of Strategic Services, precursor to the CIA (the intelligence agency, not the Culinary Institute of America), where she met her future husband, Paul Child. The worldly Paul introduced her to fine food and wine, and they began what may well be the greatest culinary love affair of all time.

After marriage they moved to France, and it was there, over lunch at La Couronne restaurant in Rouen on November 3, 1948, that Julia, dining on oysters portugaises, sole meunière, and a green salad, experienced an Epicurean epiphany.

Enthralled with French food, she enrolled at Le Cordon Bleu (the lone woman in her class) and joined Le Cercle des Gourmettes, a women's cooking club. There she met Simone Beck and Louisette Bertholle with whom, after nearly a decade of research, she co-authored the classic *Mastering the Art of French Cooking*.

It was the promotion of this 700-page tome that brought Julia Child to the attention of an America ripe for a culinary revolution. Appearing on what was then called educational television to talk about the book, she brought along a copper bowl, a whisk, and some eggs, and whipped up an omelet. The response was so overwhelming that she was given her own program, and the rest, as they say, is history. Though initially some viewers thought the show a parody, it ultimately became public television's greatest success, and in the process changed the way we cook and the way we eat.

Julia Child was the nation's premiere celebrity chef, an entity which she herself invented. Totally lacking pretension, she described herself simply as a good home cook. But really, she was a teacher. Whether unabashedly mending a dish that didn't quite come out right ("If you are alone in the kitchen," she asked, "whooooooo is going to see?") or triumphantly bringing a perfectly executed one to the dining room, she taught us to be passionate about food.

Queen of Sheba Cake, 317

KitchenAid Mixer

In 1997 Aaron Betsky, a curator at San Francisco's Museum of Modern Art, organized an exhibition around a dozen everyday objects which he believes qualify as experience-shaping icons. Among those he included were the BMW 325i and the KitchenAid mixer. Now I can see why he'd select a sexy model with all that power and so many accessories, but, frankly, I can't understand why he picked the car.

The KitchenAid stand mixer, whose very silhouette is so iconic it has been trademarked, is approaching its 100th anniversary. It remains the Cadillac, or BMW, of food-preparation appliances. I can well remember the stirring experience of buying my first one. Actually it's my only one. I fully expect it to outlast me. In fact, some of the first KitchenAid mixers produced in 1919 are still in use.

The mixer's iconic status notwithstanding, KitchenAid was not the first to market such an appliance for the home. That distinction belongs to the Hamilton Beach Company which developed a motor that, with attachments, could not only mix cake batter, but run a sewing machine, sharpen knives, and polish silver.

Nor was KitchenAid initially responsible for the popularity of the household mixer. Credit for that goes to the Sunbeam Corporation. When it launched its "Mixmaster" a dozen years after the introduction of the KitchenAid, sales went through the roof, primarily because the machine was the first of its kind to be offered at under $20. The KitchenAid, by contrast, retailed for practically ten times that amount.

What KitchenAid did, on the other hand, was to perfect the home mixer. Their secret is a "revolutionary" approach to moving the beater around the bowl—planetary action. Like a planet in the solar system, the beater rotates in one direction as it makes its revolution around the bowl in the opposite direction. Moreover, by offering a plethora of attachments, the company elevated the machine from mere mixer to food preparer. Today's attachments include a can opener, meat grinder, pasta roller, ravioli cutter, sausage stuffer, grain mill, juicer, and even an ice-cream maker.

The modern KitchenAid traces its lineage to Herbert Johnston, an engineer who, inspired by watching a baker struggle to mix bread dough by hand with a big iron spoon, developed the first commercial mixer in 1908. Before long, his 80-quart device was standard equipment in food-service operations, bakeries, and on U.S. Navy ships. A smaller home mixer was the next logical development, debuting in 1919. In 1937 the company commissioned the style guru of the day, Egmont Arens, to redesign the machine, and the classic shape, still in vogue today, was born.

The mixer earned its name when wives of company executives tested the very first KitchenAid home mixer. One remarked, "I don't care what you call it, it's the best kitchen aid I've ever had." For countless cooks, it still is.

Golden Génoise, 304

Last Meals

If you were told that your life would end tomorrow, what would be your choice of a last meal? That is the intriguing question which James L. Dickerson asked celebrities to ponder for his book, *Last Suppers*.

It is a provocative question even though, as Dickerson observes, it is one which most of us will never get to answer, or won't care to. "Most of us live for food," he says, "but in the end, it is the last thing on earth we crave. People facing their imminent demise usually request pain-killing drugs, loved ones, or one last view of the sunset."

Still, the query piques our curiosity. Would you choose a final taste of something familiar, say an old favorite like your mother's meatloaf or your wife's chocolate cake? Or would you opt for something extravagant like lobster or caviar? Surely you wouldn't need to worry about cholesterol or subsequent indigestion. And you wouldn't have to fret about seconds nor wonder about the propriety of requesting a doggy bag. (A brain-damaged death-row convict in Arkansas, however, asked to save his pie until after the execution.)

Condemned criminals are usually able to choose and savor their last meal, but the rest of us are not likely to have adequate warning or, sadly, to be in sufficiently good health. Some scholars say the tradition of offering a last meal to someone about to be executed can be traced to Jesus' Last Supper, but others disagree. Whatever the case, it is a tradition carried out in every state in which capital punishment is practiced.

Records show that the concluding culinary choices of those on death row tend to be fairly ordinary. Dickerson's research suggests that the majority of convicted killers order shrimp for their last meal. Pam Daniel, a writer for *Sarasota Magazine* who has done some research on the subject, agrees that shrimp is a popular choice as well as fried chicken and steak. Thus, as *Time* magazine reports, serial killer Ted Bundy ate steak, eggs, hash browns, and coffee before being put to death. Perry Smith and Richard Hickock, of *In Cold Blood* fame, dined on shrimp, French fries, garlic bread, ice cream, strawberries, and whipped cream. Bruno Richard Hauptmann, kidnapper of the Lindbergh baby, enjoyed a pre-electrocution repast of chicken, fries, cherries, and cake.

Not all convicts facing the death sentence made conventional choices, however. Among the truly unusual, as reported by Bill Hayes, a Florida scholar of capital punishment, was Velma Margie Barfield, who snacked on Cheez Doodles and a Coke before being executed for poisoning her lover with arsenic-laced beer. Surely the most substantial last meal, at least among convicts, was the one consumed by David Castillo in Texas. It consisted of twenty-four tacos, two cheeseburgers, two whole onions, five jalapeños, six enchiladas, six tostadas, a quart of milk, and a chocolate shake. That's what I call eating like there's no tomorrow!

Among the more elaborate last suppers of recent times was one devoured in 1995, not by a convict but by François Mitterrand, former president of France, though he broke the law in so doing. The centerpiece of the four-hour feast was the thumb-sized songbird, the ortolan, which supposedly represents the French soul. French law forbids the consumption of this member of the yellowhammer family, but that didn't stop Mitterrand from eating two of them whole, as is the custom, bones and all, beneath a large white napkin so as to heighten the sensual experience. In keeping with ritual, the birds were held captive in the dark for weeks, fed millet to fatten them, drowned in Armagnac, and then roasted whole. As a dramatic exit following the meal, Mitterrand declared he would not eat again and died eight days later.

Unlike Mitterrand, most people do not have the luxury of masterminding their last meal, yet even when unplanned, as Daniel observes, history has taken note of what famous people had for their final feed. For some reason we like to know. Thus, because patrons ask so frequently, employees at Mezzaluna, the restaurant where she ate her last dinner, are taught that Nicole Brown Simpson ordered rigatoni. Likewise, there has been much interest in what was on the menu in the dining room of the Titanic the night it sank (warm poached North Atlantic salmon with mousseline sauce and filet mignon).

Daniel reports that the last meal for Wild Bill Hickock was beans and whiskey, the specialty of the house at Nuttall & Mann's Saloon, where he was shot from behind. For U.S. President Zachary Taylor it was iced milk, cherries, and pickled cucumbers. The cherries were rumored to have been poisoned and responsible for his death five days later, though the 1991 exhumation of his body failed to confirm the allegation. For Oscar Wilde it wasn't food, but drink. Sipping champagne, the impoverished playwright announced, "I am dying as I have lived, beyond my means."

Dickerson went beyond the historical record and conducted his own investigations, for example, interviewing June Mallea, the waitress who served Ernest Hemingway his last meal at a restaurant in Ketchum, Idaho. She remembered the Nobel Prize-winning author eating a New York strip steak, baked potato, and a Caesar salad the night before he shot himself.

With the exception of Princess Diana, who last dined on asparagus and mushroom omelet and Dover sole with vegetable tempura, Dickerson reports that the last suppers of most celebrities were hastily prepared and consumed. Thus, John Candy whipped up pasta for himself and friends before going to bed where he died in his sleep. James Dean, eager to put his new Porsche through its paces, made time only for a glass of milk and an apple on the day of his death in that same vehicle. A dish of ice cream and cookies eaten at 4 AM was the last thing Elvis Presley ate. John Lennon grabbed a quick sandwich at the Stage Deli in New York before returning to his Manhattan apartment and an assassin's bullet. For her last meal, Marilyn Monroe had guacamole, stuffed mushrooms, and spicy meatballs eaten buffet style at a Brentwood restaurant.

Though we may want to know what famous people actually had for their last suppers, as Dickerson's book proves, it is equally interesting to learn what the living would request if they had the opportunity. Dickerson asked and found that Dick Clark would choose Cajun corn chowder; Vanna White, a cottage cheese salad; Helen Ruddy, raspberries with hot rum vanilla custard; Bill Clinton, chicken enchiladas; and Jack Nicklaus, Italian cream cake.

And what would I want? I thought you'd never ask. Here is my choice for a last meal: fried artichokes like they make at Kemoll's in St. Louis as an appetizer, followed by pumpkin soup, and a Greek salad. For the fish course I'd have grilled salmon and for the meat course, chateaubriand. As side dishes I'd like risotto with truffles and sautéed spinach with pine nuts and golden raisins. The cheese course would be Stilton with walnuts and port, and dessert would be chocolate cheesecake. I'd conclude with raspberry-filled white chocolate truffles and coffee. At the prospect of such a meal I can almost hear myself echoing the words of Pierette Brillat-Savarin, the aunt of the great gourmet: "I feel the end approaching. Quick, bring me my dessert, coffee, and liqueur."

The following recipe for a last request is all too good to wait until the end to fix, so try it out at your earliest opportunity. And here's hoping you'll be enjoying many more meals to come before your last supper.

Whitfield's Potato Salad, 236

Lebkuchen

What do you like most about Christmas? If it's Santa Claus and fir trees and mulled wine, you ought to thank the Germans, because these, like most of our holiday customs, are Germanic, not English. (The English themselves, for that matter, adopted them as their own, back when Queen Victoria married Prince Albert, a German.) And if, like me, you think of Christmas as a time for cookies, you ought to be especially grateful to the Germans, because they invented that custom too.

German Lebkuchen, the Cadillac (or should I say Mercedes-Benz?) of spice cookies, was probably the first cookie traditionally associated with Christmas. Certainly without Lebkuchen it wouldn't be Christmas in Germany (where 85 percent of the billion or so annually consumed are devoured between October and December), just as it wouldn't be Christmas in France without the *Buche de Noel* or in England without plum pudding.

Lebkuchen may also very well be the oldest form of cookie known to humankind. The first recorded reference to it appears in an 11th-century manuscript at a German monastery in Tegernsee, and if that's not old enough for you, its origins can be traced back even further than that—all the way back to 2000 BC and the honey and spice cakes of ancient Mesopotamia, India, and Egypt where the practice of creating decorative baked goods for special occasions began. The Greeks and then the Romans continued the practice, baking flat cakes in intricately designed molds. Just such molds have been unearthed by archaeologists from the ashes at Pompeii.

These honey cakes, the precursors of Lebkuchen (whose major ingredient is honey), were prized by the ancients for their presumably magical healing powers. They were often worn into battle or, in Egypt, buried with kings. Honey, after all, was considered a gift of the gods. The Teutonic peoples of pre-Christian Europe likewise valued honey cakes and sought them as protection against any evil spirits who might be about during the winter solstice.

According to Lebkuchen-Schmidt, one of Germany's most famous Lebkuchen makers, honey cakes changed into Lebkuchen in the 13th century. Moreover, since traditional Lebkuchen recipes call for the cookies to be baked on rounds of thin rice paper, which look and taste much like a communion wafer, it's likely that this metamorphosis took place in a monastery. Besides, most monasteries kept their own apiaries, and honey was the sweetener of choice—actually the only sweetener until 400 years ago—so it seems reasonable to conclude that the monks, who were literate and consequently could read recipes, created the first Lebkuchen.

Thus, early Lebkuchen recipes called for seven spices to symbolize the seven days of creation, and early Lebkuchen molds featured Biblical themes. Long after commercial bakeries had gotten in the act, every Lebkuchener still included as part of his equipment a mold depicting the adoration of the Magi.

Later the molds became more secular, featuring knights and noblemen, coats of arms, and outdoor scenes. So, when in 1487 the Emperor Friedrich III invited some 4,000 children to his castle and presented each with a Lebkuchen, they bore his image. Those "Little Emperor" Lebkuchen (Kaiserlein) are still being made today.

By the 19th century, elaborate Lebkuchen hearts came into vogue. Today German children are still given them to hang around their necks and nibble whenever they get hungry. During the Christmas season, of course, Lebkuchen are also cut in the shapes of St. Nicholas, angels, and stars.

Though Lebkuchen is made everywhere in Germany, there is no question that the best and most celebrated is made in Nuremberg, where as early as 1395 a bakery devoted to the delicacy opened and where during the Middle Ages a Lebkuchen Baker's Guild was established. It was only natural that production of Lebkuchen first centered there. Situated on the intersection of ancient trade routes from the Orient and surrounded by imperial woods which were home to the bee gardens of the Holy Roman Empire, Nuremberg had all the spices and honey it needed to cultivate a Lebkuchen industry.

That industry moves into high gear during the Christmas season to supply the dozens of stalls selling Lebkuchen at the city's Christmas Market, the largest, most famous, and most authentic in all of Europe. It was there, in the great medieval square in front of the Frauenkirche (Church of Our Lady), as children's choirs, hand-cranked hurdy-gurdies, and brass bands filled the air with Christmas music (much as the legendary Meistersingers must have in the 16th century, when the market was founded) that, fortified against the chilly air by a hot mug of Glühwein, I proceeded to enthusiastically sample the local Lebkuchen decked out for the holidays in all its splendor.

And it was then and there that I began to fully appreciate why Lebkuchen in German means the "cooking of life." I also quickly realized why this quintessential German Christmas cookie has for centuries been shipped to eagerly awaiting recipients in all parts of the globe. "Nuremberg trifles are exported worldwide," says an old German proverb, referring to that fact. I beg to differ. Lebkuchen is no mere trifle.

Lebkuchen Bars, 353

Lemonade

It doesn't seem that long ago that my own children went through the ritual of setting up sidewalk lemonade stands. I fondly remember helping them set up shop: preparing cardboard signs, erecting a suitable counter with a card table or, if we could find one, an orange crate, procuring paper cups, mixing the lemonade, fashioning a suitable sales strategy (our corner or a busier one?), and determining the price. Though I invariably provided the start-up capital and hardly ever got paid back, because somehow somebody always managed to drink up the profits, those little forays into the world of small business are among my most cherished memories of my kids growing up.

But you don't see very many children's lemonade stands these days, or at least I don't. Perhaps, as the *Baltimore Sun*'s humor columnist Kevin Cowherd suggested, this is because in today's world you have to think twice about even such a simple venture. As he points out, a lemonade stand could easily violate the Covenants and Restrictions clause of many community associations, and yelling at passing motorists, even just to announce the availability of your product, could be construed by some as a form of harassment. Moreover, given the 1992 multimillion-dollar judgment against McDonald's for serving coffee that was too hot, a would-be lemonade monger might be leery of taking a similar risk with a cold beverage. Finally, Cowherd warns that the media, always on the lookout for sensational and scandalous stories, might be unable to resist the possibilities inherent in a child's lemonade stand. He says, "Underage workers toiling for hours in the hot sun for less than minimum wage. The media would have a field day with that one. . . . By noon there'd be 15 satellite trucks outside our house. Sam Donaldson and Wolf Blitzer would be doing standups in front of our front door. The newspaper would come out with a three-part series on child labor practices, with a picture of me on the front page shielding my face with a raincoat."

Cowherd was being facetious, of course. Probably the real reason you don't see so many lemonade stands these days is that many children would rather stay inside where it's air conditioned than sit outside working in the heat and humidity of summer. And who can blame them? But whatever the reason for the decline of the lemonade stand, the unfortunate consequence is that many of us have forgotten, and perhaps many of today's youngsters do not even know, the pleasures of real lemonade. And that's a real shame.

Let's face it. While the powdered stuff you get out of a canister or a packet and the frozen concentrate you get from the grocer's case may make a perfectly acceptable summer drink, they are not really lemonade. Real lemonade has to be made with freshly squeezed lemons. That's because when it comes to citrus fruits, there simply is no other way to obtain that wonderful genuine taste. Generally speaking, "fresh" means better no matter what the food (fruitcakes, wine, aged cheese, and a few other things excepted), but when it comes to lemonade or limeade, the difference between fresh and other varieties is not just a difference of degree, it's a difference in kind.

This point was driven home to me recently when I visited the Ritz-Carlton Hotel in Cancun, Mexico, on the way back from a vacation in Playa del Carmen. In Mexico, of course, the citrus fruit of choice is the lime because Mexican or Key limes are both distinctive and plentiful. Many years ago I discovered the delight of Mexican limonada (limeade), a truly wonderful homemade drink that can typically be found for less than a dollar a glass at even the most humble establishments in that country. It is usually made with fresh lime juice, simple syrup, and, often, carbonated water. (I still recall vividly the hedonistic experience of lounging in the pool at our hotel in Puerto Vallarta while the children paddled back and forth to the swim-up bar for refills of my limonada.)

Imagine my surprise when our waiter at the Ritz brought to our beachside table tall glasses of limonada that turned out to have been made with a mix! One taste and I could tell. No wonder the waiter confessed immediately when interrogated, for hardly anyone could be fooled into thinking that a mix could duplicate the bracing flavor of fresh limes. I suspect the irony of it all was lost on him, but here was a fancy hotel substituting, in the name of convenience, the artificial for the real, when just down the block a native street vendor could have provided the genuine article at a fraction of the cost. I'll bet the margaritas weren't any good either, but I didn't stay long enough to find out.

No, nothing can take the place of real lemonade or limeade. To me it epitomizes summer. But sadly, most restaurants in this country no longer take the time or trouble to serve the real thing, opting instead for a mix or offering Coke and Pepsi as an alternative. (Ironically, the first flavored soda beverage, invented in 1838 by Eugene Roussel, a Philadelphia perfume dealer, was actually lemonade mixed with carbonated water.) So if you want to experience something authentic, you'll have to make it yourself.

There's nothing to making fresh lemonade or limeade, of course, except for a little extra time and some physical effort. Just be sure to choose the juiciest lemons and limes, which are the ones which are heaviest. And here's a tip for extracting the most juice from them. Simply put them in the microwave for about 15 seconds before squeezing. I recommend using carbonated water for lemonade and limeade to add a more festive touch, but if you do, it's best to sweeten the beverage with a simple syrup because all of the stirring necessary to dissolve plain sugar could make the drink go flat.

It's hard to beat the basic beverage, but there are lots of variations. And if you want something stronger, you can add alcohol. (Perhaps the most intriguing recipe I've ever seen for lemonade with a kick is something called a Lemonade Bomb. It contains lemons, vodka, and beer, and, I suspect, it's aptly named.) Perhaps the following recipes will serve as inspiration to follow the advice of Howard Gossage who said, "If you have a lemon, make lemonade."

Strawberry Lemonade, 380
Agua Fresca de Limón, 380
Iced Cucumber Limeade, 381
Frozen Lemonade Pie, 333

Lemons

"When life gives you lemons, make lemonade," the adage says. That's good advice, but there's an assumption underlying it that ought to be challenged. What's wrong with lemons? A life without them, from a culinary perspective, would be sour indeed.

I came to this deep philosophical revelation while lounging in the backyard of friends who live in California. Just a few feet from where I sat was their lemon tree, drooping with fist-sized fruit. It occurred to me that even those of us who aren't lucky enough to have them growing outside our door tend to take lemons for granted. We shouldn't.

Lemons are arguably the most versatile of fruits, certainly among the citrus family. In addition to their role in food preparation, as Sharon Tyler Herbst in the *Food Lover's Companion* reminds us, lemons have a host of other uses. They have been employed to treat epilepsy, as a bleaching agent, and even in witchcraft. Currently, cancer researchers are investigating the capacity of lemons and other citrus fruits to neutralize carcinogens. Dr. Sandra Landolt, a Toronto dermatologist consulted by the Canadian magazine *Chatelaine*, confirms the wisdom of age-old advice to use lemons to treat rough skin. (Perhaps the capuchin monkeys of Costa Rica are on to something. They like to rub themselves all over with lemons.) *Chatelaine* also advises using lemon juice as a final rinse after shampooing your hair.

And in the kitchen, lemons are no less adaptable. They can perk up a sauce, enliven fresh vegetables, add interest and perfume to desserts, or when their zest is rubbed around the edge of the glass, spell the difference between a perfect martini and one that is only near perfect. As Christopher Idone points out in *Lemons: A Country Garden Cookbook*, lemons are a lot like salt—they bring out the flavors in food. In fact, lemon juice makes a nice substitute for salt if you're watching your sodium intake, though, oddly enough, it mutes the saltiness of caviar and unmasks its flavor. Aliza Green is right when she observes in an article in *Prevention* magazine that lemons are "a bright suggestion than can accent every course from soup to dessert—adding flavor that's virtually free of fat, calories, and sodium." Try, for example, stuffing the cavity of a whole chicken with a lemon (pierce it with a fork first) or inserting some slices under the skin before roasting.

A visit to California is a particularly good way to further your appreciation of lemons (not to mention other things for that matter). It's the country's leading producer, growing nearly 25 percent of the world's crop and providing roughly 80 percent of U.S. consumption. There they take lemons seriously, and "lemon laws" don't just apply to inferior cars. (I don't know why a bad car is called a lemon any more than I know why a good one is a cream puff.) In Ventura, where we visited, you'll see commercial lemon groves everywhere, counterparts to those in virtually every backyard. They can be traced directly to William Wolfskill, a Kentucky trapper who wandered to what is now Los Angeles in 1841 and planted hundreds of lemon (and orange) seedlings on two acres at Central Avenue and East Fifth Street. Soon he had 70 acres, and, following completion of the transcontinental railroad, he pioneered shipping citrus fruit long distances across the country.

Lemon history, of course, goes back much further than that. Indeed, lemons have been cultivated for thousands of years. Tomb paintings in the Valley of the Kings reveal that the Egyptians prized lemon trees, which are native to Southeast Asia, where references to them can be found in some of the oldest of Oriental literature. From there they branched out to the rest of Asia, Persia, the Mideast, Africa, southern Europe, and, of course, to the Mediterranean where they have become an indispensable part of the trilogy of ingredients which typifies that cuisine (garlic and olive oil being the other two). In Greece, for example, they buy lemons at the market like we do potatoes, by the sack, and their most famous soup, avgolemono, is based on the fruit. Similarly, on the Amalfi coast of Italy, I found it difficult to have a meal without lemons, not that I'd want to. There, even the lemon leaves are used in cooking and they make a lemon liqueur that can be as potent as the scenery is beautiful.

Thanks to Columbus, lemons made their way across the ocean to the New World and though there are hundreds of variations, there are now three essential categories of lemons available here: commercial or acid, rough-skinned, and sweet. The most popular commercial lemon is the Eureka, probably brought from Sicily by Italian immigrants in the 1870s. The Meyer lemon is probably the most popular sweet lemon, common in California gardens. Though they seem sweeter than other lemons, they don't contain more sugar, just less acid. These were the lemons grown in Louis XIV's orangerie and sucked on by ladies of the court intent on maintaining voluptuously red lips. Rough-skinned lemons are used primarily as rootstock.

When selecting lemons, Herbst suggests looking for firm, plump fruit which is heavy for its size and which has smooth, brightly colored skin with no tinge of green. Idone advises that thin-skinned lemons produce more juice than thick-skinned ones, but the latter's zest (the fittingly named thin outer yellow layer) is more flavorful. By the way, a good trick for maximizing the amount of juice you get out of a lemon is to microwave it first for about 15–20 seconds. Though you can freeze lemon juice for future use (an ice-cube tray works nicely and provides convenient portions), there's no substitute for freshly squeezed juice. At our house we have vowed never to buy the bottled stuff. (I guess you could call that our lemon pledge.)

So when it comes to lemons, I agree with noted California chef Bradley Ogden (who started his career in Kansas City) when he says, "When life gives you lemons . . . cook with them!" The following recipes are good ways to put that philosophy into practice.

Lemon Roasted Potatoes, 297
Lemon Walnut Date Bread, 255
Penne with Asparagus and Lemon Cream Sauce, 265
Out of the Ordinary Lemon Bars, 354

Lewis and Clark

They ate nine pounds of meat per person per day. Though they took seven tons of foodstuffs with them, they supplemented their larder along the way by hunting and fishing. Thus, over the course of their journey they killed and consumed over 1,000 deer, 375 elk, 227 bison, 35 bighorn sheep, 62 antelopes, 43 grizzly bears, 113 beavers, 104 geese and brant, 46 grouse, 9 turkeys, 48 plovers, and nearly 200 dogs (a "favorite food" with most of the party and judged far superior to horse), not to mention a large assortment of exotic animals such as hawk, coyote, fox, crow, eagle, gopher, muskrat, seal, whale, turtle, mussels, crab, salmon, and trout, plus all kinds of fruits, vegetables, seeds, and nuts.

Yet there were nights when they went to bed hungry, and by the time they reached the Pacific Northwest in 1805, they may have had to resort to gnawing on beef-tallow candles. During their 7,700-mile, two-year expedition, there is scarcely a day they did not mention food in their journals. Clearly, Lewis and Clark and their Corps of Discovery were characterized by "undaunted courage," to use Thomas Jefferson's phrase, but just as clearly they possessed undaunted appetites as well.

Still, curiously, the culinary aspects of the Lewis and Clark expedition have often been overlooked by historians. That's unfortunate because the culinary dimension of the Lewis and Clark trail deserves recognition since it provides another window into the lives of the famed explorers, the native peoples they encountered, and their impact on our nation. Studying what the Corps of Discovery ate helps answer the question of whether there ever was a true American cuisine and reminds us that even frontier cooking could reach a relatively high level of sophistication.

Certainly some items on the explorers' menu seem exotic by today's standards: ingredients such as wapato (a potato-like tuber harvested from swamplands by the Chinook with their toes), cous (sometimes called "Indian celery"), camas root (a staple of the Nez Perce that tasted something like an onion), and yampah (similar to fennel). On the other hand, some elements of their bill of fare are not tempting at all, such as "portable soup," a sort of precursor to the bouillon cube, made by reconstituting a gluey condensed broth (the members of the Corps hated it) or bear grease (the Corps' favorite fat).

"May your appetite and opportunity ever coincide," said Lewis, in a toast to Clark during a birthday meal of venison, elk, and beaver tail served on the trail over a table of planks covered with red flannel pilfered from an Indian gift bundle. Examining the extent to which the two coincided or collided furthers our appreciation for what these pioneers accomplished during the most celebrated instance of trailblazing in American history. Besides, I can't think of a better way to bring history alive than through food. After all, the Corps of Discovery spent most of their time looking for it.

Charbonneau's Boudin Blanc Terrine, 218

Macadamia Nuts

Macadamia nuts, sometimes called the king of nuts because they are the sweetest Mother Nature can provide, are the only major commercial food crop native to Australia. They were growing on that continent for 50 million years before anyone besides the native aborigines took notice. In autumn the natives would gather on the slopes of the Great Divide Range and eat the seeds of the "Kindal Kindal" tree, their name for the macadamia. It wasn't until 1857 that the nuts were "discovered" by the rest of the world. According to folklore, a small boy in Brisbane was the first person, other than an aborigine, to eat a macadamia nut. Almost another century passed before they were sold commercially. (Almonds, by contrast, have been a commercial crop for more than 2,000 years.)

First described by botanists Ferdinand von Muller and Walter Hill, the hitherto unknown macadamia tree was named by them for the Scottish-born scientist and philosopher Dr. John MacAdam. Though he spearheaded the move towards cultivation of the tree's nuts, some question remains as to whether he ever even tasted one before he died at a relatively early age.

Ironically, though the macadamia nut is indigenous to Australia, farmers there did not fully realize its potential until Hawaii showed the way. Indeed, initially the tree was thought useful only for ornamental purposes. Legend has it that Australians couldn't figure out how to crack the ironlike shell of the macadamia nut and had to wait until Americans invented mechanical rollers for the purpose. Now used universally in commercial operations, they launched the industry. There is no question that the shells, encased in a thick, green husk that must be split open to reach them, are hard—the hardest of any nut. It takes 300 pounds of pressure per square inch to smash them. In the days before mechanization, people drove their cars over them to get the job done. Though other factors contribute, the fact that macadamia nuts are so troublesome to extricate from their hard covering is, in a nutshell, why they are so expensive.

Macadamias came to Hawaii in 1837 when Don Francisco de Paula Marin planted the first tree in his backyard in Honolulu. But it wasn't until 1882 when William H. Purvis introduced them to the Big Island that plantations got started. Today 10,000 acres of orchards on the slopes of the Mauna Loa volcano supply nuts to the largest processor and marketer of macadamia products in the world, the Mauna Loa Corporation. Nearly all of the state's production is now centered on the Big Island, though one grower remains on the north shore of Oahu, the charmingly rustic Tropical Farms, which I visited recently.

Though nowadays Australia's macadamia production rivals that of Hawaii, gourmets everywhere should be glad that the islands previously purloined the nut because it was word-of-mouth advertising fueled by Hawaii tourism that brought it to the attention of the culinary world.

How deprived that world would be without this luxurious nut which has been likened to caviar in its effect in a recipe. Moreover, because it's so versatile, it can add mystique to almost any dish. Macadamia nuts not only add class to a batch of cookies or brownies, or a cake or a pie, or a stack of pancakes, but they can also star as a coating for fish, lamb, or pork, punch up a pesto sauce, or impart opulence to a salad or side dish.

Furthermore, they are surprisingly healthy. Though, granted, they are high in fat, it's the good kind. In fact, macadamia-nut oil has more beneficial omega-3 fatty acid than olive oil. A daily dose of macadamia nuts can actually reduce cholesterol. They're also high in antioxidants, vitamin E, fiber, and calcium.

Truly, macadamia nuts are paradise in a shell.

Macadamia Tart with Chocolate Crust, 340

Marshmallow Peeps

Which came first, the chicken or the egg? The answer to that question is easy for Just Born, Inc., the maker of Peeps, those marshmallow chicks that signal the beginning of the Easter season. For though Peeps have been around for a long time, the company only in 1999 began making marshmallow eggs to go with them.

Peeps are the most popular nonchocolate Easter candy of all, even more popular than jelly beans. Frankly, I'm not surprised because, I must admit, I love Peeps, though this may shock some who think that Peeps are a far cry from the sort of gourmet fare a food columnist is supposed to prefer.

Certainly there's no denying that I do appreciate the more refined Cadbury eggs and Godiva chocolate bunnies. And I still miss terribly the favorite Easter candy of my childhood, the giant heavenly hash egg made by the Mavrakos Candy Company of St. Louis until it sold out some years ago to Fannie May. (Fannie May will package its heavenly hash squares in an egg-shaped box at Easter time, but that can't compare to the Mavrakos egg, filled with velvety marshmallow fluff and pecans and coated in rich milk chocolate.)

But though they may not be cultured, there's something about Peeps that makes them hard for me to resist. Maybe it's because they are such unapologetic junk food providing a sheer sugar rush. Or maybe it's because they make me nostalgic for my own childhood. (Some analysts argue that the soaring sales figures of Peeps are attributable to baby boomers trying to relive the past.)

Whatever it is, I'm not the only one. Of course, there are confirmed Peeps haters. Phillip Walsh even contends that Peeps are the "rough beast" which "slouches toward Bethlehem" described in William Butler Yeats' poem, "The Second Coming." They are made in Bethlehem, Pennsylvania, he notes. But there are at least as many who love Peeps as hate them. There are enough Peeps sold each Easter for every man, woman, and child in the United States to have at least one. Many, of course, will not get their fair share because people like me stash cartons of them away to enjoy later in the year, say, in October!

We can get away with this for two reasons. First, Peeps last forever and are practically indestructible. Recently, scientists at Emory University conducted experiments that revealed that neither freezing them in liquid nitrogen nor placing them in boiling water did much damage. And second, Peeps often improve with age. At least, a devoted legion of fans, surveys indicate about a third, think they taste better stale anyway. My daughter, for example, a Peeps patron since childhood, insists that, like fine wine, they should never be eaten before they have had a chance to age. She and others like her prefer their Peeps on the crusty side. Some even go so far as to maintain that the minimum "curing" time should be a month and that it's best to enhance the process by placing the Peeps atop a radiator or other heat source.

So there's simply no denying that, as the *Cleveland Plain Dealer* observed in a 2001 editorial, Peeps have become something of a cult candy. Peeps promoters have hatched no less than twenty unofficial websites on the Internet devoted to discussion of Peeps and their virtues. (If you use a search engine to find them, be sure to include the term "marshmallow" in your request lest you locate several "peep" sights which are not so innocent.) Even people who aren't fond of them have to acknowledge that nothing says Easter like a marshmallow Peep. As Paula Novash (who insensitively describes Peeps as looking more like wistful turkeys than chicks with their drooping beaks, beady eyes, and mushed-in faces) admitted in the *Washington Post*, "I don't really like Peeps, but the holiday feels incomplete without them."

Peeps must have something going for them, because they have been a fixture in Easter baskets, usually sticking to the grass, for nearly half a century. The company that makes them goes back even further. It was founded by Russian immigrant Samuel Born in 1910. Naming his business the Just Born company and using the motto, "A great candy isn't made, it's Just Born," he went on to invent chocolate sprinkles, hard chocolate coating for ice cream, and a machine for inserting sticks into lollipops (the Born Sucker) before he got into the Peeps business in 1953 by buying out the competitor who invented them. Born applied his ingenuity to the problem of mass-producing Peeps which originally were made by hand, squeezed out of a pastry tube one by one during a 27-hour process. Modern, trade-secret technology has trimmed that time to merely six minutes and now permits the company to manufacture Peeps at the rate of 3,500 per hour. Humans are still required to inspect the marshmallow chicks (and the more recently developed bunnies) to make sure their eyes aren't missing, crossed, or in the wrong place. Just Born's chief eye inspector (I'm not making this up) is a woman whose first name is Candy.

Over the years Peeps have become synonymous with Easter, and there's hardly anything people haven't thought of doing with them, from using them on holiday wreaths to attaching them to Easter bonnets to microwaving them for entertainment. (They swell up grotesquely.) But the best thing to do with them is to simply bite off their heads (or tails) and eat them. If you have any left after the Easter holiday and you're looking for a way to let your creativity peep through, you might try using them in the following recipes.

Marshmallows

"Last night I dreamed I ate a ten-pound marshmallow," the late Tommy Cooper used to tell his audiences. "And when I woke up, the pillow was gone."

The fez-wearing British comedian probably would not have fared very well on the marshmallow test, created by psychologists at Stanford University in the late 1960s and found to be a reliable predictor of academic success. The test gauges the extent to which children are able to delay gratification by noting whether, given a choice, they wolf down one marshmallow immediately or prefer to wait fifteen minutes if promised an extra one.

Cooper, I suspect, would have been a wolfer. And so would I. To me, what candy historian Tim Richardson aptly calls the "fabulous gooiness" of marshmallows is irresistible. (British celebrity chef Nigel Slater calls them the closest food there is to a kiss.) Easter is the nation's second-most-important candy-eating occasion, right after Halloween and well ahead of Valentine's Day, and marshmallows are the most popular nonchocolate Easter candy. We eat them at other times of the year too, of course, like in the summertime when fully 50 percent of all marshmallows sold are toasted over a fire. In May 2003, as a matter of fact, some 20,000 toasted marshmallows were used to set a record for the largest s'more ever made.

At Easter time, marshmallow treats come in a variety of forms, including marshmallow bunnies, marshmallow eggs, and, of course, marshmallow Peeps. But as good as these are, they can't hold a candle to homemade. As Sarah Carter of the *Los Angeles Times* puts it, "Handmade marshmallows have as little to do with the supermarket variety as a snow cone does with sorbet."

So what's a marshmallow aficionado to do but make his own? It's really not hard, and certainly easier these days than when a major ingredient was the namesake *Althaea officinalis*, a variety of the mallow plant called the marsh mallow because it grows in and around marshes near the sea. The root produces a mucilaginous substance that from ancient times until the middle of the 19th century was the key to marshmallows. The ancient Egyptians were the first to use the sap to flavor and thicken a honey-based candy that was the precursor to the modern variety.

Those early marshmallows, however, were really more medicine than candy. They were prescribed for colds, coughs, and sore throats. The gel from the marsh mallow plant has also been found to boost the immune system and, when applied as a poultice, to soothe cuts, scrapes, and burns.

It was the French who first thought of capitalizing on the marsh mallow plant for culinary rather than pharmaceutical purposes. They whipped up egg whites and sugar and combined it with the sap from the mallow root to create a spongy candy called *pâte de guimmauve*, their name for marshmallow. In France, marshmallows are still considered sweets sophisticated enough for adults. By the 20th century the mallow root was phased out, replaced by gelatin or imported gum.

Today, with modern ingredients, it's easy to create gourmet marshmallows like the ones that have been showing up lately on dessert plates in fashionable restaurants around the country. They're enough to make people think the Easter Bunny has been taking instruction at Le Cordon Bleu.

Mayonnaise

What do paint and mayonnaise have in common? Preferably, not much, except that both are emulsions, combinations of two liquids that do not mix.

Emulsions form due to amphiphiles, fundamental structural components of all living systems. Thus, as science writer Harold J. Morowitz points out, the microstructures of both living cells and salad dressings depend on a class of molecules every bit as important as DNA. They are central to the very origin of life. I'm not surprised, because I can't imagine life without the common emulsions used in cooking—milk, cream, butter, and especially mayonnaise.

Real mayonnaise, not Miracle Whip, has always been *de rigueur* at our house, and I've gone back to making my own ever since I paid a recent visit to the port of Mahon on the Mediterranean island of Minorca where mayonnaise originated.

Mayonnaise was invented in 1756 to celebrate the successful siege during the Seven Years War of St. Philip's Castle in Mahon by the Duc de Richelieu, who was not only an adept military leader but a gastronome as well (with a curious penchant for inviting guests to dine naked). It is hardly the only food named for a military officer or victory—Chicken Marengo, Napoleons, and Beef Wellington being just a few others. The Duke's chef, hoping to prepare a victory feast that might compare favorably with the banquets at Versailles to which the Duke was accustomed, planned on serving a sauce made of cream and eggs. But there was no cream in the kitchen, so he substituted olive oil, and in honor of the victory at Mahon christened his invention *la sauce mahonnaise.*

This is the generally accepted explanation of the origin of mayonnaise, though there are others. One theory suggests that the name is derived from the French word for stir, *manier*, since vigorous stirring is necessary to concoct real mayonnaise. Another hypothesis is that the term comes from the French word for yolk, *moyen*, egg yolks being a principal ingredient of mayonnaise. And, finally, a third posits that the name derives from yet another military figure, the Duc de Mayenne, who refused to go into battle at Arques in 1589 until he had finished his chicken salad dressed with mayonnaise, known up to that time only as cold sauce but thereafter named *mayennaise* in his memory. (He was defeated.)

Though people disagree about the origin of mayonnaise, everybody agrees there is nothing like the homemade variety. As Julee Rosso and Sheila Lukins put it, "Homemade mayonnaise is so far superior to even the best commercial product, it's a wonder they share the same name." Julia Child agrees: "The only trouble with homemade mayonnaise," she says, "is that once you've eaten your own you will never again be satisfied with anything else." As the *Joy of Cooking* notes, homemade mayonnaise is an elegant French sauce, not a mere sandwich spread.

It's too bad, then, that so many people have never tasted real mayonnaise or, worse yet, have developed a preference for the stuff that comes in a jar, a development which British food writer Elizabeth David decried, blaming commercial producers for fraudulently promoting the notion that mayonnaise is a condiment which can only be produced in a factory.

But even people who understand the difference between store-bought and homemade are often reluctant to make their own mayonnaise, either because they think it's difficult or that it's unsafe. Both fears are unfounded.

Making mayonnaise at home is actually easy, and if you use a blender or a food processor, nearly foolproof, though making it by hand produces the silkiest sauce. Besides, I always feel more like a real chef when I have a whisk in my hand. All you do is beat oil into egg yolks until everything emulsifies. The secret is to do it slowly at first, a drop at a time, until the mixture starts to thicken. Even if it separates, the intervention of a mayo clinic is unnecessary. Simply introduce another egg yolk and drizzle the separated sauce into it.

If you're worried about the safety of raw egg yolks, keep in mind that the risk is relatively slight. Only one in 30,000 eggs is tainted with salmonella. To be perfectly safe, follow a recipe that calls for whole eggs and use pasteurized liquid egg product, or use the technique advocated by the American Egg Board and combine the yolks with a little water and lemon juice, heating them to 150 degrees before adding the oil.

Ambrose Bierce called mayonnaise "one of the sauces which serve the French in place of a state religion." Try making your own to discover just how divine the real thing can be.

Homemade Mayonnaise, 224

Meringues

Perhaps you remember the 1950s horror film *The Blob*, starring Steve McQueen. In that predigital era, filmmakers could not rely on the computerized wizardry of George Lucas for their special effects. Thus, pastry chef Bill Yosses and restaurant critic Bryan Miller speculate that the menacing substance which played the title role in the movie was actually a mound of colored meringue made with several dozen egg whites.

Alas, for many cooks, meringue is almost as threatening in real life as it is in science fiction. Fearing that beating egg whites to perfect peaks is too complicated a task, they avoid it at all costs except, perhaps, when they make a lemon pie and feel they have no choice. Even then there's still the worry that tears will be shed as the meringue itself weeps. That's a shame, because meringue is one of the greatest culinary inventions of all time, and it can do a lot more than merely top a pie. Trendy chefs are even creating savory meringues flavored with peppers and serving them as a garnish to main courses.

The origin of meringue is swirled in mystery, but according to Patrick Coyle, Jr.'s *World Encyclopedia of Food*, legend has it that it was invented in 1720 by Gasparini, a Swiss pastrycook in the little town of Mehrinyghen. *The Oxford Companion to Food*, on the other hand, dismisses this account, along with the notion that the name of the substance comes from the Merovingian kings of France. Another theory is that meringue was invented by a chef in the court of the Polish King Stanislas and passed on to the French by the king's daughter. It is true that Marie Antoinette was such a fan of hard meringues that she sometimes made them herself at Versailles.

We do know that as early as the 16th century, cooks discovered that beating egg whites with a whisk made out of birch twigs would make them foam, and by the 17th century they started adding sugar to create something called "sugar puff." But the term "meringue" did not appear in print in English until 1706. Most likely the word, like many words with a similar ending, originated in Germany and was borrowed by France before being shipped to England.

Over the ensuing years, three distinct types of meringue have been developed, reflecting variations in the proportion of ingredients and in method of preparation. Perhaps the most basic is French meringue. It consists of egg whites whisked with sugar in a 2-to-1 ratio until it holds peaks. It can be baked until it's firm enough to use as a shell for fruit or ice cream or even poached to make soft puffs adrift on a sea of *crème anglaise*, a dessert called "floating islands," but it's typically used to top pies.

Next there's Italian meringue, which contains a higher proportion of sugar and is made by beating hot syrup into the whites, resulting in a more dense texture. (Usually sugar syrup is used, but maple syrup gives the meringue a whole new dimension.) It can be used to lighten a soufflé, to enrobe Baked Alaska, or to top a pie, and it's usually the basis of *dacquoise*, or baked meringue cake.

Finally, there's Swiss meringue, which is made by beating the egg whites and sugar over simmering water to create a very heavy, almost chewy meringue which is used to frost cakes. The classic seven-minute frosting is essentially a Swiss meringue.

Whichever type of meringue you make, there are some basic tips to follow for perfect results. First and foremost, the bowl in which you whip the egg whites must be immaculate. Even the slightest trace of grease or egg yolk will hinder the volume the whites can attain. For this reason, it's best not to use plastic, glass, or aluminum bowls which can easily retain fat residues, and it's a good idea to wipe the bowl with a drop or two of lemon juice before starting, just for insurance. A copper bowl works best.

Though egg whites separate more easily when chilled, they'll form more air bubbles if you let them come to room temperature before beating. Fifteen minutes should be enough to do the trick without risking bacterial infection.

Add ⅛ teaspoon of cream of tartar to each egg white before whipping for a more stable meringue, but don't add salt because it has the opposite effect.

Add sugar only after the whites reach the soft-peak stage (adding earlier will lengthen beating time), and do it slowly so the sugar can fully dissolve. Superfine sugar is preferable because it dissolves faster. You can make your own by simply whirring up regular granulated sugar in a food processor.

Start beating the whites slowly and then increase the speed. Decreasing the speed is apt to adversely affect volume.

Finally, if you want the greatest volume, use egg whites that are at least a week old because they are thinner than fresh whites and will beat more quickly. On the other hand, fresh whites will produce a more stable meringue that won't be as likely to deflate if folded into other ingredients.

Using these tactics, you'll find that mastering meringue is not all that difficult. And it's certainly worth doing because, besides providing the crowning touch to a lemon pie, meringue is the basis for three of the most spectacular desserts ever created.

First, there's Baked Alaska. Invented in the 19th century, perhaps to commemorate the U.S. purchase of what would become our 49th state, this showy dessert is elegant enough to cap off the most important of celebrations (even Spago has it on the menu), yet it is convenient and easy to make. It relies on meringue's well-known heat-insulating properties.

Second, there's Pavlova, the ethereal concoction that's as quintessential a dessert for Australians and New Zealanders as apple pie is for us. (Actually, both countries claim authorship of the dessert, but recent anthropological research has determined that New Zealand was the first to create the cake deemed as light as its namesake, the ballerina Anna Pavlova. New Zealand also holds the record for the largest Pavlova, a 45-meter one, made for a museum party.) Similar to the French Vacherin and the German schaumtorte, Pavlova too is showy yet easy to make because it's based on meringue.

Third, there's the heavenly *dacquoise*, a torte made with nutted meringue layers spread with buttercream. And as if these weren't enough, meringue can be combined with nuts, cherries, chocolate, coconut, or other ingredients and baked into cookies, appropriately called kisses. Or it can be baked and cut into chunks and used as a fondue dipper or folded into ice cream. It can be formed into decorative meringue mushrooms, baked as a pie shell, or used to provide a crunchy topping to bar cookies. The possibilities are endless.

The following recipes offer proof that, rather than an intimidating blob, meringue is a wonderful way to whip egg whites into shape.

Baked Alaska Peanut S'mores, 369
Schaumtorte, 324
Chocolate Snow Meringues, 350

Molasses

Ever been in a sticky situation? We all have. But probably none as sticky as the Great Molasses Flood, sometimes called the Molasses Massacre, which hit Boston in 1919.

The tragedy occurred when over 2 million gallons of molasses stored in a 50-foot tall tank at the Purity Distilling Company burst forth, probably as a consequence of a rapid rise in temperature from below zero one day to 40 degrees the next.

A wall of molasses estimated to be as high as 30 feet swept down Boston's Atlantic Avenue at the rate of 25–35 miles per hour, engulfing just about everything in its path. Cars were crushed, homes were toppled from their foundations, a portion of the city's elevated train line was demolished, and Boston Harbor was stained brown. As many as 150 people were injured and 21 were killed. It took six months to clean up the mess.

Additionally, I calculate that as an aftermath of the tragedy, 14 million batches of Boston baked beans, 11 million loaves of gingerbread, and over 600 million soft molasses cookies would never be made!

As this episode demonstrates, the history of molasses has not always been sweetness and light. The dark syrup also played a pivotal role in firmly establishing the slave trade in the New World. It was part of the infamous triangular trade route. Molasses would be shipped from the West Indies to New England where it would be distilled into rum. The rum would then be transported to Africa. There it would be traded for slaves who were then sent to the West Indies where they would be traded in turn for molasses and sentenced to work in the sugar plantations there. Before long, slaves were brought to the United States to work in the sugarcane fields of what is now Louisiana, where sugarcane was first established as a crop in 1751 by Jesuit priests from Santo Domingo.

The thick, brown liquid was also instrumental in abetting the American Revolution. Because France was fearful that molasses, a raw material for the distillation of rum, could jeopardize its brandy industry, it prohibited its West Indies colonies from exporting the product back to the mother country. Instead, it was shipped to the British colonies of North America where, because it was relatively cheap compared to sugar, it soon became the principal sweetener. As Margaret Guthrie, writing in *Early American Homes* magazine, observes, "Even a cursory look at early American recipes shows the extensive use of molasses." It was used in cookies, baked beans, taffy, gingerbread, and that venerable Pennsylvania Dutch specialty, shoofly pie, so named because the drops of molasses which form on its surface as it cools attract flies which, like some people, have to be chased away until the pie is ready to serve.

It didn't hurt either that rum, consumed by the typical Colonist at the rate of 4 gallons per year and thus the most significant spirit in colonial America (of the alcoholic variety anyway), can be made from molasses. In 1750, Massachusetts alone had 63 distilleries producing rum from molasses. So alluring was the syrup that the founders of the colony of Georgia offered an inducement of some 64 quarts of molasses to anyone who would settle there for a year.

It didn't take long for the British Crown, burdened with a debt from the French and Indian War, to notice this potential revenue source and slap a tax on it. The enactment of the Molasses Act of 1733, a precursor to the Sugar Act of 1764, placed a duty of 6 pence on every gallon of molasses imported to the colonies. The measure was provocative enough that John Adams called molasses "an essential ingredient in American Independence."

Not only has molasses been at times the focal point of disaster, shame, and controversy, the term is often used pejoratively to describe someone or something which is slow-moving and inefficient, as in the observation of one anonymous political pundit who noted, "Any significantly advanced bureaucracy is indistinguishable from molasses."

But despite its sweet-sour past, molasses maintained its dominance as the major sweetener in America (even being used in Cavendish brand tobacco) until after World War I when sugar prices began to fall, though as early as 1915, according to James Trager's *The Food Chronology*, U.S. per capital consumption of white granulated sugar had doubled over what it had been in the previous century, and consumption of molasses correspondingly declined.

These days molasses is used not as a general sweetener but only when its unique taste is desired. But, then, that's reason enough to use it often. In fact, you can do as the colonists did and substitute molasses for sugar in your favorite recipes for baked goods. Not only does it impart flavor, but it makes the finished product moister and helps it stay fresh longer. The general rule of thumb, according to the people who make Grandma's Molasses, is that for every cup of sugar you can substitute one cup of molasses as long as you reduce the rest of the liquid in the recipe (not counting oil) by one-third cup.

There are three grades of molasses, all of them by-products of the sugar refining process. After the sugarcane stalks are stripped of their leaves and the seedpods cut off, they are run through a mill and crushed. The juice which is squeezed out is then strained and boiled for a matter of hours. The residue that remains after crystallization is molasses. The lighter the color, the better the grade. Thus, the residue from the first boiling is light molasses; from the second, dark molasses; and from the third, the darkest of all, blackstrap molasses (identified by Gayelord Hauser in 1950 as a "wonder food"), a name derived from the Dutch word *stroop* for syrup.

We get the word "molasses" itself, by the way, from the Portuguese, who along with the Spanish began sugar production in the West having learned the agricultural techniques involved from the conquering Moors. The Portuguese word *melaco*, derived from the Latin word *mellaceus* for "honey-like," gave way to *melasus*, a term first used in 1582, according to *The Dictionary of American Food and Drink*, nearly a hundred years after Columbus brought sugarcane to the New World on his second voyage in 1493.

Ever since, to one degree or another, we have been stuck on sugar's dark and delicious derivative. If you've forgotten just how wonderful its flavor can be, try the following recipes, all oozing with the great taste of molasses.

Omelettes

Which came first, the chicken or the egg? Whatever the answer to that perennial question, surely the omelette followed not long after.

Omelettes go back to the Romans who were among the first to break the ancient taboo against eating eggs, a practice condemned in primitive times because it was seen as destroying a chicken. (Though as Samuel Butler once noted, "A hen is only an egg's way of making another egg.") Utensils for making omelettes have even been found in the ruins of Pompeii.

The first omelette recipe ever recorded was that of Apicius, the Roman epicure and glutton. His *ovemele* was a concoction of honey, eggs, and pepper, and the name may have been the derivation of the word "omelette." More likely, according to Maguelonne Toussaint-Samat in the *History of Food*, the word is a corruption of the term *lamella* meaning "a thin plate" and referring to the omelette's shape.

But Apicius was not the most famous omelette maker of all time. That title goes without question to Madame Poulard of the Hotel de la Tête d'Or on Mont-Saint-Michel. Her ethereal omelettes were renowned all over France and brought crowds of tourists to her restaurant. Ultimately, people began to conjecture as to her secret for making such extraordinary omelettes. Some speculated, for example, that she raised a breed of chickens not known in the rest of France. Others that she added foie gras to the egg mixture. And still others that her trick was using a specially made omelette pan.

Finally, as British food writer Elizabeth David tells the story, a Frenchman named M. Robert Viel wrote to Poulard in 1932, long after she had retired, and asked for her recipe. This is her reply:

> *Monsieur Viel,*
>
> *Here is the recipe for the omelette: I break some good eggs in a bowl, I beat them well, I put a good piece of butter in the pan, I throw the eggs into it, and I shake it constantly. I am happy, monsieur, if this recipe pleases you.*
>
> *Annette Poulard*

Madame Poulard's recipe confirms the assertion of *The Silver Palate Cookbook* authors Julee Rosso and Sheila Lukins that "at the bottom line, an omelet is nothing more than eggs, butter, and body English." But at the same time, it reminds us that often the simplest of dishes are the most difficult to prepare perfectly. And so it is with the omelette. Though quality ingredients are essential for a good omelette, as much as any other food I can think of, a lot depends on technique. But given a little practice, the technique for making a perfect omelette shouldn't be that daunting.

Bearing in mind Elizabeth David's dictum that "there is only one infallible recipe for the perfect omelette: your own," I recommend the procedure employed by Howard Helmer. He should know what he's doing since he's listed in the *1990 Guinness Book* as holder of the record for making the most omelettes in 30 minutes, some 427 of them using only 6 burners. In a recent issue of *Good Housekeeping* magazine, he revealed his approach.

Helmer says to heat a nonstick skillet over medium-high heat so that when a tablespoon of butter is added it melts immediately. Then pour in the egg mixture and as it begins to set at the edges, carefully push the cooked portion toward the center of the pan using an inverted pancake turner. At the same time, tilt the pan so raw egg fills any spaces. If you are using a filling, spoon it onto half of the omelette as soon as the eggs stop flowing. The egg mixture should still be moist, as it will continue cooking when removed from the pan. With pancake turner, fold omelette in half and place upside down on a plate.

Strictly speaking, this method produces what is called a folded as opposed to a classic French or rolled omelette, but I think it is just as attractive and a good deal less tricky than the latter.

Once you've got the technique down pat, consider the following tips for making the perfect omelette, taken from Narcissa G. Chamberlain's now classic little volume, *The Omelette Book*.

First, the omelette pan must have rounded sloping shoulders and must be of the proper size. If it's too small, the omelette will be too thick and difficult to cook through without making it tough. If the pan is too large, you risk producing an omelette that is too thin and dry. Chamberlain recommends a 9-inch diameter pan for a three or four egg omelette, though Helmer uses a 10-inch one for only two eggs.

Second, don't beat the eggs too long lest they become thin and toughen when cooked. Chamberlain cautions against using an egg beater, noting that 30-second's worth of beating with a fork is usually enough. Furthermore, mix the eggs with a little water to make them lighter and more tender (Helmer suggests one tablespoon per egg). Don't use milk because it has the reverse effect.

Third, don't heat the pan too quickly or let the butter get too hot. It should sizzle but not brown. And don't skimp on the butter or the omelette may stick to the pan.

And finally Chamberlain reminds us that to the other ingredients for a good omelette must be added practice and "a generous dash of self-confidence."

Keep these principles in mind the next time you try your hand at omelettes. And don't confine your omelette-making just to breakfast. An omelette makes a fine meal any time of day. In fact, in France omelettes are less likely to be found on the menu at breakfast than at lunch or dinner. Indeed, they make marvelous supper fare since they can be fixed in no time at all (many recipes take longer to read than to prepare), are a great way to use leftovers, and are eminently versatile. As Chamberlain puts it, "For the appetizing use of leftovers there is nothing to equal it. For economy in extending small luxuries to their utmost it has no peer. . . . No dish so lends itself to the inventiveness of the cook. . . ." Whip up a few omelettes and I think you'll see what she means. The following recipes are offered to egg you on.

Omelette Molière, 229
SoHo Omelette, 230
Jam Omelette, 375
Loaded Omelette, 230

Oreos

Country-western tunes are by nature plaintive, but there's no tune more mournful to me than the one Paul David Wells sings. "I'm down to my last Oreo," it goes, "playing with the cellophane." Not even "You Done Tore Out My Heart and Stomped that Sucker Flat" is more moving.

Yes, I'm addicted to Oreos. As an admitted homemade cookie snob, they're the one store-bought cookie I'll eat. (Ok, devour!) And I'm not the only one. They are, after all, America's favorite cookie and the best seller in the world. So many are sold annually, in fact, that their creme filling alone would amply cover all the wedding cakes served in the United States over the course of a year. That's even more impressive when you realize that an Oreo cookie is only 29 percent creme.

Nearly 8 billion Oreos are consumed each year, over 20 million a day. For perspective, it would take a stack of only 15,000 of them to reach the top of the Gateway Arch in St. Louis. All the Oreos sold to date stacked in a pile would reach to the moon and back—five times! No wonder Carl Icahn launched a takeover bid for Oreo's manufacturer, Nabisco, in 2000. Fortunately for those who would hate to see the company become the TWA of snack brands, smarter cookies prevailed.

The dominance of Oreos is all the more remarkable when you realize that it was not the first chocolate cookie with creme filling on the market. That distinction goes to the Hydrox Cookie. It debuted in 1908, four years before the Oreo. But its maker, Sunshine Biscuits, was no match for Nabisco's superior distribution channels and advertising budgets. Ironically, the Hydrox Cookie exists no more. It was morphed into something called Droxies when Keebler merged with Sunshine in 1996.

The Hydrox name, incidentally, was derived from abbreviations for hydrogen and oxygen, the components of water. Sunshine's founders thought water was a logical concomitant of sunshine, conveying purity. The source of the word "Oreo," on the other hand, is obscure. Even Nabisco isn't sure how it originated. One theory says the term derives from the French word for gold, "or," since the cookies initially came in gold-colored packages. Another explanation holds that since Oreos were originally hill-shaped, they were given the Greek word for mountain, "oreo." Still another hypothesis maintains that the term was created much like the cookie itself—by taking the "re" from creme and sandwiching it between two "O's" representing either the shape of the cookie or the two "O's" in chocolate.

However it got its name, the Oreo was merely one of three cookies introduced by Nabisco in 1912 to satisfy demand for English-style "biscuits." The other two, Mother Goose and Veronese, have long since disappeared, but Oreo now dominates the company's product line. In 1974, Oreo Double Stuf cookies, with twice the creme filling, debuted, followed in 1987 by Fudge Covered Oreos and in 1990 by White Fudge Covered Oreos.

Apparently unable to leave well enough alone, Nabisco also makes Oreos with colored fillings, including orange for Halloween, red and green for Christmas, and sky blue for spring. Only the color of the creme is affected, not the taste. But in 2001, Oreos with cocoa-flavored filling premiered, marking the first flavor change in the cookie's history.

For purists, only the standard version will do, and we are even set in our ways about how we eat them. Surveys indicate that 35 percent of consumers twist open their Oreos before eating them. Women are more likely to be twisters than men. Some 30 percent of consumers prefer dunking their Oreos. They are more likely to be men than women. Moreover, certain areas of the country favor one method over the other. Thus, New York, Las Vegas, and Nashville are cities where twisting is heavily practiced, whereas Chicago, Philadelphia, Buffalo, and New Orleans are cities into dunking.

By the way, dunkers can be creative. Besides the old standby of milk, they have been known to immerse their Oreos in hot chocolate, coffee, marshmallow creme, peanut butter, ice cream, whipped cream, and during the holidays, eggnog. I recommend Kahlua.

Your preferred method of eating Oreos, according to some facetious psychologists, reveals insights into your personality, a sort of culinary Rorschach test. For example, it has been suggested that dunkers obviously like to sugarcoat their experiences and may be in denial, while those who eat the whole cookie all at once are plainly carefree and reckless. As for twisters, those who break apart the cookie and eat the inside first are evidently naturally curious people who take pleasure in tearing things apart to see how they work. Of course, given the fact that they also destroy the evidence of their investigations, they may have a Machiavellian streak. On the other hand, twisters who break apart the cookie and just eat the creme filling reveal themselves to be greedy and selfish people who take what they want and throw the rest away. Twisters who break the cookie apart, discard the filling, and eat only the cookie are clearly masochists.

I doubt that even Freud would endorse such psychoanalysis, though I trust he would have agreed with me that those who don't like Oreos at all are in desperate need of therapy. One way to treat them is by using Oreos as an ingredient in other recipes. Chopped up, the cookie goes well in cheesecakes, bread pudding, parfaits, pancakes, brownies, cakes, pies, banana bread, and even other cookies, like biscotti. That's the way I like to see the cookie crumble.

Frozen Oreo White Chocolate Mousse Torte, 369

Pancakes

Archeologists have discovered evidence in tombs as old as 8,000 BC that pancakes were a significant component of the ancient Egyptian diet. And, as Maguelonne Toussaint-Samat points out in her 800-page volume, the *History of Food*, the "cakes" of the Old Testament were really pancakes. In fact, the basic pancake recipe in use today can be traced back to the Roman gourmand Apicius (who, upon realizing that he no longer could afford the lavish banquets to which he had become accustomed, committed suicide).

Though an ancient IHOP has yet to be discovered, it is clear that pancakes are one of the oldest forms of bread known to humankind. Consequently, as food writer Dorian Leigh Parker reminds us, they are steeped in tradition. As she notes, ancient cultures often celebrated the harvest with religious ceremonies associated with pancakes. For example, to Slavonic tribes, pancakes were symbolic of the sun god.

Pancake traditions are still evident today. Thus in France, the second of February is a Lenten holiday called *Chandeleurs* or Pancake Day. In England there are pancake races held on Shrove Tuesday, the day before Lent. In the Netherlands rival communities compete with each other to see which can produce the most incredible pancakes, while in Finland and Russia neighbors vie with each other in pancake-eating contests. And in Cape Girardeau, Missouri, the Lions Club annually serves thousands of pancakes on Pancake Day.

Many of us have pancake traditions of our own. At our house, for example, Sunday was always pancake day, and it was the custom for the men in the family to make them. Thus, as soon as he was able, my son was introduced to the pancake ritual, and when he went off to college, he took his dad's recipe with him.

But good pancakes require more than just a good recipe. They are as reliant on technique as any food I can think of. The proper equipment is essential too. Though you can make excellent pancakes in a skillet, I prefer a griddle, and an electric one at that, because it can be set to a precise temperature. Though some cookbooks recommend 350 degrees, I think 400 works better. Proper mixing of the batter is also crucial. It's perfectly all right if it's lumpy. In fact, it's preferable. To get a really smooth batter may require so much mixing that you end up toughening the finished product. And when it comes to flipping the pancakes, don't wait too long. They should still be wet, not dry on top when you turn them over. You'll actually be able to see them puff up.

You can practice these techniques on the following recipes which illustrate the versatility of pancakes. After all, there's not a cuisine known which doesn't have its pancake specialty, whether the crêpes of France, the *blini* of Russia, or the *palacsinta* of Hungary. And they can be eaten at any meal, from breakfast to dinner. Whatever the time of day, these are pancakes to flip over.

Papal Cuisine

Habemus Papam! Thanks to the modern mass media, at the death of John Paul II, probably never before in human history had so many people hung on those words. Consequently, as the world sat vigil for the passing of one pope and watched as a successor was chosen, almost every conceivable aspect of the papacy has been analyzed and discussed. All but one, that is. For some reason there has been scant attention paid to *La Cucina del Papa*, the Pope's Kitchen.

That's a shame, it seems to me. After all, the Apostolic See has exerted its impact on our culinary customs, and not just through its calendar of fasting days. The tradition of the Christmas Eve feast, for example, owes its existence to the 15th-century pope, Alexander VI, who had a penchant for desserts. Furthermore, legend has it that the French owe a debt to Pope Gelasius I of the 5th century for one of their national dishes, the crêpe. And Châteauneuf-du-Pape, according to some the noblest of all wines, clearly is connected to papal gourmandizing.

Granted, not every pope has been a gourmet. St. Sylvester I, the first pope to be acknowledged by the state, was a hermit given to fasting. Pope Innocent III, who first gave ecclesiastical sanction to the doctrine of transubstantiation, preached austere living and insisted that only a single dish be served at his table. Pope Sixtus IV, the architect of the inquisition, was a confirmed dieter.

But many pontiffs vowed that enjoyment at the table was not incompatible with papal duties. After all, by tradition the first thing a pope does after giving his first public blessing is to return to the conclave to share a meal with the cardinals. (According to Vatican correspondent John L. Allen, Jr., the late John Paul II uncorked the champagne himself at his first papal meal and went around the room filling everyone's glasses while singing Polish folk songs.)

In their exhaustive study of the secrets of the papal table, *Buon Appetito, Your Holiness*, culinary historians Mariangela Rinaldi and Mariangela Vicini chronicle the eating habits of some two dozen popes. Perhaps the most notorious from a gastronomic perspective was Pope Martin IV who lived in the 13th century. Nicknamed the gluttonous pope, he merits a mention in Dante's *Divine Comedy*—consigned to purgatory with other gourmands. With no small measure of understatement, Rinaldi and Vicini remark that he is "better remembered for his appetite than for his pastoral commitment."

His favorite dish was eels, a great delicacy in the Middle Ages. He had them shipped in from Lake Bolsena, whereupon they were marinated in Vernaccia wine before being roasted. Reportedly, once after devouring plate after plate of the eels to the point of discomfort, he exclaimed, "Good God, how much we must suffer for the Church of God!" Alas, his fondness for these flavorsome fish was his undoing. He died of "corpulence and indigestion" in Perugia in 1285, and in accordance with tradition, his body was washed in heated Vernaccia.

Though not as infamous as Martin, there were plenty of other epicurean popes over the years. Clement VI had 50,000 pies baked for his coronation. Leo X, who underestimated the plump Martin Luther, threw banquets consisting of twenty-five courses. Julius III appointed the great Italian cook, Bartolomeo Scappi, as his personal chef. (When Scappi catered the conclave in 1549, the food was so good the Cardinals took two months to finish their task.) Benedict XIV built Rome's first café—in the Vatican Gardens in the 18th century. Boniface IX (Pietro Tomacelli) loved *tomaselle* (liver dumplings) so much that they are said to be named after him. John XXIII, a.k.a. the "Kitchen Pope," had to have his vestments regularly altered to accommodate his ever-expanding waistline.

Truly, as Bee Wilson, writing in the *New Statesman*, notes, "The papal stomach has feasted as well as fasted." And many ate dinner as though it were their last supper.

Eggs Pope Benedict, 231

Pâte à Choux

It's the Puff Daddy of pastry. Bake it in little mounds and you have classic cream puffs or *profiteroles*, ready to be stuffed with whipped cream or ice cream. (They also make the perfect containers for escargots or, if gigantic, a Niçoise salad.) Shape it into long fingers, bake, and fill with custard and you have an éclair. Combine it with cheese, bake in a ring, and you have the hors d'oeuvre known as *gougère*. Add mashed potatoes, shape into ovals and poach, and you have *gnocchi*. Beat in puréed raw fish, cook in simmering stock, and you have the delicate French dumplings known as *quenelles*. Bake the mixture and you have fish mousse.

It's hard to believe that so many seemingly dissimilar concoctions—ranging from simple to complex and from sweet to savory—all start with the same basic dough, but they do. It's *pâte à choux* or cream-puff pastry. No wonder it's also the basis of the dessert named after the patron saint of pastry chefs, the glamorous Gâteau Saint Honoré. The dough is so versatile, you can even make a pastry cream filling out of it by adding sugar and milk.

Pâte à choux (pronounced pot-ah-shoe) is a classic French formulation that translates as "pastry for forming little cabbages" because that's what a standard cream puff resembles. Even though it is a fundamental preparation (Julia Child says that, like béchamel sauce, every cook should know how to make it), cream-puff pastry is a relatively new invention as pastries go. Whereas other pastries can be traced back to ancient times (the ancient Greeks, for instance, routinely distinguished the pastrycook from the ordinary baker), cream-puff pastry goes back only to the 16th century.

Moreover, this classic French preparation was actually invented by an Italian, Panterelli, head chef to Catherine de Medici, albeit in France where he had moved with the rest of her court upon her marriage to the Duke of Orleans. In 1540 he created the original version of the dough which he named after himself, Pâte à Panterelli. Later it would undergo some reformulation and be renamed pâte à popelini after a cake made in the shape of a woman's breast. (Those French!) Ultimately it was retitled pâte à choux because choux buns were the principal thing made from it. The recipe was finally perfected in the 19th century by the famed chef Antoine Carême.

Cream-puff pastry is essentially what is called a *panade*, a mixture of flour, water, and butter cooked together, into which are beaten whole eggs. It's the eggs that make it puff up when baked. It has no other leavening. Though it consists of flour, butter, and liquid like other pastry doughs, unlike them, pâte à choux is cooked on top of the stove before being formed and baked. It's one of the easiest pastries to make, especially with the advent of the food processor, and is practically foolproof. All you do is bring water, butter, salt, and sugar to a full boil, add flour all at once to form a ball, and beat in eggs.

Still, there are some pointers to keep in mind to ensure success when making cream-puff pastry. Rose Levy Beranbaum, the high priestess of pastry who authored *The Pie and Pastry Bible*, offers the following guidelines:

- Sift the flour after measuring to make it easier to incorporate into the liquid mixture.

- Use water rather than milk for the lightest puff because milk causes the eggs in the dough to coagulate faster.
- To make sure you have the right amount of liquid in the recipe, measure eggs by volume. Five large eggs equal one cup. Keep in mind too, as Julia Child advises, that it's better to have too little liquid than too much.
- For the most delicate cream puff, use bread flour and substitute egg whites for half the amount of eggs. Dough made this way, however, will be too delicate for large pastries.
- To encourage the pastry to puff up, spray baking sheets with water to create steam during baking.
- Lest it collapse, make sure the interior of the pastry is adequately dried out by letting it sit in the oven with the door ajar for a few minutes after baking.
- Use herb-infused oil or truffle oil in place of butter when making savory puffs for lighter texture and better flavor with no eggy taste.

Choulibiac, 287

Peaches

"An apple is an excellent thing," observed George Du Maurier, "until you have tried a peach!" He was hardly the only one to be enamored of what food historian Maguelonne Toussaint-Samat calls "the typical fruit of summer." For example, Julee Rosso and Sheila Lukins, former proprietors of Manhattan's celebrated Silver Palate gourmet food shop, claim, "A perfectly ripe peach is worth waiting for all summer long." And Alice Waters, California's apostle of utterly fresh, organic produce, goes so far as to assert, "The most perfect fruit has to be a perfect peach." Her rationale is convincing. She says about the peach, "Its texture is luscious, its aroma is intoxicating, its flavor is ravishing, and its juice runs everywhere."

No wonder peaches are among the most popular fruits in this country after apples and oranges, and no wonder that in China, where the peach originated a couple of thousand years before Christ and where wild peach trees still grow, it is revered. There it is said to offer protection from evil spirits and is the symbol of immortality. The peach tree in the Garden of Immortality, the Chinese say, is so immense that it takes a thousand men linking hands to encircle it. (Do you suppose this is where Roald Dahl got the idea for his delightful children's book *James and the Giant Peach*?)

According to legend, Xi Wang Mu, the Royal Mother, grew a peach tree in western China on whose blossoms the immortals fed. It bore fruit only once every 3,000 years. Given the stature of the peach in Chinese culture, it isn't surprising that the emperor's royal scepter, which doubled as a magic wand, was made of peach wood and that even today, Chinese brides still wear wreaths of peach blossoms to symbolize their virginity.

The Chinese, by the way, claim to have invented the espalier method, wherein trees are grown against a wall, especially for the peach tree. French legend, on the other hand, gives credit for this technique to a retired musketeer during Louis XIV's reign who, interestingly enough if you live in Cape Girardeau, Missouri, called such installations his "Girardot" walls. Whether he actually devised the method or not, the technique produced the most famous peaches of France, the internationally acclaimed Montreuil peaches grown near Paris.

Ironically, though it started out in China, the peach got its name because once it traveled to Persia, it grew so well there that it was thought to be native to that country. Alexander the Great, who took it to Greece from Persia, named it *persica* (Latin for "Persian"), a term which is still part of its scientific designation and from which its names in most other languages derive. The Romans, who called it "the Persian apple," spread it throughout Europe, and Columbus brought it to this country where by the time of the American Revolution, it grew so abundantly that it was sometimes mistakenly assumed to be native to this continent.

The peach figures not only in the legends of the Orient, but also in those of the West. Indeed, according to *The Oxford Companion to Food*, of all stone fruits (technically classified as drupes) with the possible exception of the cherry, the peach is the most celebrated in literature. Theophrastus was probably the first writer in classical antiquity to mention the peach. Pliny discussed several varieties. The Roman poet Virgil commented on the peach's silken skin. So did, much later, Emile Zola who likened the clear skin of the Montreuil peach to that of the girls of northern France, in contrast, he said, to the peaches from the Midi which were yellow and sunburned like the girls there.

Because of its plushy skin, fleshy feel, and curvaceous shape, the peach is often regarded as sensual and downright sexy. *The Oxford Companion to Food* says no other fruit is as laden with erotic metaphor. For example, quite often in literature a fruit-stealing scene represents romantic or sexual behavior, especially if peaches are involved. The French even grow a variety of peach called *Tetons de Venus* or "breasts of Venus." Perhaps that's why Renoir advised students who wanted to learn how to paint a nude woman to paint peaches first. And who knows? Maybe that's why when Escoffier wanted to honor Australian soprano Nellie Melba, he resorted to peaches. His creation, Pêches Melba, is the most famous peach dish of them all.

Despite its suggestive looks, however, a peach will not be good unless it is tree-ripened. That's because a peach will not get any sweeter once it has been picked, though it will get softer and juicier. Consequently, peaches with green undertones, the kind you are often likely to find in supermarkets these days, should be avoided. They were picked too early. Hence, as the late James Beard put it, "Your success with peaches will depend in large part on your nearness to orchards."

Peachy Keen Pie, 337

Peanut Butter

"Man cannot live by bread alone," comedian Bill Cosby once quipped. "He must have peanut butter."

The same must go for women and children too, for roughly half the peanuts consumed in North America are eaten as peanut butter. Moreover, one-third of the U.S. peanut crop goes into peanut butter, and it's on the shelf in 75 percent of American homes. Though adults actually eat more peanut butter each year than children, by the time the average child in this country graduates from high school, he or she will have eaten 1,500 peanut-butter sandwiches. No wonder peanut butter is a billion-dollar industry.

In light of these figures, it shouldn't be surprising either that thousands of people, among them Julia Child, have joined the Adult Peanut Butter Lovers' Fan Club (with headquarters in Georgia, the heart of peanut country) since it was founded about twenty years ago. Nor should it surprise us that Ruth Reichl, former restaurant critic for the *New York Times* and now editor of *Gourmet* magazine, calls the peanut-butter-and-jelly sandwich the most underrated of foods. "It's the perfect American dish," she says. "Relegating this wonderful invention to the school lunch is a terrible waste."

And it should not be a mystery why one of the hottest new restaurants in New York City is Peanut Butter & Co., where just about everything on the menu features that wonderful spread. I visited there and sampled the menu which ranges from classic and not-so-classic peanut-butter sandwiches (they'll cut the crusts off for you if you ask them) to desserts such as peanut-butter pie and even peanut-butter tiramisu. And, of course, peanut-butter cookies are perpetually available. If you like, you can wash them down with a peanut-butter-and-jelly milkshake. The restaurant grinds its own peanuts fresh every day to produce gourmet varieties such as spicy peanut butter, cinnamon-raisin peanut butter, and white-chocolate peanut butter. And when you leave, you'll find available at the cashier's counter not the ubiquitous mints or hard candies other restaurants provide, but Mary Janes, those old-fashioned chewy, peanut-butter-and-molasses taffies.

What may come as a surprise, however, is the fact that recent medical studies indicate that peanut butter, despite its high fat content, may actually be good for your heart and may even help you lose weight. *Health* magazine reports that peanut oil contains almost as much monounsaturated fat as olive oil and recounts a study conducted at Penn State in which a diet rich in monounsaturates lowered subjects' total cholesterol by 11%, their LDL (bad cholesterol) by 14%, and their triglycerides by nearly 11%. What is more, peanut butter is a good source of vitamin E and folic acid, two nutrients associated with reduced risk of heart disease. And to top it off, peanut butter contains resveratrol, the same antioxidant found in red wine. Of course, the partially hydrogenated vegetable oil in some peanut butters may mitigate these benefits, but not by much. Moreover, you can avoid the problem by sticking to old-fashioned or "natural" peanut butters which contain only peanuts and salt. *Health* magazine also reports that studies at Purdue University and at Boston's Brigham and Women's Hospital suggest that peanut butter might not necessarily make you gain weight but, by boosting the level of satisfaction and enjoyment on a diet, actually help you lose.

This good news about peanut butter, not to mention its popularity, is impressive, considering, as the Peanut Butter Lovers Club notes, that the substance started out as a protein substitute for geriatric patients who couldn't chew meat because their teeth were too bad! Though Africans used ground peanuts in their stews as early as the 15th century, and a "peanut porridge" was one of the staples of soldiers during the Civil War, it wasn't until 1890 that Dr. Ambrose W. Straub of St. Louis with the help of George A. Bayle, Jr., the owner of a food-products company, developed the first peanut butter, actually a ground peanut paste, as a nutritional supplement. Soon after, the Kellogg brothers of cereal fame began experimenting with peanut butter and actually obtained a patent for its production. (The wife of one of their employees, by the way, published the first nut cookbook.) In 1904, just a year after Dr. George Washington Carver began his research on peanuts (he found over 300 uses, including shoe polish), C. H. Sumner unveiled peanut butter to the public at his concession stand at the St. Louis World's Fair.

The real breakthrough came in 1922, however, when Joseph L. Rosefield of California developed a method for churning peanut butter which resulted in the smooth, as opposed to gritty, product we know today. Twelve years later he would create the first crunchy-style peanut butter by adding chopped peanuts to the creamy variety. (Creamy still outsells crunchy today.) Peter Pan and Skippy peanut butters, which employ Rosefield's process, are among the oldest brands on the market, though Krema Products Company of Columbus, Ohio, which began sales in 1908, is the oldest peanut butter company still in operation today. Jif, the top-selling brand made in Lexington, Kentucky, at the world's largest peanut-butter plant, is a relative newcomer, having been introduced in 1958 by Proctor and Gamble.

Clearly peanut butter's fame is still spreading. And though it is addictive right out of the jar (I've found that a Hershey bar makes a nice spoon), it can play a starring role in cakes, pies, cookies, and other desserts, and even savory dishes such as pasta and vegetables, as the following recipes demonstrate. Any of them can be a powerful antidote, should you need one, to arachibutyrophobia—fear of peanut butter sticking to the roof of your mouth.

Pepper

"The disparity between a restaurant's price and food quality," claims food critic Bryan Miller, "rises in direct proportion to the size of the pepper mill." That may be so, but the fact remains that pepper, as Plato once observed, "is small in quantity and great in virtue."

Though in the United States we tend to use pepper sparingly compared to other countries, the truth is there's hardly a food which its pungent bite does not complement. As the spice chart at the *Epicurious* website indicates, pepper goes with all salads, almost all soups (including fruit soups), all poultry, all fish, all meat, all vegetable, and almost all pasta dishes, not to mention cheese spreads, eggs, and butter sauces. I've found that it can do more for a glass of tomato juice than just about anything except a shot of vodka. As *New York Times* food writer Molly O'Neill rightly avers, "Pepper can turn the ordinary into the distinct." British newspaper columnist Josceline Dimbleby agrees, suggesting that pepper may be even more effective than salt or sugar in amplifying the taste of food.

Moreover, pepper's magic should not be limited to savory foods. For example, it is the secret ingredient in many a gingerbread recipe where it serves as a catalyst for other spices. In Italy they put it in biscotti and on fresh strawberries, in France they poach pears with it, and in India they sprinkle it on sliced oranges. At the American Restaurant in Kansas City, it's an ingredient in the caramelized topping of crème brûlée, and at the renowned La Brea Bakery in Los Angeles, they routinely put a pinch of white pepper in the holiday pumpkin pies.

With all that pepper can do for food, it's amazing that it should ever have been thought of as a way to camouflage the smell and taste of tainted meat, as it allegedly was during the Middle Ages. As it turns out, according to *The Oxford Companion to Food*, that commonly accepted notion is simply untrue. From ancient times, people have appreciated what pepper can do not to disguise flavor but to develop it. They've also employed it as a digestive, a medicine, and an aphrodisiac.

As Maguelonne Toussaint-Samat points out, relying on Sanskrit manuscripts, "The use of pepper by the peoples of India goes farther back than that of any other spice." (The word "pepper" itself comes from Sanskrit.) Before long it became the "queen of spices," sought after for more than its gastronomic credentials, a symbol of power, virility, and great wealth.

Though today pepper is cheap, throughout history it has been one of the most expensive spices. For the Romans, Pliny recorded, it was "bought by weight like gold or silver." Later, when the Visigoths conquered Rome, they demanded, in addition to gold and silver, 3,000 pounds of pepper as ransom. During the Middle Ages it was often a part of a dowry. The Ottomans used it as currency. No wonder the French have a proverb, *cher comme poivre*, "as expensive as pepper."

Not surprisingly, pepper became the most important commodity in the spice trade. Indeed, as *The Oxford Companion to Food* notes, during the 16th century the price of pepper served as a barometer for European business in general. Because of the volume sold, it is still the most valuable single commodity in the international spice trade. The largest producers are Indonesia and India (where the premium variety comes from the Malabar Coast). There's even a cartel-like community of pepper-growing countries, hearkening back to the Guild of Pepperers, one of the oldest guilds in the City of London. In 1328 they were registered as "Grossarii," the term from which the word "grocer" evolved.

Pepper's popularity ultimately changed the course of history. It was passion for pepper as much as anything else that spurred Europeans to look for trade routes to the East. Columbus was looking for pepper and, indeed, thought he had found it when he ventured into the New World. But, alas, he had unwittingly discovered chile peppers, now sometimes called "false" peppers, and the name he gave them stuck. But so-called "true" peppers belong to the genus *Piper* and are the fruit of the vine, *Piper nigrum*. They come in white, black, and green. Pink peppercorns are not truly a pepper and neither are Sichuan pepper, Melegueta pepper, Jamaican pepper or allspice, or cayenne.

Green peppercorns are picked while they are still immature and are sold either fresh or pickled in brine. Black peppercorns are picked right before they are fully ripe and are turning red. They are allowed to dry in the sun, which turns them black. White peppercorns have had their skins loosened by soaking and rubbed off. They are less powerful than black pepper and used chiefly in dishes where black specks might be unappetizing.

The most important thing to keep in mind about pepper is that it loses its punch quickly after being ground. Thus, buying ground pepper is a waste of money. To get the full impact it's essential to grind pepper right before serving. (Those pretentious waiters are on to something after all.) All kinds of devices exist for this purpose, ranging from the expensive pepper mill with a grinding mechanism made by Peugeot (the same people who went on to build French cars) and shaped like an hourglass to inexpensive plastic models that look like a tennis ball with rabbit ears. My favorite is the brass crank-top model that looks like a Middle Eastern coffee grinder. In fact, I've been so pleased with my nearly foot-high model that I've gotten a smaller one to grind salt. Whichever model you use, you'll find that what freshly ground pepper does for food is nothing to sneeze at.

Tuna Steak Au Poivre, 286

Pesto

"If the definition of poetry allowed that it could be composed with the products of the field as well as with words," Marcella Hazan observes, "pesto would be in every anthology." And, to continue the analogy, I could be a poet laureate. That's because at our house we make and freeze prodigious amounts of pesto to keep up with our bumper crops of basil.

Pesto is the Italian sauce made chiefly from basil, garlic, cheese, and olive oil, the first batch of which, as Rosso and Lukins remark in the *Silver Palate Cookbook*, officially welcomes summer back to the kitchen. But more importantly, pesto, made in large batches and frozen, is a practical way to preserve the essence of basil, a fragile herb, and, in effect, to extend the season.

Though freezing is a modern practice, pesto itself is centuries old. The first known recipe is found in Virgil. The sauce originated in the Italian region of Liguria. A narrow strip of land between the sea and the inland mountains, it's the location of the seaport of Genoa, hometown of the region's native hero, Christopher Columbus. The late Waverly Root called this area a shrine of Italian cooking because in addition to being the nurturing place of pesto, it also gave birth to minestrone and ravioli.

As Anna Del Conte notes in her massive *Gastronomy of Italy*, the region's temperate climate and the sea air have made Liguria the site of one of the most delectable vegetable gardens in all of Europe. Consequently, the Genoese people of the region have always taken pride in employing local produce in their cooking. But, argued Root, it takes more than pride in the local bounty to explain why indigenous herbs like basil figure so prominently in Genoese cuisine.

Because the Genoese so identified themselves with their role as traders, their society developed a deferential attitude toward money. This led them to view the priceless spices of the East, the transportation and selling of which made them wealthy, primarily as merchandise to be traded for gold, not as valuable in their own right. Thus, in contrast to the Venetians, they did not hold back part of their precious spice cargo for their own cooking, but sold it all and relied instead on the herbal bounty of their hills to give character to their diet. As Marchese Giuseppe Gavotti, former chancellor and national secretary of the Italian Academy of Cooking near Genoa, confirms, "Genoese cooking seldom uses spices, only herbs, and a great variety of them." Thus, pesto is essentially the culinary result of Ligurian fiscal policy.

Moreover, as Del Conte observes, pesto is the supreme example of another Ligurian principle. This one maintains that gastronomic excellence requires the perfect balance between one flavor and another, a concept which Del Conte refers to as "just rightness." Though pesto is fundamentally among the simplest of sauces, she notes, the right ingredients in proper proportions are crucial to its success.

With such attitudes well ingrained in the local consciousness, it is not surprising that the Genoese are punctilious about pesto. They've even created an organization, the Knights of the Pesto Brotherhood, to maintain standards and hold the line against mass-produced versions which, the organization contends, threaten to discredit the credibility of Ligurian cooking. The Brotherhood confers its seal of approval, a registered trademark bearing the words *Vero Tipico Pesto Genovese* ("True Typical Genoa Pesto"), only on pesto made in the classic fashion with specified ingredients, to wit, "the traditional ones used by our grandmothers."

Needless to say, members of the order are scandalized by trendy versions of pesto such as sun-dried-tomato pesto, macadamia-nut pesto, cilantro pesto, black-bean pesto, and peanut pesto, to name a few. They would surely disagree with executive chef Bruce McMillian who says, "You can make pesto out of anything."

But even when it comes to classic pesto made from basil, the Genoese are persnickety. They insist that authentic sauce can only be made with the small-leafed basil of their native region. Other varieties, like those grown in this country or in Asia, just won't do. Earlier this year they lodged a complaint with the European Commission, alleging that certain brands of packaged pesto using Vietnamese basil are essentially fakes.

Ligurian cooks further maintain, with religious conviction, that proper pesto can only be made with a mortar and pestle. (The name of the concoction, after all, comes from the Italian word *pestare*, meaning "to pound or bruise," and is a reference to the pestle itself.) They are skeptical that a blender, food processor, or even the mezzaluna, the implement of choice in neighboring Tuscany, can produce pesto with the right texture or flavor.

Some of this "pestomania" is probably well advised. Occasionally recipes, like one I saw for coconut pesto, are just too outlandish. Then, too, minty, large-leafed American basil isn't quite the same as that which grows in Liguria. And there's no question that machine-made pesto can't match the flavor, color, or consistency of that made by hand.

But in the final analysis, I think Hazan has the right attitude. She submits, "Pesto is such an inspired invention that it survives almost anything. . . ." So savor the taste of homegrown basil, add whatever else you wish to your pesto, and by all means make it in a food processor or blender (preferably the latter) in big batches to be frozen (another modern technique probably frowned upon by die-hard Italians). This winter when you use the glorious condiment on pasta, in soups, on sandwiches, on potatoes, over fish or chicken, on pizzas, or in hundreds of other dishes, one taste is all it will take to maintain a clear conscience.

Pesto, 221

Picnics

Though Southeast Missouri's muggy summer climate may occasionally test it, I've always held the conviction that there is something special about alfresco dining where, as Jean Anthelme Brillat-Savarin, one of the high priests of gastronomy, put it, the universe is your drawing room and the sun your lamp. Perhaps it's because the great outdoors enhances the appetite and produces, as Brillat-Savarin observed, "a vivacity unknown indoors."

Whatever the reason, I don't think I've ever been to a picnic I didn't enjoy, even if the affair ended in rain, as was the case when we picnicked with our son at Boreas Pass over 10,000 feet above sea level in the Rocky Mountains of Breckenridge, Colorado. It makes perfect sense to me that Webster's defines a picnic as "a pleasure outing at which a meal is eaten outdoors," but notes that the word has become slang for any pleasant experience. The word "picnic" to me has always connoted celebration, even when there was really nothing in particular to celebrate—other than the fact, of course, that the weather has changed sufficiently to permit outdoor dining in the first place.

A good picnic doesn't have to be elaborate or fancy to be successful, though as Julia Child has argued, a little luxury can make a lot of difference. "Paper plates and plastic forks have their place," she says, "in a brown bag. At a real picnic I like real cutlery. . . ." No wonder that the best picnic she ever heard of, as she reveals in her cookbook, *Julia Child & More Company*, was the one given by the Duke of Suffolk during World War II. The Duke and his squad were returning to London after a trip to one of the Channel ports to defuse some bombs following a Nazi air raid. Unbeknownst to the men, the road took them near Suffolk's country home. Suddenly, as Child tells the story, the Duke signaled the convoy to halt. "He then blew a whistle and lo, out from behind a hedge purred his Rolls Royce, laden with hampers, crystal, silver, damask, and a butler who unpacked and served a noble feast."

It would be hard to top such a scene, I'm sure, but in my experience, downscale outings can be just as memorable. Probably my favorite picnic was a relatively modest affair consisting only of crusty French bread, pâté, and wine, but the setting made all the difference. My companions and I sat on a log in the woods adjacent to Chenonceau, one of the great French châteaus in the Loire Valley. At that point I grasped fully what Sander Wolf must have had in mind when he said, "It's never been the food that makes the picnic; it's always been the attitude."

Still, the food is important. It must be able to travel well, resist spoilage outdoors, and be relatively easy to eat, perhaps even out of hand. But most importantly, as with any meal, it ought to taste good. The following recipes, I believe, meet all of these criteria and should serve you well whether your picnic is elaborate and carefully planned or simple and impromptu, and whether your destination is the riverfront, a meadow, a park, or your own backyard.

Pie

Rose Levy Beranbaum, in her best-selling book, *The Pie and Pastry Bible*, says, "There are two kinds of people: cake people and pie people." Though I have never been known to turn down a piece of chocolate layer cake, I know which category I belong in. I'm a pie person.

I'll eat pie any time of day, including breakfast (a common practice in Colonial times), and at one Cape Girardeau, Missouri, restaurant, they know my proclivity for pie so well they bring me a slice along with the menu the moment I sit down. (When it comes to pie I have always followed the sage advice, "Life is uncertain, eat dessert first.")

So for a pie lover like me, serving as a judge at the National Pie Championship was akin to being appointed to the Supreme Court for a lawyer or being elected to the College of Cardinals for a priest.

The National Pie Championship was sponsored by The American Pie Council, an organization which says it is "dedicated to preserving America's love affair with pies," and took place in Boulder, Colorado, the weekend of January 23, 2000, which is National Pie Day. There were nearly 200 entries from around the country, spanning both the amateur (or homemade) and commercial categories.

It's only fitting that such an event take place in celebration of the virtues of pie, because pie truly is the quintessential American dessert. The late James Beard, in his book *American Cookery*, tells us that apple pie has been so common in this country that many old American cookbooks did not even think it necessary to provide a recipe. It was assumed that every housewife had her own. Surveys show that apple is still the nation's most popular pie.

Surely part of pie's appeal is that it takes us back to those simpler days when people had more time to bake. Pies conjure up images of warm treats from the oven cooling on the windowsill in grandmother's kitchen. They are pure comfort food.

Unlike cakes, pies are never fussy, never ostentatious. This is not to say they aren't at home in even the most elegant of surroundings. For example, apple pie has been on the menu at Spago, Wolfgang Puck's fashionable restaurant in Los Angeles, ever since it opened in 1982 and because of the demand has never been taken off.

But there's something innately homespun about pies, even fancy ones. Cakes are aristocratic. Pies, at best, are *nouveau riche*. Even the word "pie" itself reminds us of its humble origins. According to the *Los Angeles Times*, the word derives from the name of the magpie, a bird noted for its disorderly nest. Similarly, pie fillings, especially in early times, were haphazard creations.

The simplicity inherent in a pie, of course, is one of the reasons why pie making has a longer tradition than cake baking. Baking cakes in the home is a rather contemporary development, depending as it does on fairly exact measurements and reasonably precise oven temperatures. Pies, on the other hand, are not so demanding, as I discovered to my delight some years ago when strolling on the beach at Yelapa, a little cove near Puerto Vallarta. There, genial Mexican ladies greet you, their aprons laden with some of the most wonderful pies imaginable, made using only an outdoor fire and relatively primitive utensils.

Though pies are rather basic, there is one element of them that does pose a culinary challenge: the crust. As Pat Willard, author of a delightful collection of stories and recipes called *Pie Every Day*, observes, "If pies could be made without crusts, more people would bake them." She points out that centuries ago, people were not so picky about their pie crusts because crusts originally served as cooking pots and were often nearly as hard. But with the passage of time, our standards have risen and what we now think of as the proper pie crust is something our ancestors would have made only on special occasions. This, Willard says, has left contemporary homemakers in a bind. Though they are less practiced in the art of pastry-making than their ancestors, their expectations when they do attempt to make pie crust are higher.

So while pies are essentially modest creations, we would do well to heed the advice of the wit who said, "Simple cooking cannot be trusted to a simple cook." The truth of this maxim became clear to me as I completed my judging assignment at the National Pie Championship.

The day of the contest my alarm went off at 7 AM, but, brimming with anticipation, I had already been awake for over an hour. As I left my hotel room and headed for the contest center, the aroma of freshly baked pies greeted me. My pulse quickened.

Salivating, I checked in at the judging table and received a form asking me to list my flavor preferences. This was not easy, for there isn't a pie I don't like. After some contemplation I cleverly listed the "other" category as my favorite, hoping that rather than having to taste dozens of one flavor of pie, I would be treated to a variety. And sure enough, I ended up sampling rhubarb, key lime, chocolate, mixed berry, apple cranberry, and even sweet potato pie.

I was given a code number and escorted to my judging table where I met my fellow critics. I soon realized that these were people who loved pie nearly as much as I do. For example, Beth, the judge sitting opposite me, as a contestant the previous year had awakened at 3 AM, baked her pie, and then took it on a plane from her home in Wisconsin to the contest site. She and her mother, she told me, had once baked 200 pies in a single day!

The contest began. I was in the commercial division where each pie was coded either standard, premium, or gourmet. All the pies in one category were brought to our table and carefully sliced one by one. After the first slice had been removed, the remaining pie was held up lovingly so we could see if it was too firm or runny. Appearance counted for 25 percent of the score.

Then each judge was given a slice to taste and asked to record his or her impressions as to flavor, mouthfeel, aftertaste, and overall appeal or memorability. Of course, we used a fresh plate and fork every time and cleared our palates with crackers between bites. It was only after the ninth slice that I realized that the other judges at my table were merely taking a bite or two of each pie while I instead was eating the entire slice. They were clearly less committed to the enterprise than I, but I resisted reprimanding them for their obvious lack of dedication.

Two hours and fifteen pies later, the task was finished. I tallied my score sheets, turned them in, and waited for the winners to be announced while glancing furtively at the pies I didn't get to try. We judges were surprisingly uniform in our ratings, and the pie I had picked as my favorite did, indeed, win.

Later that evening I went to dinner with a group of friends. They laughed as the waitress brought the dessert menu at the end of the meal. Surely I wouldn't be in the mood for dessert, they said. But there it was, right at the top of the menu. Banana cream pie with whipped cream and almond toffee bits. How could I resist? I was already in training for next year's contest.

Maple Pecan Pie, 334
Mississippi Mud Pie, 334
Savannah Banana Pie, 330

Pizza

As Burton Anderson in *Treasures of the Italian Table* has observed, "If Naples had managed to patent the pizza, it would now be among Italy's wealthiest cities instead of one of its poorest." He is doubtless correct.

You can now find pizza anywhere in the world. In India they top it with minced mutton; in Japan they favor eel and squid; in Russia, red herring; in Brazil, green peas; in Costa Rica, coconut; in Australia, shrimp; and in this country, of course, a wide variety of toppings bound together with tomato sauce. In fact, there was a time in the United States if a pizza did not contain tomato sauce, by law you could not label it pizza. (Such a regulation would dumbfound the crowds at Forno Campo de' Fiori, a little hole-in-the-wall in the heart of Rome where I recently discovered what is reputed to be the best *pizza bianca*, "white pizza," in the city.)

Yes, pizza is big around the world, especially in America, where it's a $30 billion a year industry. We eat an average of 46 slices per person per year, which works out to about 100 acres of pizza eaten every day. From 1998 to 2003, the demand for pizza has grown faster than for any other food item. As P. J. O'Rourke wryly notes, if everything in life were determined by majority rule, we'd have pizza for every meal.

Given such demand, there's a lot of dough to be made in pizza. For example, in 1951, Rose and James Totino borrowed $1,500 from a Minneapolis bank (after she baked a pizza for the loan officer) and launched a frozen pizza business that later would be acquired by Pillsbury for $22 million. Rose became Pillsbury's first woman vice president.

Similarly, in 1958, Dan and Frank Carney, after reading about the popularity of pizza among college students, borrowed $600 from their mother and went into business in Wichita, Kansas. Today the Pizza Hut chain is the largest purveyor of pizza in the world, with annual sales in the billions.

Likewise, in 1961, Thomas Monaghan borrowed $500 to purchase a pizzeria in Detroit that would soon revolutionize the pizza-delivery business. His Domino's Pizza is now the world leader in delivery with billions of dollars in annual sales at more than 5,000 stores in 46 international markets.

Then in 1982, pizza went gourmet when Wolfgang Puck, the third-most-famous Austrian after Mozart and Arnold Schwarzenegger, opened a restaurant on a shoe-string (hence, the name Spago, which means "string") in Los Angeles. One day when an order of first-rate smoked salmon arrived and the restaurant was out of bread, he created a smoked-salmon pizza and transformed the dish from hot to *haute*.

It is too bad for Naples that none of these entrepreneurs had to pay royalties, for they all capitalized on an idea that was born in that city. Though pizza's ancestry can be traced back to ancient times (Virgil refers to something like it in his *Aeneid*), the world's first true pizzeria, Antica Pizzeria Port Alba, opened in Naples in 1830 with ovens lined with lava from Mount Vesuvius and is still in business today. But even before that, street vendors with small tin stoves on their heads peddled pizza through-out the city, and poor Neapolitan housewives made *casa de nanza*, thin dough topped, as often as not, with leftovers. By the late 18th century, Queen Maria Carolina, wife of the King of Naples, Fernando I, had pizza ovens installed in her summer palace.

The archetype of modern pizza was invented in Naples in 1889, when Raffaele Esposito, the most popular *pizzaioli* (pizza chef) of the day, created a pizza in honor of the visit to the city by the King of Italy and his wife Queen Margherita. Using tomatoes, basil, and a new ingredient, mozzarella cheese, it bore the colors of the Italian flag—red, white, and green. The queen loved it, and Pizza Margherita became the international standard, establishing Naples as the pizza capital of the world.

Neapolitans still take their pizza seriously. They've formed the Associazione Verace Pizza Napoletana to maintain standards and have persuaded the Italian government to grant Neapolitan pizza the same protected status given Chianti. Members, whose houses display the image of Punch from Neapolitan comedy brandishing a pizza peel or paddle, vow to make pizza dough only with flour, yeast, and water, shape it by hand without a rolling pin, and cook it on the floor of a wood-burning oven, not in a pan—just the way it was made over a hundred years ago.

So perhaps Naples should be getting a commission from pizza makers around the world. Certainly during October, which is National Pizza Month, we should stop to say thanks to the city that created what has always been for Italians, and is now for the rest of us, the slice of life.

Prima Donna Pizza, 264

Plum Pudding

Christmas is the time of year when security scanners at British airports are overworked. That's because they cannot differentiate between terrorist weapons and that staple of the English Christmas dinner, plum pudding.

Plum puddings have what officials refer to as "unusual density," just the thing security monitors are designed to detect. Consequently, during the holiday season, hundreds of British travelers heading off with puddings packed in their suitcases are stopped to have their luggage searched.

The inconvenience, it seems to me, is a small price to pay for this concoction which has become virtually synonymous with Christmas. In fact, *The Oxford Companion to Food* contains no entry for plum pudding, but an entire article on the subject under the heading "Christmas Pudding." The first recorded use of that term, by the way, was in an Anthony Trollope novel published in 1858, not in Dickens' *A Christmas Carol*, written fifteen years earlier. Clearly, however, Dickens was thinking of the same thing when he had Bob Cratchit observe that the plum pudding served at the family's holiday dinner was "the greatest success achieved by Mrs. Cratchit since their marriage."

Though Dickens is responsible for shaping our current perceptions of what Christmas celebrations should be, the Christmas or plum pudding goes back much further than his era.

Plum pudding is descended from an ancient dish called plum pottage, a combination of chopped beef or mutton, root vegetables, and dried fruit, thickened with breadcrumbs and flavored with wine and spices, probably cooked in a sheep's stomach or some similar container. (The invention of the pudding cloth would come later.) One story suggests it was introduced to England by a conquering Danish king in the 10th century. Another claims it was served at the coronation of William the Conqueror.

Given its ingredients, plum pottage was usually served at the beginning of a meal, but over the years its composition changed. Meat and vegetables were left out in favor of more dried fruit, and it came to be the dessert we know today. Traces of its origins can still be found in the beef suet called for in traditional recipes for plum pudding and the token carrot specified even in many contemporary recipes. As new forms of dried fruit were introduced to England, they came to supplant the plums in plum pudding even though the term "plum" remained. Some authorities claim that true plum pudding never contained plums, but in any case, most modern recipes do not. Additionally, plum pudding is more akin to cake than pudding. (The British call most any dessert a pudding.) Indeed, fruitcake is a direct derivative.

The first recipe for modern plum pudding appeared in *Le Viander*, among the earliest works printed by Gutenberg. It was written by Taillevent, personal cook to King Charles V, who prepared plum pudding for the royal Christmas party in 1375 in response to the King's request for a "new and exciting sweet course." Thus were added two more ironies to a dessert already rich in culinary contradictions. Not really pudding and usually devoid of plums, the quintessential English Christmas dessert was perfected by a Frenchman born of Jewish parents.

But despite an attempt by Oliver Cromwell to ban it, the British have made plum pudding their signature holiday dish and devised a variety of related traditions to bolster its status as the ultimate Yuletide sweet. For example, one custom involves baking tiny good-luck charms into the pudding. Another is the practice of having every member of the house participate in the stirring of the pudding while making a wish. Stirring must always be done counterclockwise, the direction of the Magi's journey. And, finally, the pudding is typically adorned with a sprig of holly and brought to the table flaming.

In 1748 a Swedish visitor to England remarked, "The art of cooking as practised by Englishmen does not extend much beyond roast beef and plum pudding." That's no longer true, but even so, during the holiday season, who would want anything more?

Last Minute Christmas Pudding, 366
Cranberry, Orange, and White Chocolate Christmas Pudding, 367

Potatoes

Ireland was the first European country where the potato became a major food source, a fact which would ultimately have tragic repercussions in the form of the devastating Irish potato famine. That event, according to Mary Robinson, former President of Ireland, "more than any others shaped us as a people."

It's not certain just who introduced the potato to Ireland (some suggest it was Walter Raleigh, others that it simply washed up on Irish shores following the shipwreck of the Spanish Armada), but it caught on quickly, more quickly than anywhere else in Europe. This was because, more so than other European countries of the time, around 1600, Ireland was struggling to grow enough food to feed its people, and the potato promised more food per acre than any other crop. Moreover, the potato offered another advantage to Ireland, which was often torn by war during this time period. Growing hidden underground, the potato was not as often a casualty of war as other crops and livestock were. English colonization of Ireland further intensified dependence on the potato as a food source by forcing exportation of cash crops such as corn.

Thus, by the 1800s, some parts of Ireland were entirely dependent on the potato for food. Indeed, it was so abundant that it figured prominently in Ireland's tremendous population growth. By 1840, thanks in no small part to the potato, the country's population had grown to 8 million, nearly triple what it had been before the introduction of the tuber, leading some to speculate that a potato-rich diet increases fertility and that the potato is an aphrodisiac.

But beneficial though it may have been in the short term, the potato-dependent economy of Ireland eventually reaped a bitter harvest. In 1845, the fungus *Phytophthora infestans*, the potato blight, destroyed nearly half of the nation's crop and wiped it out entirely the following year. Then came "Black '47" and, incredibly, things got even worse. Black rot covered acre upon acre of Irish farmland and the people, so long reliant on the potato crop, no longer possessed the agricultural skills to save themselves. They could not pay their rent and were evicted, often ending up in overcrowded poorhouses. They ate the rotten produce and entire villages were overtaken by disease. As many as a million citizens left the Emerald Isle, making the Irish people their country's greatest export. Many did not survive the trip. In fact, conditions on the immigrant vessels were so bad that they were nicknamed "coffin ships." In the final analysis, the famine shrunk the nation's population by a million and a half. In the process, it also profoundly influenced the social and cultural structure of Ireland and, through immigration, the history of our own country as well. In fact, the impact on America is judged so vital in some states, New York for example, that the law requires that all public school children study the Irish potato famine.

Despite the experience of the famine, the Irish fondness for potatoes endures. As cookbook author Matthew Drennan writes about his native Ireland, "One thing that remains constant, wherever you go, is the potato. It is to the Irish people what pasta is to the Italians." No wonder an old Irish adage has it that there are two things too serious to joke about: marriage and potatoes. And though the Irish might well claim the potato as their national vegetable (the white potato is commonly referred to as the Irish potato), they are not alone in their admiration of the sensational spud. We Americans love them too. In the United States, one out of every three meals contains a potato. The average person in this country eats well over 100 pounds of them per year, broken down as follows: about 50 pounds fresh, another 60 pounds frozen, usually as French fries (Thomas Jefferson, by the way, is credited with introducing French fries to America by serving them at the White House), some 13 pounds dehydrated (instant potato flakes, for example), almost 2 pounds canned, and 17 pounds as potato chips. In fact, potatoes are so popular in this country that they are grown in all 50 states. Idaho, of course, is the most well known, but Maine, whose potato industry is over 240 years old and during the first half of this century produced more potatoes than any other state in the nation, is trying to change that by marketing its crop of uniform-sized tubers as the "other" potato. The potato is still Maine's number one agricultural commodity.

As deeply rooted as our appetite for potatoes is, Europeans eat even more. The typical German, for example, eats twice as many potatoes as the typical American. Europe is still the largest per capita consumer of potatoes, but there is hardly a country where they are not grown. As Dr. Robert Rhoades of the International Potato Center, appropriately headquartered in Lima, Peru, where the ancient Incas were the first people to grow and eat the potato, points out, "Cultures that may have very little else in common share the cultivation of potatoes." Its adaptability, a feature noted by Charles Darwin during his voyage on the HMS *Beagle*, allows it to grow in a wide variety of climates. This has helped to make it the world's fourth most important food crop, eaten by more than a billion people and arguably, as noted food critic Jeffrey Steingarten suggests, "the most important vegetable in the world."

This is quite an achievement for a plant which was virtually unknown to the Old World until 1532, when Spanish conquistadors came across it in the Andean Mountains of Peru. (Columbus had earlier encountered yams and sweet potatoes, but not the white potato, which is from a different botanical family.) Ironically, this vegetable, which when combined with milk supplies nearly every element required for a healthy diet, was initially greeted with suspicion if not downright fear. Because it was classified as a member of the poisonous nightshade family, it was thought to be toxic. It was even reputed to cause leprosy. At best it was thought fit only for pigs.

Today, thanks to the pioneering work of people like Antoine-Augustin Parmentier (whose name is still affixed to most any French potato dish), Luther Burbank, and Gary Johnston (inventor of the Yukon Gold), we can readily agree with the 18th-century dramatist Mercier that the potato has had "the greatest influence on Man, his liberty and his happiness." And here are some tips to keep it that way: avoid light-exposed green potatoes (even on St. Patrick's Day), do not refrigerate potatoes lest their starch turn to sugar, whenever possible cook potatoes with the skin on to preserve all their nutrients, never mash potatoes with a food processor as it makes them gummy (a ricer is the preferred tool), and finally, never bake a potato in aluminum foil because it seals in moisture, steaming the potato and making it pasty.

Keep these guidelines in mind as you prepare the following recipes, all designed to illustrate how foolish the 18th-century English garden designer Stephen Switzer was when he said potatoes were "a food fit only for Irishmen and clowns."

Lemon Roasted Potatoes, 297
Colcannon, 296
Chocolate Orange Potato Pound Cake, 309

Pumpkin Pie

I once saw Martha Stewart making pumpkin soufflés on television. They make a good alternative, she said, to pumpkin pie. They looked great, but I couldn't help wonder who in their right mind wants an alternative to pumpkin pie on Thanksgiving Day! Pumpkin pie, after all, is as American as the holiday itself.

Though Europeans knew nothing of them until Columbus dropped by, pumpkins have been a staple of this hemisphere for centuries. Evidence of them dating back as far as 7000 BC has been discovered in burial caves in Mexico.

Once colonists settled this country, pumpkin, out of necessity, became an important part of their diet. It was served at the first Thanksgiving feast in 1621. After a poor harvest of other crops the next year, Governor William Bradford ordered the Pilgrims to grow more pumpkins, and the rest, as they say, is history.

The first pumpkin pies were self-contained affairs. The top would be sliced off a pumpkin, the seeds scooped out, and the cavity filled with milk, spices, and molasses or maple sugar. Then the top was replaced and the whole thing was baked until the milk was absorbed.

Initially, however, according to food historian Charles Perry of the *Los Angeles Times*, pumpkin pie was not as highly esteemed as apple, pear, or quince pie. It was not until the 19th century, he says, that pumpkin pie and Thanksgiving became synonymous as a result of the influence of home economist Sara Josepha Hale who preached the virtues of homey food for the holiday. Moreover, the identification of mince pie and plum pudding with Great Britain enhanced the popularity of the all-American pumpkin-filled pastry.

So today it just wouldn't be Thanksgiving without pumpkin pie. But, of course, not all pumpkin pies are created equal. And on our most significant holiday, from a culinary perspective anyway, who wants to serve less than the very best version imaginable? So, as a public service to readers, I went in search of the perfect pumpkin pie. This mission, which I undertook with typical selflessness, required me to personally try about a dozen pumpkin-pie recipes culled from the hundreds in my files. Yes, it was arduous and exhausting work, but I figure somebody had to do it. After conscientious investigation, sometimes requiring me to consume not one but several slices of a given pie and mounds of whipped cream, I herewith offer what I believe to be the top recipes.

First, some background as to my methodology. Any recipe with the word "chiffon" appearing in the title was immediately rejected. There is a place for light foods like chiffon pie, but surely it is not at the Thanksgiving table. Furthermore, any recipes relying on instant pudding, Cool Whip, or related convenience foods were likewise rejected. Such products make good pies, but in my judgment they are not the real thing. That's why at our house, Cool Whip, along with margarine, has long been banned from the holiday table.

There is one convenience food which I did use, however, and that is canned pumpkin, despite the controversy surrounding it. Some purists claim you should cut up a pumpkin and make your own pumpkin purée. In fact, after *Gourmet* Magazine published an encomium to the canned product last year, an outraged reader from New Hampshire, who claims to spend entire afternoons processing her own pumpkins, wrote in to chastise the publication. "I would have expected such an article in a magazine aimed at saving working women time and guilt," she complained, "not in a gourmet magazine."

But if you take her approach, you should know that the pumpkin you find at the local supermarket, while fine for jack-o'-lanterns, is not well suited for cooking. It will produce a watery, stringy, and not particularly flavorful product. If you insist on cooking your own purée from scratch, you'll need to find a sugar pumpkin.

In truth, what is sold in cans as pumpkin typically comes from something hardly recognizable in color or shape as a pumpkin. Libby's, for example, fills its cans with a hybridized version of the Dickinson pumpkin selectively bred for texture, color, and flavor, and trademarked as the Libby's Select.

If you balk at using canned pumpkin, you might try winter squash instead. As part of my investigations, I substituted winter squash for pumpkin in my standard recipe, though even there I used frozen purée instead of making my own. The result was wonderful. Some people might even prefer the delicate taste. But I still favor canned pumpkin. After all, introduced in 1929 by Libby's, it's what most of us grew up on. And no less an authority than Rose Levy Beranbaum, author of *The Pie and Pastry Bible*, maintains, "Canned pumpkin purée is more consistent in flavor and texture than homemade."

Before presenting the recipes, here are some general tips drawn from my experiments. First, to avoid the perennial problem of soggy crusts, heat both the filling and the crust before assembling and bake on the lowest rack or even the floor of the oven. It also helps, as recommended by Beranbaum, to press a layer of gingersnap crumbs onto the bottom of the crust before baking.

Second, don't overpower the pumpkin flavor with additional ingredients. (Some recipes specify light brown instead of dark brown sugar for this very reason.) I found the chocolate pumpkin pie dense, smooth, and delicious, but I couldn't quite taste the pumpkin. Similarly, a version with black walnuts on the bottom and another with peanut butter blended into the filling were tasty, but with an eclipsed pumpkin flavor. Two additions which did work well were a half-cup of chopped candied ginger and, surprisingly, a quarter teaspoon of black pepper. The latter, the brainchild of *Ladies Home Journal*, provided a delightful kick. The former, suggested by Fifi's Kitchen on the Internet, simply involved scattering the ginger over the top of the filling and allowing it to sink during baking. It was superior to a version topped with a ginger streusel.

Finally, don't overbake the pie, or the filling will get coarse and watery. Lush ingredients also make a difference. Just by looking, I could practically distinguish between a pie made with heavy cream and one made with evaporated milk. Don't stray too far from the traditional either. For example, the frosty pumpkin pie made with ice cream was delicious but not as satisfying as conventional versions.

Now for the recipes that emerged as my favorites following a week of rigorous trials during which contracting apocolocynposis (fear of turning into a pumpkin) was a real possibility. To be honest, after all is said and done, it's still hard to beat the version on the Libby's label, but the following recipes are worthy competitors.

Quinoa

Every great ancient civilization produced a crop or a commodity which was central to its existence. For the Greeks it was wine and for the Romans it was wheat. A few thousand years from now anthropologists may look back at us and think it was the Big Mac. But whatever the case, for the Incas of South America it was a grain called quinoa (pronounced keen-wah).

Quinoa, of course, is not nearly as well known as wine or wheat, let alone the hamburger. And that's a shame. Once you sample its nutty taste, as I did on a sojourn to Peru, and realize that it comes closer than any other vegetable or animal to providing all the essential nutrients for living, you'll understand why it was considered sacred by the western hemisphere's greatest empire.

The Incan Empire, according to legend, was founded in the 12th century by Manco Capac, the son of the sun, who, along with his brothers and sisters, arose from Lake Titicaca and set out looking for the earth's navel. He established his capital there in the city of Cuzco, Peru, and by the time Columbus set sail, the Incan kingdom, inhabited by more than 6 million people, was the largest state in the New World.

The Incas are best known for their engineering feats (they built thousands of miles of roads through daunting terrain and diverse climates) and their architecture, but they were no slouches when it came to food production either. They were among the earliest peoples to develop agriculture, building intricate terraces on the Andes mountainsides to increase harvests. They probably invented peanut butter and perhaps even freeze-drying too. Because they were able to produce enough food not only for themselves but also for the tribes they conquered, they were able to subjugate dozens of different ethnic groups throughout South America.

Incan cuisine revolved around three major ingredients—corn, potatoes, and quinoa—but quinoa was clearly the most important. It was listed ahead of potatoes in a 16th-century inventory and, moreover, it can grow where corn never could, thriving at altitudes as high as 13,000 feet on as little as 2 inches of rainfall. It's also frost-resistant. No wonder the Incas called it "*chisiya mama*," the "mother grain." Packed in gold urns, it was offered to the sun god Inti.

Each year the Incan emperor planted the first quinoa seeds of the season using a gold spade, but archeological evidence from prehistoric tombs suggests the seed was a crucial part of the Andean diet long before the Incas built their empire, at least since 3000 BC. It may actually have been domesticated as early as 2,000 years before that.

Those ancient people knew what they were doing, for nutritionally quinoa is something of a "supergrain," though technically it's not a grain at all, that is, not a cultivated grass, but the botanical fruit of an herb plant, *Chenopodium quinoa*, a distant relative of spinach (with similar green leaves). It has three times as much calcium and twice as much phosphorous as wheat plus a higher proportion of essential amino acids and more iron than many other cereals. It contains as much as 50 percent more protein than most other grains. In fact, The World Health Organization rates the quality of protein in quinoa as equivalent to that in milk. Not surprisingly, NASA has considered its use in longer duration space flights. Perhaps quinoa explains why the Incas were reputed to live to 100 or 120 years of age.

Though not genuinely a grain, quinoa is essentially treated as one in cooking. Looking like a cross between sesame seed and millet, it can be substituted for just about any grain, including rice and couscous. And it can be used in all kinds of dishes including desserts. It makes a great variation, for example, on rice pudding. In the Andes they use it in soups and stews and in breads. A traditional dish is made by boiling it in water laced with llama fat. It goes well in salads and it makes an excellent pilaf, especially with dried fruit, nuts, herbs, or cheese. In Cuzco they make a drink out of it, adding corn, rice, cinnamon, anise, cloves, and sugar. In the past it has even been used as an ingredient in beer.

Quinoa couldn't be easier to cook. The process is the same as for making rice, except quinoa cooks in only half the time and expands to four times its original volume. Toasting quinoa in a dry skillet for five minutes before cooking adds to the flavor. It's essential that quinoa be thoroughly rinsed before cooking to rid it of any residue of saponin, a bitter coating that protects it from birds and insects and from the sun at high altitudes. It may be that the Spaniards did not realize this and therefore never saw in quinoa the potential they saw in corn and potatoes, even though they were well aware of the grain. Because quinoa has a higher fat content than other grains, it is more perishable, so it's wise to store it in the refrigerator. Bring it to room temperature before cooking.

While there are dozens of varieties of quinoa, there are essentially five basic types, categorized by where they grow, from the interandean valleys high above sea level to the salt flats of Bolivia. Most of it is imported from South America, but some is now being cultivated on the slopes of the Colorado Rockies. It's readily available at health-food stores and in some supermarkets. If you've never eaten quinoa, you ought to give it a try. One taste and I think you'll agree that, to put it in Quechua, the official language of the Inca Empire, quinoa is *sumaq mihuna*, "good food"!

Nutty Quinoa Salad, 234

Romantic Dinners

They say the way to a man's heart is through his stomach. I don't know how true that is, but I do know that if my wife is going to whisper something soft and sweet in my ear, I'd just as soon she say "lemon meringue pie."

Food and romance, of course, are inextricably connected and probably have been since the beginning of time. Each Valentine's Day we're reminded of that fundamental connection, an association underscored in the old French proverb that without bread and wine, love is nothing. No wonder cookbooks still outsell sex books.

Valentine's Day itself has culinary roots. It can be traced back to a pagan feast held in honor of the Roman god of fertility, Lupercus. The festival took place in mid-February and featured a lottery designed to find mates for unattached individuals. In 496 AD, Pope Gelasius, attempting to morally upgrade the celebration, replaced it with a day of tribute to the martyred Bishop Valentine, creator of the phrase "From your Valentine."

Today the interaction of palate and passion lives on in the modern custom of sharing an intimate and romantic meal with a significant other on Valentine's Day, a ritual which in its hopefulness and occasional desperation, food writer John DeMers suggests, is really just a grown-up version of exchanging valentines in grade school.

What makes a meal romantic? If you're not sure, there are plenty of books on the market to advise you. One, by Ellen and Michael Albertson, even includes detailed instructions for what is termed "an edible orgy." Others, such as the aptly titled *50 Ways to Feed Your Lover* and *A Taste for Love*, merely offer recipes, menus, and decorating ideas. Perhaps the most intriguing is Debbie and Stephen Cornwell's *Cooking in the Nude*. I trust none of the recipes in it call for a waffle iron or a veg-o-matic.

The truth of the matter is you don't need to be a cross between Dr. Ruth and Julia Child, or read a book by someone who claims to be, to know what makes a meal romantic. Intuitively we all realize that it probably depends more on the magic between two people than on any magic in the kitchen. Thus, a bowl of ice cream and a single spoon can be as idyllic as a five-course meal at the fanciest restaurant.

Still, there are some basic principles to consider if you want to make a Valentine's Day meal especially sensual, and premier restaurateurs in Cape Girardeau, Missouri, know what they are.

For example, restauranteur Jeri Wyman says that on Valentine's Day the main dining room of The Royal N'Orleans, perhaps the most beautiful in the city, glows with anticipation. The staff is eager not to disappoint, even if it means occasionally fulfilling unusual requests—like the one from the gentleman who for thirty years has been bringing in Twinkies (yes, Twinkies) and asking that they be served for dessert. For most other diners, Wyman says, nothing symbolizes Valentine's Day better than chocolate.

Mike Risch, who with Chef Matt Tygett used to run Mollie's Restaurant, suggests that some foods, like seafood, shellfish, and sushi, are more romantic than others. "Steak can be sultry," he adds. After all, red meat goes with red wine, which itself is romantic. Furthermore, the tannin in red wine can make you pucker.

James and Pat Allen of Celebrations know that the right dining environment is important. During their first year in business, one couple got engaged over a meal served in a secluded private room at the restaurant. They come back every year to commemorate their anniversary—at the same table in the same room.

The stately Rose Bed Inn, where innkeeper Eldon Nattier and Chef James Coley hold forth, has likewise been the scene of romantic encounters from the very start. Its first paying guests were honeymooners from Arkansas, reunited after losing track of each other following high school.

Coley, who maintains that a little intrigue is an essential ingredient to a romantic meal, serves luxurious Basil Chicken Wellington on Valentine's Day, just the thing to overcome inhibitions, as it did with one young man recently who insisted on proposing to his sweetheart on bended knee and in full view of the rest of the diners. Her tearful acceptance of his overtures—and five carat ring—sparked applause all around.

When it comes to romantic meals, of course, the Inn has at least one advantage over other dining venues: it's a bed and breakfast establishment, so if things go well at dinner, there are rooms upstairs where dessert, of one kind or another, can be taken.

Basil Chicken Wellington, 272

Sacher Torte

The Hotel Sacher, on the corner of Philharmonikerstrasse and Karntnerstrasse in the heart of Vienna, is so well known for its namesake chocolate dessert, the Sacher torte—perhaps the most famous cake in the world—that once some years ago a telegram from an American that was addressed simply to "Hotel Chocolate Cake, Vienna" was dutifully and without delay delivered to the place.

But the hotel's claim to be the sole purveyor of the "original" Sacher torte has not always gone unchallenged. Indeed, it took a seven-year court battle, dubbed the Sweet Seven Years War, to determine just who had the rights to this most Viennese of all cakes.

It all started back in 1832 when Austria's Prince Metternich ordered his personal chef to create a new dessert for an upcoming bash. Alas, the chef took ill and had to turn the request over to his apprentice, a sixteen-year-old named Franz Sacher. The cake he created would ultimately establish his name alongside that of Johann Strauss as a Viennese icon. Embellished with apricot preserves and glossy chocolate frosting, it was a complete success.

Catapulted to fame, Sacher was hired by the royal bakery to the emperor, now Demel's, where his torte became the best seller. Years later his grandson would open the Hotel Sacher and continue the torte tradition there.

Thus it came to pass that two different establishments, in what is arguably the torte-making capital of the world, each allegedly produced the genuine Sacher torte. Inevitably, they wound up in litigation.

The case occupied the front pages of Austria's newspapers for almost a decade and went all the way to the Supreme Court. It ultimately rested on the question of where the apricot preserves were put in the cakes. The Sacher slices its cake and puts a layer in the middle. Demel's does not. Determining that Franz Sacher's earliest recipe called for a split layer, the court awarded the hotel that still bears his name the right to adorn its product with a round chocolate seal proclaiming it as the "original."

But though the lawsuit is settled, the question remains: which of the two versions of the torte is superior? As a service to readers, I journeyed to Vienna to find out. After carefully controlled, repeated samplings at each of the pastry palaces in question, I've concluded that the court got it right. With its extra apricot filling, the hotel's version is moister. Its chocolate glaze was a bit thicker and richer too. And most decisively, unlike Demel's, the hotel routinely serves the torte with whipped cream. Case closed!

Sacher Torte, 319

Sandwiches

Whatever else he accomplished, John Montagu will go down in culinary history for what he did at London's Beef Steak Club above the Covent Garden Theatre one night in 1762. Having spent twenty-four straight hours at the gaming table without a meal, Montagu directed an underling to bring him some slices of cold roast beef and cheese between two slices of bread so that he could eat with one hand free to continue gambling. And ever since, a combination of bread and filling has carried Montagu's name, for he was the Fourth Earl of Sandwich.

The sandwich is one of the greatest culinary inventions of all time, so I think Montagu, despite his excesses, is a man worth honoring, indeed, a truly heroic Sandwich. But the truth is that long before he gave the sandwich its name, people were stuffing bread with fillings and eating it. For example, for over 2,000 years, Jews at Passover have symbolically arranged herbs, nuts, and apples between slices of matzo. Likewise, the Arab practice of packing meat into pita bread goes back centuries. Similarly, the French say that prior to Montagu's concoction, it was already common practice for field workers in their country to take with them meat or fish layered between slices of black bread. Moreover, as the *Joy of Cooking* notes, nearly every culture has its version of the sandwich, which includes, among others, the burritos of Mexico and the calzones of Italy. But though we may never know who the very first person was to eat what we now call a sandwich, the concept caught on and certain formulations have become classics.

The French Dip is a sandwich that is dipped into pan juices. Its name derives not from the fact that it is of French origin, which it decidedly is not, but from the fact that it was invented by a Frenchman, is served on a French roll, and was first eaten by a man whose last name was French. Legend has it that the first French dip sandwich was concocted by Philippe Mathieu, a French immigrant, at his Los Angeles restaurant in 1918 when he accidentally dropped a sandwich into a pan of juices as he served Officer French, a policeman. The officer said he'd eat it anyway and liked it so much he returned the next day with friends who also wanted to try it. Today the sandwich is still the signature dish at Philippe's Restaurant where you can have one that is either single or double dipped.

The Croque Monsieur really is of French origin, being a staple of many a Parisian café. Sort of an *haute cuisine* version of a grilled-cheese sandwich, it is a package of ham, cheese, and bread which is toasted or grilled. A Monte Cristo substitutes chicken for ham and is dipped in egg before grilling while a Croque Madame has an egg cooked into a hole cut out of the top of the sandwich.

A Reuben sandwich consists of corned beef, Swiss cheese, and sauerkraut on rye bread, typically slathered with Russian or Thousand Island dressing and grilled. Its origin is equally slathered with controversy. The *Joy of Cooking* credits its invention to a New York delicatessen owner, Arthur Reuben, who supposedly created the sandwich in 1914 for one of Charlie Chaplin's leading ladies. But since his sandwich utilized cole slaw instead of sauerkraut and Virginia ham instead of corned beef, I'd say the honors should go to Reuben Kulakofsky, a wholesale grocer, who is said to have devised the sandwich during a late-night poker game at the Blackstone Hotel in Omaha around 1925.

A Club sandwich is a three-decker affair of meat, bacon, lettuce, and tomato on toast typically cut into triangles. *The Oxford Companion to Food* hypothesizes that the sandwich might have originally been only a two-decker version named after the two-decker "club" cars on U.S. railroads at the turn of the century, but the *Joy of Cooking* suggests that the sandwich may actually have been invented at the Saratoga Club of Saratoga Springs, New York, around the same time.

Perhaps the Hero sandwich is my favorite because by definition it is huge. It goes by several aliases, including grinder, hoagie, poor boy, bomber, wedge, zep, torpedo, and submarine. The last term is either a reference to the shape of the oblong bread typically used or homage to a famed version served by a Connecticut deli near a submarine base. Almost anything can go into a hero as long as it is heaped on. In this regard it is similar to another favorite sandwich of mine, the Dagwood, which uses slices of bread from a conventional square loaf. This precursor to super-sizing was named, of course, after the famous comic-strip character.

Then there's New Orleans Muffuletta with its special olive salad topping, the Hot Brown from Kentucky's Brown Hotel, the Peanut Butter and Jelly sandwich (the object of a 1999 lawsuit by Smucker's), the Cheese Steak sandwich invented in South Philadelphia, the Denver sandwich (which is really an omelette on a bun), New England's Lobster Roll, and the BLT, not to mention the hamburger and the hot dog.

But perhaps the best sandwich is the one you invent yourself. For that's the beauty of this inspired creation which can serve as breakfast, lunch, or dinner—and even dessert. (What's a Napoleon, after all, but a sandwich?) The only limit to the contents of a sandwich is your imagination.

Muffuletta, 261

Serendipitous Culinary Accidents

Horace Walpole coined the term "serendipity" to refer to the talent for making desirable discoveries by accident, a talent possessed by the heroes of a fairy tale called "The Three Princes of Serendip." I don't know if the princes were good cooks, but fortuity often plays a significant role in the culinary world.

Consider, for example, pink lemonade. In her account of circus life and legends, Linda Granfield points out the reason the drink is so often associated with the big top: it was invented there.

The first batch of the stuff was concocted by the manager of a circus lemonade stand who, having run out of water, in desperation seized on a bucketful he came across in the dressing area of the bareback rider. The fact that the water was slightly pink, owing to the fact that a pair of red tights had been rinsed out in it, did not stop the enterprising mixologist. His new drink quickly sold out and soon pink lemonade became the "drink of circuses."

That story demonstrates that not only is necessity often the mother of invention but that many an invention is merely an accident encountering a receptive mind. Indeed, even if you discount Charles Lamb's satirical version of the discovery of roast pork, it's clear that the history of food is replete with such occurrences.

Not a few classic concoctions were the result of culinary misadventure. Perhaps the most elegant is puff pastry. It was invented in 1654 by a French pastrycook apprentice who forgot to add butter to a batch of dough and attempted to correct his mistake by folding lumps of butter into the dough after the fact. Imagine his surprise when the dough was baked and the butter's moisture produced steam which lifted the pastry into distinct layers.

Similarly, another emblem of haute cuisine, Crêpes Suzette, was first created by accident, according to Henri Charpentier. He claimed to have stumbled upon the classic dessert preparation while a young chef at the Café de Paris in Monte Carlo in 1895 as he was putting together an intricate sauce for crêpes. When the cordials he was using accidentally caught fire, the startled Charpentier quickly plunged the crêpes into the boiling liquid. When he served the dish to his patron, the Prince of Wales, it was a hit, and he named it after the Prince's dining companion at the time, Suzette.

Not all serendipitous culinary discoveries, of course, are French or particularly sophisticated. That All-American treat, the brownie, is a case in point. Though the origin of the bars is uncertain, everyone seems to agree they were not created on purpose. One legend has it that brownies were invented by a clumsy baker who dropped a chocolate cake. Most food historians, however, theorize that the first brownie was the result of someone forgetting to put baking powder in cake batter that might have already been overloaded with chocolate, butter, and sugar. Either way, brownies were a happy mishap.

Perhaps the greatest culinary accident of all time, at least to my mind, was the one that took place in 1933 at Whitman, Massachusetts. It was then and there that Ruth Wakefield, proprietor of the Toll House Inn, prepared a batch of her basic butter cookies and added some chopped semisweet chocolate, expecting it to melt into the batter while in the oven. It didn't. Instead the chocolate morsels retained their shape and the chocolate-chip cookie was born.

America's favorite snack food was likewise invented unintentionally, in fact, out of a fit of pique. It happened in the summer of 1853 at the Moon Lake Lodge in Saratoga Springs, New York. A dinner guest at the lodge, rumored to be Cornelius Vanderbilt, complained about the French fries he had been served. They were too thick, so he sent them back. The chef, George Crum, prepared a second batch, more thinly cut. These too were rejected. Finally, in exasperation, Crum determined to hoist the picky diner on his own petard by preparing a batch of fries cut unappetizingly paper-thin. But to his surprise, the patron loved the browned, crispy, heavily salted fries and before long, potato chips became all the rage.

Other serendipitous culinary creations include popsicles (invented by an eleven-year-old boy who mistakenly left a container of flavored soda water, with the stirring stick still in it, on the back porch in freezing weather), fudge (probably the result of a botched batch of caramel or toffee), the ice cream cone (created spontaneously at the St. Louis World's Fair when an ice-cream merchant who had run out of dishes used Persian waffles from a neighboring stand as a substitute), the French Dip sandwich (originated by a French lunch-counter worker who carelessly dropped a sandwich into a pan of juices just prior to serving it), Worcestershire sauce (the product of chance fermentation lasting several months), the Parker House roll (which came by its unique shape when a baker, angered by a quarrel with his sweetheart, threw pieces of dough into a pan, clenching each one in his fist as he did so), and St. Louis gooey butter cake (the consequence of adding the wrong proportions of ingredients to a cake batter).

In light of all these successful failures, I'm already beginning to salivate at the thought of the next culinary accident just waiting to happen.

Crêpes Suzette, 377

Shakespearean Food

"Does not our lives consist of the four elements?" Sir Toby Belch inquires in Act II, Scene 3 of William Shakespeare's *Twelfth Night*. His drinking companion, Sir Andrew Aguecheek replies, "Faith, so they say, but I think it rather consists of eating and drinking." "Thou art a scholar," Sir Toby responds, "let us therefore eat and drink."

Though others may select the balcony scene in *Romeo and Juliet*, Hamlet's soliloquy, or Bottom's transformation in *A Midsummer Night's Dream* as their favorite Shakespearean episode, this one is clearly mine. And there's reason to believe it might have been a favorite of the Bard himself, for, as Caroline Spurgeon concludes in her study of Shakespeare's imagery, he had a discriminating palate. "His interest in and acute observation of cooking operations are very marked all through his work," she maintains.

Dr. Jennie Cooper confirms that Shakespeare was mindful of the central role which food plays in the human experience. She fell in love with history's most popular playwright at the age of fourteen after seeing a production of *Hamlet* in Paducah, Kentucky, and taught courses in Shakespeare at Southeast Missouri State University for nearly forty years. Facetiously she says about the Bard, "He must have been hungry when he wrote those plays because he mentions food so often." Madge Lorwin, author of *Dining with William Shakespeare*, agrees. She says, "Shakespeare makes frequent and effective use of cooks and cooking, eating and drinking. In fact," she goes on, "there is not a play in which he has not woven some scene around food or drink."

It is perhaps no accident then, as Dr. Donald Schulte observes, that the most famous speech in dramatic literature ("All the World's a Stage") is given at a banquet. Schulte is also a lifelong fan of the plays of Stratford's most famous citizen, having appeared in many of them. Shakespeare, like any good writer, Schulte notes, relies on everyday rituals that allow the audience to identify with the action of the play, and meals are among the most familiar of rituals.

Thus, in *Troilus and Cressida*, Shakespeare describes the steps involved in bread making. In *All's Well That Ends Well*, he reveals his knowledge of pie baking (with Parolles' exclamation, "If ye pinch me like a pastry, I can say no more"). And in twenty-six of his thirty-seven plays he mentions wine, as often as not through Falstaff.

Spurgeon's analysis reveals that though food images are fairly constant throughout Shakespeare's works, their character changes considerably over time. In the earlier plays, she points out, food images are relatively crude and simple, dealing mostly with subjects such as hunger, feasting, fasting, and drinking. In the later plays, food images become more sophisticated. For example, in *Troilus and Cressida*, Shakespeare refers to a dozen different cooking processes.

This shouldn't be surprising, because just as Shakespeare was revolutionizing the English language, there was a corresponding metamorphosis going on in the kitchens of his era. Increased trade brought exotic new foods to England, the printing press allowed publication of recipes, and a growing middle class sharpened the appetite for good cuisine.

Still, the culinary scene in Elizabethan England was a far cry from today. There was no refrigeration, so meat was salted, smoked, or pickled. Roasting was done on a spit in front of an open fire. The kitchen floor was usually made of stone and sometimes the fire would be made directly on it. Wild game, obviously, was a bigger part of the diet than it is today, but cereals were a pivotal part of virtually everyone's menu. As Lorwin points out, "The greater part of England's folk rarely tasted a piece of roast beef." The typical worker's diet consisted of butter, milk, cheese, beans, and peas. Bread was hung from the ceiling to keep it out of the reach of rats and mice. There was no chocolate. Tomatoes were strictly ornamental. Baking powder had not yet been invented, so baked goods were of a coarser texture than today. Apple pie, on the other hand, was as popular then as now.

Lacking light bulbs, people went to bed early, and got up early and their meal hours were adjusted accordingly. Supper might consist of simply bread, cheese, and beer, or possibly porridge or eggs. The main meal of the day was usually taken around noon. Generally, breakfast was not served. The primary eating utensils were a spoon, a knife, and your fingers. Forks would not come into widespread use, not even among the wealthiest of families, until much later, being popularized in England in 1611 by Thomas Coryate, who initially was the object of ridicule for using them. Because clothing was expensive and not easy to clean, napkins were used in even the most humble homes. Women usually put them on their laps while men wore them folded over their shoulder. Removing food from between the teeth was an acceptable practice at the table as long as it was done with a toothpick or similar implement and not a knife. Wooden tableware was in common use, having replaced the hard slabs of bread that people previously had used for plates. Drinking mugs were typically made of waxed leather. Usually there were not enough drinking glasses to go around, so they were kept on a separate serving table and rinsed with each use.

Though feasts, particularly among the upper classes, could be lavish, lasting for hours and involving as many as fifty dishes (you were only expected to eat the ones you liked, not all of them), it's clear that dining is more pleasurable today than in Elizabethan times. Still, you might wish to go back in time with the following recipes. Not only would they complement a night of Shakespeare at the theatre, they remind us that the Bard should be honored not just for his soul but for his stomach as well.

Roast Cornish Hens with Gooseberries, 279
Sweet Potatoes with Apples, 298
Othello Petits Fours, 318

St. Louis World's Fair Foods

It was larger than Disney's Magic Kingdom. It housed over 1,500 buildings, including eleven "palaces," one alone of which required nine miles of walking to see all its displays. Among its 70,000 exhibits were the world's largest pipe organ, a giant birdcage housing every species in the nation, and the Liberty Bell, shipped in from Philadelphia for the occasion.

The St. Louis World's Fair of 1904 was the largest and arguably most impressive of them all. And this was as true from a culinary standpoint as any other. The fair offered 130 places to eat, including a restaurant that seated 5,000, another perched 150 feet above ground on a Ferris wheel, another where diners could watch a re-enactment of the Boer War, and still another that catered to people suffering from indigestion (Mrs. MacMurphy's Restaurant for Dyspeptics).

Perhaps the most popular attraction was "The Pike" (where we get the phrase "coming down the pike"), a mile-long strip of cafés, restaurants, and other concessions. As the *St. Louis Globe-Democrat* noted, it was both possible and proper to eat continuously from the time the fair gates opened until the time they closed.

Pamela J. Vaccaro, author of *Beyond the Ice Cream Cone: The Whole Scoop on Food at the 1904 World's Fair*, notes that food was important to the Fair from its first to its last days. As she points out, the very inception of the Fair occurred in the context of eating, when Fair President David R. Francis first proposed the idea over lunch with his colleagues in the St. Louis Business Men's League. Moreover, securing the resources needed to put on the Fair required thoroughly wining and dining supporters.

Food was not only plentiful at the Fair (Brazil, for example, brewed 5,000 complimentary cups of coffee every day), but many exhibits revolved around it as well. Baker's Chocolate built a replica of its factory inside the Agriculture Building, the makers of Log Cabin Syrup constructed an actual log cabin filled with thousands of cans of its product, the State of Missouri displayed a 3,000-pound round of cream cheese, and California showed off a 10-foot tall bear made of California prunes—14,265 of them to be exact. There was even a bust of President Theodore Roosevelt carved from butter and a depiction of Lot's wife carved, appropriately, from a solid block of Louisiana rock salt.

The Fair's greatest culinary claim to fame, however, was its alleged introduction of many foods still enjoyed today, among them the hamburger, the hot dog, the club sandwich, peanut butter, iced tea, Dr. Pepper, flavored coffee, puffed rice, cotton candy, the popsicle, and, most famous of all, the ice-cream cone.

Some of these claims are clearly erroneous. Hot dogs, for example, had previously been a hit at the 1893 Columbian Exposition; iced tea was already on the menu in turn-of-the-century Pullman dining cars; though making its world debut at the Fair, Dr. Pepper had been concocted some thirteen years earlier; and peanut butter, though invented in St. Louis, was being sold there as early as 1890. Though hamburgers and club sandwiches were certainly popular at the Fair, their origins are unclear.

But what about the ice-cream cone? Though the government had formerly issued a patent for a flat-bottomed edible ice-cream container in 1903, legend has it that the conical version was invented at the Fair when an ice-cream vendor ran out of dishes and substituted rolled waffles from a nearby waffle stand. Alas, there is wide disagreement about who should get credit for that inspiration, as there were some fifty ice-cream stands and over a dozen waffle sellers at the Fair. Perhaps the ice-cream cone was merely a culinary accident waiting to happen. There is little question, however, that it happened at the St. Louis World's Fair and became perhaps the greatest of its many delicious legacies.

St. Louis Frozen Custard, 370

Cajeta (Goat-Milk Caramel), page 362

Blackberry Sorbet, page 368

Cheesecake Essamplaire, page 312

Sangria Jell-O Salad, page 240

Sopa de Nopales (Cactus Soup), page 249

Last Minute Christmas Pudding, page 366

Chocolate Fondue, page 374

Fudge, page 360–361

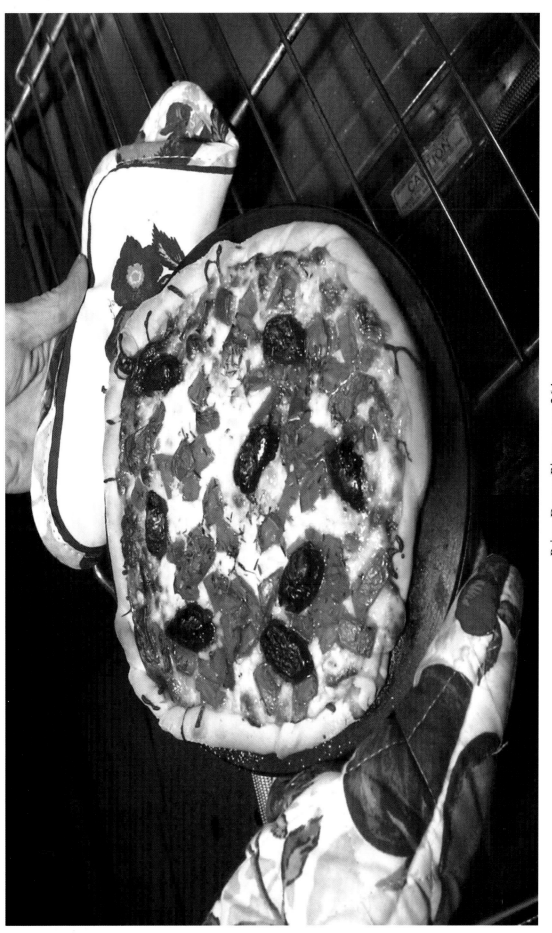

Prima Donna Pizza, page 264

Byzantine Sugarplums, page 364

Grilled Corn on the Cob with Cheese & Lime, page 292

Honeycomb, page 362

Grits Milanese, page 293

Lucky Lettuce Wraps, page 271

Flower Confetti Salad, page 234

Sacher Torte, page 319

Strange Foods

"He was a bold man who first swallowed an oyster," observed Jonathan Swift. He was right. But the first person to eat an artichoke was probably no less intrepid.

That's because our taste for most foods is acquired. Through a process of trial and error, we bravely eat something for the first time and then wait to see what happens.

Of course, some of us exhibit more culinary courage than others. Indeed, some will blithely nibble not only what is new to them but what no one else before them ever thought to taste. But most of us won't. That's because, as one anthropologist has put it, food prejudices are the most difficult of all acquired characteristics to change, along with religion and grammar. It really is true that one person's meat is often another's poison.

This notion that what one diner might consider disgusting another might simply consider supper was driven home to me when I perused *Strange Foods* by Jerry Hopkins, one of the most fascinating books I've ever read, even if it doesn't contain many recipes, and the ones it does contain (like jellyfish salad and stir-fried bat) I'm not especially eager to try.

As Hopkins points out, "Through history and around the world, what is eaten has varied greatly from time to time and place to place, from one culture to another." Part of the reason for this is simply circumstance. If you don't live near a desert, you're not likely to think of making cactus jelly. If you're landlocked, you might never develop an appreciation for filet of fish. If you've never seen a chicken, you're unlikely to wonder what one tastes like, let alone try scrambling eggs. (Which did humans eat first, I wonder, the chicken or the egg?)

But circumstance alone cannot account for everything. Otherwise we'd have a history of eating raw fish as they do in Japan, and the Japanese would not have waited until the middle of the 19th century, under the influence of the West, to start eating meat. Often religion is a critical factor. In India, for example, the steer is sacred, but here the hamburger is hallowed. Sometimes social standing makes a difference. Thus, the Beverly Hillbillies' penchant for possum marked them as lower class despite their newfound wealth.

At least one person, Ray Bruman, who maintains a website devoted to "weird and disgusting foods," suggests that our culinary preferences are not accidental or subconsciously determined but downright deliberate and perhaps a little perverse. "I have a theory," he says, "that many (all?) cultures invent a food that is weird or disgusting to non-initiates as a sort of a 'marker.' The kids start out hating it, but at some point they cross over and perpetuate it (perpetrate it) on the next generation. Then they nudge each other when foreigners gasp."

Whatever the reason for what Hopkins calls the "gastronomical gap" between one group and another, the late M.F.K. Fisher argued convincingly that it amounts to little more than prejudice. "Why," she asked, "is it worse, in the end, to see an animal's head cooked and prepared for our pleasure than a thigh or a tail or a rib?" She went on to assert, "People who feel that a lamb's cheek is gross and vulgar when a chop is not are like the medieval philosophers who argued about such hair-splitting problems as how many angels could dance on the head of a pin."

Clearly, most of us are rather prejudiced in our food habits, judging by the variety of things which are consumed by others around the world. The castaways on the television show *Survivor* may have thought they were both brave and desperate to eat a rat, but the truth is, as Hopkins points out, "rats, mice, and other members of the rodent family have a long, palatable history. . . ." In Ancient Rome, for instance, dormice were caged and fed nuts to plump them up before being served to the emperor. As Hopkins observes, "Through history, humans have eaten virtually everything that walked, including each other."

Thus, though most Americans find it horrifying, records indicate that dogs have been eaten as least since the time of Confucius. About 500 BC, American Indians such as the Arapahoe (whose name means "dog-eater") preferred puppies for their tenderness. Among the more revolting stories I remember is one told by a student who innocently ate a dish at a restaurant in Greece only to hear, upon leaving the establishment, a man beckon his dog with the same word the student had used to order his meal.

Similarly, horsemeat, a food we consider fit only for dogs, is seen as a delicacy in France where there are no less than fourteen retail horsemeat butchers still doing business. Indeed, some historians contend that horses were used as a food source long before they were domesticated as beasts of burden. The French like rabbit too, and though it now shows up routinely on menus at fashionable U.S. restaurants, many Americans recoil at the thought of eating bunnies, unless they're made of chocolate. Not surprisingly, zebra, a close relative of the horse, has been consumed for centuries in Africa. (You can purchase zebra on the hoof, by the way, at the Garrett ranch in Springfield, Missouri.) Likewise, water buffalo and yak have graced dining tables in various parts of the world, and bison was once the primary food in the American West.

In the West they also like snake meat, especially rattlesnake, and it's hard to find a restaurant in that part of the country that doesn't have it on the menu. But, according to Hopkins, it is cobra that is preferred by connoisseurs. In Guangzhou, near Hong Kong, they bring the cobra to the table and wash it in a tub of water. Then a hole is cut in its stomach allowing the heart to pop out into a dish where it continues beating. The snake blood is drained into a glass and mixed with wine made from fermented snake corpses. The heart is then added to the glass and the concoction is offered to the customer as an appetizer. And I thought tableside preparation of cherries jubilee at The Royal N'Orleans was spellbinding!

Not only snakes but iguana, alligator, crocodile, frog (not just the legs but the entire thing), snails, and even slugs are considered delicacies by some. Snails, of course, are considerably more upscale than slugs, and they may have been among the first animals ever eaten by man. As Hopkins posits, that may be because they aren't that hard to catch. Worms, grasshoppers, beetles, crickets, butterflies, and other such critters have also been known to make some people salivate. Thus, in Columbia and Venezuela, sales of beef plunge when the mopane caterpillar is in season.

Perhaps even more astonishing than the variety of species which are routinely consumed in other countries are the parts of them that are regularly cooked and devoured. Just as hog butchers claim they use every part of the pig but the "oink," there isn't any part of an animal you can think of that hasn't been tried. Though often referred to euphemistically, these include feet (trotters), pancreas (sweetbreads), lungs (lights), spleen (melt), intestine (tripe), and something called mountain or prairie oysters. (If you don't know what those are, it's probably just as well.) Moreover, in Alaska the Eskimos enjoy moose-nose jelly, and in Scotland, of course, the traditional haggis contains "parts" which, unless you're a true clansman, you ought not hear described in any greater detail than that.

Amazingly, people's appetites have not been confined just to the species that roam the earth. Sometimes people even eat the earth itself. Thus, in the Amazon, natives eat blocks of clay with their meat, and in India, silt from the Ganges River is added to a local fruit drink. And in at least one instance it isn't the animal that's the delicacy, but its lair. Birds' nest soup, a revered component of Oriental cuisine, may sell for as much as $300 a bowl.

All of this should serve to broaden our culinary horizons and make us less chauvinistic. After all, that American staple, peanut butter, really doesn't look particularly appetizing if you think about it, so maybe we shouldn't be too quick to judge the foods of other cultures. More to the point, knowing how others eat should encourage culinary adventurousness, for without a bit of daring, how will we know what we're missing?

Sopa de Nopales (Cactus Soup), 249

Sugarplums

I must have read the poem "A Visit from St. Nicholas" hundreds of times—even had to memorize it for a school play when I was in the first grade. And yet, despite all those readings, I never thought much about what sugarplums are, let alone why they were dancing.

It turns out that the question "What is a sugarplum?" is not that easy to answer. I've found at least eight distinctly different definitions of the term, some citing chocolate, some fondant, and others coriander as a chief ingredient. Part of the reason for this imprecision, no doubt, is the fact that the word "plum," according to *The Oxford Companion to Food*, has "a long history of often ill-defined use."

As far back as the Middle Ages, it referred to virtually any dried fruit, including raisins. When in the 16th century, as Francesca Greenoak observes, Little Jack Horner stuck his thumb into his Christmas pie, what he pulled out was most certainly not a plum, but a raisin. Such ambiguity is what accounts for the fact that the British holiday staple, plum pudding, typically does not contain any plums at all.

Further compounding the problem of definition, as food writer Lisa M. Sodders notes, is the fact that the meaning of many traditional Christmas foods has been lost over the centuries as tastes have changed and new ingredients have been developed. The sugarplum is no exception.

The sugarplums referred to in "A Visit from St. Nicholas" may have actually been a form of fruit, now nearly extinct, that was smaller than a regular plum, gold colored, and intensely sweet. Even then they were scarce and so were considered something rather special for a holiday stocking.

More commonly, at least since 1668 when the term was first used, sugarplums are considered a confection, or a comfit, to use an archaic English word. Probably originating in Portugal where they originally contained green plums but now are just as likely to feature black figs, they were fruits poached for days in syrup and rolled in sugar to preserve them through the winter.

Small plums were especially well suited to this preparation, but as Tim Richardson notes in his exhaustive history of candy, the term "sugarplum" was never restricted to plums alone but came to refer to practically any sweetmeat, and other fruits, seeds, and even green walnuts were candied in this fashion. Since these confections, regardless of the fruit utilized, were roughly the size and shape of plums, the name persisted.

These days the term "sugarplum" generally refers to a confection made of dried fruit and rolled into balls. As such they're easy to make, especially if you have a food processor—much easier than the poached variety which, according to 17th-century recipes, you had to "boile" for days on end.

Though you may be hard-pressed to whip up a batch of sugarplums in time for Christmas or Christmas Eve, that's ok. The best time to eat them is actually January 2, the Feast of St. Macarius, the patron saint of confectioners. A desert (or should that be dessert?) monk in Upper Egypt in the 4th century, before becoming an ascetic, he was a successful sugarplum merchant. What better way to honor him on his feast day than by gulping down a few of his favorite delicacies?

Byzantine Sugarplums, 364

Sushi

Sushi is on a roll in this country, not just on the east and west coasts where patrons stand in line for hours at places like Nobu, eagerly awaiting a raw deal, but even in the Midwest and in Southeast Missouri, where, thanks to wrap artists at Saffron Pan-Asian Restaurant in Cape Girardeau, it's holding its own against barbecued ribs and chicken-fried steak.

If you've ever tried sushi, you'd understand why. A small mound of seasoned rice and raw fish, often wrapped in seaweed, is, to my mind, perhaps the most exquisite of foods. In it is revealed the essence of Japanese culture.

But sushi didn't actually originate in Japan. Rather, it developed on the greater Asian continent, probably along the Mekong River. There, people preserved fish by fermenting it in boiled rice. The word "sushi" originally referred to the acidy taste produced by such fermentation. And to this day, rice is still the most important ingredient in any sushi.

So, sushi initially was a method of keeping fish. Though exotic to us, it was a perfectly logical development in cultures whose cuisines rely on the sea and rice cultivation.

The technique was brought to Japan around the first millennium, though Japanese legend has it that it was discovered there by accident when a fisherman's wife placed leftover rice in an osprey's nest. Returning to the nest sometime later, she discovered that the bird had filled it with fish, which, she discovered, had become quite tasty.

Once the Japanese got hold of sushi, they did what they so often do with imports. (Consider the automobile.) They perfected it and made it their own. Indeed, one variety allegedly inspired the design of the modern Japanese flag. Elaborate rituals evolved for the making and eating of sushi. For example, the *tsu* (sushi expert) is expected to try to line up each grain of rice in the same direction.

The oldest record of sushi goes back to the 8th century, but it wasn't until 600 years later that the forerunner of today's sushi was invented when, foregoing fermentation, chefs began using fresh fish and imparting the acidy taste to the rice with vinegar. Not until the 17th century would modern-day sushi, prepared while the customer waited, be created.

Today sushi chefs like Su Hill of Saffron are breaking new ground with this ancient delicacy. For example, she sometimes uses colorful soy wrap in place of the traditional seaweed, and her signature dynamite roll is, well, dynamite. With scrupulously fresh ingredients and painstaking preparation, she's proving that sometimes the best way to cook a fish is not to.

Sushi-Roll Rice Salad, 239

Tea

Recently the British Tea Council enlisted a panel of tea lovers to travel incognito aboard more than thirty of the world's major airlines. After being tutored in the methods of professional tea tasting, the panel members logged in over 300,000 miles on air routes all over the world, assessing in-flight tea service along the way. The results revealed that British airlines serve a better cup of tea than their foreign counterparts.

Even if we grant the objectivity of the researchers, this conclusion comes as no surprise. Everyone knows the British take their tea seriously. During World War II, for example, though food was severely rationed in Britain, the government took pains to ensure that tea remained widely available and, in an effort to keep morale high, dispersed tea stocks to some 500 different locations around the country to reduce the likelihood of air-raid damage.

But though the British appreciate tea, they're actually latecomers when it comes to recognizing the pleasures of the beverage. Tea's refreshing properties were first discovered, according to Chinese mythology, nearly 5,000 years ago when Shen Nung, a Chinese Emperor, noticed that a dried leaf from a wild tea plant had inadvertently blown into a vat of water his servants were boiling for drinking. Out of scientific curiosity, the emperor tried the brew and the rest, as they say, is history. Indian and Japanese legends, on the other hand, attribute the discovery of tea to Bodhi Dharma, the founder of Zen Buddhism, who after five years of sleepless meditation plucked a few leaves from a tea plant and chewed them to combat drowsiness. Whatever the case, as early as the Tang Dynasty, tea was the national drink of China, and in 780 AD, the first book on tea, by Chinese author Lu Yu, was published.

For hundreds of years thereafter, Europeans were largely ignorant of tea and its uses. One early reference, for example, suggested boiling the leaves, seasoning them with salt and butter, and eating them! But inevitably, European explorers encountered tea and brought it back home. Father Jasper de Cruz, a Jesuit priest from Portugal, is believed to have been the first European to taste tea, somewhere around 1560, while on a mission to China. The East India Trading Company formally introduced tea to England in the early 1600s, and before long it supplanted ale as the national drink. The first recorded reference to adding milk came in 1680.

In the early 1800s, while spending the summer at Belvoir Castle, Anna, the seventh Duchess of Bedford, invented that most civilized of customs, afternoon tea. "There are few hours in life more agreeable," said Henry James. Previously, the English had made do with only two main meals, breakfast and dinner. Before long, afternoon tea evolved into "high" tea, the main meal in working and farming communities. Paradoxically, high tea is not really a fancy tea. It's really supper with real food, served on a "high" dining room table. Lending to the confusion, "low" tea is the elegant tea with fancy sandwiches and sweets like you'll find at London's Ritz Hotel. (For the record, though the Ritz may have England's most famous tea, after spending several months in London a while back, I came away convinced that despite its reputation among tourists, it is not necessarily Britain's best. Actually, the perfect British afternoon tea, in my judgment, is the one served on the veranda of the old Moana Hotel on Waikiki Beach.) By the way, the popularity of tea spurred demand for teacups with handles, not the handle-less variety imported from China, and gave rise to the world-famous English pottery industry. Afternoon tea was also responsible for the custom of tipping, which began in the outdoor tea gardens of England.

Though tea was first introduced to America in the 17th century by Peter Stuyvesant, it's never been quite as popular here as in England, most likely because of the intervention of the Revolution during which the colonists resolved not to drink English tea, which was our main supply. (Even today, most tea consumed in America is imported, a little plantation in South Carolina being the only place in this country where it is grown.) America has, however, done its share to promote the enjoyment of tea, having invented both iced tea and the tea bag. But by contrast to the United Kingdom and Ireland where per-capita consumption of tea is the highest in the world (the Irish drink the most), the average American only consumes half a cup per day.

But that may be changing. As *Time* magazine reports, since 1990, tea sales in this country have more than doubled and now constitute a $4 billion a year industry. Some tea connoisseurs willingly pay $100 or more for a small bag of gourmet tea like Taiwanese Bao Jong, and trendy restaurants are engaging the services of tea sommeliers who claim that variations in the taste and quality of tea are every bit as complex as those associated with fine wine. Even Starbucks is promoting the beverage. Clearly, a Boston Tea Party now takes on an entirely different atmosphere than it did in 1773.

Part of the reason for this newfound interest in tea may be due to health concerns. Tea generally has only about half the caffeine of coffee, and there is increasing evidence that it may help prevent cancer and heart disease. Laboratory studies suggest that drinking four cups of tea per day can reduce the risk of atherosclerosis by nearly 70 percent and that green tea may inhibit the growth of cancerous tumors, especially in women, by anywhere from 20 percent to 50 percent.

But more than likely, tea is popular not because it might be good medicine, its original use, but simply because it tastes good. This fact has helped make tea the world's most frequently consumed beverage after water, and it is beginning to be rediscovered here in the United States. Americans have become interested in pairing teas with foods that bring out the best in both, and the most sophisticated drinkers may well drink two or three different teas at the same meal.

The latest trend involves cooking with tea in an attempt to infuse food with its unique flavors. Thus, trendy restaurants around the country now feature dishes such as duck with tea and cassis sauce, tea-smoked salmon or chicken, green-tea sorbet, and Earl Grey brownies. Perhaps the apotheosis of this trend is one of my favorite dining spots, Restaurant T in the basement of the SoHo branch of the Guggenheim Museum in New York City, where just about everything on the menu is made with tea. (Someday I really must go upstairs and check out the artwork.)

Typically, chefs cook with tea by brewing it and using the liquid, discarding the tea leaves themselves, whose texture is not really suited to eating. But herbal teas can be added directly to a recipe as a form of seasoning because they contain no true tea leaves but only herbs and spices. The contents of a few lemon herbal tea bags, for example, can really intensify a recipe for lemon bars or cheesecake. If you stop and think about it, using tea as an ingredient makes every bit as much sense as using wine, beer, or coffee. No wonder the Celestial Seasonings Tea Company has even published an entire book of recipes for everything from appetizers to desserts cooked with tea.

Fourteen thousands cups of tea, what the Chinese call the elixir of immortality, are drunk every second, but as the following recipes will help you discover, it's a shame to confine tea just to drinking. Try them and see if you don't agree that these are recipes literally steeped with flavor.

Tequila

"Tequila is Mexico." So says Carmelita Roman, proprietor of the San Matias tequila distillery in the state of Jalisco. Ian Chadwick of *Tequila Aficionado Magazine* agrees. Noting that no other libation is so surrounded by legend and lore (there's a brand named after Pancho Villa and another after his horse), he claims that you cannot fully appreciate Mexico without understanding tequila's place in its history and culture.

With that in mind, I recently journeyed to the namesake town of Tequila in the mountains of central Mexico, where they manufacture more than 500 brands of the stuff, to gain perspective on our neighbor to the south by pursuing the not-so-sobering task of learning as much as I could about its archetypal beverage.

The first thing I learned is that if you haven't tried tequila since your college days, when, perhaps, its taste was less important than its wallop, you're in for a surprise. No longer a crude spirit to be knocked back quickly with salt and lime to cover its raw taste, today's tequila is for connoisseurs. On a par with fine Cognac or brandy, it's made to be sipped and savored. Consequently, tequila these days can cost as much as $200 a bottle. Even the cheap stuff isn't all that cheap anymore.

Tequila's transformation from a drink that accosts to one that allures has taken awhile. North America's first distilled drink, it's made from a plant, the blue agave, that has been cultivated for 9,000 years. Long before the conquistadors arrived in the 16th century, the natives knew how to make a beverage out of it. Using more sophisticated distilling methods, the Spaniards perfected it.

That quest for perfection continues, as I learned while touring the Hacienda San José del Refugio, home of Herradura tequila, the brand which, according to my exhaustive research, is preferred by fully 50 percent of Mexican taxi drivers. (You won't find statistics like this in the *Wall Street Journal*!) Herradura is the only producer still employing natural fermentation. (In the old days they used to throw the dirtiest field hand into a vat of agave juice to introduce bacteria and encourage fermentation.) And they age their tequila in oak barrels, just like fine wine.

Thanks to the efforts of *tequileros* (tequila masters) at Herradura and other distilleries, tequila has reached the point where it's logical to consider cooking with it. After all, if you can add brandy or wine—not to mention beer or Jack Daniels—to a dish, why not fine tequila?

Try using blanco tequila (unaged) in seafood dishes or as a substitute in recipes calling for gin or vodka. Reposado tequila (rested, i.e., aged two months) works well in pork and poultry dishes and can take the place of rum, bourbon, or scotch. Añejo tequila (aged) can be exchanged for cognac or brandy and adds richness to desserts. Not surprisingly, all tequilas go well with chiles.

For me, cooking with tequila makes a lot of sense. Besides, I brought more of it back from Mexico than I should ever drink.

Jarabe Tapatío (Mexican Hat Dance) Pasta, 266

Toast

Recently we decided at our house that we needed a new toaster to replace the aging device that, long before Paul Prudhomme adapted the technique for seafood, had been reliably blackening our breads, bagels, and frozen waffles. So we set off to the nearest appliance store to make what we thought would be an easy purchase, only to discover there an astonishing array of models, especially for what is essentially a single-function contraption. Some were imposingly hefty and cost well over a hundred dollars—more than I paid for my first food processor many years ago. (They too were Cuisinarts.) Some bore digital displays; others, special defrost and reheat features; and still others, individual settings for pastries and bagels. At least one model, the one we ended up buying, was a pop-up toaster in reverse. Bread slides down through it and is deposited onto a serving tray as toast.

Clearly the electric toaster has come a long way since its invention in 1893 by Britain's Crompton and Company, and the introduction in this country in 1908 by General Electric of the first commercially successful electric toaster. Those early models were pretty Spartan compared to today's. A slice of bread was positioned close to bare electric coils and toasted on one side. You turned it by hand halfway through the process to toast the other side, and when finished you pulled the plug. Requiring constant vigilance, such appliances were used right at the breakfast table. In 1919, U.S. inventor Charles Strite patented the first automatic pop-up toaster, and the first model, the one-slice Toastmaster 1A1, was introduced in 1926. Today nearly 90 percent of American homes have a toaster.

The first electric toasters may have been primitive, but they were still a far cry from their predecessors, the toasting fork and the toasting rack. The former, which can be traced back to ancient Egypt, was used to hold bread over an open fire. The latter, a tin and wire cage enclosing sliced bread, was used over a hot burner. Today's high-tech toasters, then, are merely the latest tools in humankind's age-old quest for perfect toast.

That got me to thinking. Perhaps I haven't appreciated how significant a culinary achievement toast is. Maybe I haven't considered its Epicurean possibilities. Possibly I've taken it for granted.

Just as I was entertaining those thoughts, I came across something that soundly confirmed them: a new cookbook devoted solely to toast. Written by California food writer and caterer Jesse Ziff Cool, *Toast: 60 Ways to Butter Your Bread and Then Some* contains dozens of recipes not just for toast to be served at breakfast but for toast as an appetizer (like nasturtium-goat-cheese toast with raspberry-beet salad), a main course (such as toasted polenta corn bread with lamb and apricots), or even a dessert (for example, toast with figs and stilton cheese), not to mention lots of recipes for sandwiches.

A whole book of toast recipes might seem like overkill, but, on the other hand, maybe it's time toast finally got its due. After all, as Misty Harris, writing in the *Edmonton Journal*, observes, though it may not be hip and sexy like focaccia and brioche, toast is beautiful and unpretentious. Compared to it, the bagel is a prima donna. Alan Burdick, writing in the *New York Times*, goes even further. He claims that to toast bread is to re-enact in miniature the American dream itself. "Just as every

American child may grow to be President," he says, "so does every slice of bread, no matter how airy, white and characterless, offer the golden promise of toast."

All of this may seem like so much hyperbole, but the Brits wouldn't think so. Toast is serious business to the English. Thus, *The Oxford Companion to Food* contains about a thousand words on the subject. The hamburger, an American favorite, by contrast merits only a mere two hundred or so.

The *Companion* notes that toast is a standard component of a "proper" English breakfast and an English specialty with a long history in that country going back at least as far as the Middle Ages when "tost" was made over an open fire and used to sop up liquid mixtures or spread with toppings such as hot spiced honey or a paste of cinnamon and sugar moistened with wine. Indeed, America's penchant for cinnamon toast had its roots in 17th-century Britain. Similarly, Welsh rabbit (or *rarebit*) was an outgrowth of the 16th-century British practice of putting all manner of things, in this case melted cheese, on toast. In 18th-century Britain, burnt toast soaked in water was even used as a coffee substitute.

Why toast should have become such a staple in Britain, the *Companion* notes, is not clear, but suggests that it could be because typical English wheat bread, which keeps for several days, lends itself so much better to toasting than the close-textured rye breads of Northern Europe. Whatever the reason, toast, Ian Sansom notes in the *Guardian* of London, has become "the Englishman's bagel." I'll bet the British actually appreciate the work of so-called "toast artist" Maurice Bennett who recently constructed a billboard-sized portrait of Damc Edna made entirely from 2,989 slices of toast.

But you don't have to be English to appreciate the fact that toasting bread to caramelize its sugars and starches, what scientists call the Maillard reaction, brings out its best qualities. It can even make Wonder Bread taste good. Surely toast is the greatest thing since, well, sliced bread.

Toasted Bread and Tomato Salad with Chicken, 237

Toasted Cheese Sandwiches

"Many's the long night I've dreamed of cheese—toasted mostly," said Robert Louis Stevenson. That's a yearning which my friend and colleague, Dennis Seyer, scenic designer and technical director for Southeast Missouri State University Theatre, had no trouble satisfying.

At a silent auction to benefit Notre Dame High School in Cape Girardeau, Missouri, Dennis placed the successful bid for what was identified as five pounds of sliced American cheese. Imagine his astonishment when upon claiming his purchase he was informed that there had been a slight misprint in the sale list. What he had bought was not five pounds of sliced cheese, but five blocks of sliced cheese, each weighing four pounds—a total of twenty pounds of cheese or nearly 650 slices!

Since props wouldn't be a concern, perhaps Dennis should consider for future production Burton Cohen's play, *The Great American Cheese Sandwich*. At any rate, his experience is a symbolic reminder that as a former president of Local #421 of the International Alliance of Theatrical Stage Employees, he is a "big cheese" in technical theatre circles. (The phrase, "big cheese," has meant somebody important ever since a Massachusetts farmer delivered a 1,200-pound wheel of cheese inscribed "the greatest cheese in America for the greatest man in America" to Thomas Jefferson who served it at a White House New Year's Day reception and was still serving it three years later.)

But in the meantime Dennis, who obligingly shared some of his cheese with me, admittedly out of necessity, developed a newfound passion for toasted cheese sandwiches. He is not alone.

Just like meatloaf, bread pudding, mashed potatoes, and other so-called comfort foods, the toasted cheese sandwich has found a niche on the menus of fashionable restaurants around the country. A recent issue of *Nation's Restaurant News* reports it's selling well at San Francisco's Hawthorne Lane restaurant (where its preparation is not considered beneath the talents of two alums of Wolfgang Puck's operation), Manhattan's Bolo restaurant (where Spanish Manchego cheese is favored), Boston's Brew Moon restaurant (where chicken combines with cheddar), the East City Grill in Fort Lauderdale (where Italian ricotta salata stars), and the Avalon Grill in Portland, Oregon (where they go a step, actually three steps, beyond the competition by offering a four-cheese grilled sandwich featuring cheddar, Jack, chevre, and Brie). At California's stylish Campanile Restaurant, Thursday night is grilled-cheese-sandwich night, and not long ago one New York restaurant sponsored "The Great Grilled Cheese Meltdown," a month-long event promoting variations on the toasted cheese sandwich, including the not-so-chic Velveeta and Spam on Wonder Bread. The restaurant, which usually sells a thousand grilled cheeses a month, tripled its sales of the sandwich.

This affection for the toasted cheese sandwich is not difficult to explain. Like many comfort foods, our fondness for it probably has its roots in our childhood. As Professor Robert Thompson, president of the Popular Culture Association, notes, nostalgia exerts a powerful influence on our food choices. And there's probably no better example than the grilled cheese sandwich. It takes us back to grandmother's kitchen when life was simpler. It's the food we remember our mother making for us when we stayed home, sick from school. (My mom always served a hot bowl of Campbell's tomato soup alongside.) And when we returned to the classroom, it was a familiar and reliably satisfying item on the school cafeteria menu. It may have been the first thing we ever learned to cook all by ourselves. After all, it doesn't require many ingredients and it isn't very demanding to prepare. Even famed California chef Alice Waters warmly recalls making toasted cheese sandwiches as a kid, flattening them in the frying pan with a plate. Indeed, the grilled cheese sandwich is a perfect example of what William Hamilton, writing in *Metropolitan Home* magazine, calls feel-good food: "Not just homemade food, but food that actually makes us feel at home." It's no wonder, then, that Americans make some 2 billion toasted cheese sandwiches at home each year or that, according to the *Joy of Cooking*, the grilled cheese sandwich is our favorite hot sandwich after the hamburger.

For all its popularity, nobody seems to know for sure just who invented the toasted cheese sandwich. Perhaps it was a fortunate accident, just like the invention of cheese itself. According to the American Dairy Association, cheese was "discovered" some 4,000 years ago when an Arabian merchant journeyed across the desert and at the end of the day found that the milk he was carrying in a pouch had separated into curd and whey under the hot sun. (Cheesemaking, after all, as famed cheesemonger Steven Jenkins notes, is essentially a series of stages of controlled spoilage.) But who first thought of putting a slab of cheese between two slices of bread and then toasting it remains a mystery. *The Oxford Companion to Food* tells us that plain toast is an English specialty, a standard part of a proper English breakfast, and that towards the end of the 16th century, people began putting all manner of things—poached eggs, bacon, and, of course, melted cheese—on top of it. Welsh rabbit was one result of such experimentation. Perhaps the Swiss had something to do with creating the toasted cheese sandwich. After all, what is a toasted cheese sandwich but a fondue eaten out of hand? We do know that during the Depression, the grilled cheese sandwich, called the "cheese dream" back then, became a popular item for Sunday evening suppers. Apparently it has yet to fall out of favor.

Whether or not you have several hundred slices of cheese to get rid of, a toasted cheese sandwich can be appealing. And even though it is the height of simplicity, it can still allow you to exercise your creativity. Consider the following variations on the basic sandwich components to make your versions more than mere kids' stuff.

- Vary the cheese. No need to restrict yourself to American cheese or even cheddar. Try goat cheese, feta, fontina, jack, provolone, mozzarella, Gruyère, smoked Gouda, gorgonzola, and Brie. (At our house when making sandwiches, to Brie or not to Brie is never a difficult question.) Even cream cheese will work.
- Vary the bread. Remembering Jenkins' dictum that serious cheese requires serious bread, try rye, sourdough, and focaccia. And don't forget croissants, raisin bread, and tortillas. The latter produces a quesadilla (from *queso*, the Spanish word for cheese) which, as vegetarian-cooking expert Deborah Madison reminds us, is the grilled cheese sandwich of Mexico.
- Vary the toppings. A couple of pickle slices may be all you need to top

a regular sandwich, but to make a premium one, try caramelized onions, pecans, walnuts, macadamia nuts, roasted peppers, pepper jelly, Dijon mustard, chutney, salsa, apples, pears, watercress, spinach, fresh basil, sautéed mushrooms, roasted tomatoes, Kalamata olives, and bacon. Geoffrey Seyer, who along with his dad is doing his part to put a dent in the family's newly acquired cheese reserves, likes to insert potato chips into his sandwiches for extra crunch.

And here are some tips for making your grilled cheese perfect every time:

- Butter the outside of the sandwich before toasting. If you're concerned about the calories, you can use less butter and melt it in the pan instead or use cooking spray. Avoid low-fat margarine because it's half-water and will make the bread soggy.
- Use a heavy frying pan such as a cast-iron skillet to promote browning.
- Cook the sandwich uncovered. A covered pan holds in steam which can make the bread soggy.
- Cook over low or medium heat so the cheese melts slowly and the bread doesn't burn.
- For extra flavor, sprinkle grated Parmesan cheese over the buttered outside of the sandwich.

Finally, don't relegate the toasted cheese sandwich merely to lunch or supper. Coated in egg like French toast, before frying, a grilled cheese sandwich makes a perfect breakfast treat. Substitute pound cake for bread and add some fruit topping and you have a sandwich fit for dessert.

The following recipes rely on some of these aforementioned principles, and even if you're not a confirmed tyrophile (cheese lover), they should help you become a veritable virtuoso when it comes to making toasted cheese sandwiches, or in other words, a grilled-cheese whiz.

Grilled Four Cheese Sandwich, 260
Apple, Cheddar, and Pecan Quesadillas, 260

Turducken

The problem with tradition, Curt George Siffert notes, is that it's always dated. Apparently many feel that way even about the traditional Thanksgiving meal. Thus, the National Turkey Federation (yes, there really is one) reports that nontraditional turkey preparations are the rage. Desperate to do something different with the holiday bird, people are trying everything from smoking it to grilling it to brining it to deep frying it to stuffing it with blue corn-bread dressing.

Now for the truly daring comes the turducken, which, as the name indicates, is a turkey stuffed with a duck stuffed with a chicken. The birds are first deboned and their cavities filled with dressing—three different kinds of dressing, one for each bird, if you're a purist.

The turducken has become popular over the last few years thanks to football commentator John Madden and chef Paul Prudhomme who share a passion for the dish and, probably not coincidentally, similar somatypes. Madden first devoured a turducken during the broadcast of a Saints game and has been promoting it on air ever since, while Prudhomme claims to have invented the tri-bird back in the 60s.

Actually the concept underlying the turducken goes back much further than that. For example, a time-honored South African dish employed the turkey-duck-chicken combination but went a step further and stuffed it into an ostrich. (The result, obviously, was an osturducken.) An old feast dish in the Republic of Georgia consisted of an ox stuffed in succession with a calf, a lamb, a turkey, a goose, a duck, and finally a chicken. A traditional wedding dish in West Africa was a camel stuffed with, among other things, a couple of sheep, a few bustards, and several carp.

In fact, the technique of stuffing one animal into another can be traced back at least to the Middle Ages. A 13th-century cookbook, for example, contained a recipe for a ram stuffed with small birds. By the 19th-century, Dumas' *Le Grand Dictionnaire de Cuisine* offered a recipe for a turkey stuffed into a pig. A Southern recipe from 1832 called for a dove stuffed into a quail, then into a guinea hen, then a duck, then a capon, then a goose, and finally a peacock or a turkey. By comparison, turducken sounds like something out of *Cooking Light* magazine.

The turducken has been hailed as the first genuine advancement in Thanksgiving since the Pilgrims landed, but preparing one is not for the faint-hearted. The process is time-consuming, requires proper equipment and advanced skills, and will leave your kitchen looking like a scene from *Nightmare on Elm Street*—a vegetarian's nightmare.

Fortunately, there is an alternative that retains most of the flavor and panache of the original: a turducken roulade. You merely sandwich boneless turkey, duck, and chicken meat between layers of stuffing and roll it up. It's a delicious and attractive conversation piece and really easy. Try one for your holiday table, and the only problem you'll have is trying to figure out what wine to serve with it.

Turducken Roulade, 279

Twinkies

Years ago, fifty baboons somehow managed to escape all at once from the wildlife preserve at the Kings Island amusement park near Cincinnati. Zookeepers, sensing that this development was not good for business at the park, scrambled to lure them back, using a variety of devices. It took four days to get the job done, and though a tranquilizer gun was instrumental in the process, a far more effective tool was the Hostess Twinkie.

Those clever primates could not resist that squishy crème-filled sponge cake, what the dean of the Florida Culinary Institute calls the "gold standard" of snack foods, any more than we humans can. In fact, statistics show that someone in the United States eats a Twinkie every six seconds, which is why Hostess has to spew them out at the rate of 1,000 every minute or 500 million every year, wrapping them in some 40,000 miles of cellophane along the way. And they've been doing it now for three-quarters of a century.

The Twinkie was invented more than seventy-five years ago in Chicago (still the nation's Twinkie capital in terms of per-capita consumption) by Jimmy Dewar, the manager of the Schiller Park bakery there. (And, no, contrary to rumor, there are no leftovers from the original batch still on store shelves.) Trying to find an alternate use for the stacks of shortcake pans he had on hand and which were used only during strawberry season, Dewar landed on the idea of using them for sponge cakes which he then would inject with banana crème filling. (A shortage of bananas during WWII necessitated the switch to the vanilla crème filling still standard today.) A St. Louis billboard for Twinkle Toe shoes gave him the name for his new product which he sold for two for a nickel. Before long they were showing up in lunchboxes across the country.

But the Twinkie has become far more than a lunchbox treat. It is a veritable American icon. Thus, in 2005, a photography show in Pittsburgh revolved around Twinkies as objets d'art. Among the exhibits was "The Last Snack," inspired by DaVinci's famous painting. Moreover, in 2000 the Twinkie was chosen as "an object of enduring American symbolism" and placed in the millennium time capsule by President Clinton, along with a piece of the Berlin Wall.

"Twinkie" has even become part of our vocabulary, usually employed disparagingly. Perhaps the most notorious example is the so-called "Twinkie defense" mounted in 1979 by lawyers defending San Francisco supervisor Dan White against the charge of murder. They claimed his behavior was caused by depression fueled by bingeing on junk food. Similarly, in 1986, when Minneapolis city council candidate George Belair was indicted by a grand jury for serving Twinkies and other refreshments to citizens' groups in violation of fair campaign practices, the case was dubbed "Twinkiegate," and the new policy which resulted became known as the "Twinkie law." Likewise Paul Tsongas coined the term "Twinkie economics" during the 1992 Presidential primary campaign to refer to policies which please voters but fail to address fundamental economic problems like the deficit.

Yet such talk does not seem to have diminished enthusiasm for the Twinkie itself, even among gourmets. For example, Phil Delaplane, an instructor at the famed Culinary Institute of America, had his wedding cake made out of them. Restaurateur Christopher Sell, who trained as a French chef, created the fried Twinkie.

No doubt Twinkies will be around another seventy-five years. We know they're junk food, but like those apes, we can't help ourselves.

Twinkie-misu, 322

208

Ugly But Good

For centuries Italians have been making a chocolate meringue cookie whimsically dubbed *Brutti Ma Buoni*. The phrase means "ugly but good," and the cookie is so named because it is, if not downright unattractive, on the homely side, chunky and irregularly shaped. But it is a delicious combination of chocolate and hazelnuts that, despite its looks, is quite sophisticated in taste.

These little cookies serve as a reminder of an important principle that operates just as often in the culinary world as anywhere else: appearances can be deceiving. Some foods don't look too appetizing, but one bite and you're hooked. Conversely, others tempt you with their beauty and invariably disappoint.

This truth was driven home to me many years ago the first time I galloped through a midnight buffet on a cruise ship. Arrayed before me were dozens of gorgeous cakes, pastries, and other concoctions all made in the tradition of French haute cuisine. They were works of art. But after tireless and repeated investigation, I had to conclude that no matter how beautiful a dessert may be on the outside, it's the inside that counts.

Petits fours are perfect examples of this axiom. Maybe it's because as a rule it's easier to decorate a cake which is dry than one which is moist, but most of the time in my experience the stuff underneath all that beautiful icing is, well, just plain cake. I prefer a plebeian layer cake studded with fruits and nuts, oozing with filling and covered with a coating of frosting made bumpy by nuts, raisins, or other additions.

Similarly, many true delicacies are a little alarming, or worse, at first sight. I remember well a plate of eels I was once served in a tiny restaurant in Bordeaux, France. Though initially startling, especially to my dinner companions, they turned out to be the highlight of the meal. Oysters, perhaps, are the classic example of this aspect of the *brutti ma buoni* principle. As Henry Ward Beecher observed, "The exterior is not persuasive." Yet many people find them delectable. But even devotees would have to admit that Thomas Fuller was correct when he remarked, "He was a very valiant man who first ventured on eating oysters."

Of course, personal tastes play a role in all of this. As the Roman poet and philosopher Lucretius noted, "What is food to one may be fierce poison to others." Thus, Ambrose Bierce could describe custard, my wife's favorite dessert, as "a detestable substance produced by a malevolent conspiracy of the hen, the cow, and the cook."

And surely cultural values are involved too. While the Japanese prefer their fish raw, as José Simon reminds us, "In Mexico we have a word for sushi: bait." Likewise a true Scotsman may actually find haggis appetizing, hard as that may seem to the rest of us. On the other hand, when it comes to cajun food, a favorite of mine, a Scotsman might agree with the comedian Steve Epstein that "some of the stuff that stares out of gumbo should not be allowed out except for Halloween."

But personal preferences and cultural norms notwithstanding, the fact remains that some foods taste better than they look, some infinitely so. Here are some recipes that are perfect examples of the dictum, *brutti ma buoni*.

Velveeta

"This song's about a girl who's soft and warm and cheap. When I held her close to me, she melted right away. Velveeta was her name."

So go the lyrics to a tune by a punk band from California. The group, whose titles also include "Lawnmower of Love" and "I Love You But You're Standing On My Foot," probably won't be invited to perform at this year's Kraft Foods Inc. company picnic. Kraft, the largest packaged foods company in North America and the maker of Velveeta, wouldn't be amused. Not long ago it sued the operator of an adult website to prevent him from lampooning the Velveeta name. Clearly, the company thinks its "pasteurized prepared cheese product" deserves more respect.

But the truth is Velveeta is the Rodney Dangerfield of dairy products. Dubbed variously "Arkansas Brie" or "Spam for vegetarians," it is to cheese what John Tesh is to music. Its name has been sarcastically attached (just like Spam) to abusive practices in cyberspace. Bob Brown pronounces it a triumph of technology over conscience and declares, "The best I can say for it is that it is not poisonous."

Some people don't even regard Velveeta as real cheese, though, technically, according to Title 21 of the Code of Federal Regulations, it is. It's a processed cheese, which means it is cheese heated and mixed with other ingredients to incorporate more moisture to make it easier to spread or melt. The technique also creates a very consistent product because the heat prevents the cheese from ever ripening. Processed cheese always tastes the same because, fortunately or unfortunately, depending upon your point of view, it never ages. Likewise, processed cheese has a longer shelf life. Velveeta is even shelf stable, which is to say it does not need to be refrigerated before opening. Thus, it is not sold out of the dairy case but off a regular grocery shelf.

Those attributes of consistency and stability served J.L. Kraft well when in 1903, with just $65 in capital, a rented wagon, and a horse named Paddy, he got into the cheese business by buying it wholesale at Chicago's Water Street market and reselling it to local merchants. Today the company he founded packages over 70 major brands and is the leader in 17 of its top 20 product categories. Now the second-largest food company in the world, million-dollar-a-year brands are small potatoes to it. Twenty-five of its brands post annual sales of more than $100 million a year, and several do more than a billion dollars in sales each year.

Disappointed in the inconsistent quality of the cheese he bought, Kraft set out to remedy the situation and soon purchased a cheese factory where he began producing processed cheese in small tins. In 1916, he received a patent for his product, just in time to take advantage of a new market created by the entrance of the U.S. into World War I. The fact that his cheese didn't have to be refrigerated made it a natural for inclusion in the field rations of soldiers going overseas. And, thus, what would become Velveeta was born. The name itself wouldn't be introduced until 1928, when Kraft bought out chief rival Phenix Cheese which had earlier developed a similar product and with whom Kraft shared the patent rights. Ever since, Kraft has been a leader in processed cheese innovations, some of them even more dubious, like Cheez Whiz, a spread with over 1,000 reported uses, including as an emergency substitute for shaving cream.

Over the years, processed cheese has come to be regarded, favorably or unfavorably, as quintessentially American, and the U.S. government now promulgates standards for three major categories: "pasteurized process cheese," "pasteurized process cheese food," and "pasteurized process cheese spread." The bottom line, however, is that, generally, processed cheeses must contain at least 51% actual cheese, which qualifies Velveeta as cheese, even if just barely.

Granted, Velveeta is a far cry from, say, Brie, even the factory-produced kind most commonly available at the supermarket. (Indeed, the differences are great enough that demographers claim that a preference for one or the other is correlated with a person's political leanings.) But in the middle of what might be called the Velveeta belt, a zone that extends down the middle of the country and is centered in the Midwest with pockets of heavy concentration in Des Moines, Kansas City, Louisville, and Little Rock (which boasts the nation's highest per capital Velveeta consumption), we know that processed cheese deserves more respect.

Sure, it's not gourmet (what would you expect from the same company that brings you Cool Whip, Stove Top Stuffing, and Tang?), but it's the greatest invention since sliced bread (which made its debut at around the same time) when you're throwing a cocktail party and can't go to a lot of trouble. (No wonder its sales soar around the holidays.) That's because Velveeta can do something no other cheese can do, not even the fancy ones aged in caves over in France. It melts—effortlessly, perfectly, thoroughly. When heated, it oozes seductively out of a toasted cheese sandwich, lovingly envelops the beef patty in a cheeseburger, or embraces every strand of macaroni in a dish of mac and cheese. It never gets stringy. Thus, it's ideal for making fashionably retro hot dips which appeal to the current nostalgia for comfort foods, making it the perfect culinary centerpiece for a Super Bowl party. Armchair quarterbacks, after all, don't crave frou-frou fare, but they cannot resist tackling a vat of melted Velveeta combined with tomatoes, chiles, or refried beans.

Clifton Fadiman once remarked that cheese is milk's leap toward immortality. Velveeta has already reached that status. As long as there are football parties, there will be a market for it.

Velveeta Dips, 220

White House Food

Gesturing toward the White House, a senator once facetiously asked Calvin Coolidge, "Who lives there?" Coolidge replied, "No one. They just come and go."

But though Coolidge was correct that occupants of the White House are only temporary tenants, their impact is often felt long after they move out. And perhaps nowhere is this more the case than with dining and entertaining. For example, tiny new potatoes stuffed with sour cream and caviar became a countrywide sensation during the JFK administration. The dish was the invention of White House chef René Verdon in response to a request from Jacqueline Kennedy.

Each first family has left its own culinary imprint on the country and the executive mansion. As Henry Haller, executive chef for five presidents, observes, "No family leaves the White House exactly as it was upon their arrival. Each family, in its own personal way, leaves a special impression on the White House that forever alters the character of the President's home."

Marie Smith, a Washington reporter who wrote a book on the subject, agrees and points out that the impact has been varied. She says, "Through the years, White House hospitality has been by turns elegant, extravagant, sedate, stinted, formal, flamboyant, prim, puritanical, dignified, and at times even rowdy and rambunctious."

Certainly not every commander-in-chief has approached the dinner table with the same degree of gusto. Some, like Abraham Lincoln and William Henry Harrison, were thin or bound by restrictive diets. Harrison suffered from a digestive disorder and ate very little. Others, like Grover Cleveland who tipped the scales at 250 pounds and William Howard Taft whose weight yo-yoed between 300 and 350 pounds, had heartier appetites.

Some, like Thomas Jefferson and Herbert Hoover, had lavish tastes or were connoisseurs. For Jefferson, Marie Kimball, editor of a collection of his recipes, claims, "The selection of a cook or a maitre d'hotel was given no less thought than the choice of a minister pleni-potentiary." In his first year at the White House, Jefferson, who calculated that he needed 500 bottles of champagne annually, spent almost $11,000, nearly half the president's salary, on wine. Others, most notably Calvin Coolidge, were more frugal. He personally reviewed menus and opted for cheaper breakfast meetings over luncheon meetings. At leaving the White House, he said his greatest disappointment was never having discovered what happened to the leftovers. Then there were others, like Ulysses Grant, who simply had simple tastes. He viewed twenty-nine course dinners, the standard during his administration, as something to be merely endured. And at least one president, Theodore Roosevelt, was upset at being labeled a gourmet by the press.

Some were easier to please at the table than others. FDR, who once served hot dogs and baked beans to the King and Queen of England, derisively described White House food as "plain fare, plainly prepared." Lyndon Johnson, when first served a crabmeat salad, sternly told the White House chef, "Take the rest home to your wife." Others, like Dwight Eisenhower, were genuinely interested in cooking and knew their way around the kitchen. Ike prided himself on his homemade soups, and with typical military detail, his recipe for a plain vegetable version ran more than two pages.

It shouldn't be surprising that White House cuisine fascinates us. The first family is the next best thing we have to royalty, and who would decline an invitation to dine with the President? A few do, of course. "Ah, you'd be nuts to come," President Eisenhower once told an invitee who turned him down, but most of us would think it crazy not to show up.

Moreover, at official functions what is on the menu can sometimes be an ingredient of statecraft. Thus, when the Clintons entertained Jiang Zemin of China, the dessert was a spun-sugar orange filled with orange mousse. According to *George* magazine, the selection was no accident. Zemin loves oranges, a delicacy in China, and the President was hoping to seal a trade agreement.

Occasionally, such transparent attempts at culinary diplomacy have the potential to backfire. For example, when President Bush hosted Mexican president Carlos Salinas in 1989, a dessert consisting of an adobe house made of sweets was created. Alas, alongside was an edible stereotype: a candy Mexican boy taking a siesta. Fortunately, the President's social secretary realized the politically incorrect nature of the treat and removed it from each plate just in the nick of time.

The potential for a breach of protocol, of course, exists even before the food is served. While most of us would be happy to sit anywhere if lucky enough to get invited to a state dinner, government officials aren't always so accommodating. Thus, during the McKinley administration, the Chief Justice of the Supreme Court stormed out of a White House dinner because an ambassador had inadvertently been seated at a higher place of honor than he. The justice vowed never to accept another White House invitation again without first inspecting the seating chart.

Even what the President eats at his private table in the family quarters can have political impact. Consequently, President Ford requested that the sugar bowl be removed from the dining table, to show his concern for high sugar prices. It is not unknown for the president's lifestyle to be a campaign issue as it was when Martin Van Buren persisted in lavish entertaining despite the onset of a depression. Even the choice of presidential tableware can have political consequences, as Nancy Reagan discovered. However, she was hardly the first to have her china policy criticized. People complained that Mary Todd Lincoln thought she was royalty because she ordered purple china for the White House. Eleanor Roosevelt was also chastised for ordering a pattern with the filigree of a rose and three feathers, a foreign coat of arms.

Since John and Abigail Adams first opened the White House to the public over 200 years ago, it has been a showcase for what America stands for, in a culinary sense as much as any other. So when we unite to say "Hail to the Chief," let's not forget to say "Hail to the chef" as well.

Thomas Jefferson's Pea Soup, 248
Nancy Reagan's Veal Piccata, 281
Bess Truman's Ozark Pudding, 367

Wedding Cake

"The most dangerous food in the world is wedding cake," maintains an old American proverb. June is the month of the year—named after Juno, the patroness of marriage—when lots of people choose to live dangerously.

Contributing to the anxiety of June brides and grooms is the fact that these days nothing about planning a wedding is a piece of cake, not even the cake. Today's couples have far more to consider than just the number of layers. They may even find themselves asking whether they want a cake at all.

Thus, some newlyweds opt for tiramisu, crème brûlée, or chocolate truffles. Croquembouche, that classic tower of cream puffs, long a tradition for special occasions in France, is also popular. Not a few couples have been inspired by it to request towers of Ding Dongs or Krispy Kreme doughnuts instead. No less a connoisseur than Gale Gand, who just might be the best pastry chef in the United States, prepared a tower of cupcakes in lieu of a traditional cake for her own wedding.

Even couples not daring to depart from tradition by shedding the conventional tiers of joy are likely to choose something other than a white cake with white icing as the focal point of their first act together as husband and wife, preferring instead chocolate, carrot, or even cheesecake.

These trends are the latest in the evolution of a culinary custom that, as food historian Maguelonne Toussaint-Samat points out, goes back to Ancient Greece and Rome. Carol Wilson, writing in *Gastronomica*, describes the role played by cake back then: made of wheat or barley, it was smashed over the bride's head and the resulting crumbs eaten by the newlyweds and the wedding guests as tokens of good fortune. Over time, no doubt to the relief of new brides, the smashing evolved into mere crumbling.

By medieval times these cakes were replaced by a tall stack of sweet rolls (in parts of France they used waffles), a precursor to today's wedding cake. The bride and groom were required to kiss over this pile of buns, a challenge which, if met, insured them a prosperous future.

In his seminal work on the subject, *Wedding Cakes and Cultural History*, British anthropologist Simon Charsley reveals that the first recorded recipe for a dish specifically designed to be eaten at a wedding was actually for a pie. Called bride's pie, it was a concoction of pastry and meat into which a glass ring was inserted. The person who found the ring was destined to be the next to marry.

In the 17th century, through French influence, bride's pie evolved into bride's cake, essentially a fruitcake covered with white icing (later called "royal icing" after its use on Queen Victoria's wedding cake). Further refinements in the 19th century resulted in the familiar three-tiered cake said to have been modeled after the spire of St. Bride's Church in London.

Wedding cakes continue to evolve in the direction of greater grandiosity, making them big business today, though, as the *Joy of Cooking* suggests, baking one at home can be a "glorious undertaking," as I discovered years ago when I constructed a four-layer affair and hauled it to Dallas for a friend's nuptials. Preparing your own, however, carries additional danger, as Rose Levy Beranbaum, author of *The Cake Bible*, learned when she made a cake for her brother's wedding. It got stranded at the Newark airport by a snowstorm and was subsequently eaten by airline employees.

Wedding (Cup)Cake, 316

Whitman's Sampler

He was in the business fifteen years before Milton Hershey was even born, and he virtually invented the concept of prepackaged chocolates. The year 1992 marked the 150th anniversary of his first boxed assortment, an elegant pink and gilt affair decorated with rosebuds and curlicues with lettering proclaiming "Sugar Plums from Stephen F. Whitman."

Though the company he founded has been bought out by Missouri's own Russell Stover Candies, Inc., the Whitman name lives on in the form of the Whitman's Sampler. The Sampler has even been honored by the Smithsonian Institution. And little wonder. The Whitman story is a typically American one.

Stephen F. Whitman got into the candy business in Philadelphia back in 1842, when he was only 19. He set up a little shop on Market Street near the waterfront and went into competition with European importers. Relying on sailors who brought him the rare imported fruits, nuts, cocoa, and flavorings he needed to make his confections, his reputation soon spread as far west as Chicago.

Whitman's enterprise thrived, due as much to his high-quality products as his innovative marketing practices. By 1907 the company had begun to distribute its chocolates nationally, targeting "better drug stores" by awarding them exclusive franchises. Soon it was offering a "money-back guarantee" on its products, a novelty at the time.

The company was also responsible for two innovations in packaging which are commonplace today. The first was cellophane, which Whitman's son, Horace, brought back with him from France in 1912. The second was refrigeration. Teaming up with General Electric, Whitman's became the first to peddle chocolates out of refrigerated display cases.

Whitman's was also a pioneer in advertising, even as early as Civil War days. For years it touted celebrity endorsements from the likes of Elizabeth Taylor and Jimmy Stewart in ads in the *Saturday Evening Post*, and it was one of the first companies to use television.

But the Sampler is clearly the company's most noteworthy innovation. It was the first box of chocolates with a diagram on the lid identifying each candy. Sporting a design inspired by an old needle-worked sampler stitched by the company president's grandmother, within three years of its introduction in 1912 it was the best-selling box of candy in the country—and has been ever since.

The Sampler hasn't changed much in all those years, though now it contains just sixteen varieties, not the original thirty-seven. There's also a sugar-free version and one with low carbs. The company also makes a Presidential Tin exclusively for the White House. The Sampler box has changed a bit too. It has a tall cover that slides off instead of the old hinged one. Alas, that makes it far more difficult for me to sneak a piece of candy from the box I give my wife every Valentine's Day.

Cheesecake Essamplaire, 312

Appetizers and Accessories

This recipe, adapted from Leslie Mansfield's *The Lewis & Clark Cookbook*, is a variation of the buffalo sausage made to rave reviews by Toussaint Charbonneau, husband of Sacagawea, during the expedition of the Corps of Discovery. Meriwether Lewis called it "one of the greatest delicacies of the forest" and described its preparation in detail in his journal. Charbonneau began with six feet of buffalo intestine which he stuffed with ground meat, then ceremoniously baptized in the Missouri River and fried in bear oil. Using a food processor and serving the dish as a terrine simplify matters considerably.

> 1½ c. heavy cream
> 2 onions, chopped
> 5 shallots, chopped
> 2 cloves garlic, minced
> 5 tsp. salt
> 1 tsp. black peppercorns
> ⅛ tsp. ground nutmeg
> ⅛ tsp. thyme
> 2 tbsp. butter
> 1 lb. pork loin, cut into ½-inch cubes and chilled
> 3 eggs
> ¼ c. flour
> ¼ c. tawny port

Stir together cream, onions, two of the shallots, garlic, salt, peppercorns, nutmeg, and thyme. Bring to a boil over medium heat, then reduce heat to medium low and simmer for 20 minutes. Let stand uncovered for 1 hour, then cover and chill in refrigerator overnight. Strain cream, pressing on solids to extract maximum liquid. If there is more than 1½ cups liquid, simmer until reduced to 1½ cups. Line a 6-cup loaf pan with parchment paper, and butter parchment. Sauté remaining 3 shallots in butter over medium heat until soft. Transfer to bowl of food processor, add pork, eggs, flour, and port, and process just until smooth. With motor running, add cream mixture and process just until combined with pork. Place mixture in pan, cover with foil, and bake in water bath at 325 degrees for 1½ hours until knife inserted into center comes out clean. Uncover and let cool completely, then cover and chill. Unmold and serve. Serves 10–12.

Ravioli with Pumpkin Filling

This is not as strange as it sounds. Pumpkin, after all, is a member of the squash family, so it is right at home in this savory filling laced with Parmesan cheese. If you prefer, you can use Won Ton wrappers, but it's really very easy to make your own pasta if you have a hand-crank pasta machine, and the assembly process goes faster because you can dot a long length of rolled dough with filling, cover with another layer of dough, and use a pastry wheel to cut into several small ravioli. If you use Won Ton wrappers, make one pasta package per 3-inch square and trim with a biscuit cutter to make round ravioli which are fancier, I think, than the square variety. This recipe is adapted from *Bon Appétit* magazine.

> 2 c. all-purpose flour
> 1 c. semolina flour
> 1 tsp. salt, divided
> 6 eggs, room temperature
> 4 tbsp. olive oil, divided
> 2 tbsp. warm water
> 10 oz. solid-pack pumpkin
> ½ c. freshly grated Parmesan cheese
> 6 single amaretti (macaroons)
> ¼ tsp. ground white pepper
> ¼ tsp. grated nutmeg
> ¾ c. unsalted butter, clarified

For pasta: Combine flours and ½ teaspoon salt in processor. Add 4 eggs, 2 tablespoons olive oil, and water, and blend until dough comes together, about 20 seconds. Turn dough onto lightly floured surface and knead until smooth, about 3 minutes. Wrap in plastic and let stand 15 minutes.

For filling: Blend pumpkin, cheese, remaining 2 eggs, macaroons, pepper, nutmeg, and remaining ½ teaspoon salt in processor.

To assemble: Cut dough into six pieces. Flatten each piece, fold into thirds, and run through pasta machine at widest setting. Repeat until dough is smooth and velvety. Adjust machine to next narrower setting and run dough through without folding. Repeat, narrowing rollers after each run until dough is ¹⁄₁₆-inch thick. Dust with flour if sticky. Lay each sheet of dough on lightly floured surface and mound level teaspoons of filling at 2-inch intervals, leaving ½-inch border along edges. Brush water between filling and along edges of dough, and top with second sheet, pressing around filling to seal. Trim around filling using pasta cutter to create ravioli. Let dry until leathery around edges. Stir remaining 2 tablespoons olive oil into large pot of boiling, salted water. Add ravioli and cook until tender but firm to bite, about 8 minutes. Drain, transfer to bowl, toss with butter, divide among 8 plates, and sprinkle with Parmesan cheese and ground pepper. Makes 8 appetizer servings.

Hot Chipped Beef Dip

A common use for chipped beef these days is in cocktail snacks and appetizers like this delicious dip. This recipe is adapted from the Missouri Association of Hospital Auxiliaries' cookbook, a wonderful collection of recipes given to me by a former president of the association, Sue Meyer of Cape Girardeau, Missouri.

> 1 pkg. (8 oz.) cream cheese
> 2 tbsp. milk
> ¾ c. snipped dried beef
> 1 tbsp. minced onion
> 2 tbsp. chopped green pepper
> ¼ tsp. seasoned pepper
> ½ c. sour cream
> ¼ c. sliced almonds

Blend together cream cheese and milk. Mix in beef, onion, green pepper, seasoned pepper, sour cream, and almonds. Spoon into a 2-cup ungreased casserole and bake at 350 degrees for 15 minutes. Garnish with additional almonds and serve with raw vegetables or crackers.

Velveeta Dips

You can make a comforting hot dip by combining Velveeta with almost anything, even cheese! Simply cut up one pound of Velveeta and melt in the microwave on low power or in a saucepan over low heat. Add whatever ingredients you like, stirring to combine. The following are time-honored variations.

Con Queso Dip: add 1 can (10 oz.) diced tomatoes and green chiles, drained.

Cheesy Chili Dip: add 1 can (15 oz.) chili.

Ranch Dip: add 8 oz. sour cream and 1 c. ranch dressing.

Spinach Dip: add 1 can (14½ oz.) tomatoes, cut up; 1 pkg. (10 oz.) frozen spinach, thawed and drained; and ¼ tsp. crushed red pepper.

Pizza Dip: add 1 med. chopped tomato and 1½ oz. chopped pepperoni.

Bean Dip: add 1 can (16 oz.) refried beans and ½ c. salsa.

Crab Dip: add ½ stick melted butter and 1 can (4¼ oz.) crabmeat, drained.

Sausage Dip: add 1 lb. bulk sausage, browned and drained, and ¼ c. salsa.

Pesto

These days pesto can be made from almost any herb, including thyme, parsley, cilantro, mint, and a wide variety of other ingredients, including sun-dried tomatoes, sunflower seeds, green olives, red peppers, raisins, almonds, hazelnuts, and even avocados. But this is the classic recipe adapted from the *Joy of Cooking*. Pesto is traditionally served with trenette, a flat ribbon pasta, but it can also be used with other pasta shapes and in lots of other dishes as well. Try it, for example, slathered on a French baguette as a change of pace from garlic bread.

> 2 c. loosely packed fresh basil leaves
> ⅓ c. pine nuts
> 2 med. cloves garlic, peeled
> ½ c. grated Parmesan cheese
> ½ c. olive oil

Place all ingredients except olive oil in food processor and process to a rough paste. With machine running, slowly pour olive oil through feed tube until incorporated. If sauce seems dry (it should be a thick paste), add a little more olive oil. Season with salt and pepper to taste. May be kept in covered glass jar in refrigerator for 1 week or frozen. If freezing, add nuts and cheese after thawing.

Cranberry Chutney

I like to make this by the vat and serve it instead of the traditional cranberry sauce at Thanksgiving dinner. It's also nice served over a block of cream cheese as an appetizer spread. Chutney, of course, is an East Indian sweet-and-sour condiment that can be made out of almost any fruit and which includes vinegar, sugar, and spices. This recipe is based on one from Julia Child which I clipped from *Parade Magazine* years ago. I've opted for minced ginger rather than grated, and whereas she called for currants, I substitute raisins because I think the smaller currants tend to get lost in this mixture. Besides, raisins are cheaper.

> 1 c. sliced onions
> 1 c. water
> ¾ c. dark brown sugar
> ½ c. granulated sugar
> ¾ c. cider vinegar
> 2 tart apples, peeled, seeded, and diced
> ½ tsp. salt
> 1 tsp. fresh minced ginger
> ½ tsp. mace
> ½ tsp. curry powder
> 2 oranges
> 1 lb. cranberries
> ½ c. raisins

Simmer onions, water, and sugars for 30 minutes. Add vinegar, apples, salt, ginger, mace, curry powder, and the grated rind of the oranges. Simmer another 30 minutes. Add cranberries, raisins, and the strained juice of the oranges. Boil slowly for about 10 minutes until cranberries burst. Makes 1 quart.

Flavored Honeys

The National Honey Board, headquartered in Colorado, suggests that these gourmet honeys are an appropriate way to honor the work of the honeybee. They couldn't be easier to produce and would make a unique gift.

> 1½ c. honey
> **One** of the following:
>   1 tbsp. grated orange, lemon, lime, or grapefruit peel
>   ¼ c. chopped fresh mint
>   1 tbsp. julienned ginger
>   1 tbsp. whole allspice
>   1½ tsp. dried crushed red pepper

Add flavoring to honey, warm over low heat for 5–10 minutes, being careful to avoid boiling or scorching. Remove from heat and let stand 2 hours. Strain into 8-ounce jar with lid.

Spicy-Sweet Peanut Dressing

This Thai-style dressing is terrific served over chilled pasta or raw vegetables. The recipe is adapted from *Bon Appétit* magazine.

> 1 c. smooth old-fashioned peanut butter
> ½ c. freshly brewed black tea at room temperature
> ½ c. orange juice
> 3 tbsp. sesame oil
> 3 tbsp. honey
> 2 tbsp. soy sauce
> 2 tbsp. rice vinegar
> 1 tbsp. minced fresh ginger
> 2 tsp. grated orange peel
> 3 minced garlic cloves
> 1½ tsp. minced canned chipotle chiles

Mix all ingredients until blended and smooth.

Low-fat Blue Cheese Dressing

The use of reduced-fat sour cream and mayonnaise along with buttermilk makes this recipe, adapted from *Eating Well* magazine, surprisingly low in fat. When making this or any other blue-cheese dressing, consider cheesemonger Steve Jenkins' advice: "I have never cottoned to the practice of blending Roquefort into a dressing for salad. For this purpose, any blue cheese, such as Danish Blue, will do, and at one-third to one-fourth of the price."

> ¼ c. crumbled blue cheese
> 2 tbsp. reduced-fat sour cream
> 2 tbsp. reduced-fat mayonnaise
> ¼ c. buttermilk
> 1 tbsp. white wine vinegar
> 1 tbsp. chopped fresh parsley
> 1 tbsp. chopped scallions
> salt and pepper to taste

In a small bowl, whisk together blue cheese, sour cream, and mayonnaise. Stir in buttermilk, vinegar, parsley, and scallions. Season with salt and pepper.

Homemade Mayonnaise

Do not use aluminum or copper bowls when making this classic recipe, adapted from the venerable *Joy of Cooking*, because they will react with the acid ingredients and affect color and flavor. The suggestions for variations can also be employed in a pinch to perk up store-bought mayonnaise.

>2 lg. egg yolks
>1–2 tbsp. lemon juice
>¼ tsp. salt
>pinch of ground white pepper
>1 c. vegetable oil, at room temperature
>1½ tsp. Dijon mustard

Whisk together the egg yolks, the lemon juice, salt, and white pepper until smooth and light. Whisk in oil a drop at a time until the mixture starts to thicken. After about one-third of the oil has been incorporated, whisk in remainder a tablespoon at a time until thoroughly blended. Stir in Dijon mustard and further salt and pepper to taste.

Variations:

Green Curry Mayonnaise: to 1 c. mayonnaise add 2–3 tsp. Thai green-curry paste, 1 tbsp. lime juice, ⅛ tsp. Thai fish sauce, and 1 tbsp. chopped fresh cilantro.

Chutney Mayonnaise: to 1 c. mayonnaise add ½ c. Major Grey Chutney (chop the large chunks of fruit), 1 tbsp. lime juice, and the green part of one green onion, finely chopped.

Chipotle Mayonnaise: to 1 c. mayonnaise add 1 finely chopped chipotle chile in adobo sauce, 1 clove minced garlic, and 2 tbsp. chopped cilantro.

Herb Mayonnaise: to 1 c. mayonnaise add 2–3 tbsp. minced fresh herbs, such as tarragon, basil, chervil, chives, parsley, dill, or oregano.

Tomato Basil Mayonnaise: to 1 c. mayonnaise add 1 tbsp. tomato paste, 3 tbsp. finely chopped basil, a dash of Tabasco, and salt and pepper to taste.

Orange and Ginger Mayonnaise: to 1 c. mayonnaise add 2 tsp. grated orange peel, 4 tsp. minced peeled fresh ginger, and 2 tbsp. lime juice.

Blueberry or Raspberry Mayonnaise: substitute blueberry or raspberry vinegar for lemon juice in basic recipe, adding additional vinegar to finished product to taste.

Breakfast

Chocolate Chip
Cookie Dough Pancakes

This recipe is my version of one of the signature dishes at the Marathon Grill on Rittenhouse Square in Philadelphia, a wonderful restaurant just a block from the famed Curtis Institute of Music. The inspired combination of pancake batter and cookie dough is so rich you hardly need syrup or even butter for that matter.

1 tube (16–18 oz.) prepared chocolate chip cookie dough
2 c. flour
1 tbsp. baking powder
½ tsp. baking soda
1 tsp. salt
2 eggs
2 c. soured milk
¼ c. oil

Slice cookie dough into ½-inch thick slices. Cut each slice into quarters. Combine flour, baking powder and soda, and salt. Beat eggs lightly and mix in milk and oil. Add liquid mixture to flour mixture and stir just until combined. Pour about ¼ cup batter at a time onto hot (400 degrees) griddle and scatter cookie dough pieces over top. Bake until bubbles form and edges just start to dry out. Turn and bake other side. Dust with powdered sugar.

Giant Sunday Pancakes

These pancakes, adapted from *Bon Appétit* magazine, are reminiscent of the ones served at my son's favorite place for pancakes (other than home), New York City's Canadian Pancake House. There the pancakes fill an entire plate and require two spatulas for turning.

    3 eggs
    ½ c. sugar
    6 tbsp. melted butter
    1½ c. flour
    1 c. milk
    1 tbsp. baking powder
    ¼ tsp. salt

Whisk eggs, sugar, and butter until blended. Add flour alternately with milk in 3 additions, whisking to blend after each addition. Whisk in baking powder and salt. Melt just enough butter to coat bottom in heavy medium nonstick skillet over medium heat. Ladle scant ¾ cup batter into skillet, rotating skillet to spread batter to about 6-inch diameter. Cook pancake until bubbles form on surface and bottom is brown, about 1 minute. Turn over pancake and cook until bottom is brown and pancake is cooked through, about 1 minute. Makes 5 pancakes. Pancakes may be kept warm on baking sheet in 250-degree oven.

 # Biscuits and Shiitake Mushroom Gravy

I must confess that I have an aversion to biscuits and gravy even if it is a classic dish. But this upscale version made with shiitake mushrooms and Madeira wine is appealing. It's still not pretty to look at, but with an attractive salad, it could even be served for supper. The recipe is adapted from *Bon Appétit* magazine.

    1 tube (5 oz.) refrigerator biscuits
    2 tbsp. butter
    12 oz. fresh shiitake mushrooms, stems trimmed, caps sliced
    2 tbsp. flour
    2 tbsp. chopped fresh thyme or 2 tsp. dried
    1 can (14½ oz.) vegetable broth
    ½ c. Madeira
    salt and pepper to taste

Bake biscuits according to package directions. Melt butter over medium-high heat. Add mushrooms and sauté until brown and soft, about 6 minutes. Add flour and thyme, and stir 1 minute. Whisk in broth, then Madeira. Boil until mixture thickens to gravy consistency, whisking occasionally, about 8 minutes. Season to taste with salt and pepper. Split open 4 biscuits (save remaining for another time), place on 2 plates, and spoon gravy over. Makes 2 servings.

Kahlua Compote
with Sweet Potato Biscuits

The Barrett family, formerly of Cape Girardeau, Missouri—Kimberly, Terry, and Terrance—have been celebrating Kwanzaa for years. In that time, this sumptuous breakfast dish, a specialty of Terry's, has become a family holiday tradition.

        2 c. water
        1 c. sugar
        ½ c. Kahlua
        1 stick butter
        2 tbsp. lemon zest
        ¾ tsp. cinnamon
        1 tbsp. cornstarch
        1 pkg. (18–24 oz.) mixed dried fruit

Mix together all ingredients except dried fruit, and bring to a boil, stirring frequently. Add dried fruit, return to a boil, then simmer until syrupy, about 10–12 minutes. Cool, and refrigerate until serving.

See recipe for Sweet Potato Biscuits, page 256.

Franklin School Doughnuts

This recipe is courtesy of Mrs. Katy Proctor, who for over twenty years worked in the Franklin School kitchen in Cape Girardeau, Missouri, to make wholesome meals and treats that are still recalled fondly by alums of the school and their parents, like me.

        ¾ c. water, divided
        1 tbsp. active dry yeast
        ¼ c. plus ½ tsp. sugar, divided
        1 tsp. vanilla
        5¼ c. flour, divided
        ¾ tsp. salt
        ¼ c. dry milk, heaping
        1½ sticks butter, melted
        2 eggs

Combine 6 tablespoons water, the yeast, and ½ teaspoon sugar, and stir until dissolved. Add 6 tablespoons remaining water and vanilla. Mix together 2½ cups flour, remaining ¼ cup sugar, salt, and dry milk. Add some of this mixture to yeast mixture. Add eggs and butter and rest of dry mixture, plus 2¾ cup flour or as much as needed to make a soft sticky dough. Let rise until doubled. Punch down, roll out, and cut with a doughnut cutter. Let rise and deep fry. Dip in sugar or glaze. Makes 1½ to 2 dozen.

Jimmy Carter's Baked Cheese Grits

Grits experienced something of a resurgence during the administration of President Jimmy Carter who was known to serve them even to foreign dignitaries. Alas, their popularity faded before long. Nonetheless, this recipe, adapted from Henry Haller's *White House Family Cookbook*, deserves another term.

> 4 c. chicken stock
> 1 c. enriched white hominy grits
> 1 tsp. Worcestershire sauce
> 1 stick butter
> 2 c. grated sharp cheddar cheese
> 4 eggs, separated
> ¼ to ½ c. cold milk

Bring stock to a boil and whisk in grits gradually. Reduce heat, stir, and cook until mixture thickens. Cover and cook another 15 minutes, stirring occasionally. Remove from heat and add Worcestershire sauce, butter, and 1½ cups of the cheese. Stir until blended. Blend egg yolks with ¼ cup milk and mix into grits, adding more milk if needed to thin to consistency of Cream of Wheat. Beat egg whites until stiff and fold into grits. Place mixture into a greased 2-quart dish, sprinkle with remaining cheese, and bake for 30 minutes at 350 degrees until browned. Serves 6.

Omelette Molière

This recipe, adapted from one printed in Elizabeth David's 1959 essay, "An Omelette and a Glass of Wine," originated with the proprietress of the restaurant Molière, a small restaurant in Avignon where this cheese omelette was the house specialty.

> 3 eggs
> 1 tbsp. grated Parmesan cheese
> pepper to taste
> 1 tbsp. butter
> 1 tbsp. diced Gruyère cheese
> 1 tbsp. cream

Beat eggs with Parmesan cheese and pepper. Heat a nonstick skillet over medium-high heat so that when a tablespoon of butter is added, it melts immediately. Pour in the egg mixture and add Gruyère and cream. As mixture begins to set at the edges, carefully push the cooked portion toward the center of the pan using an inverted pancake turner. At the same time, tilt the pan so egg mixture fills any spaces. When cheese melts and egg mixture is set but still moist, fold omelette in half using pancake turner and place upside down on a plate.

Loaded Omelette

When it comes to omelettes, the Italians take the easy way out. They mix the filling ingredients with the eggs rather than folding them inside, and they cook the top under the broiler. The result is called a frittata which is essentially what this recipe, adapted from *Bon Appétit* magazine, appears to be. Whether you call it a frittata or an omelette, there's no question that the word "loaded" is appropriate, for this dish is brimming with flavors.

2 tbsp. butter
½ c. finely chopped onion
6 eggs, beaten to blend
2 green onions, sliced
2 oz. cream cheese, cut into small pieces
2 oz. smoked salmon, chopped
⅓ c. grated mozzarella
1 oz. caviar

Preheat broiler. Melt 1 tablespoon butter in heavy large skillet over medium-high heat. Add onion and sauté until translucent, about 4 minutes. Remove onion. Melt remaining 1 tablespoon butter in skillet. Add eggs and season with salt and pepper. Cook until edges of omelette are set, about 1 minute. Lift edges of omelette and tilt skillet, allowing uncooked eggs to flow under cooked eggs. Continue cooking until eggs are almost set, about 2 minutes. Sprinkle sautéed onion, green onions, cream cheese, smoked salmon, and mozzarella over omelette. Broil until mozzarella melts, about 3 minutes. Cut omelette into wedges and top with caviar. Serves 4.

SoHo Omelette

This omelette suggestion, adapted from *The Silver Palate Cookbook*, doesn't call for precise measurements, but the cookbook authors, Rosso and Lukins, advise a proportion of ¼–⅓ cup of filling per three-egg omelette. The heat of the eggs is sufficient to cook the spinach, so it can be added raw to the omelette.

Basic omelette recipe
crisp-cooked bacon
grated sharp cheddar cheese
spinach leaves

Prepare basic omelette and fill with a combination of bacon, cheese, and spinach leaves. When cheese begins to melt and spinach starts to wilt, fold omelette in half and serve.

Eggs Pope Benedict

This recipe, adapted from famed Seattle chef Don Curtiss, seems an appropriate culinary tribute to the pope. Relying on Italian ingredients like ciabatta, prosciutto, and tomatoes makes the dish all the more heavenly.

    1 c. hollandaise sauce
    4 tsp. tomato purée
    1 tsp. tomato paste
    4 eggs
    4 slices ciabatta
    8 slices prosciutto

Combine tomato purée and tomato paste with hollandaise. Toast ciabatta. Lightly grill prosciutto. Poach eggs. Place 2 slices prosciutto atop each ciabatta slice and top with egg. Ladle with sauce. Makes 4 servings.

Emancipation Proclamation Breakfast Cake

This pastry, traditionally served on New Year's Day, which is also Emancipation Proclamation Day, tastes good year-round. The recipe is adapted from *The Historical Cookbook of the American Negro*, a collection of recipes arranged to commemorate dates significant to the African-American community. First published by The National Council of Negro Women in 1958 and reprinted in 2000, the book, containing historical facts, photos, and anecdotes as well as recipes, offers a delicious way to learn about African-American history.

    ⅓ c. butter
    ⅓ c. sugar
    1 egg
    2 c. flour
    1 tbsp. baking powder
    ½ tsp. salt
    ¼ tsp. cinnamon
    1½ c. blueberries
    ½ c. milk
    ¼ c. honey
    grated orange and lemon rinds

Cream butter and sugar. Beat in egg. Sift dry ingredients, add blueberries, and add to butter mixture alternately with milk to make a dough. On a floured surface, pat dough out to ½-inch thickness. Cut into rounds and arrange overlapping in greased pie pan. Spread with honey, sprinkle with rinds, and bake at 400 degrees for 20 minutes or until browned. Serves 6.

Salads

Flower Confetti Salad

Choose nasturtiums, calendulas, violets, pansies, rose petals, or chrysanthemums for this simple salad served at the Bellevue Bed & Breakfast in Cape Girardeau, Missouri. The recipe is adapted from Rosalind Creasy's *The Edible Flower Garden*.

> 1 lg. head Bibb lettuce
> 1 lg. handful mixed baby greens
> 2 tbsp. rice-wine vinegar
> salt and pepper
> 1 tsp. frozen white-grape juice concentrate
> 3–4 tbsp. olive oil
> 6–8 edible flowers

Wash the lettuce and baby greens and dry them. Break lettuce leaves into bite-size pieces and place in a salad bowl along with the greens. Combine vinegar, salt, pepper, and juice concentrate. Whisk in oil until blended. Carefully wash flowers, pat dry with paper towels, and gently pull off petals. Mix petals together to make a confetti. You will need about ⅓ cup of loosely packed petals. Lightly dress the lettuce and greens, divide among four plates, and scatter a small handful of flower confetti over each serving. Serves 4.

 # Nutty Quinoa Salad

This recipe, adapted from *The New Basics Cookbook* by Julee Rosso and Sheila Lukins, substitutes quinoa for the customary wild rice. The result is a lighter salad that's perfect for hot summer days. It is best served at room temperature.

> 1 c. quinoa
> 2 c. water
> ½ c. golden raisins
> ¼ c. sesame oil
> 3 green onions (bulb and 3 inches of green, sliced)
> ½ c. roasted peanuts
> ½ c. mandarin orange sections
> 2 tbsp. chopped mint
> 2 tsp. grated orange zest

Place quinoa in a fine strainer and rinse under cold running water. Drain thoroughly. Bring quinoa and water to boil. Reduce heat, cover, and simmer 10 minutes. Add raisins and continue cooking until all liquid is evaporated, another 5 minutes. Spread mixture out on platter or baking sheet and allow to cool completely. Combine with remaining ingredients, tossing gently. Serves 4–6.

Lemon Cookie Chicken Salad

A few years ago, *The Joplin Globe* sponsored a contest in which local chefs were invited to invent a new dish using Girl Scout Cookies. This recipe, adapted from Tom Danner of T.J. Mot's Restaurant, was one of the winners in the "Cookie Cook-off."

> 6 Girl Scout Lemon Pastry Creme cookies
> ¼ c. olive oil
> 1 med. onion, slivered
> 1 tsp. garlic
> 4 artichoke hearts, quartered
> 2 boneless chicken breasts, diced
> 1 tomato, diced
> 1½ tbsp. balsamic vinegar
> 1 head Romaine lettuce, torn into bite-sized pieces
> 1 sm. bunch green onions, chopped
> ¼ c. Parmesan cheese, grated

Scrape creme centers from cookies, reserving both centers and cookies. Heat olive oil to moderate temperature. Add slivered onion, garlic, artichokes, and chicken, and sauté until chicken is just cooked through. Add tomatoes, lemon creme centers, and vinegar. Blend mixture to make sauce. Add olive oil as needed to make sauce desired consistency. Toss with lettuce and green onions and top with grated cheese. Serve with reserved cookies in place of crackers. Serves 6.

 # Pasta Insalata Caprese

Caprese, the classic tomato and mozzarella salad from Capri is, I have happily discovered, found everywhere in Italy, sort of the equivalent (in ubiquity only) of our chef salad. Invented in the 1950s at the Trattoria da Vincenzo, it consists simply of tomatoes, basil, and mozzarella drizzled with olive oil. In the summer we enjoy the following recipe adapted from *Bon Appétit* magazine for a "pastafied" version of the salad.

> 1½ lbs. plum tomatoes, seeded, coarsely chopped
> 8 oz. fresh mozzarella cheese, cut into 1x½-inch strips
> 3 tbsp. olive oil
> 2 tsp. red wine vinegar
> salt and pepper to taste
> ½ c. chopped fresh basil
> 12 oz. penne pasta

Mix tomatoes, mozzarella, oil, and vinegar in medium bowl. Season with salt and pepper, and let stand 1 hour at room temperature. Mix in basil. Cook pasta, drain, add tomato mixture, and toss gently to blend. Serves 4.

Peeps Waldorf Salad

This recipe, adapted from *Salon* magazine, is best made with yellow or pink peeps. Lavender ones tend to turn the entire salad gray. You may prefer to dice the Peeps into small pieces. Peeps also work well in an ambrosia salad containing oranges, grapefruit, and coconut. Pink ones are especially "Spring-y."

    10 Peeps, whole
    3 ripe bananas, diced into ½-inch pieces
    2 lg. navel oranges, sectioned into ½-inch pieces
    juice of one orange
    12 maraschino cherries, halved
    ½ c. shredded coconut
    2 tbsp. fresh lemon juice
    1 tbsp. orange liqueur
    ¼ c. finely chopped macadamia nuts, pecans, or almonds

Mix all ingredients and allow to macerate for 2 hours, stirring occasionally.

Whitfield's Potato Salad

If she had the choice, this excellent potato salad would be an essential component of Cape Girardeau, Missouri, caterer Elma Staten's last meal, which would also include fried chicken, collard greens, cornbread, and bread pudding.

    12 med. red potatoes
    6 boiled eggs
    1 chicken breast, poached and finely chopped
    2 stalks celery, finely chopped
    1 med. white onion, chopped
    1 tsp. celery salt
    ½ c. Miracle Whip
    ½ c. sour cream
    1 tsp. sugar
    ½ c. sweet pickle relish
    salt to taste
    paprika

Boil potatoes until fork tender, drain, and let sit until room temperature. Chop potatoes into small cubes and combine with remaining ingredients. Sprinkle with paprika.

Quick and Easy Pasta Salad

This simple pasta salad recipe from Debbie Cannon of Cape Girardeau, Missouri, makes a big hit. Debbie recommends adding shrimp or other vegetables if you want to dress up the salad even more. I suspect some cheese cubes wouldn't hurt either.

    4 c. pasta shells
    1 pkg. ranch-dressing mix
    1 c. buttermilk
    1 c. mayonnaise
    3–4 lg. carrots, grated
    1 c. frozen peas

Combine the mix, mayonnaise, and milk. Add peas and carrots. Cook shells, drain, and combine all ingredients. Chill.

 # Toasted Bread and Tomato Salad with Chicken

This dish, what Italians call *panzanella*, is perfect for warm summer evenings. After fresh tomatoes are no longer at their peak, substitute canned ones, preferably the fire-roasted variety. Because you'll need lots of juice to moisten the toasted bread, they'll work nearly as well. The recipe is adapted from Jesse Ziff Cool's cookbook *Toast: 60 Ways to Butter Your Bread and Then Some.*

    3 lg. very ripe tomatoes or 1 can (24 oz.) canned whole tomatoes
    1 red onion
    1 med. cucumber
    2 cloves garlic
    1½ c. chopped fresh basil
    ½ c. olive oil
    3 tbsp. red wine vinegar
    3 tbsp. balsamic vinegar
    2 tbsp. sugar
    2 tbsp. capers
    2 c. shredded skinless chicken
    salt and pepper
    1 loaf (1 lb.) crusty white bread

Chop tomatoes, reserving juices. Thinly slice onion. Peel, halve, and seed cucumber and slice thinly. Mince garlic. Combine all ingredients except the bread and tomato juice, and refrigerate. Tear bread into bite-sized pieces and toast in oven at 400 degrees for 10–15 minutes or until lightly browned. About 15 minutes before serving, add bread to salad mixture and toss thoroughly. Drizzle with tomato juice to moisten bread to desired texture. Serves 4–6.

Technicolor Bean Salad

This recipe, adapted from the now classic *Silver Palate Cookbook* by Julee Rosso and Sheila Lukins, goes considerably further than the traditional three-bean salad. The fact that it shouldn't be served chilled makes it more likely to arrive at a picnic site at the right temperature. The fresh green beans are a nice touch, but if you're in a hurry, canned ones could be substituted. If you're concerned about the raw egg yolk in the dressing, you can substitute two hard-cooked yolks, but the texture of the dressing will not be the same.

> 1 can (1 lb.) garbanzos
> 1 can (1 lb.) white kidney beans
> 1 can (1 lb.) red kidney beans
> 1 can (1 lb.) baby lima beans
> 1 can (1 lb.) black-eyed peas
> 1 lb. fresh green beans (or half green and half yellow wax beans)
> 1 egg yolk
> ⅓ c. red wine vinegar
> 1 tbsp. sugar
> 1 tbsp. chopped garlic
> salt and pepper to taste
> 1 c. olive oil
> 1 c. chopped green onions
> ½ c. chopped Italian parsley

Drain canned beans, rinse thoroughly, and drain again. Cook fresh beans uncovered in boiling salted water until done but still crunchy. Cool beans in ice water. Drain, pat dry, and cut into 2-inch lengths. Toss canned and fresh beans together. Combine egg yolk, vinegar, sugar, garlic, and salt and pepper in bowl of food processor fitted with a steel blade. Process briefly. With motor running, slowly dribble in olive oil. Pour dressing over beans, add onions, and toss. Cover and refrigerate overnight. Garnish with parsley and serve at room temperature.

Sushi-Roll Rice Salad

Though it's fun to try your hand at making sushi, it's not easy. On the other hand, this terrific salad, a deconstructed version of a sushi roll, contains mostly the same constituents but requires a whole lot less work. The recipe is adapted from *Gourmet* magazine.

1½ c. short-grain sushi rice
1¾ c. plus 1½ tbsp. water
¼ c. seasoned rice vinegar
1 tbsp. sugar
1 tsp. salt
1 med. carrot
½ lg. seedless cucumber
3 scallions
3 tbsp. sliced Japanese pickled ginger
1¼ tbsp. wasabi paste
1½ tbsp. vegetable oil
1 tbsp. toasted sesame seeds
1 ripe avocado
1 sq. (6-inch) toasted nori (dried seaweed)

Rinse rice in several changes of cold water until almost clear, then drain for 30 minutes. Bring rice and 1¾ cups water to a boil in a 3–4 quart saucepan, then simmer, covered, 2 minutes. Remove from heat and let stand covered for 10 minutes. Meanwhile, bring vinegar, sugar, and salt just to a boil, stirring constantly until sugar is dissolved. Cool 2 minutes. Spread rice in shallow baking pan and sprinkle with vinegar mixture, tossing with a wooden spoon. Shave thin lengthwise slices from carrot using a vegetable peeler, then cut diagonally into ¼-inch-wide strips. Peel cucumber, halve lengthwise, core, and chop. Thinly slice scallions diagonally. Drain ginger slices and coarsely chop. Whisk together wasabi, remaining water, and oil. Add rice, carrot, cucumber, scallions, ginger, and sesame seeds, and toss gently. Halve, pit, and peel avocado, and cut crosswise into ¼-inch thick slices. Place avocado and rice mixture on plate. Cut nori into very thin strips with scissors and sprinkle over top. Serves 4.

Elvera Weber's Jell-O Salad

I have to admit I don't regard Jell-O as a special dish, except when it's prepared and served by the ladies at Trinity Lutheran Church in Altenburg, Missouri. Not surprisingly, their cookbook has an entire section on Jell-O salad with nearly forty wonderful recipes. This one, from a fine Altenburg cook who used to be the mainstay of the production line at My Daddy's Cheesecake in downtown Cape Girardeau, Missouri, is especially refreshing.

> 4 c. apple cider
> 2 sm. boxes lemon Jell-O
> 2 c. diced apples, unpeeled
> ½ c. pecan pieces
> ½ c. diced celery

Heat 2 cups of the cider and dissolve Jell-O in it. Add rest of cider and chill until partially set. Add remaining ingredients and chill until firm.

 # Sangria Jell-O Salad

Incorporating the fruity flavors of sangria, this Jell-O mold is designed for grown-ups. Served either as a side dish or as a dessert, it would be perfect for Thanksgiving—or any time of year. The recipe is adapted from *Bon Appétit* magazine.

> 1¾ c. fruity red wine
> 1 pkg. (6 oz.) raspberry Jell-O
> 1 c. orange juice
> ¼ c. lemon juice
> 1 c. green seedless grapes
> 1 c. strawberries
> 1 can (8 oz.) mandarin oranges, drained
> 1 tbsp. grated orange peel

Bring wine to a simmer. Place Jell-O in large bowl and pour wine over, stirring until dissolved. Add orange and lemon juices, and stir to combine. Place bowl in larger bowl filled with ice water and chill until set slightly, about 20 minutes. Halve grapes, slice strawberries, and add along with oranges and orange peel, blending well. Pour into a lightly oiled 6-cup ring mold and chill overnight. Unmold and garnish with additional fruit.

Soups

Barbara Bauerle's Chili

Many years ago I had the good fortune to take a culinary course taught by the late Barbara Bauerle, an exuberant cook who passed this recipe along to the class. It has been my favorite chili recipe ever since. In classic Mexican fashion, it calls for unsweetened chocolate to add depth to the dish.

1 lb. ground beef
1 med. onion, chopped
1 green pepper, chopped
2 cans (16 oz. each) stewed tomatoes
1 sm. can tomato paste
2 tsp. chili powder
½ tsp. salt
1½ tsp. ground coriander
1 tsp. ground cumin
½ tsp. thyme
1 tsp. dried oregano leaves
2 tsp. wine vinegar
½ oz. unsweetened chocolate
1 clove garlic, minced
1 can (1 lb.) red kidney beans, drained

In a large kettle, cook beef over medium heat until crumbly. Add onion and green pepper, and sauté until onion is limp. Stir and add next 11 ingredients and 1½ cups water. Bring to a boil and simmer, stirring occasionally, for 1¼ hours. Add beans and cook ¼ hour longer.

White Bean and Chicken Chili

This trendy recipe adapted from the *Lighter Tastes of Aspen* might horrify purists who insist on a "bowl of red," but it's a delicious alternative to beef chili that could complement the regular offering at your next chili party.

> 4 c. green chiles, diced
> 6 c. cooked Northern beans
> 2 lbs. boneless chicken breast, cooked and chopped
> 1 lg. yellow onion, diced
> ¼ c. cumin
> 2 qts. chicken stock
> ½ c. cilantro, chopped
> 1 tsp. salt
> 1 tsp. pepper
> ½ c. cream

Combine all ingredients in a pot, bring to a boil and simmer for 1 hour, stirring often. Serve topped with sour cream and cheddar cheese.

Sweet and Sour Chili

This recipe provides a unique twist on conventional chili and could hardly be easier to make. A favorite of my wife's, it is adapted from *Better Homes and Gardens* magazine.

> 1 lb. lean ground beef
> ¼ c. chopped onion
> 1 clove garlic, minced
> 1–1½ c. water
> 1 can (6 oz.) tomato paste
> 1 tbsp. grated Parmesan cheese
> 1 tsp. sugar
> ½–1 tsp. chili powder
> ½ tsp. salt
> ½ tsp. dried parsley flakes
> ¼ tsp. pepper
> 2 cans (15 oz. each) three-bean salad

In large saucepan, cook ground beef, onion, and garlic until meat is browned and onion is tender. Drain if necessary. Add 1 cup water and remaining ingredients except three-bean salad and mix well. Add undrained three-bean salad and bring to boiling. Reduce heat, cover, and simmer 30 minutes, adding additional water if needed and stirring occasionally.

Mike Bennett's Beanless Chili

Nearly everyone has a chili recipe they swear by, and Cape Girardeau, Missouri, dentist Dr. Michael Bennett is no exception. This one, which he has been making for over 20 years, clearly reveals where he stands in the beans vs. no beans debate.

1 lb. bacon, cooked and broken into small bits
5 tbsp. bacon fat (from cooked bacon)
4 med. onions, chopped
5 cloves garlic, chopped
2 lbs. round steak, cut into bite-sized pieces
2 lbs. ground beef
4 tbsp. chili powder
2 tbsp. flour
3 cans (14½ oz. each) tomatoes with juice
1 can (14½ oz.) salsa tomatoes with green chiles
5 bay leaves
2 tbsp. salt
2 tbsp. oregano
3 tbsp. red wine vinegar
3 tbsp. light brown sugar
1 lb. fresh mushrooms, sliced
1 pt. ripe olives (optional)

Brown onions in bacon fat. Add garlic and meat; brown. Mix chili powder with flour and add to meat mixture, stirring until smooth. Add all tomatoes and cook gently for 20 minutes. Add remaining ingredients except mushrooms and olives, cover, and cook slowly for 2 hours. Add mushrooms and olives, and cook 30 minutes longer before serving.

Barbecue Bean Soup

The use of molasses in barbecue sauces and in baked beans has been traditional at least since the mid-19th century, especially in New England. This soup recipe, adapted from *Gourmet* magazine, capitalizes nicely on that heritage.

3 cloves garlic
3 c. chopped onion
¼ c. vegetable oil
2 tbsp. chili powder
2 tbsp. ground cumin
1 tsp. ground allspice
¼ tsp. ground cloves
2 cans (32 oz. each) tomatoes
3 cans (16 oz. each) pinto beans
2 bottles (7 oz. each) roasted red peppers
3½ c. beef broth
¼ c. molasses
1 tbsp. Tabasco
2 tsp. cider vinegar

Mince the garlic and cook with the onion in oil over moderate heat, stirring until onion is softened. Add spices and simmer for 1 minute. Chop the tomatoes and add with their juice. Rinse and drain the beans and add. Rinse and drain the peppers, chop, and add. Add remaining ingredients except vinegar and simmer, partially covered, for 1½ hours, stirring occasionally. Stir in the vinegar and heat through. Makes 8 servings.

Purée Crecy (Cream of Carrot Soup)

Though waiters had it better during Escoffier's day than cooks, they too experienced occupational hazards. One account tells of a waiter who spilled soup down the front of a woman's dress and then frantically began blotting it with a cloth, whereupon her outraged male companion chivalrously knocked him to the floor, an incident similar to one which Escoffier recalled as his greatest culinary mishap, only in that story it was a plate of peas that was upset. Whatever the case, this Escoffier recipe for soup, adapted from a modernized version by Anne Willan, makes a dish you'll want to take care not to spill. It's too good to waste.

> 4 tbsp. butter, divided
> 5–6 med. carrots, chopped
> 1 med. onion, chopped
> salt
> pinch of sugar
> 4–5 c. beef or chicken stock
> ½ c. rice
> ¾ c. heavy cream

Melt 2 tablespoons butter and add carrots, onion, salt, and sugar. Cover and cook over low heat for 5–7 minutes until butter is absorbed and vegetables are soft. Add 4 cups of stock and the rice, bring to a boil, cover, and simmer 25–30 minutes until rice and carrots are tender. Purée soup in a blender, bring just to a boil, and add more stock if necessary to achieve the consistency of thin cream. Add cream, bring back to boil, remove from heat, and stir in remaining 2 tablespoons butter. Serve with croutons. Serves 6.

Cranberry Pear Soup

Recipes for cranberry soup are rare. I could only find one in my collection. Even my favorite cranberry cookbook, put out by Ocean Spray and containing some 200 recipes, had none for soup. Similarly, I could track down but one on the Internet despite the huge database accessible there. So I developed the following recipe, a streamlined version inspired by one I ran across in my search. It's a pretty soup that can be served either hot or cold with a dollop of sour cream or yogurt.

> 1 c. cranberries
> 2 c. cranberry juice cocktail
> 1 can (15 oz.) pear halves
> ½ tsp. cinnamon
> ½ tsp. nutmeg
> ½ tsp. ginger

Simmer cranberries in juice for 10 minutes. Drain, saving juice, and place in food processor. Drain pears and add to processor. Add spices and process until smooth. Add reserved juice until desired consistency. Serves 4–6.

Cheddar and Blue Cheese
Potato Chowder

Potatoes were first cultivated by the ancient Incas around 3000 BC. They would doubtless scorn today's instant potato flakes, and, I must admit, I don't have much use for them either. But they work fine and make preparation a snap in this recipe adapted from the National Dairy Board.

> 1 tbsp. butter
> ¾ c. chopped onion
> ½ c. chopped green pepper
> 3 c. low-fat milk
> 1 c. chicken broth
> ⅛ tsp. ground black pepper
> 1½ c. instant mashed-potato flakes (not granules)
> ⅓ c. shredded sharp cheddar cheese, divided
> 3 tbsp. crumbled blue cheese, divided

In medium saucepan, melt butter. Add onion and green pepper. Cook and stir until softened, about 5 minutes. Stir in milk, broth, and black pepper, and bring to a boil. Stir in potato flakes. Cook and stir until thickened, about 1 minute. Set aside 1 tablespoon of each cheese. Stir in remaining cheeses and heat until melted. Sprinkle with reserved cheeses just before serving. Serves 4.

Famous-Barr Onion Soup

This is arguably the most famous dish ever served in any Missouri department store. The store always graciously consented to share the recipe and even had it printed for distribution. This rendition was obtained by Alice Dye, formerly of Cape Girardeau, Missouri, who used to work at Famous-Barr in St. Louis.

> 3 lbs. onions
> 1 stick butter
> 1½ tsp. pepper
> 2 tbsp. paprika
> 1 bay leaf
> ¾ c. flour
> 3 qts. beef bouillon
> 1 c. white wine (optional)
> 2 tsp. salt
> ½ lb. Swiss cheese
> French bread

Slice onions ⅛-inch thick. Slowly sauté onions in butter for 1½ hours. Add pepper, paprika, bay leaf, and flour, and sauté over low heat 10 more minutes. Add bouillon and wine and simmer for 2 hours. Season to taste with salt. Refrigerate overnight. To serve, heat soup in individual casseroles, top each with a slice of French bread and Swiss cheese and broil.

 # *Thomas Jefferson's Pea Soup*

Without question, Thomas Jefferson was the greatest epicure to ever occupy the White House. Even as president he would often accompany his executive chef to the market to help in selecting supplies. An inveterate gardener, he cultivated some thirty types of peas, his favorite vegetable. This recipe is adapted from *Thomas Jefferson's Cook Book* by Marie Kimball.

> 2½ c. water
> 1 c. peas
> ½ tsp. sugar
> ½ tbsp. chopped parsley
> 1 tbsp. flour
> 1 tbsp. butter
> 2 egg yolks

Bring water to a boil and add peas, cooking until tender. Drain peas, reserving water. Purée peas and add back to water with sugar and parsley. Combine flour and butter to form a paste and add to soup to thicken. Beat egg yolks and add to mixture.

Sopa de Nopales (Cactus Soup)

Could anything look more forbidding than cactus? Yet it's been a part of the human diet for 9,000 years. It can be peeled and eaten raw, dried, roasted, or turned into wine or jelly. And, as this recipe adapted from *Sunset* magazine shows, it can be the basis for a delicious soup. Cans of the vegetable are not that hard to find at major supermarkets.

    1 lg. onion
    1 tbsp. oil
    1 lb. tomatillos
    6 c. chicken broth
    1 can (28 oz.) sliced cactus (nopales)
    2 tbsp. lime juice
    2 tbsp. minced cilantro
    2 oz. crumbled feta cheese

Chop onion and sauté in oil over medium heat until golden, about 15 minutes. Husk tomatillos, coarsely chop, add to onion mixture and cook until soft, 5–6 minutes. Add broth and bring to boil. Drain and rinse cactus and add with lime juice and cilantro. Heat through, ladle into bowls, and top with cheese. Serves 6.

Pumpkin Soup

This is unquestionably one of the best pumpkin soups I've ever eaten, and it's a snap to prepare. The recipe is adapted from *Saint Louis Days . . . St. Louis Nights*, an excellent cookbook published by the Junior League of St. Louis.

    ½ stick butter
    1 c. chopped onion
    1 clove garlic, crushed
    1 tsp. curry powder
    ⅛ tsp. salt
    ⅛ tsp. ground coriander
    ⅛ tsp. red pepper
    3 c. chicken broth
    1 can (16 oz.) pumpkin
    1 c. half-and-half

Sauté onion and garlic in butter until soft. Add curry powder, salt, coriander, and red pepper; cook 1 minute. Add broth; boil gently, uncovered, for 15–20 minutes. Stir in pumpkin and half-and-half; cook 5 minutes. Purée in blender until creamy. Garnish with sour cream and chopped chives. Makes 6 cups.

Black-Eyed Pea Soup
with Smoked Turkey

Black-eyed peas are indigenous to Africa. They make a wonderful soup in this recipe adapted from Barbara Smith of B. Smith's restaurant in New York City (she's sometimes called the black Martha Stewart, presumably affectionately). The soup has been lightened up by *Heart and Soul* magazine so that it contains less than 30% of calories from fat.

> 1¼ c. dried black-eyed peas (about 10 oz.)
> 2 tbsp. vegetable oil
> 1 lg. onion, chopped
> 1 tsp. minced garlic
> 1 c. chopped green bell pepper
> 5 c. reduced-fat chicken stock
> 1 bay leaf
> 1 tsp. salt
> ¼ tsp. dried red-pepper flakes
> ¾ c. diced smoked turkey

Place peas in large bowl; cover with cold water and soak overnight. Drain, rinse, drain again, and set aside. Heat oil over medium-high heat, and sauté onion and garlic until soft. Add peas, bell pepper, stock, bay leaf, salt, and red-pepper flakes. Cover, bring to boil, and simmer over low heat for 1 hour or until peas are tender. Stir in turkey and cook 15 minutes more. Remove bay leaf before serving. Top with nonfat sour cream and cilantro if desired. Serves 6.

Breads

Asparagus and Ham Brunch Bread

This recipe, adapted from one devised by Foodland Ontario, makes a delicious main course that needs only a light salad as an accompaniment.

> 3 c. biscuit mix
> 1 tsp. dried tarragon
> ½ tsp. dry mustard
> ½ tsp. pepper
> 2 eggs
> 1½ c. milk
> 2 lbs. fresh asparagus
> 1 c. diced ham
> 1 onion, chopped
> 1 c. grated Parmesan cheese

Combine biscuit mix and seasonings. Beat eggs slightly and combine with milk. Pour over dry mixture and stir until smooth. Spread half of batter in a greased 9x13-inch pan. Trim asparagus and place half of it over batter in a single layer. Sprinkle with ham, onion, and half of cheese. Pour remaining batter over top. Place remaining asparagus spears over batter and sprinkle with remaining cheese. Bake at 375 degrees for 35–40 minutes, until golden brown and wooden pick inserted in center tests clean. Cool 20 minutes before serving. Serves 6.

 # Georganne Syler's
Boston Brown Bread

I don't know if you're required to be cheerful to be a nutritionist, but all the ones I know are, especially Dr. Georganne Syler of Southeast Missouri State University. Her effervescent personality could probably get even me to eat health food. Fortunately, her healthy recipes also taste great, and this one for an American classic is no exception. It's low in fat, but because of the inclusion of molasses, it's high in flavor.

> 2 c. whole-wheat flour
> 1 c. all-purpose flour
> 2 tsp. baking soda
> ½ c. sugar
> ½ c. molasses
> 2 c. buttermilk
> 1 c. raisins
> 1 c. chopped walnuts

Mix together all dry ingredients except nuts and raisins. Add wet ingredients and blend thoroughly. Blend in raisins and nuts. Let stand 1 hour. Bake in muffin cups at 350 degrees for about 30 minutes.

Golden-Raisin Irish Soda Bread

Of all the recipes for Irish soda bread I've run across, this one, adapted from a recipe which appeared in *Gourmet* magazine, may very well be the best. It comes from County Cork.

> 2 c. unbleached flour
> ¼ c. toasted wheat germ
> 1 tsp. baking soda
> ½ tsp. salt
> ½ stick cold butter
> 1 c. golden raisins
> 1 c. buttermilk

Whisk together flour, wheat germ, baking soda, and salt. Cut butter into bits, add to flour mixture, and toss to coat. Using fingertips, rub butter into flour until mixture resembles coarse meal. Add raisins and toss to coat. Add buttermilk and stir until dough is evenly moistened. Knead dough for 1 minute on floured surface, sprinkling with additional flour as needed to prevent sticking. Dough should remain soft. Shape dough into a ball and pat out into a 6-inch round on a lightly floured baking sheet. Sprinkle with flour and spread lightly over top. Cut a shallow X in the top and bake at 400 degrees for 35–45 minutes until golden brown. Wrap in a kitchen towel and cool on rack for 1 hour. Unwrap and cool at least another hour before slicing.

 # Banana Pecan Muffins

Though adapted from a recipe by Diane Mott Davidson, whose novels such as *Dying for Chocolate*, *The Cereal Murders*, and *Killer Pancake* have earned her the title of foremost practitioner of the culinary whodunit, the only mystery about these muffins is how they achieve high taste and low fat at the same time.

> 4½ c. flour
> 1¾ c. sugar
> 5 tsp. baking powder
> 1¾ tsp. salt
> 1¾ c. mashed overripe banana
> ¼ c. vegetable oil
> 2 eggs
> 1⅓ c. skim milk
> 2 c. pecans

Whisk together dry ingredients except pecans. Whisk together wet ingredients. Combine wet and dry ingredients just until moistened. Add nuts. Spoon into greased muffin tins to three-fourths full, and bake at 350 degrees for 25 minutes until brown.

Cranberry Pecan Cornbread

This wonderful bread has become obligatory at our Thanksgiving table. It features two food gifts from Native Americans: corn, called Indian corn by colonists, and cranberries, one of only three major fruits indigenous to this continent. I always substitute nonfat yogurt for the sour cream originally called for in this recipe, adapted from *Bon Appétit* magazine, thereby reducing the fat content considerably with no discernible impact on taste.

 1 c. (packed) dried cranberries
 ½ c. fresh orange juice
 1 c. flour
 1 c. yellow cornmeal
 2 tsp. baking powder
 1¼ tsp. salt
 1 tsp. ground cardamom
 ½ tsp. baking soda
 2 eggs
 1½ c. nonfat yogurt
 ⅓ c. pure maple syrup
 6 tbsp. melted butter, slightly cooled
 2 tsp. (packed) grated orange peel
 ½ c. chopped toasted pecans

Combine cranberries and orange juice and let stand, stirring occasionally, about 30 minutes until cranberries are softened. Drain and discard juice. Mix flour, cornmeal, baking powder, salt, cardamom, and baking soda. Whisk eggs to blend. Add yogurt, syrup, butter, and orange peel to eggs and blend well. Add yogurt mixture to dry ingredients, stirring just until blended. Mix in pecans and cranberries, and transfer batter to a buttered 10-inch springform pan. (Wrap outside of pan with foil to prevent leaking.) Bake at 400 degrees for 35 minutes or until golden and tester inserted into center comes out clean. Cool, release from pan, and cut into 12 wedges.

Lemon Walnut Date Bread

You're bound to love this fantastic quick bread if you're a lemon lover. It calls for a whole lemon, peel and all. The recipe is adapted from *Sunset* magazine.

> 1 lemon (about 5 oz.)
> 1 c. chopped pitted dates
> 1¼ c. sugar, divided
> 2 tbsp. butter, room temperature
> 1 egg
> 1¾ c. flour
> 1 tsp. baking soda
> 1 tsp. salt
> 1 c. chopped walnuts
> ½ c. lemon juice

Coarsely chop lemon, discard seeds, place in food processor with dates, and process until evenly chopped. Add ¾ cup sugar, butter, and egg, and process until blended and lemon and dates are finely chopped. Mix flour, baking soda, and salt, and add to mixture, processing until blended. Stir in nuts. Spread into greased and floured 4x8-inch glass loaf pan and bake at 325 degrees about 1 hour or until tester comes out clean. Combine remaining ½ cup sugar and lemon juice, and stir over medium heat until sugar dissolves. When bread is done, poke holes over surface and pour hot syrup over, letting stand until absorbed, about 2 hours. Chill overnight.

 # Ham and Black-Pepper Biscuits

These sensational biscuits, adapted from a recipe by Marcelle Bienvenu of the *New Orleans Times-Picayune*, are a good example of a drop biscuit. I recommend a heavy hand with the pepper mill.

> 2 c. flour
> 1 tbsp. baking powder
> 1 tsp. salt
> ¼ tsp. freshly ground pepper
> 2 tbsp. chilled butter
> 2 tbsp. chilled shortening
> 2 oz. finely chopped boiled ham
> 1½ c. milk

Sift together flour, baking powder, salt, and pepper, and cut in butter and shortening until mixture resembles coarse meal. Stir in ham. Add milk and stir until just mixed. Drop dough by large spoonfuls (about ¼ cup) onto greased baking sheet about 1 inch apart and bake at 450 degrees for 10–12 minutes until lightly browned. Makes 12.

Sweet Potato Biscuits

Terry Barrett, formerly of Cape Girardeau, Missouri, serves these biscuits with his Kahlua Compote, but they are also mighty good just by themselves.

> 1 med. sweet potato, unpeeled
> 6 tbsp. butter
> ½ c. milk
> 2 tbsp. sugar
> 1 egg
> 2½ c. flour
> 1 tbsp. plus ½ tsp. baking powder
> 1 tsp. salt

Cook potato in water until tender. Cool, peel, and mash. (Do not use a food processor.) You should have 1 cup mashed sweet potato. Cook mashed potato and butter until butter is incorporated and mixture is smooth. Stir in remaining ingredients. Knead dough until soft. Roll out ¾-inch thick, cut with biscuit cutter, and bake at 425 degrees for 15–20 minutes.

See recipe for Kahlua Compote on page 228.

Blue Cheese Biscuits

These are "worse than popcorn, cookies, or potato chips—you can't keep out of them," declares Barbara Rose Rust of Cape Girardeau, Missouri, who shares her variation on a recipe which, she says, is so old she cannot remember where she got it. She says the biscuits are also great cold in case there are leftovers, which at her house, there usually aren't.

> 4 pkgs. refrigerated biscuits
> 2 sticks butter
> 4 oz. crumbled blue cheese

Cut biscuits into quarters and arrange in one layer in 10x15 oblong baking pan. Melt together butter and cheese and pour over biscuit pieces, being sure to coat all. Bake at 400 degrees for 15–20 minutes or until brown. (Watch carefully at end because they brown quickly.)

Flying Biscuits

These biscuits, along with lots of other great food, have made their namesake restaurant, The Flying Biscuit Café, which bakes nearly 5,000 of them each week, one of the most popular places in all of Atlanta. They are the creation of Chef April Moon and are adapted from her cookbook.

> 3 c. extra-fine flour (such as White Lily)
> 1½ tbsp. baking powder
> ¾ tsp. salt
> 2½ tsp. sugar
> 6 tbsp. butter at room temperature, cut into bits
> ⅔ c. heavy cream
> ⅔ c. half-and-half
> 2 tbsp. half-and-half for brushing on top of biscuits
> 1 tbsp. sugar for sprinkling on top of biscuits

Combine flour, baking powder, salt, and sugar, and work in butter until mixture resembles coarse meal. Make a well in center of flour, pour in cream and half-and-half, and mix just until dough begins to come together into a ball. Knead dough 2 or 3 times on lightly floured surface and roll to 1-inch thickness. Cut dough with biscuit cutter. Place ¼-inch apart on sheet pan lined with parchment paper, brush with half-and-half, and sprinkle with sugar. Bake at 375 degrees for 20 minutes until lightly browned. Makes 8–12.

Lucille's Caramel/Cinnamon Rolls

These rolls are the perfect showcase for cinnamon, says Dr. Jim Dufek of the Communication Department at Southeast Missouri State University. A cinnamon aficionado (he prefers Penzey's Chinese Cassia), he has been making them for years from a recipe handed down by his mother whose renditions of these rolls in years past have sold at church auctions for as much as $500 per pan. One bite and you'll see why.

    5 c. flour
    2 pkg. instant dry yeast
    2 c. milk
    ½ c. soft margarine, plus additional for spreading
    ½ c. sugar
    2 tsp. salt
    2 eggs
    2½ c. brown sugar, divided
    2 tbsp. cinnamon
    1 c. heavy cream
    1 tsp. vanilla

Sift 3 cups of the flour and mix with the yeast. Warm milk to 125–130 degrees. Melt ½ cup margarine and add to milk along with sugar and salt. Add milk mixture to flour and yeast mixture. Mix well. Beat eggs until frothy and add to mixture. Add remaining flour a little at a time to form soft dough. Knead dough until smooth, place in a covered greased bowl and let rise until doubled. Punch down dough, let rise again, and punch down again. Roll half of dough out onto a floured surface and spread with additional margarine. Sprinkle generously with ¼ cup brown sugar and 1 tablespoon cinnamon. Roll up tightly and cut into 1-inch slices. Repeat with remaining dough. Place rolls in a greased 9x13-inch pan and let rise until doubled. Combine 2 cups brown sugar, heavy cream, and vanilla, and heat just to the boil. Remove from heat and let cool. Pour over rolls and bake at 375 degrees for 20 minutes or until topping begins to bubble. Serve warm. Makes two dozen rolls.

Entrées

Apple, Cheddar, and Pecan Quesadillas

I was reminded just how delicious quesadillas can be, toasty on the outside and oozing with cheese, when I shared one with my wife at a little Mexican restaurant near Chicago. You can make your quesadilla with one tortilla folded, or flat with two tortillas, as in this recipe inspired by *The Essential Cook Book* by Caroline and Terence Conran and Simon Hopkinson.

> 2 flour tortillas (6-inch size)
> ½ c. shredded cheddar cheese
> 1 quarter of a Granny Smith apple
> 1 tbsp. finely chopped pecans

Sprinkle one tortilla with ¼ cup of cheese. Core apple and slice thinly. Arrange slices in spoke pattern atop cheese. Sprinkle with 1 tablespoon pecans and top with remaining ¼ cup cheese. Cover with other tortilla and cook in large frying pan over medium heat, turning once, until browned and cheese has melted, about 3 minutes. Cut into wedges.

Grilled Four Cheese Sandwich

This sandwich, based on a recipe from Angie Toole in *The Buffalo News*, has real appeal to a lifelong proponent of culinary overkill like me. I suspect you'll like it too.

> 2 slices wheat bread
> 2 tbsp. cream cheese, softened
> 2 tbsp. butter, softened
> 2 slices Monterey Jack cheese
> 2 slices cheddar cheese
> red onion slices
> tomato slices
> 2 tbsp. grated Parmesan cheese

Spread bread slices with cream cheese on one side, butter on the other. On the cream cheese side of one slice, layer remaining ingredients except Parmesan. Top with other slice of bread, cream cheese side down. Sprinkle assembled sandwich on both sides with Parmesan cheese. Grill until golden and cheese is melted, about 2–3 minutes per side.

Muffuletta

You'd expect a place with the culinary reputation of New Orleans to produce a sandwich of Epicurean dimensions, and this is it. I've found that this recipe, adapted from the *Joy of Cooking*, serves nicely between visits to the city's Central Grocery, home of the definitive version. Feel free to vary the ingredients, but the olives are essential for authenticity.

1 c. chopped pitted green olives
1 c. chopped pitted black olives
½ c. olive oil
⅓ c. chopped parsley
¾ tsp. dried oregano
1 clove garlic, minced
1 roasted red pepper, chopped
1 tbsp. lemon juice
1 lg. round loaf Italian bread
2 c. salad greens
4 oz. sliced soft salami
4 oz. sliced hard salami
4 oz. sliced provolone cheese
½ c. oil-packed sun-dried tomatoes, drained and chopped

Combine first 8 ingredients (through lemon juice) and refrigerate 8 hours. Slice bread in half horizontally, removing and discarding most of soft inner bread. Drain olive mixture, saving the marinade. Generously coat cut sides of bread with the marinade. Spread half of olive mixture onto one slice of bread and layer in remaining ingredients. Top with remaining bread, wrap in plastic, weight down and refrigerate for at least 30 minutes before slicing into wedges.

Missouri Sirloin
and Blue Cheese Burger

This recipe adapted from Marcel Desaulniers' book, *The Burger Meisters*, a collection of burger recipes from America's best chefs, was developed by Bill Cardwell of St. Louis restaurant fame. I have doubled the amount of blue cheese originally called for. Cardwell's serves the burger on cornmeal black-pepper bread.

> 1½ lbs. ground sirloin
> 2 oz. blue cheese
> salt and pepper to taste
> 4 slices (1 oz. each) white cheddar cheese
> 8 crisp slices bacon
> tomato relish

Form meat into 8 patties. Make an indentation in the center of 4 patties and fill each with a ½-ounce ball of blue cheese. Top each with another patty and seal edges. Grill or sauté until done. Top each burger with cheddar and bacon, and serve on bun with tomato relish.

 # New American Bistro Burger

This recipe, adapted from Rick Rodgers' book, *365 Ways to Cook Hamburger and Other Ground Meats*, is admittedly trendy, but it still satisfies the basic hamburger craving.

> 1⅓ lbs. lean ground lamb or sirloin
> 3 tbsp. pesto
> 2 tbsp. grated Parmesan
> ½ tsp. salt
> ¼ tsp. pepper
> 4 oz. goat cheese, cut into 8 slices

Mix meat, pesto, Parmesan, salt, and pepper, and form into 4 patties and grill. Thirty seconds before done, top each burger with 2 slices of cheese. Serve with arugula on toasted sourdough French bread.

Chicago Beer Burger

This recipe, adapted from Marcel Desaulniers' *The Burger Meisters*, is the creation of Carlyn Berghoff of the famous Chicago restaurant family. Any beer will work, but I prefer something fairly dark. On the assumption that you can't have too much of a good thing, Berghoff recommends serving the burgers with onions that have been braised in beer.

> 1½ lbs. ground chuck
> 2 tbsp. beer
> ½ tsp. Tabasco sauce
> ¼ tsp. Worcestershire sauce
> salt and pepper to taste
> 4 slices (½ oz. each) brick cheese

Combine all ingredients except cheese and form into 6 patties. Grill or sauté until desired doneness. Top with cheese, allow to melt, and serve on toasted buns.

 # Tex-Mex Dried Beef Supreme

This recipe adapted from the Knauss Dried Beef Company, the world's largest producer of naturally cured dried beef, is easy to make and would no doubt work equally well with Spam in place of the beef. It can be served cold or heated in the microwave for 15–20 seconds.

> 4 oz. chopped dried beef
> 2 c. shredded lettuce
> 1 tomato, chopped
> 4 oz. shredded cheddar cheese
> ¾ c. sour cream
> ⅓ c. chopped onion
> ¼ c. Italian salad dressing
> ¼ c. chopped black olives
> ¼ tsp. Worcestershire sauce
> 6–8 soft tortilla shells

Mix all ingredients except tortillas together in a large bowl and refrigerate until needed. When ready to serve, scoop mixture onto soft tortilla shells and fold.

Prima Donna Pizza

This recipe is the specialty of Barbara Herbert, Southeast Public Radio's opera maven, whose taste in pizza, as in music, veers toward the authentically Italian. In this case, however, she has added a few classic Greek ingredients to the traditional Pizza Margherita to produce a dish that is worth singing about. For best results, Barb advises baking the pie on a hot stone in a convection oven. For added atmosphere, of course, eat while listening to Barb's Sunday Night at the Opera, every Sunday at 7 PM on Southeast Public Radio.

> 1 tbsp. active dry yeast
> ¾ c. plus 2 tbsp. lukewarm water
> 2¾ c. flour
> 1 tsp. salt
> 3 c. grated Sargento brand 6-cheese blend
> 1 c. crumbled feta cheese
> 1⅓ c. chopped, peeled plum tomatoes
> 24 pitted Kalamata olives
> fresh basil leaves

Dissolve yeast in water and let stand 10 minutes or until slightly foamy. Stir together flour and salt and form into a mound with a well in the center. Add yeast mixture to well and stir with a fork in a circular motion, gradually pulling flour into yeast mixture to form a dough. Knead dough on a floured surface for about 10 minutes until smooth and elastic. Place in oiled bowl, cover with plastic wrap, and let rise until doubled, 1–2 hours. Turn dough out onto floured surface, punch down, and roll out to desired shape and thickness (¼-inch for crispy pizza, ½-inch for softer crust). Roll the edges to form a small rim. Cover with cheese blend and crumbled feta. Scatter tomatoes, olives, and basil over cheese. Bake on a cornmeal-dusted pan or pizza stone at 450 degrees for 10 minutes, then lower oven temperature to 400 degrees and bake about 10 minutes longer, or until crust is golden. Makes 1 large pizza or 4 small ones.

Balsamic Glazed Pasta

This simple dish, which I adapted from a clipping in my files, is quick and easy, would be especially good when tomatoes are in season.

 1 tsp. olive oil
 1 c. chopped onion
 ½ lb. kielbasa, sliced
 ½ lb. mushrooms, halved
 2 tsp. minced garlic
 ½ c. balsamic vinegar
 3 Roma tomatoes
 ½ c. parsley
 8 oz. bellflower, gemelli, or similar pasta
 ¼ c. grated Parmesan cheese

Sauté onion in olive oil at medium-high heat until it begins to soften. Add kielbasa and brown for 2–3 minutes. Add mushrooms and garlic, and cook, stirring frequently, until mushrooms release their liquid. Reduce heat to low, add vinegar, and simmer 4–5 minutes. Quarter tomatoes, then cut each quarter in half. Chop parsley. Cook pasta in boiling water until tender, and drain. Combine pasta, balsamic mixture, tomatoes, parsley, and Parmesan and toss. Season with salt and pepper and additional Parmesan if desired. Serves 4.

Penne with Asparagus
and Lemon Cream Sauce

This low-fat recipe, adapted from *Eating Well* magazine, was a real hit when we made it at our California friends' house using lemons picked from their tree. It will taste just as good at your house made with lemons from the supermarket, and it can be thrown together in minutes.

 1 lb. asparagus
 2 bunches scallions
 1 tsp. olive oil
 ¾ c. part-skim ricotta cheese
 2 tsp. grated lemon zest
 12 oz. penne pasta
 ¼ c. slivered fresh basil

Trim asparagus and scallions, and cut into 1-inch diagonal pieces. Cook in oil over medium heat, stirring occasionally, until tender and browned, about 10 minutes. Whisk together ricotta and lemon zest. Cook penne. Stir ¼ cup of pasta cooking-water into ricotta mixture and toss with drained pasta. Add vegetables and toss well. Season with salt and pepper and garnish with basil. Serves 4.

Jarabe Tapatío
(Mexican Hat Dance) Pasta

This recipe is based on a favorite old dish, from the venerable *Silver Palate Cookbook*, which has been doctored with a little tequila.

2 tbsp. olive oil
½ c. finely chopped onion
1 can (35 oz.) tomatoes
2 tsp. tarragon
salt and pepper
1 c. heavy cream
pinch of cayenne pepper
1½ c. shrimp, crab, or lobster
1 lb. pasta, preferably sombrerini (little hats)
½ c. 100% agave blanco tequila
½ c. fresh cilantro leaves

Cook onion in oil, covered, over low heat until tender. Chop and drain tomatoes, and add to onions along with tarragon. Season to taste with salt and pepper, and bring to a boil. Reduce heat, cover, and simmer, stirring occasionally, for 30 minutes. Let mixture cool slightly and purée in food processor. Return to saucepan, stir in cream, and simmer over medium heat for about 15 minutes until slightly reduced. Stir in cayenne and seafood, and continue simmering until seafood is heated through. Meanwhile, cook the pasta. Add tequila to sauce and cook only long enough to warm it, but not so long as to evaporate all of the alcohol. Serve sauce over drained pasta and garnish with cilantro. Serves 4.

Linguine with Lobster

Linguine ought to be the lexicographer's favorite pasta since it is Italian for "little tongues" and is related to words like "language," "linguist," and "lingo." This recipe, an upscale version of the clam linguine we thrived on in graduate-school days, is adapted from Diane Seed's *Italian Cooking with Olive Oil*.

> 2 (1½ lb. each) live lobsters
> 3 tbsp. delicate extra-virgin olive oil
> 2 garlic cloves, minced
> 8 ripe plum tomatoes (1 lb.), peeled, seeded, and finely chopped
> ½ c. chopped fresh flat-leaf parsley
> 1 lb. linguine
> salt and pepper

Partially cook lobsters covered in rapidly boiling water for 3–4 minutes. Drain, cool, remove meat, and cut into ½-inch pieces, reserving juices. Heat oil over medium heat, add garlic, and cook until barely colored, about 1 minute. Stir in tomatoes and parsley, bring to a simmer, reduce heat to low, and cook for 10 minutes. Add lobster and its juices and cook for another 3 minutes. Meanwhile, cook linguine in boiling water until barely tender. Drain, toss with lobster sauce, and season with salt and pepper. Serves 4–6.

 # Spicy Thai Pasta with Chicken

This recipe is adapted from one by Kerry Bullette, which placed in a recent *Joplin Globe*'s "Cookie Cook-off." The crushed cookies take the place of the chopped peanuts which would normally adorn such a dish.

> 1 lb. linguine
> 1 clove minced garlic
> ¼ c. sesame oil
> ¼ tsp. ground ginger
> 4 tbsp. crunchy peanut butter
> ¼ tsp. soy sauce
> 1 tbsp. honey
> juice of ½ lime
> 1 tsp. red-pepper flakes
> 2 boneless chicken breasts
> ½ c. crushed Girl Scout peanut-butter sandwich cookies

Prepare linguine according to package directions. While pasta cooks, mix together garlic, oil, ginger, peanut butter, soy sauce, honey, lime juice, and red-pepper flakes. Grill chicken breasts, julienne, and toss in bowl with drained pasta and sauce. Sprinkle crushed cookies over top. Serves 4.

Upscale Macaroni and Cheese

The addition of blue cheese makes this favorite childhood dish elegant enough for the most sophisticated adult. Any blue cheese will work well in this recipe adapted from *Bon Appétit* magazine, but I prefer one of the stronger varieties.

> 2 tbsp. butter
> 3 lg. red bell peppers, cut into ½-inch pieces
> 5 celery stalks, chopped
> salt and pepper
> 1½ c. whipping cream
> 1½ c. half-and-half
> 1 lb. crumbled blue cheese
> 1 tsp. celery seeds
> cayenne pepper
> 3 egg yolks
> ½ c. chopped celery leaves
> 1 lb. penne pasta
> ¾ c. grated Parmesan cheese

Sauté peppers and celery in butter until just beginning to soften. Remove from heat. Season with salt and pepper. Combine cream, half-and-half, and blue cheese, and stir over low heat until cheese melts. Remove from heat. Add celery seeds. Season sauce with cayenne, salt, and pepper. Beat yolks to blend and gradually whisk in half of cheese sauce. Return mixture to saucepan and whisk into remaining sauce to blend. Add celery leaves. Cook pasta until tender but firm to bite. Drain. Add sauce and vegetables, and stir to blend. Transfer to a buttered 4-quart oval baking dish and sprinkle with Parmesan. Bake at 400 degrees until sauce is bubbling and top is starting to brown, about 25 minutes. Serves 12.

Pasta with Tomatoes and Four Cheeses

Ever since we first ran across it more than a decade ago, we've been making this wonderful pasta dish adapted from *Bon Appétit* magazine. It's so simple you don't even have to cook the sauce.

2¾ lbs. diced tomatoes
½ c. shredded fresh basil
1½ tsp. coarse kosher salt
1 lg. garlic clove, minced
1 c. ricotta cheese, room temperature
2 tbsp. whipping cream
fresh ground pepper
fresh ground nutmeg
½ c. Fontina cheese, diced
½ c. mozzarella cheese, diced
1 lb. rotelle or other short pasta
2 tbsp. olive oil
1 c. freshly grated Parmesan cheese

Combine first 4 ingredients in bowl and let stand 1–2 hours, stirring occasionally. Fluff ricotta with fork and thin to creamy consistency with cream. Season with pepper and nutmeg. Mix in Fontina and mozzarella. Drain most of liquid from tomatoes, leaving just enough to keep moist. Cook pasta until tender but firm to bite. Drain well and toss with oil. Add cheese mixture and toss until cheese begins to melt. Spoon tomato mixture over top. Toss at table and sprinkle each serving with Parmesan. Serves 4.

Stir-fry of Asparagus with Pears and Chicken

In this country if you want to get rid of somebody, you might say, "Go fly a kite!" But in Spain they say, "¡*Vete a freir espárragos!*" which means "Go fry asparagus!" This dish, adapted from one developed for the *Executive Health's Good Health Report*, is a delicious way to comply with such a request. Serve it with rice, couscous, or better yet, German pancakes.

> 2 c. sliced pears
> 2 tbsp. lemon juice
> ½ lb. chicken fingers
> 1 tbsp. oil
> 2 c. sliced asparagus
> 1 c. sliced mushrooms
> 1 c. sliced red bell peppers
> ½ c. sliced onion
> ½ tsp. salt
> 2 tbsp. fresh tarragon or 1 tbsp. dried

Toss pears with lemon juice. Sauté chicken pieces in oil until cooked through. Add asparagus, mushrooms, peppers, onion, salt, and tarragon, and cook until crisp-tender. Add pears and cook until heated through. Serves 4.

Lucky Lettuce Wraps

The Chinese word for lettuce, *sang choi*, sounds like the word meaning "to bring about wealth and riches," making these lettuce wraps a perfect choice for Chinese New Year. The recipe is adapted from the About.com website.

1 head iceberg or romaine lettuce
1 tbsp. sesame oil
1 garlic clove
1 slice ginger
2 green onions
1 lb. boneless and skinless chicken breasts
1 red pepper
1 can water chestnuts
1 stalk celery
1 tbsp. soy sauce
2 tbsp. oyster sauce
1 tbsp. dry sherry
1 tsp. sugar
1 tbsp. cornstarch
2 tbsp. water

Wash and dry lettuce. Separate leaves and set aside. Heat sesame oil over high heat. Mince garlic and ginger, chop green onions, and add to pan, frying until garlic and ginger are aromatic. Slice chicken and add to pan, cooking until browned. Seed and dice red pepper, rinse water chestnuts and chop, and dice celery; add to pan. Mix together soy sauce, oyster sauce, sherry, and sugar, add to pan, and cook over medium heat for a few minutes. Combine cornstarch and water, and add to sauce, stirring to thicken. Lay out lettuce leaves, spoon tablespoon of mixture into middle of each, and fold into a package.

Basil Chicken Wellington

This elegant entrée, a specialty of Chef James F. Coley of Cape Girardeau, Missouri's Rose Bed Inn, is perfect for any romantic occasion, especially Valentine's Day. If you really want to impress your dining companion, decorate the dish with heart shapes cut out of additional puff pastry and secured to the Wellington with egg wash for the last 10 minutes of baking.

        2 sticks butter
        1 tbsp. olive oil
        1 c. white wine
        2 med. onions, diced
        1 bulb garlic, crushed
        2 cans (3½ oz. each) sliced mushrooms
        2 tsp. diced fresh basil
        6 oz. Swiss cheese, shredded
        6 boneless, skinless chicken breasts
        10x15-inch sheet of puff pastry
        2 eggs, beaten
        2 tbsp. honey
        ½ tsp. salt
        ½ tsp. ground white pepper
        ½ c. heavy cream

Melt together 1 stick butter, the olive oil, and ¼ cup of the wine. Add the onions and half the garlic, and sauté until onions are translucent. Drain mushrooms and add along with 1 teaspoon of the basil, and sauté another 5 minutes. Drain liquid and chill mixture. Once chilled, stir in cheese and set aside. Trim chicken breasts and pound between sheets of plastic wrap until uniform thickness of about ½-inch. Place a 2-oz. scoop of the mushroom and cheese mixture in the middle of each breast and gather edges over to form a ball. Place breasts in cups or large muffin tin and freeze just until they hold their shape. Cut puff pastry into 5-inch squares and roll out a bit to increase size. Cover each breast with pastry using beaten egg to seal all edges. Bake at 350 degrees on lightly greased baking sheet for 1 hour. While chicken bakes, sauté remaining garlic in remaining 1 stick butter until golden. Add remaining ¾ cup wine and 1 teaspoon basil, honey, and salt and pepper. Simmer until alcohol boils off. Add cream, bring to a boil, lower heat and simmer until reduced by one-third. To serve, ladle sauce onto plate, place chicken in center, and garnish with fresh basil. Makes 6 servings.

Basil Grilled Chicken

This recipe adapted from *McCall's Magazine* calls for basil oil, which you can buy at gourmet stores such as Williams-Sonoma, but it's easy to make yourself. Simply put ½ cup packed basil leaves into ½ cup olive oil and cook in the lower third of a 300-degree oven for an hour. Strain the oil into a glass jar and keep covered loosely and refrigerated at all times for up to one month. This chicken would go well sliced and served over salad greens.

> 1 tbsp. plus 1 tsp. basil oil
> ½ tsp. minced garlic
> ¼ tsp. hot red pepper flakes
> 4 boneless, skinless chicken breast halves
> ¼ tsp. each salt and pepper

Combine 1 tablespoon oil, garlic, and pepper flakes in glass pie plate. Add chicken and turn to coat evenly. Let stand 15 minutes. Sprinkle both sides of chicken with salt and pepper, and grill over medium heat 3 4 minutes until cooked through. Drizzle with remaining teaspoon basil oil.

Orange Tea Chicken

This recipe, inspired by one in Jennifer and Mo Siegel's book, *Cooking With Tea*, would work well with any orange-flavored tea, such as Celestial Seasonings' Mandarin Orange Spice or Bigelow's Constant Comment.

> 4 orange-flavored tea bags
> 1 c. flour
> ½ tsp. garlic powder
> ½ tsp. ground pepper
> 4 boneless chicken breasts, halved
> 4 tbsp. butter
> 3½ c. water
> 2 tsp. sherry
> ¾ c. orange marmalade

Brew tea in water, letting steep for at least 5 minutes. Remove bags, squeezing out liquid. Combine flour, garlic powder, and pepper, and coat breasts lightly with mixture. Brown breasts in butter over medium heat. Add sherry and marmalade to tea and pour over breasts. Simmer 15–20 minutes or until cooked through.

Thelma Stone's Apricot Chicken

Chicken and fruit make a great combination, as this easy recipe from the River Heritage Quilters' Guild cookbook demonstrates. Mrs. Stone, one of only a very few certified quilt appraisers in Southeast Missouri, suggests serving this dish with rice and a green salad.

12 boneless chicken breast halves, skinned
1 can (12 oz.) apricot nectar
¼ tsp. ground ginger
¼ tsp. pepper
1 tsp. ground allspice
½ tsp. salt
¾ c. apricot preserves
½ c. chopped toasted pecans

Place breasts in 13x9 baking dish. Combine nectar and spices, and pour over chicken. Cover and chill 8 hours. Remove from refrigerator and let stand 30 minutes. Drain liquid and discard. Heat preserves over low heat until warm and brush over chicken. Bake uncovered at 350 degrees for 25 minutes, basting with preserves. Sprinkle with pecans; garnish with celery leaves if desired.

Picnic Chicken

This recipe adapted from *Bon Appétit* magazine is easy to prepare, and though it is excellent hot, it's just as flavorful when served cold, hence its name.

½ c. fresh lemon juice
6 garlic cloves
1 bay leaf
½ tsp. dried thyme
½ tsp. dried marjoram
½ tsp. dried summer savory
1 (5 lb.) roasting chicken

Combine first 6 ingredients in blender and blend until garlic and bay leaf are finely chopped. Transfer mixture to bowl. Add chicken to bowl and turn to coat. Marinate chicken in bowl in refrigerator, breast-side down, overnight. Place rack in roasting pan. Remove chicken from marinade, reserving marinade. Place chicken on prepared rack and season with salt and pepper. Roast in 375-degree oven until chicken is cooked through, basting occasionally with reserved marinade, about 1 hour and 20 minutes.

Roast Chicken and Potatoes
with Balsamic Black-Pepper Sauce

This dish used to be served at the old Rainbow Room in New York. The recipe is adapted from a version which appeared in *Bon Appétit* magazine.

½ c. olive oil
¾ c. chopped onions
1 tbsp. thyme
2 tbsp. flour
3½ c. chicken broth
1¾ c. beef broth
2½ tbsp. balsamic vinegar
½ tsp. ground black pepper
2 lbs. red potatoes
1½ tbsp. chopped garlic
1 tbsp. fresh rosemary, chopped
1 cut up fryer chicken (5 lbs.)

Sauté onions and thyme in 2 tablespoons oil over medium-high heat until onions begin to brown. Add flour and stir 1 minute. Gradually whisk in broths and boil until reduced to 1½ cups, stirring occasionally. Add vinegar and pepper. Cut potatoes lengthwise into 1-inch wedges and toss with garlic, rosemary, and 1 tablespoon oil. Arrange, rounded-side down, on baking sheet. Brown chicken skin-side down in remaining oil, about 15 minutes. Turn over and cook another 5 minutes. Place skillet with chicken on rack in bottom third of a 375-degree oven, and place potatoes on rack in top third. Roast 45 minutes or until potatoes and chicken are cooked through. Serve with sauce.

Paella Rapida

Traditional paella, that magnificent dish from Spain, can be a lot of trouble to make, but not in this streamlined recipe adapted from *Eating Well* magazine which, because it substitutes smoked mussels for the customary pork sausage, is also low in fat.

2 c. defatted reduced-sodium chicken stock
¼ tsp. saffron threads, crushed, or pinch-powdered
1 tbsp. olive oil
½ lb. medium shrimp, peeled and deveined
½ lb. boneless, skinned chicken breast, cut into ½-inch-thick strips
salt and pepper to taste
1 onion, chopped
2 cloves garlic, minced
1 can (14½ oz.) tomatoes with juice
⅛ tsp. red-pepper flakes
1 c. arborio rice
1 c. artichoke hearts, canned in water or frozen and thawed
1 c. frozen peas, thawed
⅓ c. bottled roasted red pepper, cut into strips
⅓ c. smoked mussels (2 oz.), not packed in oil

Bring chicken stock and saffron to simmer and set aside. In large nonstick skillet, heat 1 teaspoon oil over high heat, add shrimp, and sauté until pink, 3–4 minutes, and set aside. Add 1 teaspoon oil to skillet and sauté chicken until lightly browned and opaque, 3–4 minutes. Remove from skillet. Season chicken and shrimp with salt and pepper. Reduce heat to medium and add remaining 1 teaspoon oil, stir in onions and garlic, and sauté until softened. Add 1–2 tablespoons water if they become too dry. Stir in tomatoes and pepper flakes, simmer uncovered for 3 minutes, breaking up tomatoes with a wooden spoon. Add rice and stir to coat well with tomato mixture. Stir in stock, bring to a simmer, and cook covered over low heat for 20 minutes. Gently stir in artichoke hearts, peas, red peppers, and mussels, and cook covered for 5–10 minutes until rice is tender, and shrimp and chicken are heated through, stirring occasionally. Serves 4.

King Ranch Chicken Casserole

The King Ranch, where this dish originated, is considered the birthplace of American ranching. Founded in 1853 by Captain Richard King, it is the largest ranch in the world. The dish, a common one in Texas, is typically loaded with fat and calories, but has been slimmed down considerably in this recipe adapted from *Vegetarian Times*. The magazine, true to its mission, recommends using vegetable stock and substituting tofu for the chicken, but I have put the meat back in while retaining the other healthy modifications.

3 c. cooked chicken, cubed (or tofu if you prefer)
1 c. onions, finely chopped
1 c. green pepper, finely chopped
1 clove garlic, chopped
½ tsp. chili powder, divided
¼ tsp. ground cumin
2½ tbsp. flour
1½ c. chicken or vegetable stock
¼ c. reduced-fat sour cream or yogurt
salt to taste
8 flour tortillas (6-inch size)
1 can (14½ oz.) diced tomatoes with green chiles, drained
1½ c. shredded reduced-fat cheddar cheese
paprika for garnish

Combine chicken or tofu, onions, pepper, garlic, ¼ teaspoon chili powder, and cumin, and set aside. Whisk flour into stock and cook over medium heat, whisking constantly, until sauce is thick enough to coat the back of a spoon. Remove from heat and whisk in sour cream or yogurt, remaining chili powder, and salt. In casserole dish, layer tortillas, chicken or tofu mixture, and tomatoes alternately, beginning and ending with tortillas. Pour sauce over casserole, sprinkle with cheese and paprika, and bake at 350 degrees about 30–35 minutes until hot and bubbly. Serves 8.

Duck Breast
with Moroccan Honey Sauce

This beautiful dish adapted from *A Taste of Honey*, a lovely book by Jane Charlton and Jane Newdick, showcases duck's affinity for sweet sauces and was inspired by the Moroccan fondness for honey. The recipe should work almost as well with chicken.

> 1 cinnamon stick
> 1 tbsp. hot strong coffee
> ¼ tsp. allspice
> ¼ tsp. nutmeg
> ¼ tsp. cloves
> 2 tsp. sugar
> 4¼ tbsp. honey
> 4 duck breasts, skin on
> 1 stick butter
> 1¼ c. chicken broth

Break cinnamon stick in half and place in shallow container. Pour coffee over it and let stand for 15 minutes. Combine allspice, nutmeg, cloves, sugar, and 2 teaspoons honey. Add coffee, discarding cinnamon stick, and mix well. Brush duck breasts with mixture and let marinate for 2–3 hours. Pan-fry breasts skin-side down over high heat for 5 minutes, then turn and fry 2–3 minutes more. Remove from pan and keep warm. Pour off all but 2 teaspoons fat, add butter, and when melted, add remaining marinade, the broth, and remaining half of cinnamon stick. Simmer 8–10 minutes until sauce thickens. Discard cinnamon stick and serve sauce over breasts.

Roast Cornish Hens with Gooseberries

Squab, or pigeon, was enjoyed by English families in Shakespeare's day regardless of their station. The lowly farmer would raise them in the rafters of his tiny cottage, while the wealthy landowner maintained dovecotes. Pigeon is still considered a delicacy in France, but most Americans haven't tried it nor care to, so this variation on an Elizabethan recipe, adapted from the *Joy of Cooking*, employs Cornish hens instead.

    4 Cornish hens
    1½ tsp. thyme
    1 tsp. salt
    1 tsp. pepper
    4 tbsp. melted butter
    4 sprigs rosemary
    1 c. gooseberries

Remove giblets from hens, rinse, and pat dry. Combine thyme, salt, and pepper, and rub over hens. Insert rosemary into body cavities. Brush with melted butter and bake in 400-degree oven about 30 minutes or until done. Garnish with gooseberries and serve.

Turducken Roulade

This recipe makes 6–8 servings. If you need more, rather than making a larger roll, simply make another roulade of this same, more manageable, size. Any stuffing will do, though cornbread dressing is perhaps the most authentic, given the turducken's Southern roots. If you want to go all out, you can use three different flavors of stuffing, as is often done for a classic turducken.

    1 boneless turkey breast (about 2 lbs.)
    1 boneless duck breast
    1 boneless chicken thigh
    3 c. stuffing
    8 slices bacon

Butterfly turkey breast, and with a heavy mallet or rolling pin, pound to an even thickness of about ½ inch. Similarly pound duck breast and chicken thigh. Cover turkey breast with a layer of stuffing. Lay duck breast on top and cover with additional stuffing. Top with chicken thigh and cover with remaining stuffing. Roll up tightly, jelly-roll style. Lay bacon slices side-by-side over roll. Wrap tightly in parchment paper, twisting ends to seal. Wrap in aluminum foil. Bake at 350 degrees until internal temperature reaches 155 degrees, about 1½ hours. Remove from oven, let rest 20 minutes, remove foil, paper, and bacon strips. Slice and serve.

Steak and Guinness Pie

This easy recipe, an adaptation of one on the Irish website Ireland-Information.com, is a typical Irish favorite.

> double-crust pie pastry
> 2 lbs. round steak, cubed
> 1 tbsp. flour
> 3 tbsp. shortening
> 8 slices bacon, chopped
> 5 sm. onions, peeled and chopped
> 1 tbsp. brown sugar
> 1 tbsp. raisins
> 1 bottle Guinness Stout

Roll steak in flour and brown in shortening with bacon. Cook onion until golden and add to meat. Add rest of ingredients, cover tightly, and simmer over low heat or in 325-degree oven for 2½ hours, stirring occasionally and adding more Guinness if gravy gets too thick. Line deep pie dish with half the crust and bake at 425 degrees until just starting to color. Add beef mixture, cover with top crust, and bake until golden, about 10 minutes.

 # Saltimbocca

The name of this dish is a contraction of the Italian *salta in bocca* or "it leaps into the mouth" because it is so tasty. The name comes from the Latin *saltare*, meaning "to leap or jump," which is also the basis for the French word *sauté*, or "jumped," a reference to how the contents of the pan should be tossed during this cooking procedure. This recipe is adapted from Rosso and Lukins' *The New Basics Cookbook*.

> 8 oz. veal scallopini (4 pieces), pounded thin
> salt and pepper
> flour
> 4 tbsp. butter
> ¼ c. Parmesan cheese shavings
> 4 thin slices prosciutto, cut to fit scallopine
> 4 fresh sage leaves
> ⅓ c. dry Italian white wine
> 1 tsp. minced fresh sage leaves

Season veal with salt and pepper, and dust with flour, shaking off excess. Sauté veal in 2 tablespoons butter over medium-high heat until lightly browned. Transfer to baking dish and sprinkle cheese over. Cover each slice of veal with 1 slice prosciutto and a sage leaf. Bake at 375 degrees until cooked through, about 5 minutes. Meanwhile, add wine to skillet, cook over high heat, scraping up brown bits until reduced to 3 tablespoons. Lower heat and swirl in remaining butter and minced sage. Arrange veal on plate and pour sauce over. Serves 2.

Nancy Reagan's Veal Piccata

Mrs. Reagan especially liked veal piccata because it was simple and light, yet elegant enough for state occasions. If you'd rather not use veal, you could substitute chicken breast in this recipe adapted from Henry Haller's *White House Family Cookbook*.

        12 slices veal tenderloin
        ½ c. flour
        1 tbsp. salt
        ½ tsp. white pepper
        2 eggs
        1 tbsp. Worcestershire sauce
        1 tbsp. chopped parsley
        ¼ c. grated Romano cheese
        ¾ c. clarified butter
        6 thin lemon slices
        pinch of paprika
        pinch of finely chopped parsley

Pound veal between sheets of wax paper to a thickness of ⅛ inch. Combine flour, salt, and pepper. Beat eggs with Worcestershire sauce, chopped parsley, and cheese. Dredge veal slices in flour mixture, then dip in egg mixture to coat. Sauté veal in butter in heavy skillet over medium-high heat until browned, about 3 minutes per side. Drain on paper towels. Sprinkle one half of each lemon slice with paprika and the other with finely chopped parsley and use for garnish.

Tournedos Rossini

There couldn't be a more elegant way to celebrate a special occasion than this classic dish, though it's quite a splurge. This recipe, based on one from Julee Rosso and Sheila Lukins of *Silver Palate* fame, calls for serving the beef on a bed of celery root, instead of the traditional crouton, and puts the truffle slices in the sauce. For such an aristocratic entrée, the preparation is really quite simple and easy.

> 2 tbsp. fresh lemon juice
> 2 sm. bulbs celery root
> 1 tbsp. butter
> 2 beef tournedos (5–6 oz.)
> salt and pepper to taste
> 2 slices foie gras, ¼-inch thick
> 1 c. Madeira sauce (use bottled or your own recipe)
> 3 sm. truffles, sliced

Peel celery root and cut into ¼-inch slices, placing into mixture of lemon juice and water to keep from turning brown. Simmer in boiling water until tender, then drain and sauté in butter until golden. Arrange slices overlapping on two dinner plates. Season tournedos with salt and pepper, and sauté over medium heat until medium-rare (about 4 minutes per side). Place on sliced celery root and keep warm. Sauté foie gras over medium heat about 1 minute per side and place a slice on each tournedos. Whisk Madeira sauce into skillet, scraping up brown bits, add truffle slices, bring to a boil, and spoon over fillets.

Flank Steak with Crispy Polenta and Roasted Shallot Vinaigrette

This elegant recipe, adapted from a cookbook by Charlie Trotter, whose Chicago restaurant houses the best known "chef's table" in the country, is easy enough that you can serve it at your own table any time you want.

> 2 tbsp. chopped garlic
> ¼ c. butter
> 2 c. hot polenta
> salt and pepper
> 4 shallots
> 1 c. olive oil
> 3 tbsp. balsamic vinegar
> 2 tbsp. chopped chives
> 4 (4 oz. each) pieces flank steak
> 10 sprigs thyme

Sauté garlic in 3 tablespoons of the butter for 1 minute. Fold into polenta and season with salt and pepper. Spread on a sheet pan into a ½-inch-thick layer, cover with plastic wrap, and chill for 2 hours. Meanwhile, peel shallots and place in an ovenproof pan with ¾ cup of the olive oil. Bake at 350 degrees for 50–60 minutes until soft. Let cool, remove shallots, and reserve oil. Julienne the shallots and put in a bowl. Add vinegar and slowly whisk in reserved oil. Add chopped chives and season with salt and pepper. Cut polenta into four 3-inch discs and sauté in remaining tablespoon of butter in a hot, nonstick pan for 2–3 minutes on each side until golden brown and crispy. Blot with paper towels. Season steak with salt and pepper, and rub with remaining ¼ cup olive oil. Remove thyme leaves from their stems and rub onto beef. Grill for 5–7 minutes on each side until medium-rare. Place a piece of polenta in the center of each plate and top with a piece of steak. Spoon vinaigrette over and around plates, and top with a grinding of fresh pepper. Serves 4.

Tagine of Lamb with Prunes

The word "tagine," like the word "casserole," can refer both to a cooking vessel and the dish that's cooked in it. The pot usually has a conical lid and is made of earthenware. The dish is a Moroccan specialty. This particular version, adapted from Kitty Morse's *Cooking at the Kasbah*, is an exceptional one that doesn't taste as sweet as you might expect. You can leave out the saffron for economy's sake if you wish, and I suspect the dish would be just as good with pork instead of lamb.

        2 tbsp. olive oil
        1 tsp. ground turmeric
        1 tsp. ground ginger
        2 lbs. leg of lamb, trimmed and cut into 2-inch chunks
        2 onions
        1 c. chicken broth
        15 fresh cilantro sprigs, tied with cotton string
        8 threads saffron
        1 c. pitted prunes
        2 tbsp. honey
        1 tsp. ground cinnamon
        ½ tsp. pepper
        salt to taste
        1 tbsp. toasted unhulled sesame seeds

In Dutch oven over medium-high heat, sauté turmeric, ginger, and lamb in olive oil until meat is well coated and lightly browned. Finely dice one onion and add to meat. Add broth, cilantro, and saffron. (If using saffron, toast 2–3 minutes in a nonstick pan, stirring constantly, before crushing into pot.) Cover, reduce heat to medium-low, and cook for an hour or so until meat is tender. Discard cilantro and remove meat, keeping warm. Bring sauce in pot to a simmer and add prunes, honey, cinnamon, pepper, and remaining onion, sliced, and season with salt. Cook until mixture thickens, about 6–8 minutes and spoon sauce over meat. Sprinkle with sesame seeds. Serves 4.

Pork Chops with Guinness Stout and Onion Gravy

This recipe, adapted from Guiness' official American home page, calls for a cup of stout, which means that if you use a standard 14.9-ounce can of Guinness draught, you should have almost another cup left over to consume as you prepare the dish.

> 8 pork chops, 1-inch thick
> salt and pepper to taste
> all-purpose flour
> 1 tbsp. butter
> 1 tbsp. oil
> 3 lg. onions, sliced
> 3 lg. garlic cloves, minced
> 1 c. Guinness Stout
> 1 c. chicken stock
> 1 tbsp. coarse-grained mustard
> 1 tbsp. fresh parsley
> 1½ tsp. balsamic vinegar

Season pork with salt and pepper, and dredge in flour, shaking off excess. Melt butter and half the oil in heavy skillet and brown pork in batches, about 6 minutes per side. Set aside. Dredge onions in flour, shake off excess, and sauté with garlic in remaining oil. Cover and cook 8–10 minutes, stirring occasionally. Add stout and ¾ cup stock, and bring to boil, scraping up brown bits. Return pork to skillet, add additional stock and stout to bring liquid halfway up sides of pork, cover, and simmer 20 minutes. Turn pork over and cook 25 minutes more. Transfer pork and onions to platter, boil pan juices until thickened slightly, whisk in mustard, parsley, and vinegar, and pour over meat.

Barbecued Ribs, Missouri Style

This recipe, adapted from Chris Schlesinger and John Willoughby's informative book *The Thrill of the Grill*, comes about as close to true barbecuing as you can get at home. The secret is cooking the ribs slowly in the oven, then finishing them on the grill. The term "3/down" refers to the weight of the ribs, 3 pounds or under for each slab of 10–12 ribs.

> 2 tbsp. salt
> 4 tbsp. sugar
> 2 tbsp. freshly ground pepper
> 2 tbsp. ground cumin
> 2 tbsp. chili powder
> 4 tbsp. paprika
> 2 full racks of 3/down pork spareribs

Combine salt, sugar, pepper, cumin, chili powder, and paprika, and rub thoroughly onto ribs. Bake at 180 degrees for 3 hours. Remove from oven and place on grill with rack set as high as possible over a very low charcoal fire. Cook until a light crust forms and ribs are heated throughout, about 30 minutes per side. Serve "dry" with your favorite barbecue sauce on the side or "wet," coating with sauce just before removing from grill. Serves 5.

 # Tuna Steak Au Poivre

Fresh tuna, along with swordfish, benefits from the classic treatment usually reserved for beef in this recipe adapted from the *Joy of Cooking*. Because you want the peppercorns very coarsely cracked, the best approach is to abandon the pepper mill and crush them with a heavy rolling pin or the side of a wide chef's knife.

> 4 tuna steaks
> 3 tbsp. coarsely cracked black peppercorns
> 1 c. red wine
> 1 tbsp. minced shallots
> 2 tbsp. butter
> 1 tsp. salt
> 2 tbsp. minced parsley

Press peppercorns onto each side of tuna steaks. Sear steaks in a pan over high heat on both sides until done (approximately 2 minutes per side). Remove steaks from pan and keep warm. Reduce heat to medium and add wine and shallots, stirring until wine is reduced by one-third. Stir in butter and salt, and when incorporated, add parsley. Spoon sauce over fish. Serves 4.

Choulibiac

This elegant dish may well be the ultimate choux pastry concoction. Not only is it encased in pâte à choux, but the dough is the basis for the mousse filling. Inspired by an old recipe from Julia Child, but substituting salmon in keeping with its name—a pun on *coulibiac*, a fancy Russian pastry stuffed with salmon—it is really far easier to prepare than it looks.

> 2¾ lbs. salmon fillet
> 1½ c. water
> 1½ sticks butter
> 1½ tsp. salt
> 1 c. flour
> 6 eggs
> ¾ c. cream
> salt and pepper
> 2 tbsp. chopped fresh dill
> 2 tbsp. capers

Trim salmon to produce one long 2-pound fillet. Cut remaining ¾ pounds of salmon into ½-inch pieces. Bring the water, butter, and salt slowly to a boil. As soon as the butter melts, remove from heat and add flour all at once, beating with a spoon until smooth. Set over moderately high heat and continue to beat until mixture begins to film bottom of the pan. Scrape mixture into food processor. Turn on processor and, while it is running, quickly add five eggs in sequence, stopping machine after last egg is added. Remove ½ cup of mixture to a metal bowl and place over ice water. Put remaining mixture back in saucepan and cover to keep warm. Stir reserved ½ cup mixture over ice until well chilled. Return to processor, add the cut-up salmon chunks, cream, salt and pepper to taste, and process until smooth. Mousse should be just firm enough to hold its shape when spread. If too stiff, dribble in additional cream until desired consistency is reached. Lay salmon fillet on a lightly greased cookie sheet. Sprinkle evenly with dill and capers. Cover top with mousse, mounding in center. Using a flexible-blade spatula, encase salmon and mousse with remaining pastry mixture, using a pastry bag to pipe decorative shapes on top. Beat remaining egg with 1 teaspoon water, and use to glaze top and sides of structure. Bake at 425 degrees for 15–20 minutes until lightly browned and puffed slightly. Turn oven temperature down to 375 degrees and bake for 20–25 minutes longer, being careful not to overbake. Serve warm or cold with hollandaise or other sauce if desired. Serves 6–8.

Scallops Sautéed with Garlic and Herbs

At dinner on a cruise, I ordered the scallops after strategically asking the waiter if the portion was ample. "I'll take care of you, sir," he replied. And he did. I was delighted with the colossal helping he served me, but no sooner had I devoured it, than, looking over my shoulder, I saw him coming to the table with another plateful. Not wanting to insult him, I ate that too. The scallops were reminiscent of those prepared by the late Julia Child on a crossing of the *Queen Elizabeth 2* during a celebrity chef demonstration. The recipe, adapted from *The French Chef Cookbook*, makes four servings—or two if you're on a cruise!

> 1 lb. fresh or frozen scallops
> lemon juice, salt, and pepper
> ½ c. flour
> 2 tbsp. olive oil
> 2 tbsp. minced scallions
> 1 clove garlic, mashed
> 2 tbsp. butter
> 2 tbsp. minced parsley

Dry scallops on paper towels. (If frozen, first blanch by dropping into rapidly boiling water and bringing immediately back to the boil, then draining.) Sprinkle with lemon juice, salt, and pepper. Heat oil to very hot in nonstick frying pan. Dredge scallops in flour, shaking off excess, and sauté in a single layer 4–5 minutes until lightly browned. Add scallions and garlic, and toss. Finally toss with butter and parsley, and serve.

Shrimp and Spinach Pancakes

These savory pancakes remind me of my favorite pancake house in all the world, the Pannekoekenhuisje, a tiny restaurant in a 16th-century brick building on a side street in romantic Brugge, Belgium. The friendly staff there serves nothing but appetizer, main course, and dessert pancakes in an atmosphere that is positively enchanting. The recipe is adapted from Dorian Leigh Parker's book, *Pancakes: From Flapjacks to Crêpes*.

> 4 oz. spinach, cooked and minced
> 4 oz. small shrimp, cooked and coarsely chopped
> 4 eggs
> ¾ c. milk
> 2½ c. flour
> salt, pepper, and nutmeg to taste

Thoroughly mix spinach and shrimp. Beat in eggs, then milk. Stir in flour and beat well. Season to taste, cover, and let stand for 30 minutes. Use ¼ cup batter to make pancakes and brown on both sides. Makes 12 small pancakes.

Hot and Spicy Spam Stir-fry

Hawaiians are the leading consumers of Spam worldwide, a tradition dating back to the time when canned food was a status symbol there. Thus, you'll find Spam Musubi, a sushi-style dish, on the menu at the Ala Moana Hotel, and there's an annual Spam cook-off on the island of Maui. This recipe, adapted from Hormel, the creator of Spam, is a colorful Polynesian dish so good that your guests may not guess the secret ingredient.

⅓ c. reduced-sodium teriyaki sauce
⅓ c. water
2–3 tbsp. Chinese hot oil
½ tsp. ground ginger
1 can (12 oz.) Spam Lite, cubed
1 c. broccoli florets
1 c. chopped onion
1 c. pea pods
1 red bell pepper, cut in strips
1½ tbsp. vegetable oil
1 can (14 oz.) whole baby corn, drained and halved
1 jar (7 oz.) mushrooms, drained
6 c. hot cooked rice

Combine teriyaki sauce, water, hot oil, and ginger, and set aside. In wok or skillet, stir-fry Spam, broccoli, onion, pea pods, and red pepper in oil for 2 minutes. Add sauce mixture and cook until bubbly. Add baby corn and mushrooms. Heat thoroughly. Serve over hot rice. Serves 6.

Sides

Grilled Corn on the Cob
with Cheese and Lime

Try this messy Mexican street snack and you'll understand why in Latin America they consider corn sacred. This recipe, adapted from *Gourmet* magazine, calls for cotija cheese. Feta cheese is an acceptable substitute.

    4 ears of corn in the husk
    ¼ c. mayonnaise
    ⅛ tsp. cayenne
    ¾ c. shredded cotija cheese
    lime wedges

Soak corn in husks in cold water for 10 minutes. Drain and grill over glowing coals until husks are charred. Shuck corn and grill 10 minutes longer, or until kernels are browned in spots. Meanwhile, whisk together mayonnaise and cayenne. Brush onto hot corn and sprinkle with cheese. Serve with lime wedges.

Baked Grits
with Sun Dried Tomatoes

Though on the trendy side, this dish goes over well in the Mecca of Low Country Cooking: Charleston, South Carolina. The recipe, adapted from the *New York Times*, is a favorite at the Charleston Grill. You can speed up the preparation by using quick grits, but at the sacrifice of some flavor.

    2 c. chicken stock
    1 c. water
    4 tbsp. butter
    1 c. stone-ground grits
    1 c. heavy cream
    1 tbsp. chopped garlic
    2 tsp. thyme
    ½ c. diced sun-dried tomatoes
    white pepper
    ½ c. goat cheese
    chopped chives

Bring stock, water, and butter to a boil. Whisk in grits, return to boil, and simmer 35 minutes, stirring occasionally. (Add more water if mixture becomes too stiff.) Stir in cream and continue to cook at low heat for another 25 minutes until mixture becomes very thick. Fold in garlic, thyme, tomatoes, and white pepper to taste. Spoon mixture into greased 8-inch square baking dish, crumble cheese on top, and bake 15 minutes at 375 degrees. Garnish with chives. Serves 4.

Grits Milanese

This inventive recipe, adapted from *Blue Corn and Chocolate* by Elisabeth Rozin, a cookbook which concentrates on New World foods, calls for preparing grits in the style of Italian risotto. The dish, which is excellent by itself, goes especially well with chicken.

> 1 tbsp. butter
> 1 tbsp. olive oil
> 1 med. onion, chopped
> 2 c. chicken stock
> black pepper to taste
> ½ tsp. sage
> ½ tsp. rosemary
> ½ c. grits
> ⅓ c. frozen peas
> 2–3 tbsp. chopped Italian parsley
> ½ c. chopped mushrooms, sautéed
> 1 tbsp. grated Parmesan cheese

Sauté the onion in the butter and oil over moderate heat until golden. Add the stock, pepper, sage, and rosemary, and bring to a boil. Gradually whisk in grits. Reduce heat, cover, and cook 15–20 minutes (12–14 minutes if using quick grits), stirring occasionally, adding peas during last 5 minutes of cooking. Remove from heat, stir in parsley, mushrooms, and cheese. Cover and let stand 10 minutes before serving. Serves 4.

Cranberry Pecan Couscous

If there's such a thing as Christmas couscous, this is it. It's what we'll be serving with the holiday turkey, instead of stuffing, at our house this year. If you don't have a couscoussiére, you can substitute a steamer basket or fine-holed colander and a stockpot. The basic procedures in this recipe were adapted from Paula Wolfert's *Couscous and Other Good Food from Morocco*.

> 1½ c. couscous
> 1 tsp. salt
> 1 tbsp. olive oil
> 1 tbsp. butter
> 1 c. diced onion
> 1 c. dried cranberries
> 1 c. chopped pecans
> 1 c. chopped cilantro
> ½ c. chopped green onions

Wash couscous in 4½ cups water and drain through a sieve. Place grains in a large, shallow pan, smooth them out, and let rest for 10 minutes. Scoop up handfuls of couscous, breaking up lumps, and rub between your hands. Rake the couscous with your fingers and let swell another 10 minutes. Mound one-fourth of couscous in top part of couscoussiére set over simmering water, and steam uncovered for 5 minutes. Add remainder and steam 20 minutes longer. Return to pan, spread out, and sprinkle with 1 cup cold water and 1 teaspoon salt. Break up lumps and, with oiled hands, work the grains again. Smooth out couscous and let dry for 10 minutes. Steam for another 20 minutes. Meanwhile, sauté onions in butter and oil until translucent. Add cranberries and pecans. Combine with prepared couscous. Stir in cilantro and green onions. Serves 4.

Miss Hulling's Creamed Spinach

Miss Hulling was a real person, an Illinois farm girl who came to St. Louis in 1930 looking for a job as a telephone operator and ended up presiding over a restaurant empire which included two downtown cafeterias, now closed. This creamed spinach, adapted from her cookbook, was the most popular item at her 8th and Olive location.

> 2 boxes (10 oz. each) frozen chopped spinach, thawed
> 1½ tbsp. bacon fat
> 1½ tbsp. chopped onion
> 2 tbsp. flour
> ½ c. milk
> ½ c. water pressed from spinach
> 1½ tsp. salt
> 1⁄16 tsp. white pepper

Squeeze out all water from spinach, reserving ½ cup. Sauté onions in fat until clear but not brown. Add flour and blend. Add milk and water, stirring rapidly until sauce thickens. Simmer slowly for 5–7 minutes. Add seasoning and strain. Add spinach and heat until barely serving temperature. Do not overcook.

 # Szechuan Spinach Sauté

It's a real mystery to me why old recipes for spinach call for as many as 30 minutes of cooking. Today we know that heat decomposes chlorophyll, the green pigment in leaf cells, destroying its color. So green vegetables, especially spinach, should be cooked quickly, as in this recipe adapted from Sharon Tyler Herbst's sophisticated but uncomplicated book, *Cooking Smart*.

> 1 tbsp. hot-pepper oil
> 2 garlic cloves
> 1 fennel bulb
> 2 lbs. spinach
> 1 c. sliced radishes
> 1 tbsp. toasted sesame seeds

Mince garlic and combine with oil in skillet or wok, and cook over medium-high heat until it sizzles. Remove stalks from fennel, trim bulb, and dice. Add to pan and cook, stirring often, 3 minutes. Add spinach and cook just until wilted. Add radishes and sesame seeds, toss and cook 1 minute, season with salt and pepper, and serve immediately.

Colcannon

This dish, typical of southern Ireland, would make an excellent St. Patrick's Day feast served, as it traditionally is, with grilled sausages and bacon. The recipe is adapted from one in Matthew Drennan's wonderful tribute to Irish home cooking, *Classic Irish*, a book my wife brought back as a souvenir from a trip to Ireland.

> 2 lbs. potatoes
> 1 savory cabbage
> 4 tbsp. butter
> 1 sm. onion, finely chopped
> 1 tbsp. chopped parsley
> salt and pepper

Peel and cut potatoes into even pieces. Place in pan, cover with cold water, bring to a boil, and simmer for 20 minutes. Drain and dry out over high heat for 1 minute. Mash. Meanwhile, trim cabbage and tear into pieces. Cook in boiling water just until tender, about 15 minutes, and drain. Heat butter and sauté onions until soft. Add mashed potato and cabbage, and fry for 5 minutes, stirring occasionally, until brown around edges. Sprinkle with parsley and season with salt and pepper.

Bubble and Squeak

The traditional English dish Bubble and Squeak is so named because it does just that while frying. It's not the only British dish named for the noises it makes while cooking. Singing hinny ("hinny" is northern English dialect for "honey") is a spice cake that sings while baking on a griddle; and the famous English breakfast sausages, "bangers," get their name from the fact that they tend to explode like a firecracker (a banger in England) if they are not pricked before cooking. This recipe for the classic potato and cabbage dish is based on the one in *Cooking with the Two Fat Ladies* by Clarissa Dickson Wright and the late Jennifer Paterson, British stars of a BBC cooking series shown in this country on the Food Network.

> ¼ c. lard
> 1 minced onion
> 3 c. chopped **cold** cooked potatoes
> 1½ c. chopped cooked cabbage

In heavy frying pan, melt half the fat and fry the onion in it. Slightly crush the potatoes and add to pan along with the cabbage. Add a bit more lard, press the mixture into the hot fat, and fry over moderate heat until browned. Turn over, add remaining lard, and fry until other side is browned.

Pennsylvania Dutch Potato Stuffing

This stuffing recipe is based on one in James Beard's book, *American Cookery*. He says it is unusual, delicious, and typical of the region.

    1 lg. onion, chopped
    1 clove garlic, chopped
    ⅓ c. butter
    1 c. chopped turkey or chicken liver
    ⅓ c. chopped celery
    ½ tsp. baking powder
    2½ c. mashed potatoes
    4 c. dry croutons or breadcrumbs
    ¼ c. chopped parsley
    1 tbsp. salt
    1 tsp. thyme
    ½ tsp. pepper
    ½ tsp. Tabasco sauce

Sauté onion and garlic in butter until browned. Add liver and cook until it just changes color. Add celery and cook another 3 minutes. Blend baking powder into mashed potatoes and stir in onion mixture. Add croutons and seasonings, and blend well. Turn into large, shallow, buttered baking dish and bake at 350 degrees for 30–40 minutes until browned and bubbly.

Lemon Roasted Potatoes

This is my favorite way to prepare potatoes. They're even good cold, and you can't say that about French fries. The recipe is based on one in the best potato cookbook I know, *Beyond Burlap*, compiled by the Junior League of Boise.

    4 med. potatoes
    2 tbsp. olive oil
    ½ tsp. salt
    ⅛ tsp. pepper
    2 lemons, sliced very thinly
    2 sprigs fresh rosemary
    1 garlic clove, minced

Wash and pat dry potatoes, and cut into ¾-inch pieces. Mix with remaining ingredients, spread in a shallow pan, and bake at 450 degrees for 45–60 minutes or until tender, turning every 15 minutes.

Lemon Blossom Mashed Potatoes

This recipe, adapted from the Stash Tea Company website, uses both brewed and raw tea to give mashed potatoes an extra kick.

> 3 lbs. potatoes
> 6 lemon herb teabags
> 1 tbsp. garlic, finely sliced
> 1 stick butter
> 2 tbsp. milk

Peel and cube potatoes and put in large pan with 4 teabags and garlic. Cover with water and boil until tender. Drain, add butter, milk, and contents of remaining two teabags and mash.

 # Sweet Potatoes with Apples

White potatoes were little known in Shakespeare's day, so most recipes calling for potatoes were for the sweet variety. Few cookbooks gave recipes for preparing them other than as desserts. Apples, on the other hand, had been known for centuries in England and were often brought to the playhouse by young fops who would take a bite out of one and then throw it into the pit where youths would fight over it. This recipe is adapted from an updated version of the 17th-century dish by Madge Lorwin.

> 1½ lb. sweet potatoes
> 1 lb. tart cooking apples
> 4 tbsp. butter
> 5 tbsp. brown sugar
> ¼ tsp. cinnamon
> ½ tsp. ginger
> ⅓ c. white wine vinegar
> ¼ c. diced candied orange peel

Bake the potatoes at 400 degrees for 30 minutes. Peel and slice thinly. Peel and core the apples and slice thinly. Grease a casserole dish with 1 tablespoon butter and place a layer of apples into it. Combine 3 tablespoons brown sugar with spices, and sprinkle a little over apples. Dot with butter. Cover with a layer of potatoes, sprinkle with sugar mixture, and dot with butter. Continue with remaining apples and potatoes. Pour vinegar over and sprinkle with remaining 2 tablespoons brown sugar. Bake covered at 350 degrees for 40 minutes until tender. Scatter orange peel over top and serve.

Baked Apples in Blue Cheese
with Walnuts and Leeks

This dish, adapted from Karla Fisher, executive chef of the River Lane Inn in Brown Deer, Wisconsin, is recommended as a side dish for lamb chops or other roasted meats. But leave out the leek and the salt and pepper, and you have a marvelous dessert. You could even peel and slice the apples, increasing the amount to 6, add some sugar and flour (¾ cup sugar and about 3 tablespoons flour should do it), and bake it all in a pastry shell as a double-crust pie. (Bake at 425 degrees for 15 minutes and then at 375 degrees for 35–40 minutes or until done.)

> 1 leek, rinsed well and finely diced
> ½ tbsp. butter
> 4 tbsp. chopped walnuts
> salt and pepper
> 4 tart apples, cored
> 4 oz. blue cheese, crumbled
> 4 tbsp. ruby port

Sauté leek in butter. Add walnuts and continue to sauté until golden brown. Lightly salt and pepper to taste. Place apples in buttered baking dish. In center of each apple, insert 1 tablespoon leek-walnut mixture. Add a small amount of blue cheese. Continue layering leek-walnut mixture and blue cheese in each apple until all is used. Bake uncovered for 30 minutes. Remove from oven, pour 1 tablespoon port over each apple, and continue baking until tender, about 5–10 minutes.

Desserts

Better than Better-than-Sex Cake

This seductive dessert is an enhanced version of the original Better-Than-Sex Cake, a staple of American community cookbooks. It's adapted from Elaine Corn's irresistibly titled book, *Gooey Desserts*, which also contains recipes for Better-Than-Robert-Redford Cake and Better-Than-Tom-Selleck Cake.

> 2½ sticks butter, divided
> 1 c. plus 2 tbsp. sugar, divided
> 2¼ c. flour, divided
> 2 c. milk
> 3 egg yolks
> 6½ tsp. vanilla, divided
> 8 oz. cream cheese
> 1 tsp. lemon juice
> 2½ c. cream, divided
> 20-oz. can crushed pineapple, drained
> 1 jar caramel sauce
> 3 tbsp. powdered sugar
> ⅓ c. chocolate chips

Cut up 2 sticks butter and place in food processor with 2 tablespoons sugar and 2 cups flour. Process until a coarse mixture results. Press mixture on bottom of a buttered 9x13-inch pan. Bake for 20 minutes at 350 degrees until golden. Cool completely. Meanwhile, whisk together ½ cup sugar, ¼ cup flour, and 2 cups milk, and cook over medium heat, stirring constantly, until mixture just comes to a boil. Remove from heat. Beat egg yolks to blend and whisk into them a little of the hot mixture. Whisk yolk mixture back into remaining hot mixture and cook another 1–2 minutes, stirring constantly, until thick. Remove from heat and stir in 2 teaspoons vanilla and 2 tablespoons butter until incorporated. Pour pudding into a bowl, cover with plastic wrap directly on surface, and chill. Beat cream cheese, ½ cup sugar, 1 teaspoon vanilla, and lemon juice until fluffy. Whip 1 cup cream to medium-stiff peaks. Stir a scoop of whipped cream into cream cheese mixture to lighten, and fold in remainder. Spread cream cheese mixture over baked crust. Top with pineapple. Pour caramel sauce over. Spread with pudding. Beat remaining 1½ cups cream with powdered sugar and 1 tablespoon vanilla until stiff peaks form. Spread over top of cake. Melt chocolate chips with remaining 2 tablespoons butter. Add remaining ½ teaspoon vanilla and drizzle decoratively over top of cake. Serves 12.

Nany's Caramel Peanut Butter Cake

This recipe is adapted from one by Terri Spitler of Dothan, Alabama, which won the grand prize at a National Peanut Festival Recipe Contest. Try it and you'll understand that the judges weren't crazy, just nuts over peanut butter.

1 c. shortening
2½ c. granulated sugar
6 eggs
3 c. sifted flour
1 tsp. baking powder
1 c. buttermilk
2½ tsp. vanilla, divided
½ tsp. salt
1½ sticks margarine, divided
8 oz. cream cheese
2 lbs. powdered sugar
⅓ c. plus 2 tbsp. evaporated milk, divided
½ c. creamy peanut butter
1½ c. brown sugar
4 tbsp. light corn syrup
1 c. crunchy peanut butter

Cream shortening and granulated sugar. Add eggs one at a time, mixing well. Sift together flour and baking powder. Add to egg mixture alternately with buttermilk. Add 1 teaspoon vanilla and salt, and mix only until combined. Do not overbeat. Line 5 round 8-inch baking pans with wax paper and place 8–9 tablespoons of the batter in each. Bake at 400 degrees until tester comes out clean. Cool completely. Cream ½ stick margarine and cream cheese. Add 1 pound powdered sugar and beat until creamy. Add ½ teaspoon vanilla, 2 tablespoons evaporated milk, and ½ cup creamy peanut butter. Spread between cake layers. Melt remaining stick margarine, brown sugar, and syrup, and bring to boil. Remove from heat, add remaining ⅓ cup evaporated milk, remaining pound powdered sugar, remaining teaspoon vanilla, and 1 cup crunchy peanut butter. Beat until creamy and spread on top and sides of cake.

Golden Génoise

The KitchenAid stand mixer is perfectly suited to making this classic recipe adapted from Rose Levy Beranbaum's *Cake Bible*. You could use a hand mixer, but it will take you twice as long to beat the egg yolks and you'll be limited to only one step at a time.

> 9 tbsp. butter
> 1 tsp. vanilla
> 12 egg yolks
> ⅞ c. sugar
> 1 c. sifted cake flour
> 3 tbsp. cornstarch
> ¼ c. water

Melt butter over medium heat, and when it looks clear, cook until it turns deep brown. Strain and add vanilla. Heat egg yolks and sugar over simmering water, stirring constantly, until almost hot to the touch. Using whisk attachment, beat at high speed for 5 minutes or until triple in volume. (If using a hand mixer, you will need to beat at least 10 minutes.) While the eggs are beating, sift together flour and cornstarch. Decrease mixer speed and beat water into yolk mixture. Sift half of flour mixture over yolk mixture and fold in with a spatula until almost all of the flour has disappeared. Repeat with remaining flour mixture until flour disappears completely. Fold in browned butter in two batches just until incorporated. Pour into greased and floured 9-cup fluted tube pan. Bake at 350 degrees until cake shrinks slightly from sides of pan, about 40 minutes. Unmold immediately and let cool. Sprinkle with liqueur if desired.

 # Melted Ice Cream Cake

This recipe adapted from Anne Byrn's *The Cake Mix Doctor* cleverly uses melted ice cream to both enrich and flavor cake mix, and the possibilities are endless. Make sure you measure the ice cream after melting, because it will contain some air. You can gild the lily by serving this cake with a scoop of the ice cream that was added to it.

> 1 pkg. white cake mix without pudding
> 2 c. melted ice cream
> 3 eggs

Blend together the cake mix, melted ice cream, and eggs on low speed of electric mixer for 1 minute. Scrape down sides of bowl and beat at medium speed for 2 minutes longer until batter is thick and well blended. Pour batter into a greased Bundt pan and bake at 350 degrees until cake springs back lightly when pressed, about 40 minutes. Cool cake 20 minutes before removing from pan. Dust with powdered sugar or frost with the glaze of your choice.

Blackberry Cake

This marvelous cake from Faye Huey Sanders of Chaffee, Missouri, is actually a spice cake to which blackberries are added. Slathered in cream cheese and coconut, it's no wonder this dessert has for years been the most sought-after item at the Sanders family reunion. (Some family members head for the cake first, before they select their entrée, just to make sure they get a slice.) One taste may make you wish to be adopted by the Sanders family in time for the next reunion.

> 3 eggs
> 1½ sticks margarine, divided
> 2 c. granulated sugar
> 3 c. flour
> 1 tsp. cinnamon
> 1 tsp. ground cloves
> 1 tsp. allspice
> 1 tsp. nutmeg
> 1 tsp. baking soda
> 2 tsp. baking powder
> 2 heaping c. blackberries
> 1 pkg. (8 oz.) cream cheese
> 1 tsp. vanilla
> 1 lb. powdered sugar
> 1 pkg. (14 oz.) flaked coconut

Combine eggs, 1 stick margarine, and granulated sugar, and beat well. Add flour, spices, baking soda, and baking powder, and mix thoroughly. Fold in berries. (If necessary, thin batter with berry juice.) Bake in three greased and floured 9-inch pans at 350 degrees for 20–25 minutes or until done. Cool thoroughly. Mix cream cheese, remaining ½ stick margarine, vanilla, and powdered sugar until light and fluffy. Frost cake and sprinkle with coconut, pressing lightly to adhere.

Consummate Carrot Cake

Ever since Viola Schlicting of Texas created the first carrot cake in the 1960s, a reworking of her German carrot-nut bread, people have been perfecting the recipe. This version is adapted from *Cooks Illustrated* magazine where, after numerous experiments, it was concluded that draining the carrots of excess moisture and substituting browned butter for oil are the secrets for making the best carrot cake.

    7 c. finely grated carrots
    1⅔ c. granulated sugar
    2⅔ c. flour
    4 tsp. baking powder
    ½ tsp. baking soda
    2 tsp. cinnamon
    1 tsp. salt
    3¼ sticks butter, divided
    1 c. light brown sugar
    5 eggs
    1½ tsp. vanilla
    ¾ c. toasted walnuts
    ¾ c. raisins
    1 lb. cream cheese
    2½ c. powdered sugar
    2½ tbsp. sour cream

Toss the carrots with 1 cup granulated sugar and set in a colander to drain until 1 cup of liquid has collected, about 20–30 minutes. Whisk together flour, baking powder and soda, cinnamon, and salt. Melt 2 sticks of the butter over medium-low heat, stirring frequently, and cook until golden brown, 8–10 minutes. Transfer to large bowl and cool 10 minutes. Whisk in remaining ⅔ cups granulated sugar and the brown sugar. Add eggs one at a time, whisking each in thoroughly. Add vanilla. Blend in flour mixture, stirring just until almost combined. Mix in carrots, nuts, and raisins. Divide batter between two greased and floured 9-inch cake pans, and bake at 350 degrees until toothpick inserted in center tests clean, about 40–50 minutes. Cool 10 minutes, remove from pans and cool completely. For frosting, beat cream cheese and remaining 10 tablespoons butter until smooth. Add powdered sugar and sour cream, and blend well.

Blueberry and Nectarine Buckle

This recipe adapted from *Gourmet* magazine takes traditional blueberry buckle to a new level with the addition of nectarines. Peaches also work well. Whipped cream makes a nice accompaniment. Though the name "buckle" refers to the appearance of the dessert, it could just as easily refer to one's belt buckle which will surely need adjustment following a few helpings of this dessert.

> 2 sticks butter, divided
> 1¼ c. sugar, divided
> 1⅔ c. flour, divided
> ½ tsp. cinnamon
> ½ tsp. nutmeg
> 1 tsp. vanilla
> ¼ tsp. baking powder
> ½ tsp. salt
> 3 eggs
> 2 c. blueberries
> 2 nectarines, pitted and cut into 1-inch wedges

Cut ½ stick butter into pieces and blend together with ½ cup sugar, ⅓ cup flour, the cinnamon, and the nutmeg, until mixture resembles coarse meal. Chill. Cream remaining 1½ sticks butter with remaining ¾ cup sugar and beat in vanilla. Stir together baking powder, remaining 1⅓ cups flour, and salt, and beat into butter mixture alternately with eggs. Fold in fruit. Spread batter in 10-inch cake pan, sprinkle chilled topping mixture over, and bake at 350 degrees for 45–50 minutes until tester comes out clean and topping is crisp and golden.

Blueberry Torte

You won't believe that this sensational cheesecake-like torte adapted from *Eating Well* magazine is actually low in fat, but at 7 grams per slice, it is. Moreover, though it is beautiful enough to make others think you spent hours on it, it's really easy to prepare.

 1½ c. flour
 1½ c. sugar
 ½ tsp. cinnamon
 1½ tsp. baking powder
 ¼ tsp. salt
 ¼ c. canola oil
 2 egg whites, lightly beaten
 1 tbsp. melted butter
 2 tsp. vanilla, divided
 1 egg
 ⅔ c. low-fat sweetened condensed milk
 2 tbsp. cornstarch
 1½ c. nonfat plain yogurt
 grated zest of 1 lemon
 3 c. blueberries

Spray 9-inch springform pan with cooking spray. Mix together flour, sugar, cinnamon, baking powder, and salt. Add oil, egg whites, butter, and 1 teaspoon vanilla, and mix with fork until well blended. Press into bottom of pan. Whisk together whole egg, condensed milk, and cornstarch until smooth. Add yogurt and whisk until smooth. Blend in lemon zest and remaining 1 teaspoon vanilla. Pour over crust. Sprinkle blueberries over top. Bake at 300 degrees for 1¼–1½ hours until top is just set and center quivers slightly when shaken. Cool in pan. Serve warm or chilled, dusted with powdered sugar. Serves 12.

Apple Brown Betty

Here's the classic recipe for this distinctly American dessert, adapted from the *Joy of Cooking*. If you'd like to defy tradition, try using blueberries instead of apples.

> 1½ c. dry bread crumbs
> 6 tbsp. melted butter
> 1¼ c. packed dark brown sugar
> 1 tsp. cinnamon
> ¼ tsp. ground nutmeg
> ¼ tsp. ground cloves
> 3 med. apples, peeled, cored, and sliced
> 3 tbsp. lemon juice

Stir together bread crumbs and butter. In another bowl, whisk together brown sugar and spices. Spread one-third crumb mixture evenly in bottom of a 9-inch pie pan. Distribute half of apples over. Sprinkle with half of sugar mixture and then half of lemon juice. Cover with another third of crumb mixture, the remaining apples, the remaining sugar mixture, and the remaining lemon juice. Cover with remaining crumb mixture. Cover dish with foil and bake at 350 degrees until apples are nearly tender, about 40 minutes. Increase temperature to 400 degrees and bake until browned, about 15 minutes. Serve warm in bowls.

 # Chocolate Orange Potato Pound Cake

If you love desserts as I do, this spud's for you! Potatoes can make for a wonderfully moist cake, a richly dense fudge, and, with the aid of crushed potato chips, a provocative chocolate-chip cookie. This recipe is adapted from the Idaho Potato Commission.

> 3 c. sugar
> 3 sticks butter
> 3 c. flour
> 1 c. sour cream
> 1 c. mashed potatoes
> ½ c. cocoa powder
> ½ c. orange juice
> 1 tsp. baking soda
> 2 tsp. orange extract
> ¼ tsp. salt
> 5 eggs

Cream butter and sugar. Add remaining ingredients and beat until well blended. Beat at high speed for 2 minutes. Bake at 350 degrees in greased 10-inch tube pan for 1½ hours or until tester comes out clean. Cool 15 minutes, remove from pan, and glaze with favorite icing.

Funnel Cake

This recipe is adapted from one of my favorite cookbooks, the *Sugar Beach Cookbook* put out by the Junior League of Fort Walton Beach, Florida. It's fairly conventional except for the inclusion of a little cinnamon which I think is a nice touch. Though the recipe calls for the traditional funnel, you'll get equally good results pouring the batter from a teapot, and it's less cumbersome. A spiral pattern is the typical design, but a crosshatch pattern is just as authentic and doesn't require quite as much precision.

> 2½ c. flour
> 1 tsp. baking powder
> ¼ tsp. salt
> ¼ tsp. cinnamon
> 2 eggs
> 2 c. milk

Sift together flour, baking powder, salt, and cinnamon. Beat eggs and add to milk, and combine with the flour mixture, beating until smooth. Pour ⅓–½ cup batter into a large funnel, holding finger over spout. Release, spiraling batter into hot oil. Lightly brown one side, turn, and brown the other. Drain and sprinkle with powdered sugar or top with fruit or maple syrup.

Graham Cracker Streusel Cake

This recipe is a variation of one on allrecipes.com, an Internet recipe site. It can be made in a 9x13 pan, but I think the Bundt version is more attractive.

> 1⅓ c. graham-cracker crumbs
> ¾ c. chopped nuts
> ¾ c. brown sugar
> 1½ tsp. cinnamon
> ⅔ c. melted butter
> 1 pkg. yellow-cake mix (18.5 oz)
> 1 c. water
> ¼ c. oil
> 3 eggs

Combine crumbs, nuts, brown sugar, and cinnamon. Stir in melted butter. Combine cake mix, water, oil, and eggs, and beat for 2 minutes. Place half of streusel mixture around bottom of greased Bundt pan. Spread half of cake batter over top, sprinkle with remaining streusel, and cover with remaining batter. Bake at 350 degrees for 35–40 minutes or until tester inserted into cake tests clean. Cool 15 minutes before removing from pan. Drizzle with frosting if desired. Serves 12–16.

Gooey Butter Cake

Like so many great culinary discoveries, this one was an accident. According to legend, a German baker in St. Louis in the 1930s mistakenly added the wrong proportions of ingredients to his cake batter, and the result became a city tradition. This recipe, adapted from the Junior League cookbook *St. Louis Days . . . St. Louis Nights*, is the one used at the venerable Heimburger Bakery.

> 2 c. flour, divided
> 1¼ c. plus 3 tbsp. sugar, divided
> 1½ sticks plus ⅓ c. butter, divided
> 1 egg
> ⅔ c. evaporated milk
> ¼ c. light corn syrup
> 1 tsp. vanilla
> powdered sugar

Combine 1 cup flour and 3 tablespoons sugar. Cut in ⅓ cup butter until mixture resembles fine crumbs and starts to cling together. Pat into bottom of 9x9-inch greased pan. Beat remaining 1¼ cups sugar and remaining stick and a half of butter until light and fluffy. Mix in egg. Alternately add remaining cup of flour and evaporated milk, mixing in after each addition. Add corn syrup and vanilla, and blend well. Pour batter over crust, sprinkle with powdered sugar, and bake at 350 degrees for 25–35 minutes until nearly set. Do not overbake. Cool before serving.

Cheesecake Essamplaire

The word "sampler," first used in 1502 in the account book of Elizabeth of York, derives from the Old French word *essamplaire*. Here the word refers to a cheesecake with Whitman's Sampler chocolates buried inside. You can use any combination of chocolates you desire, but those with soft centers work best. Save the solid chocolate messenger boy for decoration.

1½ c. graham cracker crumbs
5 tbsp. melted butter
1¾ c. sugar, divided
3 pkgs. (8 oz. each) cream cheese
1 stick softened butter
3 eggs
2 tsp. grated lemon rind
1 box (1 lb.) Whitman's Sampler assorted chocolates
¾ c. chocolate chips
1 c. sour cream

Combine graham-cracker crumbs, melted butter, and ¼ cup of the sugar, and press firmly into the bottom of a 9-inch springform pan. Beat cream cheese until smooth. Add 1 cup of sugar and beat until fluffy. Cut up stick of butter and beat into cream-cheese mixture until smooth. Add eggs one at a time, beating well after each addition. Beat in lemon rind. Pour half of mixture into prepared pan and freeze for 30 minutes. Remove from freezer and distribute assorted chocolates over top of frozen batter. Pour remaining batter over chocolates to cover completely. Bake at 350 degrees until set, about 1 hour. Let cake cool 10 minutes. Melt chocolate chips and combine with sour cream and remaining ½ cup sugar. Spread carefully over cake. Return to oven for 5 minutes until topping is set. Cool cake completely and refrigerate overnight.

Gingerbread Cheesecake Swirl

If you like to gild the lily, this is the recipe for you. It is adapted from a recipe by cookbook author Linda Merinoff that appeared in *Food and Wine* magazine.

>1 lb. cream cheese, at room temperature
>½ tsp. vanilla extract
>4 eggs
>½ c. plus 2 tbsp. sugar
>¼ c. light molasses
>4 tbsp. butter at room temperature
>1 tsp. ground ginger
>1 tsp. ground cinnamon
>¼ tsp. ground nutmeg
>⅛ tsp. ground cloves
>¼ tsp. salt
>½ c. light brown sugar
>1½ tsp. baking soda
>1 c. flour

Beat cream cheese until light and smooth. Beat in vanilla and 2 of the eggs, one at a time. Gradually add sugar and beat until light and fluffy. Heat molasses until it starts to bubble, remove from heat, and stir in butter 1 tablespoon at a time until incorporated. Stir in spices, add the brown sugar, and beat until smooth. Let cool to room temperature and beat in remaining 2 eggs one at a time. Stir in baking soda, then beat in flour a third at a time until incorporated. Butter a 9-inch springform pan and dollop half of gingerbread batter in tablespoons on bottom of pan. Fill in empty spaces with ¼ of cream cheese mixture. Dollop remaining gingerbread batter on top of cream cheese mounds. Fill in with another ¼ of cream cheese mixture. Swirl to marbleize. Smooth remaining cream cheese mixture over the top and bake at 350 degrees for 50 minutes, until top of cake begins to crack. Cool and refrigerate before serving.

Johanne Killeen's
Gingerbread Johnnycakes

I saw Johanne Killeen of Al Forno Restaurant in Providence, Rhode Island, demonstrate this recipe on an episode of Julia Child's television program, *Baking with Julia*, and ran to get a pad and pencil to copy it down. Julia pronounced it the best gingerbread she had ever eaten, though I personally prefer versions with less molasses and more ginger. But there's no denying that this recipe, with its use of coffee, cocoa, and ground pepper, and calling for the batter, which is thicker than most, to be baked in individual molds, elevates plain gingerbread to opulent heights.

        2 c. flour
        ¼ c. instant espresso powder
        3 tbsp. cocoa
        1 tbsp. ground ginger
        1 tsp. ground pepper
        ½ tsp. baking powder
        1 tsp. salt
        2 sticks butter
        1 c. dark brown sugar
        4 eggs
        3 tbsp. grated fresh ginger
        2 c. molasses

Whisk together dry ingredients, except sugar. Cream butter and sugar until fluffy. Add eggs one at a time, mixing well after each addition. Add grated ginger to butter/sugar mixture and mix in. Add molasses and mix well. Stir in dry ingredients. Bake in greased and floured 4-inch molds or soufflé dishes at 350 degrees until tops crack and cake springs back when lightly touched (25–35 minutes). Do not overbake.

Low-fat Triple Ginger Pound Cake

The typical list of ingredients for pound cake suggests that it is aptly named. It doesn't take many slices to put on extra pounds. Though a low-fat pound cake can never equal that of the real thing, I have found the following recipe, adapted from *Cooking Light* magazine, to be tasty. As in all low-fat baking, cake flour is essential here to avoid a rubbery texture.

> 6 tbsp. softened margarine
> ⅔ c. sugar
> 3 egg whites
> 2½ c. sifted cake flour
> ¾ tsp. baking soda
> ¼ tsp. salt
> 1 tsp. ground ginger
> 1 carton (8 oz.) lemon nonfat yogurt
> ¼ c. finely chopped crystallized ginger
> 1 tbsp. peeled, minced fresh ginger
> 2 tsp. vanilla

Cream margarine and sugar, add egg whites, and beat at medium mixer speed 4 minutes or until well blended. Combine flour, baking soda, salt, and ground ginger, and add to margarine mixture alternately with yogurt, beginning and ending with flour mixture. Stir in remaining ingredients. Bake in 8x4x3 loaf pan coated with cooking spray and dusted with flour at 350 degrees for 55–60 minutes or until tester comes out clean. Cool 10 minutes before removing from pan. Makes 16 servings at 4.5 fat grams each, which means you can eat two slices and still consume less than 10 grams of fat.

Fresh Ginger Cake

This recipe comes closest of any I've found to that wonderful gingerbread I had at the Aloha Theatre in Hawaii. It's based on a recipe in the new edition of the *Joy of Cooking*, but I prefer to use light brown rather than dark brown sugar, and light corn syrup instead of anything darker so that the full flavor of that whole half cup (yes a half cup!) of fresh ginger dominates.

> 1½ c. flour
> 1 tsp. baking soda
> ¼ tsp. salt
> ½ c. light brown sugar
> ¼ c. light molasses
> ¼ c. light corn syrup
> 1 egg
> ½ c. packed finely minced fresh ginger
> 1 stick butter
> ½ c. water

Whisk together flour, baking soda, and salt. In another bowl, whisk together sugar, molasses, syrup, and egg. Stir in ginger. Melt together butter and water, and add to molasses mixture. Stir in flour mixture just until incorporated. Bake in greased and floured 9-inch square pan at 350 degrees for 25–30 minutes or until tester inserted into center of cake comes out clean.

 # Wedding (Cup)Cake

A tower of cupcakes makes a surprisingly impressive bridal cake. And what could be easier to serve at the reception? There's no cutting! Even if you're not celebrating a wedding, this recipe, adapted from Gale Gand, makes the perfect yellow cupcake for any occasion.

> 2 sticks butter
> 2 c. sugar
> 1¼ tsp. vanilla
> 4 eggs
> 3 c. sifted cake flour
> 1 tbsp. baking powder
> ½ tsp. salt
> 1 c. milk

Cream together butter and sugar. Gradually add vanilla and eggs, and mix well. Sift together dry ingredients and add to butter mixture alternately with milk. Bake in paper-lined muffin tins, filling three-fourths full, at 350 degrees for 20–25 minutes until golden brown. Frost and decorate cupcakes as desired (Gand suggests butter-cream frosting, pearlized fondant balls, and Victorian cake pull charms) and arrange on stacked, graduated cake stands.

Queen of Sheba Cake

If the fundamental test of a good recipe is that it makes you want to prepare it, this one passes with flying colors. Within minutes of watching Julia Child prepare this dessert on the 100th episode of her pioneering television show, *The French Chef*, I was in the kitchen trying my hand at it. That was many years ago, and I've made it many times since. Like most French cakes, it is only a single layer, but it is as decadent as any two-layer cake you'll ever eat. The recipe is adapted from Child's *The French Chef Cookbook*.

> 1 tbsp. instant coffee
> 2 tbsp. boiling water
> ⅔ plus ½ c. semisweet chocolate chips
> 1 stick plus 6 tbsp. soft butter
> ⅔ c. plus 2 tbsp. sugar
> 3 eggs, separated
> ¼ tsp. cream of tartar
> pinch of salt
> ⅓ c. pulverized blanched almonds
> ¼ tsp. almond extract
> ¾ c. cake flour
> 1½ tbsp. dark rum

Dissolve instant coffee in boiling water and add ⅔ cup chocolate morsels. Stir over very low heat or microwave until chocolate is melted. Cream 1 stick butter and ⅔ cup sugar until fluffy. Beat in egg yolks. Whip egg whites with cream of tartar and salt at low speed, and when they begin to foam, gradually add 2 tablespoons sugar and beat at high speed until whites hold their shape but are still smooth and shiny. Stir chocolate into butter mixture and add almonds, extract, and flour, stirring well. Stir in one-fourth of egg whites to lighten batter and then carefully and rapidly fold in remaining whites. Turn batter into a round 8-inch greased and floured cake pan, and bake at 350 degrees for about 25 minutes until cake is puffed on top and tests clean around circumference. The center should not test clean and may move slightly when shaken. Cool 10 minutes, run a knife around edge of pan, and unmold cake. Let cool completely. Melt remaining ½ cup chocolate chips in the rum and beat in 6 tablespoons butter 1 tablespoon at a time until icing is smooth and of spreading consistency, beating over cold water if necessary. Pour icing over cake to cover top and sides, and decorate with whole almonds. Makes 6–8 servings.

Othello Petits Fours

Serve these little cakes for dessert and your guests will surely agree that all's well that ends well. These aren't the only petits fours to be named after a character in Shakespeare's *Othello*. There are also Desdemona petits fours, which are white for purity, and Iago petits fours, which are green for jealousy. This recipe is based on one in Pamela Asquith's *Ultimate Chocolate Cake Book*.

> 4 eggs, separated
> ½ c. sugar
> ⅝ c. sifted cake flour
> 2 tbsp. cocoa
> ¼ c. brandy
> ½ c. apricot jam
> 2 tbsp. plus 2 tsp. heavy cream
> 1 c. chocolate chips
> 2 tbsp. butter
> 25 whole blanched almonds

Butter a 12x18-inch baking sheet, line with wax paper, and butter again. Flour the pan. Beat egg whites with ¼ cup sugar until peaks form. Beat the yolks with remaining sugar to the ribbon stage. Sift together flour and cocoa. Alternately, a third at a time, fold egg whites and flour mixture into yolks. Mix until smooth. Do not overmix. Spread batter evenly in pan and bake at 325 degrees until set, about 12–15 minutes. Cool and cut the cake in half into two 9x12-inch pieces and sprinkle with brandy. Spread jam on one layer and invert other layer on top. Chill. Melt cream and chocolate together in microwave. Stir in butter. Remove wax paper from cake, cut into diamond shapes, and glaze with chocolate mixture. Decorate with almonds.

Sacher Torte

Though the original Sacher Torte recipe is still locked up in a safe in the Hotel Sacher, this one, adapted from Rick Rodgers' beautiful book, *Kaffeehaus*, and based on one in *The Big Sacher Baking Book*, is a close approximation.

10½ oz. bittersweet chocolate, divided
9 tbsp. butter
1 c. powdered sugar
6 eggs, separated
1 tsp. vanilla
2 c. granulated sugar, divided
1 c. flour
2 tbsp. rum
1¼ c. apricot preserves
¾ c. water

Melt 4½ ounces of the chocolate and let cool. Cream together butter and powdered sugar. Beat in egg yolks one at a time. Beat in melted chocolate and vanilla. Beat egg whites and ½ cup granulated sugar to soft, shiny peaks. Stir ¼ whites into chocolate mixture, then fold in remainder. Fold in flour in two stages. Spread batter in 9-inch greased springform pan lined on the bottom with parchment paper. Bake at 400 degrees until tester comes out clean, about 45 minutes. Cool 10 minutes before removing from pan, then cool completely. Boil rum and preserves over medium heat, stirring often, until very sticky. Strain. Slice cake horizontally into two layers, leveling the top layer if necessary. Brush top of each layer with the apricot glaze, reassemble, and brush sides with remaining glaze. Cool until glaze sets. Bring remaining 1½ cups sugar, remaining 6 ounces chocolate, and water to boil over high heat, stirring occasionally. Reduce heat to medium and cook, stirring until mixture reaches 234 degrees. Cool 1 minute and pour over cake to completely coat. Cool until glaze is barely set and refrigerate at least 1 hour. Remove cake from refrigerator 1 hour before serving with whipped cream. Makes 12–16 servings.

Parker House Boston Cream Pie

According to the Omni Hotel chain, which now owns Boston's Parker House Hotel, this is the authentic recipe for Boston Cream Pie (except for the icing which is a substitute for the more difficult to make fondant originally used) right down to the use of only two instead of the three layers sometimes seen in commercially prepared versions. The dessert is pretty simple and basic, but you can vary it by adding additional flavoring to the pastry cream (in Seattle, for example, they like to spike the filling with coffee), soaking the cake layers in rum or flavored syrup, or using the batter to make cupcakes which are then injected with the pastry cream, creating a sort of high-class Twinkie. The recipe is adapted from the *Boston Herald*.

> 13 eggs
> 1½ c. sugar
> 1 c. flour
> 3 tbsp. butter
> 2 c. milk
> 2 c. light cream
> 3½ tbsp. cornstarch
> 1 tbsp. dark rum
> 6 oz. chocolate chips
> 5 tbsp. warm water
> 1 c. powdered sugar
> 1 tbsp. light corn syrup
> 4 oz. toasted almonds

Separate 7 of the eggs and combine the yolks with ½ cup of the sugar, beating until light. Beat the whites, adding ½ cup sugar, until stiff peaks form. Fold the whites into the yolk mixture and mix in the flour. Melt 2 tablespoons of the butter and incorporate into the batter. Pour batter into a 10-inch greased cake pan and bake at 350 degrees for 20 minutes, until golden. Cool completely. Meanwhile, combine remaining tablespoon butter, milk, and cream in saucepan, and bring to a boil. While mixture is cooking, combine remaining ½ cup sugar, cornstarch, and remaining 6 eggs, and beat to the ribbon stage. When cream mixture reaches boiling point, whisk in the egg-cornstarch mixture and heat to boiling. Boil for 1 minute, then pour into a bowl and cover the surface with plastic wrap. Chill thoroughly. Cut the cake into two layers. Whisk the pastry cream to smooth out, and add the rum. Generously spread pastry cream over bottom cake layer, reserving a small amount for the sides of the pie. Top with the second layer. Melt the chocolate with 4 tablespoons of the warm water to make an icing and spread a thin layer on the top of the cake. Combine the powdered sugar, corn syrup, and remaining tablespoon water to make a free-flowing icing, warming the ingredients if necessary. Pipe white icing in spiral pattern on top of cake and score with a knife to make decorative, web-like pattern. Spread sides of cake with thin coating of reserved pastry cream and press on toasted almonds.

Light Tiramisu

Tiramisu, the ubiquitous and very rich Italian dessert, can be made relatively light when angel food cake is its base. The use of whole eggs rather than egg yolks and light sour cream and cream cheese also helps to bring down the calorie count in this recipe adapted from *Bon Appétit* magazine.

¼ c. plus 1 tbsp. dry marsala
¼ c. plus 2 tbsp. sugar
2 extra-large eggs
3 tbsp. light sour cream
8 oz. light cream cheese
1 loaf angel cake (11 oz.), cut into ½-inch slices
½ c. strong brewed coffee
2 tbsp. dark rum
1 oz. grated semisweet chocolate

Combine marsala, 1 tablespoon sugar, and eggs in top of double boiler, and whisk gently over simmering water until thickened and foamy and mixture registers 160 degrees on candy thermometer, about 2 minutes. Remove from heat, whisk in sour cream, and cool to room temperature. Beat cream cheese until light and fluffy. Beat in one-third of egg mixture. Fold in remaining egg mixture in two additions. Line bottom and sides of 9x5-inch loaf pan with plastic wrap. Line bottom of pan with angel food cake slices, trimming to fit. Combine coffee, rum, and remaining sugar and brush generously over cake in pan. Pour filling over cake, brush additional cake slices with coffee mixture, and place coffee-side down over filling. Brush top of cake generously with coffee mixture, sprinkle with grated chocolate. Cover and refrigerate 8 hours or overnight.

Twinkie-misu

This is what you get when you substitute Twinkies for the conventional ladyfingers in the classic Italian dessert, tiramisu.

> 18 Twinkies
> 2 tbsp. instant coffee
> 1 tbsp. sugar
> 1 c. boiling water
> 1 lb. cream cheese
> 2 cans (14 oz. each) sweetened condensed milk
> 16 oz. whipped topping
> 2 tsp. unsweetened cocoa powder

Slice Twinkies in half lengthwise. Line the bottom of a 9x13-inch pan with half of the split Twinkies, filling-side up. Dissolve coffee and sugar in boiling water. Brush ½ cup of coffee mixture over Twinkies. Beat cream cheese until smooth. Blend in condensed milk. Fold in whipped topping. Spread half of the cheese mixture over Twinkies. Place remaining split Twinkies over top of cheese mixture, filling-side down. Brush with remaining coffee mixture. Cover with remaining cream cheese mixture. Dust with cocoa powder. Chill at least 5 hours.

Chocolate Indulgence

The chocolate which Columbus tasted was not at all like this concoction. Introduced in the 1970s and sometimes referred to as Chocolate Decadence, this dense, practically flourless cake is aptly named, since it contains an entire pound of chocolate. The recipe is adapted from *Chocolatier* magazine.

> 1 lb. coarsely chopped bittersweet chocolate
> 10 tbsp. butter
> 4 eggs
> 1 tbsp. sugar
> 1 tbsp. flour

Butter bottom and sides of springform pan, line bottom with circle of waxed paper, and dust sides with flour. Melt butter and chocolate together until smooth. Let cool 15 minutes. In large heatproof bowl, whisk eggs and sugar until frothy. Set bowl over hot water and whisk egg mixture for 2–3 minutes until sugar dissolves. Remove from heat and beat mixture at medium-high speed of electric mixer until it triples in volume and soft peaks form. Gently fold in flour. Fold one-fourth of batter into chocolate mixture to lighten, then fold in remaining batter. Pour into pan and bake at 400 degrees for 15 minutes or until tester inserted into center comes out slightly moist. Cool, cut into wedges, and serve with raspberry sauce and whipped cream. Serves 8.

Mississippi Mud Cake

This cake, made in an oblong pan, is too unpretentious to ever win a beauty contest, but what it lacks in looks it more than makes up for in taste. The recipe, from Darline Kaufmann, was published in the 1974 edition of the Cape Girardeau, Missouri, Evangelical United Church of Christ cookbook.

    2 c. sugar
    3 sticks margarine, divided
    ⅓ c. plus 2 tbsp. cocoa, divided
    4 eggs
    1 tsp. vanilla
    1⅓ c. flour
    1½ plus ⅓ c. coconut, divided
    1½ c. nuts
    1 pt. jar marshmallow creme
    1 box powdered sugar
    ⅓ c. evaporated milk

Cream together sugar, 2 sticks margarine, and 2 tablespoons cocoa. Add eggs, vanilla, flour, 1½ cups coconut, and nuts; mix. Bake in greased and floured 9x13-inch pan at 350 degrees for about 45 minutes. While warm, spread with marshmallow creme. When cool, spread with frosting made by combining powdered sugar, 1 stick margarine, milk, and remaining cocoa and coconut.

Death by Chocolate

With a pound and a half of chocolate, two sticks of butter, nearly a cup of heavy cream, and more than a half-dozen eggs, this is, indeed, a real killer—but what a way to go! This recipe is adapted from the Apricot Systematic website.

    4 c. chocolate chips, divided
    2 sticks butter
    ⅔ c. heavy cream
    7 eggs

Spray a springform pan with cooking spray, then enclose with foil to make watertight. Melt butter and 2⅔ cups chocolate chips and stir to blend. Gently warm eggs over hot water, then beat until thick and fluffy. By hand, carefully fold chocolate mixture into eggs and pour into pan. Place pan in water bath and bake at 425 degrees for 5 minutes. Cover with foil and bake 12–15 minutes longer, until puffed up slightly. Melt remaining 1⅓ cups chocolate chips and cream, and stir until smooth. Let cool 5 minutes, then carefully pour on top of cake. Refrigerate several hours before serving.

Schaumtorte

Schaum is German for foam and refers to the meringue which constitutes the top and bottom layers of this torte. The recipe, based on one in the *Joy of Cooking*, is somewhat easier to execute than the similar Vacherin or Pavlova because you don't have to form the meringue shells free-handed, but instead use two springform pans as molds.

     6 egg whites
     ¾ tsp. cream of tartar
     1 c. superfine sugar
     1 c. powdered sugar
     1½ c. heavy cream
     1 pint strawberries

Combine whites with cream of tartar and beat until soft peaks form. Gradually add superfine sugar until meringue holds stiff peaks. Sift powdered sugar over meringue and fold in with spatula. Grease and flour two 8-inch springform pans and line bottoms with parchment paper. Divide meringue between pans and spread evenly. Bake for 2 hours at 225 degrees, turn off oven, and let meringues cool in oven. Remove meringues from pans and remove parchment paper. Wash and dry one pan, and place one meringue layer on bottom. Whip 1 cup cream and spread over meringue layer. Place second meringue layer over top. Beat remaining cream and spread over top layer. Decorate with strawberries.

Stout Cake

This traditional spiced fruitcake adapted from *The Baking Book*, a beautiful work by Linda Collister and Anthony Blake, will keep well and, in fact, should be stored in an airtight tin for 3–5 days before cutting.

     1¼ c. raisins
     1¼ c. golden raisins
     7 tbsp. stout
     ¾ c. butter
     ¾ c. dark brown sugar, packed
     3 eggs
     1⅔ c. flour
     1½ tsp. apple-pie spice
     ⅓ c. chopped mixed candied peel
     ¾ c. walnut pieces

Soak raisins in stout overnight. Beat butter until light, then gradually beat in sugar until fluffy. Gradually beat in eggs. Sift flour and spice, and fold in. Add fruit and soaking liquid, then the peel and walnuts. Pour into deep 8-inch round cake pan, greased and lined with greased parchment paper. Bake at 350 degrees for 1½ hours until tester comes out clean. Cool and turn out of pan. Wrap in wax paper to store.

Bittersweet Chocolate
Fruitcake Torte

This is not your ordinary fruitcake, but a fruit-and-nut filled torte, glazed with chocolate that makes a spectacular Christmas dessert. The recipe is based on a version that first appeared in *Bon Appétit* magazine.

½ c. dried apricots, chopped
½ c. dried Calimyrna figs, chopped
½ c. candied cherries
⅓ c. currants or raisins
½ c. plus 2 tbsp. bourbon
1½ c. whole almonds
16 oz. semisweet chocolate, divided
2 sticks butter, room temperature
1 c. plus 2 tbsp. sugar
4 eggs, separated
½ c. flour
pinch of salt
½ c. toasted hazelnuts, chopped
½ c. plus 2½ tsp. whipping cream
¼ c. powdered sugar

Combine first four ingredients and ½ cup bourbon, and let stand 2 hours or overnight. Butter 10-inch springform pan with 3-inch sides, sprinkle with sugar, and tap out excess. Finely grind almonds and set aside. Melt 8 ounces chocolate. Cream butter and 1 cup sugar until light and fluffy. Add egg yolks one at a time, beating well after each addition. Stir in flour and salt. Add melted chocolate, then fruit mixture, ground almonds, and hazelnuts. Mix well. Beat egg whites until foamy. Gradually beat in remaining 2 tablespoons sugar and beat until stiff peaks form. Fold egg whites into batter in two additions. Pour batter into prepared pan, smooth top, and bake at 325 degrees until toothpick inserted into center comes out clean, about 1 hour and 10 minutes. Cool on rack 20 minutes. Brush fruitcake with remaining 2 tablespoons bourbon. Cool. Release pan sides. Remove bottom and sides of pan from fruitcake. Wrap tightly in plastic, then in foil. Refrigerate overnight. (Can be made 1 week ahead.) To glaze, chop remaining 8 ounces chocolate. Bring ½ cup cream to boil, remove from heat, and add chocolate. Whisk until smooth and melted. Let stand 15 minutes until warm to touch. Meanwhile, whisk powdered sugar and remaining cream in small bowl until smooth. Set rack over rimmed cookie sheet and place fruitcake on rack flat-side up. Spoon glaze over sides and top of fruitcake, and smooth with spatula. Pour white icing into parchment cone and cut off tip to form small opening. Pipe even spiral of icing atop torte, spacing lines about ¾-inch apart. Draw sharp knife from center of torte to edge to create spiderweb design dividing torte into 8 even sections. Refrigerate torte until glaze is set. Serve at room temperature.

Mixed Nut Fruitcake

This fruitcake was the favorite of my father, a true fruitcake aficionado. It is adapted from *Good Housekeeping* magazine. It's mostly fruit and nuts with just enough cake to hold it together. Though, perhaps, a bit on the extravagant side, it is easy to make.

2 containers (6–8 oz. each) candied red cherries
1 pkg. (12 oz.) pitted prunes
1 container (10 oz.) pitted dates
1 container (3–4 oz.) candied green cherries
½ c. cream sherry
6 c. salted mixed nuts
1½ c. pecans
1½ c. flour
1 c. sugar
1 tsp. baking powder
6 eggs, slightly beaten

In large bowl, combine first 5 ingredients; let stand 15 minutes or until all liquid is absorbed, stirring occasionally. Meanwhile, line 10-inch tube pan with foil; press out wrinkles as much as possible. Stir mixed nuts and pecans into fruit mixture. Remove 1½ cups mixture and set aside. Stir flour, sugar, and baking powder into remaining fruit and nut mixture until well coated. Stir in eggs until well mixed. Spoon batter into prepared pan, packing firmly to eliminate air pockets. Sprinkle reserved fruit and nut mixture on top. Cover pan loosely with foil. Bake at 300 degrees for 2 hours. Remove foil and bake 30 minutes longer or until knife inserted into center of cake comes out clean and top of cake is lightly browned. Cool cake in pan on wire rack 30 minutes. Remove from pan and carefully peel off foil. Cool cake completely, wrap tightly in foil or plastic wrap, and refrigerate.

Mrs. Fitzpatrick's Fruitcake

Adelaide Heyde Parsons shares this recipe for a fruitcake that her grandmother, a widow with two young children, used to make to sell at Vandeven's Grocery Store in Cape Girardeau, Missouri, during the Depression. She says that since Prohibition was also in force at that time, her grandmother would manage to get a "prescription" from the doctor for the whiskey. Adelaide credits the cake with helping to lure a marriage proposal from her husband Bob. "I first learned to make this cake when I was dating Bob," she says. "He loves fruitcake and my mother was hoping that a surprise homemade fruitcake would assist me in getting a proposal from him. It may have, since he proposed soon after the Christmas holiday!"

⅔ c. sugar
⅓ c. butter
2 eggs
1⅓ c. flour
½ tsp. nutmeg
½ tsp. baking powder
¼ c. whiskey or brandy
½ c. fruitcake fruit mix
1¾ c. raisins
¾ c. chopped dates
¾ c. dried figs
1⅓ c. pecans, chopped

Cream sugar and butter, add eggs, and beat until fluffy. Sift together flour, nutmeg, and baking powder, and add gradually. Batter will be quite thick. Add brandy or whiskey, then fold in fruits and nuts. Transfer batter to greased and floured 9x5x3-inch loaf pan and bake at 350 degrees for 45–50 minutes until light golden color. Do not overbake. Cool thoroughly, baste with brandy or whiskey, and wrap in cheesecloth or waxed paper. Place in tin. Baste once a week and let ripen for up to 1 month.

Rose's Less Fruity
Fruitcake Cupcakes

This recipe adapted from noted food writer Rose Levy Beranbaum emphasizes the cake in the word "fruitcake." And no ordinary cake it is. It's moist and almost pudding-like. Baking the batter in muffin tins means no ripening is required. The cakes can be eaten right from the pan. For an especially attractive presentation, use mini Bundt-style pans.

> ½ c. small mixed candied fruit
> 2 tbsp. candied citron
> ¼ c. dried currants
> ¼ c. broken pecans
> ½ c. Meyers's dark rum
> ½ c. unsifted cake flour
> ¼ tsp. cinnamon
> ⅛ tsp. baking soda
> ¼ tsp. salt
> 1 stick butter, softened
> ¼ c. dark brown sugar
> 1 egg
> ¼ c. molasses
> 2 tbsp. milk

At least 24 hours ahead, mince the candied fruit and citron, and soak with the currants and nuts in ¼ cup rum. Cover and store at room temperature. Whisk flour, cinnamon, baking soda, and salt to combine. Cream butter and sugar until light and fluffy. Beat in the egg and then the flour mixture in 3 batches, alternating with the molasses and milk. Add the candied fruit mixture with the soaking rum and beat until blended. The batter will be slightly curdled, but this will not affect cake texture. Fill greased and floured muffin tins three-fourths full with batter and bake 20 minutes at 325 degrees until cake tester inserted in center comes out clean. Sprinkle each cupcake with 1 teaspoon rum, unmold after 5 minutes, and store airtight at room temperature for up to 6 weeks. Makes 11 cupcakes.

Mrs. Sharp's Pumpkin Pie

This unique recipe, made on top of the stove instead of baked, was a favorite of the late Mrs. Ellen Sharp, mother of retired Southeast Missouri State University history professor Dr. Charles Sharp. For twenty-five years she was a dietician and school cafeteria manager in California.

  1 can (15 oz.) pumpkin
  ⅔ c. miniature marshmallows
  ¼ c. brown sugar
  1 c. granulated sugar
  ½ tsp. salt
  ½ tsp. cinnamon
  ⅛ tsp. allspice
  2 tbsp. flour
  ¾ c. evaporated milk
  1 tbsp. butter
  2 eggs
  ½ tsp. vanilla
  1 baked pie shell

Heat pumpkin and stir in marshmallows until dissolved. Combine sugars, spices, and flour, and add milk, mixing well. Add some of pumpkin mixture to milk mixture, stirring rapidly. Add back to remaining pumpkin mixture and cook until thickened. Stir in butter. Beat eggs and add some of the hot pumpkin mixture, beating well. Add back to rest of pumpkin mixture and boil a few minutes. Remove from heat, add vanilla, cool, and pour into pie crust. Chill and serve.

Caramelized Pecan Pumpkin Pie

If some people at your Thanksgiving table prefer pumpkin pie and others pecan, this delicious concoction should please them both. The recipe is adapted from *Bon Appétit* magazine.

  ⅔ c. brown sugar
  ½ c. chopped pecans
  3 tbsp. butter
  1 baked pumpkin pie, chilled

Combine sugar and pecans, and cut in butter until mixture resembles coarse meal. Sprinkle evenly over pie. Broil until sugar melts and bubbles, about 1 minute. Cool 15 minutes before serving.

Pumpkin Cheesecake Pie

If there's anything that rivals pumpkin pie, it's pumpkin cheesecake. This recipe combines the best of both. Any crust works well, including a graham-cracker or gingersnap crust, but a cornmeal crust is especially good. The recipe is adapted from *Bon Appétit* magazine.

>6 oz. cream cheese
>½ c. granulated sugar
>½ c. brown sugar
>2 eggs
>1 egg yolk
>1 c. pumpkin purée
>¾ c. half-and-half
>1 tsp. cinnamon
>1 tsp. nutmeg
>½ tsp. lemon peel
>½ tsp. ginger
>¼ tsp. salt
>1 pie shell

Beat cream cheese with sugars until fluffy. Beat in eggs and yolk, and add remaining ingredients, combining well. Pour filling into crust and bake at 350 degrees for 55 minutes until slightly puffed and just set in center. Cool and refrigerate at least 4 hours before serving.

 # Savannah Banana Pie

This recipe, a streamlined version of one from Maida Heatter, is, as she says, out of this world. You can use already caramelized Mexican *cajeta*, available at international food stores, instead of the condensed milk.

>1 baked 9-inch pie shell
>1 can (14 oz.) sweetened condensed milk
>3–4 ripe bananas
>1½ c. whipping cream
>2 tbsp. powdered sugar
>1 c. chopped English toffee bars

Pour milk into 2-quart glass pie plate and microwave at 50% power for 4 minutes, stirring briskly every 2 minutes, until smooth. Cook on 30% power 12–18 minutes or until very thick and caramel colored, stirring briskly every 2 minutes, until smooth. Cool. Slice bananas evenly over crust. Place spoonfuls of caramelized milk evenly over bananas and smooth top to cover. Refrigerate 4–8 hours. Whip cream, spread over pie, and top with toffee.

Cranberry Walnut Pie

Native Americans enjoyed eating cranberries with maple syrup. That wonderful combination is at the heart of this recipe based on one from *Bon Appétit* magazine in which, not surprisingly, I have doubled the number of cranberries called for. The crunch and flavor of the walnuts when added to the other ingredients make this a dessert that will challenge pumpkin pie as the obvious way to end your Thanksgiving meal.

    1 single pie crust
    ¾ c. golden brown sugar
    2 eggs
    ¾ c. maple syrup
    2 tbsp. melted butter
    1 tsp. vanilla
    ¼ tsp. salt
    2 c. coarsely chopped walnuts
    2 c. coarsely chopped cranberries

Beat sugar and eggs to blend. Whisk in syrup, butter, vanilla, and salt. Stir in walnuts and cranberries. Pour filling into prepared crust and bake at 400 degrees for 10 minutes. Reduce oven temperature to 350 degrees and bake until filling is set, about 35–45 minutes longer. Cool before serving.

Sawdust Pie

This recipe gets its name from the fact that crushed graham crackers are the texture of sawdust. (Sylvester Graham's hometown newspaper, in fact, called him "the philosopher of sawdust pudding.") The dessert is a staple at Patti's restaurant in Grand Rivers, Kentucky, where they really know how to do pies. The recipe first appeared nearly twenty years ago in *Bon Appétit* magazine. This adaptation calls for cinnamon-flavored graham crackers. (Chocolate grahams might be an interesting variation as well.)

    1½ c. sugar
    1½ c. coconut
    1½ c. chopped pecans
    1½ c. cinnamon graham-cracker crumbs
    7 egg whites
    1 unbaked 10-inch pie shell
    1 banana, sliced thinly
    whipped cream

Combine sugar, coconut, pecans, crumbs, and egg whites, and mix well without beating. Turn into pie shell and bake at 350 degrees for 35 minutes or until just set. Top with whipped cream and banana slices.

Earl Grey Chocolate Pie

Earl Charles Grey was Prime Minister of England during the reign of William IV. The tea named after him, the second-most-popular in the world, is flavored with bergamot oil from a small acidic orange, making it an excellent companion to chocolate. Try topping this pie with whipped cream, which has been infused with the tea. The recipe is modified from one in the Lipton collection.

      1 pie shell, unbaked
      2 c. half-and-half
      2 tbsp. sugar
      6 bags Earl Grey tea
      ¾ c. chocolate chips
      2 eggs
      2 egg yolks
      2 tsp. vanilla

Combine half-and-half and sugar, and bring to the boiling point. Add tea bags and brew for 10 minutes. Remove bags, squeezing out liquid. Add chocolate chips, and stir over low heat until melted. Let cool. Blend eggs, yolks, and vanilla, and whisk into chocolate mixture. Pour into crust and bake at 325 degrees for 45 minutes or until set. Cool 30 minutes before serving.

Peeps Pie

The hardest thing about this recipe, adapted from one given to National Public Radio by Peeps aficionado Howard Yoon, is avoiding feelings of guilt as you melt down the Peeps, their eyes looking out pitiably from the saucepan at you. At least lobsters put up a fight.

      1 graham-cracker pie crust
      ⅓ c. milk
      30 Peeps (color optional)
      1½ c. cream
      ¼ tsp. brandy
      ⅓ c. chocolate chips, chilled

Bake crust at 350 degrees until golden. Cool. Heat milk, add Peeps, and stir until completely melted. Cool to room temperature, but do not allow to stiffen. Whip cream to stiff peaks, adding brandy. Fold whipped cream and chocolate chips into Peeps mixture until fully incorporated. Pour into crust and refrigerate several hours before serving. Garnish with whole Peeps if desired.

Chocolate Coconut Caramel Dessert

This recipe is adapted from ABC Bakers of Richmond, Virginia, the oldest of two bakeries licensed to supply Girl Scout Cookies nationwide. Their affiliation with the Girl Scouts dates back to 1939.

    1 box Girl Scout Caramel deLites
    3 tbsp. margarine, melted
    1 pkg. (8 oz.) cream cheese, softened
    ¼ c. sugar
    1¼ c. plus 2 tbsp. milk, divided
    1½ c. thawed nondairy whipped topping, divided
    1 pkg. (4-serving) instant coconut cream pudding mix
    ¼ c. toasted coconut
    3 tbsp. semisweet chocolate mini morsels

Place cookies in processor or blender and process into fine crumbs. Spray bottom of a 9-inch square pan with nonstick cooking spray. Combine cookie crumbs and margarine, and press evenly in bottom of pan. Beat cream cheese with sugar and 2 tablespoons milk until smooth. Blend in ¾ cup whipped topping. Spread evenly over cookie layer. Combine pudding mix and remaining milk, and beat 1–2 minutes until smooth. Pour over cream cheese layer. Chill several hours or overnight. Just before serving, spread remaining whipped topping over top of dessert, and sprinkle with toasted coconut and mini morsels. Serves 12.

 # Frozen Lemonade Pie

If you can't get enough lemonade just by drinking, try this refreshing pie from Mrs. ElLouise Kollman, whose daughter, Susan Janzow of Cape Girardeau, Missouri, brought back the recipe from a visit. Mrs. Kollman, a doting great grandmother, is a talented cook and craftsperson who still lives on the family farm in Clark, Missouri.

    1 can (6 oz.) frozen lemonade concentrate
    1 pkg. (8 oz.) cream cheese
    1 can sweetened condensed milk
    1 tub (8 oz.) Cool Whip
    1 graham-cracker pie crust

Put concentrate, cream cheese, and milk in a blender, and whir until smooth and creamy. Pour into bowl and fold in Cool Whip. Pour into crust and refrigerate 2–3 hours.

Mississippi Mud Pie

This recipe was given to me long ago by Nell Beall who used to be the housemother at the since razed Leming Hall on the Southeast Missouri State University campus. Over the years, it has become a favorite at our house. It's easy to make, but baking can be a little tricky. If you overbake the pie, it will still be good, but it will lose the silky texture which makes it outstanding.

> 1 unbaked 9-inch pie shell
> 1 stick butter
> ½ c. chocolate chips
> 4 eggs, beaten
> 3 tbsp. light corn syrup
> 1½ c. sugar
> ¼ tsp. salt
> 1 tsp. vanilla

Melt butter and chocolate, and cool slightly. Add remaining ingredients and blend thoroughly. Pour into pie shell and bake at 325 degrees for 30–40 minutes or until top is crusty and filling is just set.

 # Maple Pecan Pie

You might think that winning three awards at the National Pie Championship constitutes pie in the sky, but it was a reality for Marles Riessland of Riverdale, Nebraska. She won first prize in the nut and custard categories and took the cake, so to speak, winning best of show for this pecan pie spiked with maple syrup.

> 1 unbaked 9-inch pie shell
> 4 eggs, well beaten
> ¾ c. sugar
> ½ c. maple syrup
> ½ c. light corn syrup
> ½ c. dark corn syrup
> 2½ tsp. vanilla
> ¼ tsp. salt
> 1¼ c. broken pecans
> ⅓ c. melted butter

Mix sugar, syrups, vanilla, and salt with eggs until blended. Stir in pecans and butter. Pour filling into shell. Bake at 350 degrees for 45–55 minutes until center is set. Brush hot pie with maple syrup and cool.

Asparagus and Rhubarb Custard Pie

Believe it or not, asparagus can function as dessert under the right circumstances. An asparagus and rhubarb pie even took the grand prize one year at the National Asparagus Festival. This is my take on the combination, adapted to my preference for custard pies.

  1 unbaked 9-inch pie shell
  2 c. diced asparagus
  2 c. diced rhubarb
  ⅔ c. sugar
  2 eggs
  1 c. cream
  1 tbsp. cornstarch

Parboil asparagus for 4 minutes and combine with rhubarb and sugar, tossing to coat until sugar is fully moistened. Transfer to pie shell. Combine eggs, cream, and cornstarch, and pour over rhubarb mixture. Bake at 425 degrees for 10 minutes. Reduce oven temperature to 400 degrees and bake until puffed and golden, and knife inserted in center comes out clean, 35–40 minutes. Serves 6.

Blintz Casserole

This recipe, which is a lot easier than making individual blintzes, is from one of my favorite cookbooks, *Cooking in Clover*, published by the hospital auxiliary of the old Jewish Hospital in St. Louis and given to me years ago by the late Mrs. Ruth Bygel, who used to work in the hospital flower shop. I still consult the book regularly.

  1 c. butter, melted
  6 eggs, divided
  ¼ c. milk
  1 tsp. vanilla
  1 c. flour
  ¾ cup sugar, divided
  3 tsp. baking powder
  dash salt
  2 lbs. small-curd cottage cheese, blended until smooth
  juice of 1 lemon

Make batter by mixing butter, 3 eggs, milk, vanilla, flour, ½ cup sugar, baking powder, and salt. Pour half of batter into buttered 2-quart baking dish. Make filling by mixing cottage cheese, remaining 3 eggs, remaining ¼ cup sugar, and lemon juice. Pour over batter in dish. Top with remaining batter. Bake at 300 degrees for 1½ hours. Serve with sour cream or blueberry sauce.

Strawberry Rhubarb Cobbler with Cornmeal Biscuit Topping

Biscuits, of course, don't have to be relegated to the breakfast table, as this recipe adapted from *Bon Appétit* magazine demonstrates. Biscuit dough is a classic topping for cobblers and can be used for shortcakes as well. Here, the crunch of the cornmeal adds an extra dimension to a favorite summer dessert.

½ plus ⅓ c. sugar, divided
1 c. plus 2 tbsp. flour, divided
⅛ tsp. ground cloves
2 baskets (12 oz.) hulled strawberries, halved
1½ c. fresh or frozen rhubarb, cut in ½-inch slices
¼ c. yellow cornmeal
1 tbsp. baking powder
1 tsp. baking soda
pinch of salt
3 tbsp. chilled butter, diced
½ c. buttermilk

Mix ½ cup sugar, 2 tablespoons flour, and cloves. Add fruit and toss to coat. Transfer to 10-inch glass pie plate. Mix remaining 1 cup flour, remaining ⅓ cup sugar, cornmeal, baking powder and soda, and salt, and cut in butter until mixture resembles coarse meal. Gradually add buttermilk, tossing with fork until moist clumps form. Spoon topping evenly over fruit and bake at 400 degrees until golden brown and filling is tender, about 25 minutes. Serves 6.

 # Raspberry Cheese Tart

I've been making the filling for this tart for over 25 years, ever since I first saw the basic recipe in *Family Circle* magazine. There's nothing to it, yet you couldn't ask for a more impressive showcase for fresh raspberries or, for that matter, fresh fruit of any kind.

1 pie shell baked in 9-inch round fluted tart pan
1 pkg. (8 oz.) cream cheese
¼ c. sugar
1 tbsp. heavy cream
1½ tbsp. orange liqueur
1 pint raspberries
¼ c. apple jelly

Beat cream cheese until fluffy and add sugar, cream, and liqueur. Spread over pastry and refrigerate 1 hour. Arrange berries over tart and brush lightly with melted apple jelly to glaze.

Tart Tatin

This dessert was a specialty of the Tatin sisters, Stephanie and Caroline, at their hotel in the Loire Valley of France in the 19th century. Though now a classic, the original was quite probably a salvaged culinary disaster, the result of a harried cook mistakenly baking the tart upside-down. There's no mistaking this recipe, adapted from Rose Levy Beranbaum's *The Pie and Pastry Bible*, as the definitive version.

     Pastry for a one-crust pie
     10 c. thickly sliced apples
     1 tbsp. fresh lemon juice
     ½ c. sugar
     ½ stick butter

Combine apples, lemon juice, and sugar. Toss and let sit for 30 minutes. Drain the liquid from the apples (there should be about ½ cup) and pour in a skillet along with the butter. Cook over medium heat, stirring often, until caramelized, about 5 minutes. Remove pan from heat and arrange apple slices in slightly overlapping circles over the caramel, heaping them in the middle. Cook, covered, over medium heat for 10 minutes. Uncover and continue cooking over high heat, stirring constantly, until apples are almost tender, about 10 minutes longer. Remove from heat and cool 20 minutes. Place pastry evenly over the apples, tucking the edges into the pan. Cut a few steam vents near the center of the crust and bake in a 425-degree oven for 30 minutes until golden. Cool 10 minutes. Using a small knife, loosen crust from side of pan and invert the tart onto serving plate. Serve warm with crème fraîche.

 # *Peachy Keen Pie*

On those occasions when the juiciness of a fresh peach eaten out of hand threatens both decorum and clothing, the next best thing is a fresh peach pie. There couldn't be an easier way to make one than this recipe, adapted from one of Shirley Beggs' (of Beggs' Orchards) favorite volumes, the *Passion for Peaches* cookbook by Gail McPherson. You don't even have to peel the fruit! If you want to enhance the pie's appearance and flavor even further, add a cup of fresh blueberries to the filling.

     1 nine-inch baked pie shell
     3½ c. sliced fresh peaches, unpeeled
     ½ c. orange juice
     1 c. sugar
     2½ tbsp. cornstarch

Arrange 2 cups of the sliced peaches in the pie shell. Process remaining 1½ cups peaches, skin and all, in food processor for a few seconds until mashed. (You should have 1 cup mashed peaches.) Combine mashed peaches, orange juice, sugar, and cornstarch, and bring to a boil. Cook until mixture is clear and slightly thickened. Pour over peaches in pie shell, let cool, and chill. Serve with whipped cream.

Peach Berry Cobbler

This classic recipe is from the late Hulda Lehne Hengst of Cape Girardeau, Missouri, an avid recipe collector who regularly exchanged recipes with her sister, the late Meta Lehne Hengst (they married brothers) of Egypt Mills. Their recipe collection has been lovingly preserved for posterity in a booklet assembled by nephew and grandson Rick Borchelt who formerly lived in Cape Girardeau.

14 tbsp. sugar, divided
¼ c. brown sugar
1 tbsp. cornstarch
½ c. water
1 tbsp. lemon juice
2 c. sliced peaches
1 c. blueberries
1 c. sifted flour
1½ tsp. baking powder
½ tsp. salt
¼ c. soft butter
½ c. milk
¼ tsp. nutmeg

Combine 4 tablespoons sugar, brown sugar, and cornstarch, and add water, blending well. Cook over medium heat, stirring constantly, until thick. Add lemon juice, peaches, and berries, and turn into 2-quart baking dish. Sift together flour, 8 tablespoons sugar, baking powder, and salt, and add butter and milk, beating until smooth. Spoon mixture over fruit and sprinkle with remaining 2 tablespoons sugar and the nutmeg. Bake at 375 degrees for 40–45 minutes.

Plum Crisp

Though crisps are homey desserts by definition, the use of plums, it seems to me, makes this dish just a little more sophisticated. Though plums may not have the glamour of summer fruits like strawberries and peaches, the Italian prune variety, available at the end of summer and in the fall, is especially superb when baked in a cake, tart, clafouti, cobbler, or, as in this recipe adapted from *Gourmet* magazine, a crisp.

> ¾ c. sliced almonds
> ¾ c. flour
> ¾ c. light brown sugar
> ¾ c. old-fashioned rolled oats
> ¾ tsp. cinnamon
> ½ tsp. salt
> 1 stick cold butter, cut into bits
> ¾ c. water
> 4 tsp. cornstarch
> 3 lbs. Italian prune plums, halved and pitted
> ½ c. sugar

Toast almonds until golden. In food processor, blend flour, brown sugar, ½ cup oats, cinnamon, salt, and butter until mixture resembles coarse meal. In a bowl, stir together flour mixture, remaining oats, and almonds. Combine water and cornstarch. Cook plums with sugar in skillet over moderate heat, stirring, until sugar melts. Stir in cornstarch mixture and simmer, stirring, 15 minutes or until thickened. Transfer to 3-quart baking dish and sprinkle with topping. Bake at 375 degrees for 40–45 minutes or until topping is crisp and golden. Cool 10 minutes before serving warm with ice cream.

Macadamia Tart
with Chocolate Crust

After tirelessly sampling as many macadamia-nut pies as I could find during a visit to the Big Island of Hawaii where nearly 90 percent of the state's macadamia nuts are grown, I've concluded that this version is still the best I've ever tasted, and why shouldn't it be? It's the one they serve at Spago, Wolfgang Puck's award-winning restaurant. The recipe is adapted from *Spago Desserts* authored by Mary Bergin and Judy Gethers.

> 2 c. flour
> ½ c. cocoa
> 1 c. sugar
> 15 tbsp. chilled butter, divided
> 5 egg yolks, divided
> 2 tbsp. cream
> 1 lb. macadamia nuts
> 1 tsp. vanilla
> 1⅓ c. light corn syrup
> ⅔ c. brown sugar
> 1 egg
> 1 tbsp. Frangelico

Place flour, cocoa, and sugar in food processor and pulse to combine. Add 12 table-spoons butter cut into pieces and process just until combined. Whisk together 2 of the egg yolks and the cream, and, with the processor running, pour through the feed tube. Process until dough begins to come together, about 1 minute. Flatten dough into a round, wrap, and refrigerate 2–3 hours. Lightly grease a 9-inch tart pan. Roll out dough on a lightly floured surface to an 11-inch circle, press into pan, and trim edges. Refrigerate 30 minutes. Toast nuts at 375 degrees, stirring occasionally, until golden brown, about 10 minutes. Melt remaining 3 tablespoons butter over medium heat and cook until it turns golden brown. Remove from heat, add vanilla, corn syrup, brown sugar, egg, remaining 3 yolks, and Frangelico, and whisk until well combined. Fill tart shell with nuts, then ladle filling over. Bake at 375 degrees until golden brown and firm to the touch, 40–45 minutes. Cool 20 minutes and remove sides of pan. Cool tart completely before serving. Serve with caramel sauce and whipped cream if desired.

Peeps S'mores Napoleon

This recipe is adapted from one served at Prego Italian Restaurant in Houston. You can omit the mousse topping for a standard s'more.

> 5 oz. white chocolate
> 2 tbsp. cold milk
> 1¼ c. whipping cream, whipped
> 16 graham crackers
> 16 Peeps, varied colors
> 4 Hershey's chocolate bars (1.55 oz. each)

Melt white chocolate and stir in milk. Let cool. Fold in whipped cream. For each s'more, place 3 squares of the chocolate bar atop half a graham cracker, and microwave until chocolate begins to melt (about 45 seconds). Place one Peep on top of chocolate and microwave until Peep begins to swell. Top with another half of a graham cracker and press down to set. Top with dollop of the white chocolate mousse.

 # Baklava

This classic recipe is adapted from Rose Levy Beranbaum's *The Pie and Pastry Bible*. She swears by pistachio nuts, but almonds, walnuts, or a mixture can also be used.

> 1¼ c. sugar, divided
> 6 tbsp. honey
> ½ c. water
> 1 tbsp. light corn syrup
> 1 tbsp. lemon juice
> 1½ c. nuts
> ½ tsp. cinnamon
> 12 sheets filo
> 12 tbsp. clarified melted butter

Mix 1 cup sugar, water, honey, and syrup, and bring to a simmer over medium heat, stirring constantly. Lower heat and simmer 30 minutes, stirring occasionally. Add lemon juice and let cool. Chop nuts finely, add cinnamon, and remaining ¼ cup sugar. Lightly coat a 9x13-inch pan with some butter. Brush one sheet filo with 1 teaspoon butter and fold in half to fit pan. Brush with another teaspoon butter. Lay a total of 4 folded sheets in pan, brushing each with 2 teaspoons butter in this manner. Spread half of nut mixture in pan and top with 2 more folded and buttered filo sheets. Sprinkle remaining nut mixture over top and add 6 more folded and buttered filo sheets. Score top sheets of filo into diamond pattern using a sharp knife. Bake at 300 degrees for 30 minutes or until golden. Spoon syrup mixture over baklava and let stand until absorbed.

Chocolate Date Nut Baklava

This recipe adapted from *Bon Appétit* magazine is so decadent you might as well go all out and serve it with ice cream!

> 1 c. plus 2 tbsp. sugar
> ½ c. water
> pinch of ground allspice
> pinch of ground ginger
> pinch of ground cloves
> 2 c. walnuts
> 1 c. chocolate chips
> 1 c. pitted dates
> 1 tbsp. cinnamon
> 1 egg
> 11 sheets filo
> 1½ sticks clarified melted butter

Bring 1 cup sugar, water, allspice, ginger, and cloves to boil, stirring until sugar dissolves. Boil 1 minute and cool completely. Combine nuts, chocolate chips, dates, remaining 2 tablespoons sugar, and cinnamon in processor and coarsely chop. Mix in egg by hand. Lightly butter 9x13-inch pan. Brush 1 sheet filo with butter. Top with second sheet, brush with butter, and arrange in pan. Brush another sheet filo with butter, fold in half, brush with butter, and place in pan. Repeat with another 2 sheets filo. Sprinkle half of filling over top. Butter another sheet filo, fold in half, and place on top of filling. Sprinkle remaining filling over top. Place 3 more buttered and folded filo sheets over top. Butter remaining 2 sheets filo and place lengthwise in pan, tucking in sides and ends. Score top layers of filo into squares and bake at 350 degrees until golden, about 45 minutes. Spoon syrup over, cool, and let stand overnight at room temperature.

Pineapple Cheese Baklava

This recipe, adapted from a little paperback book by Sylvia Schur, is really a cross between cheesecake and baklava, and offers a tasty change of pace from the nut-filled versions of the sweet.

> 1 can (20 oz.) crushed pineapple
> 1 c. ricotta cheese
> 8 oz. softened cream cheese
> 1 c. sugar, divided
> 2 egg yolks
> 1 tsp. grated lemon peel
> 1 tsp. vanilla
> 8 filo leaves
> 1 stick clarified melted butter
> 1 tsp. lemon juice

Strain juice from pineapple and reserve. Mix together ricotta, cream cheese, ½ cup sugar, egg yolks, peel, and vanilla. Stir in drained pineapple. Place 1 sheet filo in well-greased 9x13-inch pan and brush with butter. Repeat using 3 more leaves. Spread cheese mixture over pastry. Top with remaining filo leaves, brushing each with butter. Mark pastry into diamonds and bake 50 minutes at 350 degrees until golden brown. Combine reserved syrup, remaining ½ cup sugar, and lemon juice. Bring to a boil, reduce heat, and cook to a thick syrup. Spoon over baklava. Cool.

Basic Danish Pastry Dough

D'Angleterre is the grand dame of Copenhagen hotels and the place where the late G. L. Wennberg, the acknowledged master of *Weinerbrod*, worked his magic. This recipe is based on his version as printed in the Glasgow *Herald*.

> 2 pkg. active dry yeast
> ¾ c. milk
> 1 tbsp. sugar
> 1 egg
> 1 egg yolk
> ¼ tsp. salt
> 1 tsp. ground cardamom
> 1 lb. butter
> 4 c. flour

Dissolve yeast in ¼ cup of the milk. Heat remaining milk to lukewarm and add sugar, egg, yolk, salt, cardamom, and 6 tablespoons of the butter. Stir in the yeast mixture. Add flour, and knead until smooth and pliable. Cover and let rise until doubled. Punch down dough and roll out into a 12-inch square. Pound remaining butter with a rolling pin to soften it and knead until pliable. Shape into a square and place on dough, making sure entire surface of dough is covered. Cover with parchment or wax paper and roll into an oblong shape. Remove paper and fold dough into thirds like a business letter. Refrigerate 10 minutes. Repeat rolling and chilling two more times. Roll dough into a half-inch thick oblong and fold in half. Chill at least 30 minutes before rolling and shaping into pastries.

Mock Danish Pastry

Though not a true Danish pastry dough, this facsimile works quite well and is far easier to manage than the authentic variety. The recipe is based on one that appeared on an Internet site devoted to Danish pastries and managed by Joan Ross.

> 4–6 c. flour
> ½ tsp. salt
> 3 sticks butter
> 2 tbsp. sugar
> 1 pkg. active dry yeast
> 1 c. warm milk
> 3 eggs, slightly beaten
> 1 tsp. vanilla
> 3 jars thick preserves
> 3 c. chopped nuts
> powdered sugar

Sift together 4 cups of the flour with the salt. Cut in butter until mixture resembles coarse meal. Dissolve sugar and yeast in milk and let sit until foamy. Add to flour mixture along with eggs and vanilla and mix thoroughly. Add additional flour to make a soft dough. Knead until smooth and elastic. Cover and refrigerate overnight. Divide dough into three parts and roll each on a lightly floured surface into a large rectangle. Spread 1 jar of preserves over each rectangle of dough and sprinkle with 1 cup of the nuts. Bring up both long sides of the rectangle towards the center, overlapping slightly. Tuck under side edges. Bake on greased cookie sheet at 350 degrees for 20–25 minutes until golden. Dust with powdered sugar.

Cheese Danish Puffs

This clever concoction mimics real Danish pastry by using a standard pastry crust on the bottom and cream puff pastry on the top. The recipe, to which I couldn't resist the temptation to add cream cheese, is a variation of one found in April Moon's wonderful *The Flying Biscuit Cafe Cookbook*.

> 2 sticks butter, divided
> 2 c. flour, divided
> 1 c. plus 2 tbsp. water, divided
> 1 lb. cream cheese
> 1⅓ c. powdered sugar, divided
> 1 tsp. almond extract
> 3 eggs
> 2 tbsp. cream

Cut 1 stick butter into 1 cup flour until mixture resembles coarse meal. Add 2 tablespoons water and mix until dough forms a ball. Pat dough into a 12x6-inch rectangle and place on baking sheet. Beat cream cheese and 1 cup powdered sugar until smooth and soft. Spread over rectangle. Bring remaining 1 stick butter and remaining 1 cup water to a boil. Remove from heat, add extract, then whisk in remaining flour all at once until mixture pulls away from pan. Beat in eggs one at a time. Spread over cream cheese. Bake at 375 degrees for 45–50 minutes until brown. Let cool. Combine remaining ⅓ cup powdered sugar with cream and beat until smooth. Drizzle over pastry and cut into 3 strips. Cut each strip into serving pieces.

Brioches aux Gouttes de Chocolat

Doubtless these unique chocolate-chip *brioches*, developed by Parisian *pâtissier* Gérard Mulot, were not what Marie Antoinette had in mind when she uttered her famous phrase as peasants stormed the Bastille, but she surely would have loved them. The recipe is adapted from Linda Dannenberg's marvelous book, *Paris Boulangerie-Pâtisserie*.

> 5 tbsp. cream, divided
> ½ tsp. sugar
> 1 pkg. active dry yeast
> 2 c. flour
> 1 tsp. salt
> 3 eggs
> 1 stick melted butter, cooled
> 1 c. thick pastry cream
> ⅔ c. chocolate chips
> 1 egg yolk

Warm 4 tablespoons cream to 105 degrees and stir in sugar and yeast. Let proof 5 minutes. In a food processor, mix yeast mixture, flour, salt, eggs, and butter for 10 seconds. Knead dough by hand on lightly floured surface until slightly sticky yet smooth and manageable. Transfer dough to greased bowl, turning to coat all sides, and let rise, covered, until doubled, about 1½ hours. Punch down dough and roll out on lightly floured surface to a 10x15-inch rectangle. Spread with pastry cream. Sprinkle with chocolate chips. Fold short ends of rectangle toward the middle until they meet in the center. Cut dough in half along center seam. Cut each half into six strips. Place on parchment-lined baking sheets and let rise until puffy, about 1½ hours. Combine yolk and remaining 1 tablespoon cream, and brush on top of pastries. Bake at 400 degrees for 10 minutes. Reduce heat to 350 degrees and bake 5–10 minutes longer until golden brown.

Brutti Ma Buoni al Cacao
(Ugly But Good Chocolate Cookies)

While these cookies are not as chic as Florentines, biscotti, or pizzelle, they are every bit as delicious. The recipe is adapted from *The International Cookie Cookbook* by Nancy Baggett.

½ c. whole, unblanched hazelnuts
½ c. slivered blanched almonds
1 oz. unsweetened chocolate
3 egg whites
pinch of salt
½ tsp. instant coffee powder
2¾ c. powdered sugar
6 tbsp. unsweetened cocoa powder
½ tsp. almond extract
½ tsp. vanilla extract

Toast nuts separately in oven at 325 degrees, stirring occasionally; set aside to cool. (Almonds should take about 6 minutes, hazelnuts about 17.) Melt chocolate and set aside to cool until barely warm. Line baking sheets with baking parchment. Remove hulls from hazelnuts and chop along with almonds. Combine egg whites, salt, and coffee powder, and let stand 5 minutes. Beat with electric mixer on medium speed until frothy. Increase mixer speed to high and beat until well mixed and fluffy. Continue beating, gradually adding sugar, cocoa, and extracts. Beat until stiff, smooth, and glossy. Stir in melted chocolate and nuts until incorporated. Do not overmix. Drop dough by heaping teaspoonfuls onto baking sheets, spacing 1½ inches apart. Bake at 350 degrees 11–13 minutes until almost firm to touch. (Underbake for chewy cookies; overbake for crispy ones.) Let stand for 1–2 minutes, then slide parchment from baking sheets and let cookies cool completely before carefully peeling off.

Versatile Chocolate Chip Cookies

This recipe, adapted from Shirley O. Corriher, makes a thin, crisp cookie, but as she reveals in her book *CookWise*, there's no mystery about how to alter it for soft cookies as well. Simply substitute shortening for the butter, use 1½ teaspoons baking powder in place of the baking soda, leave out the milk and corn syrup, replace the sugars with 1 cup brown sugar, add an egg, and use cake flour.

    10 tbsp. butter
    ½ c. sugar
    ⅓ c. brown sugar
    3 tbsp. light corn syrup
    2 tbsp. milk
    1 tbsp. vanilla
    1½ c. flour
    ¾ tsp. salt
    ¾ tsp. baking soda
    1 cup toasted pecans
    1 c. chocolate chips

Cream butter and sugars until fluffy, add corn syrup, milk, and vanilla, and beat thoroughly. Combine flour, salt, and baking soda, and mix into butter mixture. Add nuts and chocolate chips. Drop tablespoons of batter onto greased cookie sheets and bake at 375 degrees for 12 minutes or until just starting to brown. Cool slightly before removing from sheets.

Millennial Chocolate Chip Cookies

This chocolate-chip cookie inspired by *Chocolatier* magazine is an appropriate way to usher in the new millennium and to celebrate the old one. The recipe, after all, is indebted to many breakthroughs of the last ten centuries, including the discovery of new ingredients like chocolate, advances in the production of already known ones, the invention of appliances like the temperature-regulated oven, and, of course, the experimentation of Ruth Wakefield.

    2 sticks butter
    1 c. granulated sugar
    ½ c. brown sugar
    2 tbsp. grated orange zest
    2 tsp. vanilla
    2 eggs
    1 tsp. baking soda
    1 tsp. salt
    2 c. flour
    1 c. pecan halves
    3 giant (8-oz.) milk-chocolate bars, cut into chunks

Cream butter, sugars, and zest until fluffy. Beat in vanilla and eggs. Stir in combined baking soda, salt, and flour. Stir in pecans and chocolate chunks. Spoon dough onto greased cookie sheets and bake at 350 degrees 10–12 minutes. Cool slightly before removing from cookie sheets.

 # Chocolate Snow Meringues

This recipe for meringue cookies, or kisses, based on one recently reprinted in the *Atlanta Journal-Constitution*, makes a confection which is crisp on the outside but chewy on the inside.

    4 egg whites
    ¼ tsp. cream of tartar
    1½ c. superfine sugar
    1 c. chopped walnuts or pecans
    1½ c. chocolate chips
    1 tsp. vanilla

Beat whites until foamy. Add cream of tartar and beat until stiff peaks form. Add sugar, 2 tablespoons at a time, beating well after each addition. Fold in nuts, chocolate chips, and vanilla. Drop by teaspoonfuls onto parchment-paper-lined baking sheets. Bake for 20–25 minutes or until golden. Remove from pan to cool.

Spago's Peanut Butter Cookies

What could be more comforting than classic peanut-butter cookies and a glass of milk? These are elegant enough to serve at Spago, Wolfgang Puck's landmark restaurant in Los Angeles. The recipe is adapted from *Spago Desserts* authored by Mary Bergin and Judy Gethers.

     2 c. plus 1 tbsp. flour
     2 tsp. baking soda
     2 sticks butter
     1 c. granulated sugar
     1 c. brown sugar
     1 c. peanut butter (chunky or smooth)
     2 eggs
     1½ c. dried currants

Sift together flour and baking soda. Cream butter and sugars until fluffy. Add peanut butter and beat until combined. Add eggs one at a time, beating at medium speed. Add sifted ingredients, beating at low speed just until combined. Fold in currants by hand. Wrap dough in plastic wrap and refrigerate 2–3 hours or overnight. Divide dough into 1-ounce pieces and roll between palms to form 48 small balls. Arrange 2 inches apart on parchment-lined baking sheets and bake at 350 degrees until slightly firm to the touch, about 12–14 minutes. Remove cookies from pans and cool on racks. Makes 4 dozen.

The Ultimate Molasses Cookie

For my wife, nothing brings back fond childhood memories better than molasses cookies, the kind her late grandmother used to make. This recipe, adapted from *Bon Appétit* magazine, updates the classic homey cookie with the addition of white chocolate and cashews. Someday these, too, might make a future grandchild wistful.

        2 sticks butter
        1 c. sugar
        ¼ c. molasses
        2 eggs
        2½ c. flour
        1 tsp. baking soda
        ¼ tsp. nutmeg
        1½ c. salted cashew pieces
        ½ c. white chocolate chips

Cream butter, sugar, and molasses until fluffy. Beat in eggs. Sift together flour, baking soda, and nutmeg, and add to butter mixture, combining well. Stir in cashews and chips. If dough is too soft, refrigerate until firm. Drop by heaping teaspoonfuls onto greased baking sheets and bake at 350 degrees for 10–12 minutes, until golden. Cool slightly before removing from sheets. Makes 4 dozen.

 # Nordy Bars

Though urban legend has it that it was a Neiman Marcus cookie recipe with a $250 price tag, these cookies, reminiscent of those available at Nordstrom's, might fetch a high price, too.

        1 stick butter
        1⅔ c. butterscotch chips
        ½ c. brown sugar
        2 eggs
        1½ c. flour
        2 tsp. baking powder
        ½ tsp. salt
        2 tsp. vanilla
        2 c. chocolate chips
        2 c. mini marshmallows
        1 c. chopped nuts

Place butter, butterscotch chips, and brown sugar in microwave-safe bowl and heat at full power until melted, about 2½ minutes, stirring once or twice. Beat in eggs one at a time. Add flour, baking powder, and salt. Stir in vanilla. Let cool. Stir in chocolate chips, marshmallows, and nuts. Spread batter in greased 9x13-inch pan and bake at 350 degrees for 25–28 minutes. Cut into squares when cool.

Lebkuchen Bars

Authentic Lebkuchen is traditionally baked on a wafer base and may be formed into all shapes and sizes, though bars, as in this recipe adapted from *German Life* magazine, are obviously the easiest version to make. But even using this simple approach, it is essential that the dough be refrigerated overnight to develop the proper flavor and texture.

>1 c. honey
>¾ c. dark brown sugar
>1 egg
>½ c. golden raisins
>½ c. finely chopped almonds
>¼ c. finely chopped candied orange peel
>¼ c. finely chopped candied citron
>1 tbsp. grated lemon zest
>4 tbsp. lemon juice, divided
>1 tbsp. allspice
>2 c. sifted flour
>½ tsp. baking soda
>¼ tsp. salt
>2 tbsp. milk
>32 whole blanched almonds, toasted
>1½ c. powdered sugar
>1 tsp. vanilla

Heat honey and brown sugar over low heat, stirring constantly, until sugar dissolves and mixture is thin. Let cool until only slightly warm and whisk in the egg. Add raisins, chopped almonds, candied fruit, lemon peel, 1 tablespoon lemon juice, and the allspice, and mix well. Sift together flour, baking soda, and salt, and stir into honey mixture ½ cup at a time until all ingredients are combined. Cover with plastic wrap and refrigerate overnight. Divide dough in half and press evenly into two buttered 9-inch square pans. Brush surface with milk and bake at 350 degrees for 30 minutes until tester inserted in the center comes out clean. While warm, score each pan into 16 bars, pressing a whole almond into the center of each. Combine powdered sugar, remaining 3 tablespoons lemon juice, and vanilla, and brush evenly over bars. Let cool completely before cutting. Store in a tightly covered tin. Do not store in plastic bags.

Out of the Ordinary Lemon Bars

Chocolate and citrus is such a sublime combination, as these cookies demonstrate, that I don't know why it is not more common. The thin layer of chocolate under the lemon curd makes this variation on the classic lemon bar truly special. The recipe is adapted from *Bon Appétit* columnist Marie Simmons' book, *Bar Cookies A to Z.*

  1¾ plus ⅓ c. flour, divided
  ½ c. powdered sugar
  ¼ tsp. salt
  2 sticks cold butter, cut into small pieces
  1 tsp. vanilla
  4 oz. semisweet chocolate
  4 eggs
  2 c. granulated sugar
  2 tsp. grated lemon zest
  ¾ c. fresh lemon juice

Process 1¾ cups flour, powdered sugar, and salt in food processor until blended. With motor running, add butter and vanilla, and process until mixture forms a ball. Press dough in even layer over greased 13x9-inch baking pan, and bake at 350 degrees for 20 minutes, until edges are golden. Melt chocolate and spread over crust. Refrigerate until chocolate is firm. Beat eggs. Combine sugar, remaining ⅓ cup flour, and lemon zest, and beat into eggs until just blended. Stir in lemon juice. Pour over chocolate-cookie layer and bake at 350 degrees for 25–30 minutes until set. Cool and sprinkle with more powdered sugar.

Homemade Graham Crackers

Though Nabisco has for years been manufacturing graham crackers based on Sylvester Graham's recipe, sometimes, when the Martha Stewart bug bites, it's nice to make your own. This version is adapted from one printed in *Highlights for Children* magazine.

> 6 tbsp. butter
> ⅔ c. brown sugar
> ¼ c. honey
> ½ c. yogurt
> 1 tsp. vanilla
> 3 c. whole-wheat flour
> 1 tsp. baking soda
> 1 tsp. baking powder
> ½ tsp. salt

Cream together butter and sugar. Blend in honey, yogurt, and vanilla. Stir together remaining dry ingredients and combine with butter mixture. Roll between sheets of waxed paper to ⅛-inch thickness. Place on floured cookie sheet, score into squares, and prick with a fork. Bake at 350 degrees until golden, about 8 minutes.

Extra Fudgy Brownies

According to the editors at *Gourmet* magazine, these are the fudgiest brownies they've ever tried; quite a claim, considering the magazine must have published hundreds of brownie recipes over the years. This version is an adaptation of the original recipe used at The Farm of Beverly Hills where they serve the brownies in giant squares. *Gourmet* recommends cutting them into smaller portions because they are so rich. I don't!

> 3 sticks butter
> 2 c. semisweet chocolate chips
> 6 eggs
> 1¼ c. cake flour
> 1 c. plus 2 tbsp. cocoa powder
> 3 c. sugar
> ½ tsp. salt

Melt butter and chocolate until smooth. Remove from heat and whisk in eggs, one at a time. Combine flour, cocoa, sugar and salt, and stir into chocolate mixture. Bake in greased and floured 9x13-inch pan at 350 degrees for 40–45 minutes, until top is firm and toothpick inserted into center comes out with crumbs adhering. Cool at least 2 hours before cutting into squares.

Marge Janssen's Brown Sugar Brownies

When Marge Janssen of the Southeast Public Radio Circle brings a pan of these brownies to the station during its fund drive, they go faster than a 30-second spot announcement. She got the recipe from her sister over 40 years ago.

> 2 c. brown sugar
> 2 eggs, beaten
> 1 stick butter, slightly melted
> 1 tsp. vanilla
> 1 c. flour, sifted
> ½ tsp. salt
> 1 tsp. baking powder
> ½ c. broken nuts
> ½ c. chocolate chips

Beat sugar, eggs, butter, and vanilla until light and smooth. Add flour, salt, and baking powder. Stir in nuts and chocolate chips. Bake in a greased 9x13-inch pan at 350 degrees for 30 minutes. Cut into squares while warm. Cool before removing from pan.

Sacher Brownies

The Viennese Sacher torte is world famous, and the impetus for a prolonged court trial (the "Sweet Seven Years' War") to determine who had exclusive rights to it, the Sacher Hotel or Demel's pastry shop. But as one who has visited both places for some firsthand comparison tasting, I honestly believe this brownie version is even better than the original. I've adapted the recipe from one that first appeared in *Ladies Home Journal*.

    4 sticks butter, divided
    ¾ c. powdered sugar
    2¾ c. flour, divided
    1 c. toasted hazelnuts, finely chopped
    1 jar (12 oz.) apricot preserves
    5 oz. unsweetened chocolate
    3 eggs
    2 c. sugar
    ¼ tsp. salt
    2 c. semisweet chocolate chips
    2 oz. white chocolate
    1 tsp. vanilla

Cream 2 sticks butter with powdered sugar until light and fluffy. Beat in 1¾ cups flour and nuts, and spread in foil-lined 10x15-inch jellyroll pan. Bake at 350 degrees for 25 minutes. Purée preserves in a food processor, and spread over baked crust. Refrigerate 20 minutes. Melt remaining 2 sticks butter with unsweetened chocolate and cool 10 minutes. Beat eggs, sugar, and salt to ribbon stage, then beat in chocolate, vanilla, and remaining 1 cup flour. Pour over preserve-glazed crust and bake at 350 degrees for 20–25 minutes until tester comes out just barely clean. Cool. Melt semisweet chocolate and spread over brownies. When set, melt white chocolate and drizzle decoratively over top.

Pumpkin Brownies

These dense, cream-cheese-swirled brownies, adapted from a recipe by Betty Ros-bottom, are wonderful by themselves, but Rosbottom, director of La Belle Pomme Cooking School in Columbus, Ohio, recommends serving them with vanilla ice cream and warm caramel sauce.

> 1 stick butter
> 1 c. brown sugar
> 1 egg
> 1½ tsp. vanilla extract
> 1 c. flour
> 1 tsp. baking powder
> ¾ tsp. ground cinnamon
> ¼ tsp. ground ginger
> ⅛ tsp. ground cloves
> ¼ tsp. salt
> ¾ c. canned solid-pack pumpkin
> ½ c. coarsely chopped pecans
> ¼ c. softened cream cheese
> 2 tbsp. sugar
> 1 egg yolk
> 2 tsp. whipping cream

Preheat oven to 350 degrees. Butter and flour 8-inch square glass baking dish. Beat butter in large bowl until light. Gradually add brown sugar and beat until well blended. Add egg and 1 teaspoon vanilla and blend. Add flour, baking powder, spices, and salt, and beat until well mixed. Beat in pumpkin. Stir in nuts. Spread batter in pan. (Batter will be thick.) Mix cream cheese, 2 tablespoons sugar, egg yolk, cream, and remaining ½ teaspoon vanilla in bowl to blend. Drop cream cheese mixture by heaping tablespoons atop batter and gently swirl with knife. Bake until tester comes out clean and top is firm, about 35 minutes. Makes 10.

Chocolate Syrup Brownies

These moist and chocolatey brownies make a perfect ending to a summer picnic. When Professor Janice Rainwater, now retired, would bring a batch of them to the teachers' lounge on the second floor of the Grauel Building on the Southeast Missouri State University campus, as she often did, word spread quickly. You only have to take one bite to know why. Though there is a recipe for chocolate syrup brownies in *Hershey's 1934 Cookbook*, revised in 1993, this one is better. The real secret to its success, however, is the wonderfully fudgy icing which, by the way, can be used on other cakes and cookies too.

14 tbsp. margarine, divided
2⅓ c. sugar, divided
4 eggs
1 lg. (1 lb.) can chocolate syrup
1 c. flour
⅔ c. nuts (optional)
6 tbsp. milk
½ c. semisweet chocolate chips

Cream 1 stick (8 tablespoons) margarine and 1 cup sugar. Add eggs and syrup, and beat thoroughly. Blend in flour and nuts. Pour batter into a large, greased jellyroll pan (sided cookie sheet) and bake at 350 degrees for 25 minutes. Cool. Bring remaining 6 tablespoons margarine, milk, and remaining 1⅓ cups sugar to a boil, and boil for 1 minute. Remove from heat and add chocolate chips. Beat until chips are melted and icing is slightly thick. Rapidly spread on cooled brownies.

Vassar Fudge

This is the modern version of the fudge introduced at Vassar in 1887. The recipe is adapted from Lee Edwards Benning whose encyclopedic work *Oh, Fudge!* took many hours and over 200 pounds of sugar to write.

> 2 c. sugar
> 1 c. heavy cream
> 2 oz. grated unsweetened chocolate
> 1 tbsp. butter, frozen

Combine sugar, cream, and chocolate in heavy 2-quart saucepan and stir over low heat until chocolate melts. Bring to a boil over medium heat and cook to soft ball stage (234–240 degrees). Remove from heat and place pan in cold water. Add butter and let mixture cool to 110 degrees. Stir fudge by hand or with electric mixer until it thickens and loses its sheen. Chopped nuts may be added at this point if desired. Pour into a greased 5x10-inch pan and cool completely.

 # *Cookies and Cream Fudge*

Fudge doesn't always have to contain chocolate. In fact, some of the earliest recipes referred to chocolate merely as a variation on plain white, or what is sometimes called Opera, fudge. This contemporary take on white fudge is adapted from the Nestle Company's website.

> 3 c. sugar
> 1½ sticks butter
> ⅔ c. white chocolate chips
> 1 jar (7 oz.) marshmallow creme
> 1½ c. crumbled Oreo cookies
> 1 tsp. vanilla

Bring sugar, butter, and milk to a roiling boil, stirring constantly. Boil 3 minutes, remove from heat, and stir in remaining ingredients. Pour into 9-inch square foil-lined pan and refrigerate until firm. Cut into squares.

Pumpkin Fudge

This fudge would make a perfect treat to hand out on Halloween night. The recipe is adapted from *The Perfect Pumpkin* by Gail Damerow, who says that recipes for fudge are the most frequently requested type of recipe by visitors to roadside pumpkin stands.

    12 oz. butterscotch chips
    2 c. mini marshmallows
    1 c. chopped nuts
    1 tsp. vanilla
    3 c. sugar
    ¾ c. butter
    5 oz. evaporated milk
    ½ c. pumpkin purée
    1 tsp. pumpkin-pie spice

Place marshmallows, butterscotch chips, nuts, and vanilla in a Pyrex dish. Combine remaining ingredients in heavy saucepan and bring to a boil, stirring constantly. Reduce heat and cook to 234 degrees. Pour over ingredients in Pyrex dish and combine thoroughly. Spread into greased 7x11-inch pan. Cool and cut into squares.

Delma Williams'
Peanut Butter Fudge

This family recipe is from Delma Williams of Bernie, Missouri, who has been cooking since she was barely tall enough reach the stovetop. When her son Glen, who has been eating this fudge since he was a toddler, brings a pan of it to work with him, he is instantly mobbed by his coworkers. One bite and you'll understand why.

    4 c. sugar
    1 can evaporated milk
    1 stick butter
    1 jar marshmallow creme
    2 c. peanut butter (smooth or chunky)

Bring sugar, milk, and butter to boil. Cook to 236 degrees, stirring frequently. Remove from heat and immediately add marshmallow creme and peanut butter. Stir until candy loses its gloss and is thoroughly blended. Pour into a large pan, let cool, and mark into squares. Makes about 4 pounds.

Cajeta (Goat-Milk Caramel)

This recipe, adapted from Rick Bayless' marvelous book *Mexico: One Plate at a Time*, uses cow's milk to offset the tang of traditional goat's milk which is, nonetheless, essential to authentic *cajeta*. Do not use a smaller pan than the one specified, lest the mixture boil over, nor a larger one that might allow the mixture to reduce too quickly to develop proper color and flavor. The traditional vessel for making this recipe is an unlined copper pan or *cazo*, but any heavy pan, such as an enameled cast-iron one, will work fine. Just be sure to regulate the heat carefully so that the mixture simmers slowly and not too rapidly.

> 4 c. goat's milk
> 4 c. cow's milk
> 2 c. sugar
> 2-inch piece cinnamon
> ½ tsp. baking soda
> 1 tbsp. water

In a 6-quart pot combine first 4 ingredients and cook, stirring occasionally, over medium heat until mixture begins to simmer and sugar is dissolved. Combine baking soda and water, and add to mixture off heat. Mixture will foam up. After foam subsides, return to heat and cook at a brisk simmer, stirring regularly, for about 1 hour until mixture turns pale golden. Continue cooking, stirring frequently, until mixture turns deep brown and when tested on a cold plate is the thickness of medium-thick caramel sauce. Strain mixture when cool. Makes 3 cups.

 # *Honeycomb*

With its porous honeycomb-like structure, this candy is aptly named. It's reminiscent of peanut brittle, only without the peanuts. The recipe is adapted from *A Taste of Honey* by Jane Charlton and Jane Newdick, who suggest serving the confection with vanilla ice cream.

> 3 tbsp. honey
> ¾ c. sugar
> 1 tbsp. light corn syrup
> 3 tbsp. water
> 1¾ tsp. baking soda

Combine all ingredients except baking soda in a high-sided pan and place over low heat until sugar is completely dissolved. Bring to a boil and cook until syrup reaches 300 degrees (hard crack stage). Immediately remove pan from heat and stir in baking soda. Pour syrup onto lightly greased baking pan, and let cool until set, about 1 hour. Crack into pieces.

Homemade Peeps

If you've got a little Martha Stewart in you, you might find it fun to try making your own Peeps. This recipe is adapted from one offered by Martha herself.

> 1 envelope unflavored gelatin
> ⅓ plus ¼ c. water
> 1 c. sugar
> colored granulated sugar
> chocolate icing

Soften gelatin in ⅓ cup water. Combine sugar and ¼ cup water, and stir over medium-high heat until sugar is dissolved. Boil to 238 degrees and stir into gelatin. Cool slightly and beat on medium-high speed of mixer until soft peaks form and mixture holds its shape. Transfer to a pastry bag fitted with a ½-inch tip. Pipe small mounds of marshmallow onto baking sheet covered with colored sugar. Pipe smaller mounds on either end for head and tail. Pipe ears, starting from top of head onto body, pulling forward and off to finish. Pat down with damp fingers if necessary. Sprinkle sugar over entire surface of Peeps and allow to set. Pipe on faces with icing. Store in airtight container.

 # *Homemade Marshmallow Eggs*

This recipe is adapted from famed chocolatier Jacques Torres. Rather than covering the eggs, he merely decorates them with chocolate, an approach which is not only easier, but which has the benefit of increasing the marshmallow-to-chocolate ratio. You can flavor the marshmallow with almond, lemon, peppermint, or other extracts instead of vanilla, if you desire.

> 1½ c. sugar
> ¼ c. plus ⅓ c. corn syrup
> ¾ c. water
> 3 tbsp. powdered gelatin
> 2–3 drops vanilla
> cornstarch
> 4 oz. melted milk chocolate

Place sugar, ¼ cup of the corn syrup, and ½ cup of the water in a saucepan and cook to 110 degrees. Soak gelatin in the remaining ¼ cup water for 5 minutes, then melt over very low heat. Place remaining ⅓ cup corn syrup in a mixing bowl, and add the warm sugar mixture and the gelatin. Whip until fluffy. Add vanilla. Spray egg molds with cooking spray and dust with cornstarch. Spoon mixture into molds and let sit overnight or until firm. Unmold eggs and, using a fork, splatter decoratively with melted chocolate.

Byzantine Sugarplums

You can use whatever dried fruits and nuts you like in this recipe, adapted from a little Christmas cookbook by Mimi Sheraton, *Visions of Sugarplums*. The ones listed here and their proportions are what I like best, but after some experimentation, you'll surely develop your own vision of the perfect sugarplum.

> 1¾ c. dates
> 1½ c. figs
> 1½ c. raisins
> 1 c. dried apricots
> 1 c. crystallized ginger
> 1 c. walnuts
> 1 c. almonds
> 2 tbsp. brandy
> sugar

Coarsely chop dried fruits, add ginger, and place in food processor along with brandy. Pulse until mixture just starts to stick together. Add nuts and pulse until chopped and incorporated. Shape mixture into balls about 1½ inches in diameter. Roll in sugar. Makes about 4 dozen. Store in airtight container in refrigerator.

 # *Louisiana General Store's Pralines*

This recipe, adapted from Joe Cahn of the New Orleans School of Cooking and Louisiana General Store, is said by some to be New Orleans' best praline. It's adaptable to several variations. For instance, try adding ½ teaspoon ground red pepper, or 3 tablespoons orange liqueur, or five chocolate-covered peppermint patties (½ ounce) to the mixture before cooking.

> 1½ c. sugar
> 1 tsp. vanilla
> ¾ stick butter
> ¾ c. light brown sugar
> ½ c. milk
> 1½ c. pecans

Combine all ingredients and bring to soft ball stage. Remove from heat and stir until mixture cools and thickens. Spoon out onto waxed paper and cool until firm.

Apple Apricot Noodle Pudding

This recipe, adapted from Faye Levy's *The New Casserole* demonstrates that casseroles don't always have to be main courses. Some, such as Jewish sweet noodle kugels, are enjoyed as desserts.

> 14 oz. med. egg noodles
> 3 Golden Delicious apples (about 1.5 lbs.)
> ¼ c. plus 2 tbsp. butter
> 1 tsp. ground ginger
> ¼ c. plus 2 tbsp. sugar
> 1 tsp. ground cinnamon
> ½ c. blanched almonds, chopped
> ½ c. diced dried apricots
> 4 eggs, separated

Cook noodles in boiling water until barely tender. Rinse with cold water and drain. Peel, core, and slice apples, and sauté in two batches in 2 tablespoons butter for about 5 minutes. Combine apples, ginger, 2 tablespoons of sugar, and ½ teaspoon cinnamon, and sauté 1 minute longer, tossing to coat. Melt remaining butter. Add 3 tablespoons butter, almonds, and apricots to the noodles and mix well. Beat egg whites to soft peaks, beat in remaining ¼ cup sugar, and beat until stiff but not dry. Stir egg yolks into noodles, stir in one-fourth of the whites, and fold in remaining whites. Spread half of noodle mixture in baking dish, top with apples, and top with remaining noodle mixture, spreading evenly. Sprinkle with remaining ½ teaspoon cinnamon and drizzle with remaining tablespoon butter. Cover and bake for 30 minutes. Uncover and bake 15–20 minutes or until set. Serve hot. Serves 8.

Last Minute Christmas Pudding

It's never too early to make a plum pudding because it improves with age. I found one recipe that even encourages starting a year in advance. But this recipe, adapted from Britain's leading food magazine, *Good Food*, can be made on the same day you serve it.

⅓ c. glace cherries, quartered
¾ c. mixed dried fruits
¾ c. chopped figs
⅔ c. dried apricots, chopped
⅔ c. pitted prunes, chopped
2 tbsp. brandy
3 tbsp. port wine
grated zest and juice of 1 lemon
grated zest and juice of 1 orange
1 stick butter
⅔ c. brown sugar
¼ c. chopped almonds
2 eggs, beaten
1 apple, peeled and diced
10 tbsp. self-rising flour
½ tsp. ginger
½ tsp. nutmeg
½ tsp. cinnamon
1 tsp. allspice
1½ c. fresh breadcrumbs

Put fruits, liquors, zests, juices, butter, and sugar in a saucepan, boil until butter melts, and simmer uncovered for 5 minutes. Cool slightly and stir in almonds, eggs, and apple. Stir in flour and spices. Add breadcrumbs and mix well. Spoon into greased, one-quart mold, and cover with a double thickness of wax paper, pleated in the center. Tie down with string and overwrap with aluminum foil. Steam for 3 hours in a covered pan of simmering water. (A Crockpot is ideal for this.) Serve warm with whipped cream or hard sauce.

Cranberry, Orange, and White Chocolate Christmas Pudding

This contemporary take on Christmas pudding is not as heavy as its plum counterpart, but it's every bit as festive. You can serve it with whipped cream or a *coulis* made of cranberry sauce thinned with orange juice and strained. The recipe is adapted from one by cookbook author Elinor Klivans.

>1 stick butter
>1 c. sugar
>3 eggs
>1 c. white chocolate chips
>1 tsp. vanilla
>1 tbsp. orange liqueur
>1¼ c. flour
>1½ tsp. baking powder
>½ tsp. salt
>1 c. cranberries
>⅓ c. orange marmalade

Cream butter and sugar until fluffy. Add eggs one at a time, beating well. Melt white chocolate and mix in, along with vanilla and liqueur. Combine flour, baking powder, and salt, and add, mixing until just incorporated. Chop cranberries and stir in along with marmalade. Pour batter into two-quart mold, greased and dusted with powdered sugar, and cover tightly with foil. Steam for 2 hours in a covered pan of simmering water until tester comes out clean. (A Crockpot is ideal for this.) Cool 10 minutes before unmolding. Serve warm.

Bess Truman's Ozark Pudding

Harry Truman preferred home cooking to fancy fare. Though he was most fond of buttermilk pie, Mrs. Truman's favorite dessert was this one, not really a pudding in the traditional sense, but a chewy cake-like concoction, not unlike a *dacquoise*. Served with ice cream or whipped cream, it can be addictive.

>2 eggs
>1½ c. sugar
>6 heaping tbsp. flour
>½ tsp. baking powder
>¼ tsp. salt
>2 tsp. vanilla
>1 c. chopped pecans
>1 c. chopped apples

Beat eggs. Add sugar gradually, beating until light and fluffy. Combine flour, baking powder, and salt, and blend into egg mixture. Fold in nuts and apples, and spread in a greased 8x11½-inch pan. Bake at 350 degrees for 25–30 minutes.

Blackberry Sorbet

This recipe is simplicity itself, yet it produces a beautiful and intensely flavored dessert which, incredibly, is fat-free. My inspiration for the sorbet was an article on fruit slushes published in one of those so-called women's magazines you get at the supermarket. I've also successfully substituted strawberries, raspberries, and kiwi fruit for the blackberries. In fact, the recipe is so easy, it's no trouble at all to make three flavors which can then be served as a trio, perhaps scooped out onto a plate of complementary sauce, for a finale elegant enough for even the most sophisticated meal.

> 1 lb. (2¼ c.) frozen blackberries
> 3–4 tbsp. sugar
> 1 c. fat-free half-and-half (or evaporated skim milk)

Place berries in bowl of food processor fitted with a metal blade. Add sugar and half-and-half. Process until mixture is smooth and the consistency of soft-serve ice cream. Freeze until firm. Makes about 1 pint.

Grappa Semifreddo

Originally a peasant's drink but now one of the biggest things in distilled spirits, grappa is a potent form of Italian brandy distilled from the skins and seeds left over from winemaking. Semifreddo is a chilled, mousse-like dessert. This recipe, adapted from *Gourmet* magazine, offers a good lesson on both of them. When making it, use pasteurized egg whites from a carton so you won't have to ponder the culinary question, "What is salmonella?"

> 3 egg yolks
> ½ c. sugar
> ⅓ c. plus 6 tsp. grappa
> 2 egg whites
> 1 c. cream

Beat egg yolks, sugar, and ⅓ cup grappa in a bowl set over simmering water until thick and pale and mixture registers 170 degrees, about 10 minutes. Place bowl in ice bath and beat mixture until cold. Beat egg whites with a pinch of salt until they just hold stiff peaks. Beat cream to soft peaks. Whisk one-third of whites into yolk mixture, then fold in remaining whites and cream. Spoon mixture into six ½-cup molds, cover with plastic wrap, and freeze until firm. Chill the remaining grappa. When ready to serve, dip molds in hot water for 5 seconds, run a knife around edges, and unmold, spooning a teaspoon of chilled grappa on top of each. Can be garnished with chocolate or caramel sauce or warm espresso.

Frozen Oreo White Chocolate Mousse Torte

Oreos with red filling, available during the holidays, make this dessert particularly festive, but the contrast between the chocolate cookies and the white mousse is sophisticated any time of year. The recipe is adapted from Nabisco's *Oreo with a Twist* cookbook.

    1 pkg. (20 oz.) Oreos
    6 tbsp. butter
    1 envelope unflavored gelatin
    1¼ c. milk
    1 pkg. (11 oz.) white chocolate chips
    2 c. heavy cream

Finely crush 24 cookies. Melt butter and mix with cookie crumbs. Press mixture firmly on bottom and 1 inch up the side of a 9-inch springform pan. Pour milk into large saucepan and sprinkle gelatin over top. Let stand 1 minute. Cook over low heat for 3 minutes, stirring, until gelatin is completely dissolved. Add white chocolate chips and continue cooking until chips are melted. Place saucepan over bowl of ice water and stir mixture frequently until it is slightly thickened, about 8–10 minutes. Coarsely chop remaining cookies. Whip cream and fold along with chopped cookies into gelatin mixture. Spoon into crust and freeze. Let thaw slightly before serving, garnishing with cookie halves. Serves 12.

Baked Alaska Peanut S'mores

Perhaps this delightful and imaginative treat is what Eskimo scouts eat around the campfire. The recipe is based on one in *Gourmet* magazine.

    6 tbsp. butter
    1½ c. graham-cracker crumbs
    7 tbsp. sugar, divided
    1½ pt. chocolate ice cream
    ½ c. peanuts
    2 egg whites

Melt butter, and combine with crumbs and 2 tablespoons sugar. Reserve ¼ of mixture and press remainder onto bottom of an 8x8-inch baking pan. Bake at 350 degrees for 12 minutes until golden. Cool completely. Soften ice cream, stir in peanuts, and spread on top of crust. Sprinkle reserved crumb mixture evenly over top, pressing lightly. Freeze until firm. Combine whites with remaining sugar and heat over simmering water until sugar is dissolved. Remove from heat and beat to stiff, glossy peaks. Spread meringue over ice cream and broil 4 inches from heat for 30 seconds until golden. Freeze to harden. Cut into 8 triangles.

Risotto Gelato

Several years ago, my wife discovered a sublime rice-pudding gelato at a little gelateria in the Cannery in San Francisco. Being a rice-pudding devotee, she has been looking all over for something like it ever since, but to no avail. Happily, this recipe, adapted from Patricia Wells' wonderful book, *Trattoria*, seems to be the genuine article.

> ¼ c. arborio rice
> 3½ c. whole milk, divided
> 1¼ c. vanilla-scented sugar
> ¼ tsp. fine sea salt
> 2 plump, moist vanilla beans
> 6 egg yolks
> 1 c. heavy cream

Combine rice, 1½ cups milk, ½ cup sugar, and salt, and bring to a simmer over moderate heat, stirring often. Reduce heat and simmer until rice is cooked, about 20 minutes, stirring often. Cool to room temperature, strain, and discard the liquid. Set aside. Remove seeds from vanilla beans and reserve. Combine the remaining 2 cups milk and the vanilla pods over moderate heat. Scald the milk, remove from heat, cover, and let steep for 15 minutes. Remove pods. Using an electric mixer, whisk the vanilla seeds, egg yolks, and remaining ¾ cup sugar until thick, fluffy, and a pale lemon color, 2–3 minutes. Mixture should form a ribbon when whisk is lifted. Return simmered milk to high heat and bring just to boil. Remove from heat and pour ⅓ of the boiling milk into the egg-yolk mixture, whisking constantly. Return milk and yolk mixture to remaining milk in saucepan, reduce heat to low, and cook, stirring constantly, until mixture thickens to a creamy consistency (registering 185 degrees on a candy thermometer), about 5 minutes. Remove from heat and immediately stir in cream to stop the cooking. Pass through a sieve and cool completely. Stir in the cooled rice, transfer to an ice-cream maker, and freeze according to manufacturer's instructions. Makes 1 quart.

St. Louis Frozen Custard

This recipe for frozen custard, another St. Louis favorite, is adapted from *The World's Fair Souvenir Cook Book* which sold at the fairgrounds for 50 cents.

> 1 qt. milk
> 4 eggs
> 1 c. sugar
> 1 tbsp. vanilla

Heat milk in a double boiler. Beat together eggs and sugar, and stir into hot milk. Cook 1 minute. Strain, cool, and add vanilla. Freeze in ice-cream maker according to manufacturer's instructions.

Thomas Jefferson's
Recipe for Ice Cream

The first American recipe for ice cream is in Thomas Jefferson's own handwriting, copied by him and brought back from France. It was so intricately detailed that it involved eighteen separate procedures. This updated version, adapted from a recipe by Marie Kimball, editor of *Thomas Jefferson's Cook Book*, streamlines the operations without sacrificing any of the richness and flavor of the original.

> 6 egg yolks
> 1 c. sugar
> pinch of salt
> 1 qt. cream
> 2 tsp. vanilla

Beat yolks until thick and lemon colored. Gradually add sugar and salt. Bring cream to a boil and add slowly to egg mixture. Cook in the top of a double boiler until thickened. Strain mixture and let cool. Add vanilla and freeze in ice-cream freezer according to manufacturer's directions.

Pêches Melba

Escoffier first served this dish at the Hotel Savoy in London in 1892 to honor the Australian soprano, Nellie Melba, after her performance in *Lohengrin*. Thus, it was originally served in an ice swan reminiscent of the swan in the opera. It was not until several years later, however, that Escoffier added the raspberry sauce. The dish is now so well known that recipes for it can be found in almost any good basic cookbook. This easy version is adapted from Pillsbury's. Fresh peaches and raspberries, of course, make the most authentic version.

> 1 (10 oz.) pkg. frozen sweetened raspberries
> 2 tsp. cornstarch
> ½ c. currant jelly
> 6 fresh peach halves (or a 29 oz. can peach halves)
> 1 qt. vanilla ice cream

Thaw and drain raspberries. Combine with cornstarch and jelly, and cook over medium heat until mixture boils and thickens, stirring frequently. Place peach halves in individual serving dishes, top with ice cream, and spoon cooled sauce over.

Golden Cream

Though I have seen a recipe for Guinness ice cream, this concoction strikes me as a quicker way to get the same result. Invented by Tim and Ned Gamble, it won a Guinness recipe contest in 1986. The brothers advise that the ice cream should never be put in the glass first.

> 8–10 oz. bottled Guinness
> several scoops vanilla ice cream

Pour Guinness into glass and allow to settle so there is no head. Slowly add ice cream. Wait 1 minute and serve.

Grilled Banana Split

The banana split was invented at Strickler's Drug Store in Pennsylvania in 1904. This contemporary version, adapted from Elizabeth Karmel, who has been dubbed the "Queen of the Grill," makes a great ending to a summer night's cookout.

> 4 firm, ripe bananas
> 1 tbsp. sugar
> ½ tsp. cinnamon
> 8 scoops vanilla ice cream
> 1 c. fudge sauce
> ½ c. chopped walnuts
> whipped cream
> Maraschino cherries

Without peeling, slice bananas in half lengthwise and cut each half in two to produce four pieces in all. Combine sugar and cinnamon, sprinkle on cut sides of bananas, and let stand for 5 minutes. Place bananas cut-side down on grate over a charcoal fire and cook for 2 minutes over direct low heat, until grill marks appear. Turn and cook on other side for 5 minutes, until skins pull away from the banana. Remove skins and place four banana pieces in each of four bowls. Top each serving with two scoops of ice cream. Warm sauce and ladle ¼ cup over each serving. Sprinkle with nuts and whipped cream, and top with a cherry. Serves 4.

Peanut Rocky Road

This recipe, adapted from the *St. Louis Post-Dispatch*, has been a favorite ice-cream dessert at our house ever since we first came across it many years ago. If you like "drumsticks," those frozen ice-cream novelty cones, you'll love this.

> 1 c. chopped cocktail peanuts
> 1 c. chopped chocolate chips
> 2 c. miniature marshmallows
> 3 pt. vanilla ice cream, cut up
> 1½ c. peanut butter

Toss together peanuts, chocolate chips, and marshmallows. Stir ice cream until smooth. Swirl peanut butter into ice cream. Spoon half of ice-cream mixture into a chilled 8-inch square pan and spread evenly. Sprinkle half of peanut-chocolate-marshmallow mixture over ice cream and cover with layer of remaining ice-cream mixture. Sprinkle with remaining peanut-chocolate-marshmallow mixture, pressing lightly into top. Freeze until set and cut into squares.

 # Strawberries and Ice Cream with Balsamic Vinegar

No, this isn't a misprint. The rich, fruity taste of balsamic vinegar makes a wonderful contrast to the sweet strawberries. At our house, we often just splash a little of the vinegar on top of a dish of strawberries, but this recipe, adapted from *Gourmet* magazine, goes a step beyond by adding ice cream and a brown-sugar glaze.

> 6 lg. ripe strawberries
> 2 tbsp. balsamic vinegar
> 2 tbsp. brown sugar
> 1½ c. vanilla ice cream

Trim berries and cut into wedges. Heat vinegar and brown sugar over moderate heat, stirring, until sugar is dissolved. Simmer 1 minute. Remove pan from heat and add berries, tossing to coat. Serve over ice cream. Serves 2.

Chocolate Fondue

Though cheese fondue was invented in Switzerland, chocolate fondue, like chocolate itself, originated in the New World. It was invented in 1964 by Konrad Egli, the Swiss-born chef at New York's Chalet Swiss restaurant. You can spike this recipe, adapted from Judith Olney's *The Joy of Chocolate*, with a couple of tablespoons of Grand Marnier, Kahlua, Chambord, or other liqueur.

> 12 oz. semisweet chocolate
> ¾ c. heavy cream
> assorted dippers (pound cake, fresh fruit, or even chocolate cookies)

Melt chocolate with the cream over low heat (or in a microwave). Transfer to fondue pot or bowl, and invite guests to skewer dippers and dunk them into the chocolate.

 # Poached Pears with Ricotta, Walnuts, and Balsamic Vinegar

This elegant recipe, adapted from an Internet site devoted to balsamic vinegar, demonstrates that it not only enhances salads and main courses, but desserts as well.

> 1 c. water
> ½ c. sugar
> 4 pears
> 1 c. Ricotta cheese
> ¼ c. toasted walnuts, chopped
> 4 tbsp. balsamic vinegar

Combine water and sugar, and bring to a boil. Peel, core, and halve pears, and place in baking dish. Pour syrup over and bake at 350 degrees until tender, 20–25 minutes. Cool slightly and serve with a dollop of ricotta, a sprinkling of walnuts, and a drizzle of vinegar.

Sweet Hominy Chimichangas with Fruit Purées

The origin of the word *chimichanga*, a fried burrito, is uncertain, though *The Dictionary of American Food and Drink* reports that it may be based on an expletive. That analysis is perhaps compatible with the story that the first of these treats was the result of an accident in which a cook dropped a burrito into hot fat and yelled, "Chimichanga!" This recipe for a dessert chimichanga is adapted from *The Well-Filled Tortilla Cookbook* by Victoria Wise and Susanna Hoffman.

        1 can (29 oz.) white hominy, drained
        4 tsp. powdered sugar
        2 tbsp. whipping cream
        6 flour tortillas
        1 pt. strawberries, hulled
        2 ripe mangos, peeled and pitted
        4 tbsp. butter
        2 tbsp. dark brown sugar

Purée hominy, stir in powdered sugar and cream, and place ⅓ cup of the mixture in the center of each tortilla. Fold up envelope style. Purée the strawberries and mangos separately. Melt butter and brown sugar in skillet until butter foams and sugar melts, stirring to blend. Add filled tortillas and fry 1 minute per side. To serve, spoon strawberry purée over one end of each chimichanga and mango purée over the other.

Jam Omelette

Omelettes make great desserts when filled with fruits, preserves, or other treats. There are even chocolate omelettes. This recipe, adapted from Narcissa Chamberlain's *The Omelette Book*, has as many variations as there are jams and jellies.

        6-egg omelette recipe
        2 tbsp. sugar
        jam

Add 2 tablespoons sugar to 6-egg omelette recipe along with a small pinch of salt, and grated lemon rind if desired. Make omelette and fill with apricot, strawberry, peach, raspberry, or other jam. Fold omelette, sprinkle with sugar and glaze under broiler. If desired, flame with 2 tablespoons warm rum or brandy.

Lime Fool
with Strawberries and Kiwi

With the addition of white chocolate, this fool is both classic and contemporary. The recipe is adapted from *Bon Appétit* magazine.

    1 c. whipping cream, divided
    ¼ c. fresh lime juice
    1 tsp. grated lime peel
    6 oz. white chocolate, chopped
    3 tbsp. sugar
    2 c. sliced hulled strawberries
    2 kiwi fruit, peeled, thinly sliced
    4 whole strawberries
    4 lime slices

Bring ¼ cup cream, lime juice, and peel to a simmer. Reduce heat to low. Add chocolate and stir until melted and smooth. Refrigerate until cool but not set, stirring occasionally, about 25 minutes. Beat remaining cream to soft peaks. Add sugar and beat until stiff. Fold cream into white-chocolate mixture. Place scant ¼ cup sliced berries in each of four 8-ounce wineglasses. Press 3 kiwi slices against sides of each glass. Spoon ⅓ cup cream mixture in each glass. Spoon ¼ cup sliced berries in center of each, pressing into center so berries do not show at sides of glasses. Spoon remaining cream over; smooth tops. Cover and chill at least 2 hours. To serve, make lengthwise cuts in whole strawberries without cutting through stem ends. Fan 1 strawberry atop each dessert and attach lime slice to rim of each glass.

Gooseberry Fool

This recipe is adapted from Elizabeth David, who has been called "Britain's most inspirational cookery writer." Though it will work well with uncooked strawberries, uncooked raspberries, or blackberries cooked like the gooseberries, David, in her delightful book *An Omelette and a Glass of Wine*, says, "I give precedence to those dishes made from the gooseberry, because green gooseberry fool is—to me at any rate—the most delicious as well as the most characteristic of all these simple, almost childlike, English dishes."

    2¼ qt. gooseberries (about 2 lbs.)
    1 c. superfine sugar
    1–2 c. heavy cream whipped to soft peaks

Wash the berries. Put them with the sugar in the top half of a double boiler and steam them for about 30 minutes until they are quite soft. Strain off the surplus liquid and purée the berries in a food mill or processor. When the purée is quite cold, add the cream. Serve in a stemmed glass. Serves 6–8.

Low-fat Rhubarb Fool

Who says you can't fool all of the people all of the time? Using low-fat yogurt in place of heavy cream, this recipe adapted from *Bon Appétit* magazine will deceive even the most indifferent diet fools and have them rushing in for more.

> 16 oz. rhubarb stalks, trimmed, cut crosswise into ½-inch slices
> ½ c. sugar
> 6 tbsp. orange juice
> 4 tbsp. Grand Marnier
> 2 c. low-fat vanilla yogurt

Bring rhubarb, sugar, and orange juice to simmer over medium-low heat, stirring until sugar dissolves. Partially cover pan and cook until rhubarb is very soft. Mix in Grand Marnier. Refrigerate until cold, about 15 minutes. Alternate layers of rhubarb mixture and yogurt in 4 large wine goblets. Using knife, swirl mixtures together. Serve immediately or refrigerate up to 1 hour. Frozen rhubarb can be substituted for fresh.

Crêpes Suzette

This dessert is so famous, as Julia Child notes in her classic *The French Chef Cookbook*, that few of us can say "crêpes" without automatically adding "Suzette." Once considered the epitome of sophisticated desserts and to require the experienced hand of a maître d'hôtel, preparation of this dish has been made somewhat easier by the advent of ready-made crêpes which are now regularly available at the supermarket. This recipe is adapted from the *Joy of Cooking*.

> ½ stick butter
> ½ c. fresh orange juice
> 1 tsp. fresh lemon juice
> ⅓ c. sugar
> zest of 1 orange
> 10 tbsp. Grand Marnier
> 2 tbsp. Cognac
> 12 sweet crêpes

Put butter, juices, sugar, and zest in a skillet or chafing dish, and bring to a boil, stirring until sugar is melted. Continue to boil until slightly thickened, about 2–3 minutes. Stir in 2 tablespoons of the Grand Marnier and the Cognac, and boil for another 30 seconds. One by one, place the crêpes in the sauce for about 15 seconds, allowing each to heat through. Fold each crêpe into quarters to form a ruffle-edged triangle with browned side facing out. Place two folded crêpes on each of six plates, overlapping slightly in the center, and pour remaining sauce over. Heat remaining ½ cup Grand Marnier, pour over crêpes, and ignite. Serves 6.

Drinks

Agua Fresca de Limón

This unique lime drink is popular in the state of Oaxaca in southern Mexico where *agua frescas* or "cool waters" are so well liked that there is a special day dedicated to them. On the fourth Friday of Lent, the citizens of Oaxaca City drink this and similar concoctions in memory of the Samaritan woman who met Christ at the well. The recipe, adapted from Zarela Martínez's lovely book, *The Food and Life of Oaxaca*, uses no juice, only the rind of the fruit.

> 6 c. cold water
> ⅓ c. sugar
> 2 lg. dark green limes

In a pitcher, combine the water and sugar, stirring to dissolve. Refrigerate until very cold. Just before serving, grate the rind of the lime into the pitcher. Serve over ice cubes.

 # *Strawberry Lemonade*

Flavored lemonades have become the rage at The City Bakery in New York. Owner Maury Rubin even put on a lemonade festival there a few years ago. The adaptation of his version of pink lemonade (which usually gets its color from the addition of grenadine) is tart, so you may want to adjust it to taste. You might also try experimenting with additions of other puréed fruits such as blueberries, raspberries, mangos, kiwis, and peaches.

> 1½ c. sugar
> 1¼ c. water
> 3 c. freshly squeezed lemon juice (about 16 lemons)
> 1 pint fresh strawberries, hulled

In a pitcher or container, whisk together the sugar and water until the sugar dissolves. Add lemon juice and stir. Purée the berries and strain to remove seeds. Add purée to lemon mixture and stir. To serve, pour into 10-ounce glasses filled with ice. Serves 7.

Iced Cucumber Limeade

This unique recipe, adapted from *Prevention* magazine, is from the Ponkok Laguna restaurant in Jakarta, Indonesia, where iced drinks are so popular, and on hot days so welcome, that an entire section of the kitchen is dedicated to their preparation. Like the restaurant, you may want to serve this drink with a spoon as well as a straw.

    ½ c. freshly squeezed lime juice
    3 tbsp. honey
    1 good-size cucumber
    10 ice cubes

Mix juice and honey thoroughly and pour equal quantities into two glasses. Peel cucumber, remove seeds, and chop coarsely. Put into blender and blend until smooth. Put in ice cubes and blend until mushy. Pour equal quantities into the two glasses with the lime juice and mix thoroughly. Garnish with mint sprigs if desired.

Iced Mochaccino

This drink might be the ultimate in trendiness: the uniting of the coffee bar with the smoothie bar. Inspired by a recipe from *Smoothies and Other Blended Drinks*, by Elsa Petersen-Schepelern, which used chocolate syrup and vanilla ice cream, I set out to develop something similar, but easier to make and with less fat and fewer calories. After numerous experiments and many sleepless nights, this is the result.

    1 pkg. hot-cocoa mix, such as Swiss Miss
    1 c. skim milk
    1 heaping tsp. instant coffee
    8 ice cubes

Place all ingredients in blender and blend until thick and slushy. Serve topped with whipped cream if desired or dusted with cinnamon or cocoa. Makes 1 generous serving.

Castillian Hot Chocolate

The Spanish prefer their hot chocolate thick, and so do I. Typical thickeners are eggs or cornstarch. This recipe, posted on the Internet by Tovah Hollander who first tasted it while on a choir tour of northern Spain, uses the latter which helps to keep fat and cholesterol content in check. The concoction, whose consistency is that of unset pudding, is addictive. I drank several mugs just while writing down the recipe.

> ½ c. cocoa powder
> 1 c. sugar
> 7 tsp. cornstarch
> ½ c. water
> 4 c. milk

Mix cocoa and sugar. Dissolve cornstarch in water and combine with cocoa mixture to make a smooth paste. Heat, stirring continuously, gradually adding milk. Simmer for 10 minutes until thick and glossy. Serves 6.

Mexican Hot Chocolate

We have the Spanish missionaries and nuns to thank for adding cinnamon and sugar to the native chocolate of Mexico to produce a unique drink. This recipe, adapted from *Chocolatier* magazine, can be embellished by adding 4 tablespoons orange liqueur to produce a drink called a Nun's Habit, or 2 tablespoons hazelnut liqueur and 3 tablespoons brandy to create a drink called Monastery Madness. Adding coffee and a little rum, brandy, and crème de cacao makes Café Ole.

> 4 c. milk
> ½ c. dark brown sugar
> 2 oz. chopped unsweetened chocolate
> 2 egg whites
> ¾ tsp. cinnamon
> ¾ tsp. vanilla
> ¾ tsp. almond extract

Cook milk, sugar, and chocolate over medium heat until smooth, stirring frequently. Bring mixture to boil and remove pan from heat. Beat egg whites for 30 seconds until frothy. Beat whites into chocolate mixture until frothy. Stir in remaining ingredients and heat for 1 minute before serving.

Parisian Hot Chocolate

This rich and creamy hot chocolate is reminiscent of the one served at the famous Paris tea salon, Angelina. The recipe is adapted from a wonderful book, *All About Chocolate*, by the unfortunately named Carole Bloom. (Bloom is the term used to refer to the unsightly but harmless condition of chocolate in which the cocoa butter has separated from the rest of the ingredients leaving white streaks.)

> 2 c. milk
> ½ c. heavy cream
> ¼ c. Dutch-processed cocoa powder
> 6 oz. bittersweet chocolate, finely chopped
> 1 tsp. vanilla

Combine milk, cream, and cocoa powder, and warm over medium heat, stirring to dissolve cocoa. Add chocolate and stir until completely melted. Bring mixture to simmer, return heat to medium, and cook 5 minutes. Add vanilla. Serve garnished with sweetened whipped cream.

White Hot Chocolate

White chocolate technically isn't chocolate at all because it doesn't contain any chocolate liquor, the thick nonalcoholic liquid produced by grinding the interior nibs of cocoa beans, a fascinating process I was privileged to observe once at the Guittard Chocolate Factory in San Francisco, a supplier of ours when we were in the cheesecake business. But true chocolate or not, white chocolate makes a wonderful drink as in this recipe adapted from *The Ultimate Encyclopedia of Chocolate*.

> 7½ c. milk
> 6 oz. genuine white chocolate, chopped
> 2 tsp. coffee powder
> 2 tsp. orange-flavored liqueur (optional)

Heat milk until almost boiling. Remove from heat and add remaining ingredients. Stir until chocolate is melted and mixture is smooth. Pour into four mugs, top with whipped cream, and sprinkle with ground cinnamon.

Recipe Index

T

Tea
    Earl Grey Chocolate Pie, 332
    Lemon Blossom Mashed Potatoes, 298
    Orange Tea Chicken, 273

Tomato
    Baked Grits with Sun Dried Tomatoes, 292
    Balsamic Glazed Pasta, 265
    Pasta with Tomatoes and Four Cheeses, 269
    Toasted Bread and Tomato Salad with Chicken, 237

Turkey
    Black-Eyed Pea Soup with Smoked Turkey, 250
    Turducken Roulade, 279